D0413722

GIMME DANGER: THE STORY OF

iGGY POP

JOE AMBROSE

OMNIBUS PRESS

Exclusive Distributors
Music Sales Limited,
8/9 Frith Street,
London W1D 3JB, UK.

Music Sales Corporation,
257 Park Avenue South,
New York, NY 10010, USA.

Macmillan Distribution Services,
53 Park West Drive,
Derrimut, Vic 3030,
Australia.

To the Music Trade only
Music Sales Limited,
8/9 Frith Street,
London W1D 3JB, UK.

Every effort has been made to trace the copyright holders of the photographs in this
book but one or two were unreachable. We would be grateful if the photographers
concerned would contact us.

Typesetting by Galleon Typesetting, Ipswich.
Printed by Creative Print & Design, Ebbw Vale, Wales.

A catalogue record for this book is available from the British Library.

Visit Omnibus Press on the web at omnibuspress.com

Contents

Foreword

Patti Smith came up with the equation "art + electricity = rock'n'roll". When I was a student in Dublin in the late Seventies it was generally perceived, in student circles, that Iggy Pop fitted into that equation perfectly. In the damp impoverished provincial city of those times he seemed an outstanding presence, right up there with the Lou Reeds and Bob Dylans of this world. Only that, while art made them rich and famous, Iggy was one of our own. We imagined that his bank account didn't run into four figures, that his stance was somehow more extreme or brave than others. We guzzled the bottomless pit of pro-Iggy propaganda that *NME*, then the most important style bible in rock, spewed out. We imagined ourselves to be playing some part in an heroic anti-adventure. Or else Iggy seemed to be playing that part for us.

This was just so much wishful thinking, a wishful thinking that helped Pop survive, and which eventually facilitated his emergence as punk's Tina Turner. The spin is much the same. A sexy past. Great achievements back in the days. Tough times and tragedy. The world's forgotten boy. Never got a fair shake. And isn't it great that he's still around to show us how things once were? So what if he's past his sell-by date? So what if he appeared in *Crocodile Dundee II* and endorses Reebok? He deserves everything he gets, good luck to him, says a compliant media and a mendacious entertainment power elite happy to go along with the notion that he was done out of his crown back in the Seventies.

There is something to this argument. Except that Iggy has been getting a fair shake all his life. Some of the most powerful (and richest) people in music and art bent over backwards to help him. Some of the most beautiful and intelligent women (many of them rich too) put themselves entirely at his disposal. He was an abuser of other people, "a dedicated user" as he once self-described.

His fans would be horrified by his occasional political views. The sort of people who checked out junk rock and fag rock, the territories where he once ruled supreme, never had anything to do with the sexual politics which informed both his private life and his music. Those same people might be surprised to know that their seemingly anti-heroic icon – his image forever incarcerated in a needle infested Berlin transvestite whorehouse of the imagination – actually lives in Southern splendour and drives a Rolls-Royce Corniche when not buying antiques or discussing with his gardener what they should do next to improve the grounds.

In 1979 Pop told Nick Kent that he was a leader who does not want to be followed, that he was exactly the sort of man that Nietzsche could only write about. An important critique of misogyny in rock music, *The Sex Revolts* by Simon Reynolds and Joy Press (which looks at rock clichés like the born-to-run syndrome, the rock singer as soldier or warrior, and "self-aggrandizing fantasies of man machine omnipotence") attributes a sexual fascism to Pop, claiming that his work portrays a kind of rapist without victim, burning for total connection with reality.

"Iggy's whole aesthetic," say Reynolds and Press, "was based around the quest for blackout and bloody miasma. Though he often hurled himself into combat with the audience, the main target of his aggression was his own body."

Pop is an old school sexist and misogynist. There are so many "chicks" in this book that one might be forgiven for thinking that it's about poultry farming. Leee Black Childers, who shared a house with him, can quite distinctly remember Pop saying that he hated women. Pop told Nick Kent, "Well, I hate women. I mean, why do I even have to have a reason for that? It's like, why are people repelled by insects? I use 'em because they are lying, dirty, treacherous and their ambitions all too often involve using me!" This anti-women stance is not merely confined to long-ago doped-out interviews and extravagant rock lyrics. His treatment of women in real life has been lamentable too. He still encourages girls to get naked on his stage for the delight of the crowd.

No rapper would get away with the kind of bitch-hating which characterises Pop's life and work. The white middle-class liberal media never misses an opportunity to point the racist finger at smart aleck black kids who are often being entirely ironic. But when Pop shows up in town, telling journalists what difficult books he's reading (he usually seems to be reading *The Decline and Fall of the Roman Empire*) and how much he likes fine wines, he is rarely challenged on his past right-wing politics or attitudes towards women. In code, he is one of us. White, bookish, and comfortably off. So leave him alone. He has product to push.

I was never an Iggy fanatic. I don't think I'd be an appropriate person to write a whole book about him if I were. When I was a student advocate of Pop my knowledge of his music was just about as sketchy as the next guy. I knew him from hearing the Bowie/Berlin stuff and the *Raw Power* album at parties and in other people's bedsitters. I didn't own any of his records. I first heard *Metallic KO* while walking through a flea market in Dublin in 1993. His rent boy face or Tom of Finland physique on the cover of *Raw Power* or *Creem* magazine was the most of what I knew about him. This image tied in with my taste for sleazy drug-addled outsider rock'n'roll.

Later his Arista albums showed up in Dublin remainder bins for next to nothing so I picked them up and brought them home. Two of these – *Soldier* and *New Values* – were accurate insights into the real Iggy. He was the Ugly American, standing up for blue-collar values while not believing in fairies anymore. I liked those records very much despite, and because of, their stance.

Twelve years ago I met him. I was involved in writing a book about Brion Gysin, the important William Burroughs collaborator. I was told that Gysin had had a relationship of some sort with Pop so I went hunting for that story. Pop's manager was contacted, and he persuaded Iggy to fax through a freshly written text on Gysin which made its way into the book.

When the book came out Iggy was doing his Instinct World Tour and I met up with him after one of those shows. He gamely sang the tune Gysin had written for him back in lost time, 'Blue Baboon'. He looked old at the aftershow party where every lowlife on the local music scene was vying for his attention. He was extraordinarily courteous, like most Americans are, but he was obviously a burnt-out shell of a man. Uptight, sick of this showbiz shit, working his music biz crowd. Working.

I caught him working again two years back. He was headlining a gig at London's Brixton Academy. The venue was far from sold out, the show was OK if somewhat dry. It was certainly better than the previous time I saw him, somewhere down the middle of a nu-metal bill in the middle of a field at an open-air festival. That was an atrocious one-for-the-money effort, providing a unique opportunity for most of the young crowd to go have a piss or pick up a veggie burger before the contemporary big boys took to the stage.

The Brixton crowd were mainly 30-something, shaved-headed, suburban fat boys and frat boys who, clearly, were not familiar with his back catalogue. There was nothing romantic or glamorous about it. The fat boys were there to see the freak show. The guy who did that tune from *Trainspotting* and had a hit with 'Real Wild Child'. Success had stranded him in the middle of a Frankenstein of his own creation.

To some extent Pop had sold himself cheap. To some extent he'd bartered his integrity for a lucrative career in advertising and commercial movies. If you whore yourself to Hollywood, the catwalks, and the ad agencies it's tough going holding on to integrity. The sad thing about this was that his records could still be very good. His 2001 white noise attack, *Beat 'Em Up*, is one of his finest. Not that anybody paid it too much attention; like its predecessor, the much-lauded but soporific *Avenue B*, it sold fuck-all.

Initially nobody paid all that much attention either when, in 2003, Pop got back together with the Asheton brothers to record some of his *Skull Ring* album and to tour once more as Iggy & The Stooges. The sound experiments abandoned long ago in the last century suddenly recommenced with a vigour both youthful and mature. The usual Stooge suspects – fashionista rock hacks, sexy bitches, bitter 30- and 40-something guys with receding hairlines from moneymaking indie bands, queers and junkies – got their collective knickers in a twist about the enterprise.

It was once said of the MC5 – by a member of a megaselling rock group – that they "chopped down the trees to clear the dirt roads to pave the streets to build the highway so the rest of us could drive by in Cadillacs." This is an honourable role in music, one fulfilled by The Ramones, Woody Guthrie, Horslips (who respectively chopped down forests on behalf of Pearl Jam, Bob Dylan and U2), and innumerable other musicians/ bands who never got to lodge the money in the bank but who surely showed the rest of us how to make the art. The crazy thing about Iggy is that he seems to need to be relaxing in the exclusive limousine, cruising down the highway at the end of the movie, having torn down the trees with his bare hands and teeth in the first reel.

But he has a great story to tell. One of the greatest in rock history. Up until the age of 40 he testified consistently and admirably on behalf of a compelling, beguiling, self-destructive lifestyle. I can only endorse that testimony, so eloquently and elegantly lived out through his life and art. Bob Dylan and Lou Reed may have passed their years making better albums and being more consistent. But Iggy went out and lived the life. Read here about degradation, cruelty, sex beyond one's wildest imaginings, Scarface-style quantities of drugs, life lived beyond the edge and beyond the law. Why is Iggy Pop important? Because he is rock'n'roll made flesh.

Joe Ambrose, Marrakesh, March 2004

CHAPTER 1

Rock'n'roll High School

IF you take Iggy's explanation seriously, Jim Osterberg from Ann
Arbor and Iggy Pop from Hell share one body but multiple personalities, much like Superman/Clark Kent or Jesus Christ/God. Jim
Osterberg is allegedly a clubbable, well-read, methodical, glasses-wearing,
quiet fellow, given to golf, money, and regular-guy politics. Iggy Pop, a
"charming fucker" according to one of his many women, is a well hung
rock'n'roll asshole; albeit, at the time of writing, a semi-retired asshole.

Everybody called him Jim until his band The Stooges were in full
flight. Then he began calling himself Iggy Pop and a manager caused
him to be known, briefly, as Iggy Stooge, a formulation he detested. To
this day his real pals know him as Jim. Iggy is a name reserved for his
public persona and for those he wants to keep at arm's length. He says
that the people who call him Jim are "people I've known a long time or
smart alecks."

The creature eventually known as Iggy Pop was born James Newell
Osterberg on April 21, 1947 at Muskegon Osteopathic Hospital,
Michigan. When he was one and a half year's old the family moved from
Muskegon to Ypsilanti, an industrial centre on the outskirts of Ann
Arbor, a significant university town replete with the coffee shops, dives,
and record shops one associates with provincial university towns. In a

1

1996 interview Iggy said he'd "never figured out what this guy Ypsilanti did. He's some obscure Greek hero. It's a really strange name for a town in Michigan. The most famous thing in Ypsilanti is this big water tower made out of brick, about 175 years old. It looks like this big penis."

His mother Louella (nee Christensen) was of Danish and Norwegian descent. Dad Osterberg – another Newell – claimed Irish and English lineage, but he'd been adopted by a Swedish family living in America. Tough-assed Newell – in his day a first class debt collector – was a professional athlete before World War II, playing in the minor leagues on farm teams for the Brooklyn Dodgers. He was regarded as being a good first baseman and hitter. After the War he went back to college and trained to be a teacher. Louella worked as a controller/executive secretary for Bendix Aerospace while Newell was an English teacher at Ypsilanti High. Louella died in 1996. Newell, aged 84, now lives in what they call "an assisted living facility" in Myrtle Beach, South Carolina, where his only child visits him whenever he can.

Dad was a stern disciplinarian as teachers often are and, like many men of his generation, he believed in trailer life. "This is the way to live!" Newell confidently opined. He instilled in young James, generally called Jim, traditional American values concerning sport and hard work, values which would remain buried within Jim during the turbulent decades ahead only to re-emerge in the Nineties when the son wholly embraced his old man's flinty, puritanical approach to work, money and life. In an autobiographical sketch Iggy described his parents as being "hardworking and arrow-straight". Iggy's childhood was passed in trailer parks which remained his relatively prosperous parents' home of choice.

The Osterberg trailer from when Jim was eight until he was 13 was a New Moon model, 45 feet long and 8 feet wide, the trailer used in the hugely influential family movie of the Fifties, *The Long, Long Trailer*, starring Lucille Ball, Desi Arnez, and "40 feet of train". Iggy's parents subsequently traded up into a spacious 50 foot by 10 Vagabond trailer with which they were content for a long time. The Osterbergs lived at Lot Ninety-six, Coachville Gardens Mobile Park, which Iggy later described as being "on the outskirts of the outskirts". There were 113 trailers in the trailer camp, and the only people there with a college education were the Osterbergs. Young Jim slept on a shelf above the kitchenette.

Iggy: "In a well designed trailer, to save space, the doors don't open and close hinge-wise – they're sliding doors and generally without locks. So I had no lock on my door. A boy without a lock on his door and without at least one storey separating him from his parents goes through some funny shit. So I used to spend a lot of time in the bathroom, or out in the cornfields."

He was never particularly enthusiastic about his Ann Arbor roots. "It's a dry town," he complained. "I never cared for Ann Arbor very much. I went to school there really and that's all. I'm from Ypsilanti which is more like a town. It's oakies, bunch of oakies."

In Ypsilanti the Osterberg's trailer was planted right across from a big shopping centre, located in the middle of a huge cornfield. It was the repressive post-war America of J.D. Salinger, Pat Boone and Eisenhower. The malign forces of American optimism seemed unassailable. Vietnam was still France's problem. America was strong. The transcendent Frank Sinatra dominated the airwaves while Rock Hudson was the very essence of American manhood. After 20 years in the belly of the grungey rock'n'roll beast, these influences would re-emerge to shape the Iggy Pop who now provides soundtrack material for corporate advertising campaigns, drives a vintage Cadillac, and shows up in a tuxedo at the Oscars.

During his childhood and early teens Jim had bronchial asthma which caused him to lead a sheltered life under pretty constant maternal supervision. His mother Louella remembered him as being a well liked and happy child: "He was definitely a very normal kid, and he had lots of friends. He would get along with them well even as a very small child. He enjoyed his friendships and got along very, very well."

The Osterbergs were located significantly close to the University of Michigan at Ann Arbor campus, a centre for independent and influential cultural thinking. SDS (Students for a Democratic Society), the powerful radical student organisation, was founded in Ann Arbor in 1959 by Tom Hayden. Composer Robert Ashley – busy forging the future of American opera – was working in the University's Music Department. By the late Sixties Ann Arbor was a major hub for drug distribution and consumption throughout the Midwest.

Any full-blooded American boy – and wimpy, geeky, asthma-scarred, young Jim Osterberg was just about full-blooded enough when it came to conventional male pursuits – would've been thrilled to have his trailer parked around the corner from a Sixties campus then cooking up a tough potent stew of pussy, protest, and pot. It was entirely relevant to the emergent noise merchant that Ann Arbor was 40 miles from the legendary motor city of Detroit, the centre of the American automobile industry, a big music town, and an important port. The State of Michigan was heavily industrialised and fertile. It's a cold, bleak, and isolated place in the winter.

Iggy says that his father was a difficult customer who couldn't stand the "buddy-buddy suburbs shit, watering the lawn, talking to the guy next door. I'm kinda cantankerous too. Born on the cusp of Aries and Taurus: stubborn, miserable, never satisfied. My father was very highly strung. Very shy man. A disciplinarian. Kept his army haircut, made me get these military haircuts, quarter-inch all round, bought my clothes. Didn't drink. Didn't smoke or cuss or fool around with women." The Osterbergs were definitely the most literate occupants of the entire trailer park. Their neighbours were mainly drivers of heavy trucks or low-wage unskilled workers who were often migratory. "Guys," according to Iggy, "who would come up from the South when they heard there was some work in Detroit."

It was an incredibly isolated environment. He never met kids who lived in houses. He never felt like the other kids anyway. He felt weird. "We lived near this gravel pit," he said. "I never knew when I was a kid why I always felt so melancholy. But it was because I was looking at this slag heap every day . . . Even later, I hardly hung out with anybody, even the guys in my group."

He got good grades in English, Communications, and Mathematics. Mother Louella said that all the other mothers she knew would come up to her and say, "I wish my son was as well-behaved and nice to talk to as your Jim."

A hyper-intelligent kid with some health problems whose curiosity was encouraged by bookish parents, the adolescent Jim grew active in civics and student government, and got involved with both music and drama at school. Although subsequently a vocal supporter of far-right President Ronald Reagan, the young Jim was, like most other smart kids of his generation, a fan of the neo-liberal John F. Kennedy. Jim was made Vice President of his class in Ninth Grade and, according to Louella, chosen to represent a foreign country in a statewide school civics project known as The Model U.N.: "I can't remember which country Jim was supposed to be involved with, but they would go away for about three days and they actually had a model United Nations organisation. They spoke on the particular issues that were in the real U.N. at the time."

Jim got interested in music in the fourth grade when he started playing drums. He found himself fascinated by the industrial home environment that was always around him, by everything from his father's electric shaver through to the electric space heater in their metal trailer. When he was nine years old he was taken on a tour of Ford's main assembly plant in River Rouge and there he saw his first machine press. "A machine press is basically a metal foundation," he said, "a great piece of very heavy metal cut in a form. You put what's to become a fender in the middle, it crashes down, you pull out the form of metal and put another piece in. I loved that sound!" The sound gave birth, 20 years later, to a song about his background, 'Mass Production'.

The industrial and industrialised noises of his childhood and early adolescence made Jim crave for something nastier and less acceptable than the rather conventional aspirations of other Sixties R&B buffs: "A large part of me remains like this kid listening really close to some of this stuff and going, 'I like this and I like this. This is shit, and I hate it and I wanna blow it up.' A lot of Mishima in me – *Confessions of A Mask*. The day I was out of school; platinum hair shoulder length as soon as possible. Wrecking cars, breaking into houses, drugs . . . the wildest thing."

His father initially opposed his son's interest in drumming, and his nascent desire to be in a band. Newell, a big man, said to Jim, "You're gonna have to push me out this door if you wanna go off and play the drums with these bums instead of going to school." Jim said, "OK Dad, here I come." At that moment, when Newell realised that his son was serious and committed – not to mention scared – he was very graceful about it, and let the drumming continue.

Louella was more indulgent: "We always encouraged him in everything he did. We have always supported him, and we gave him a lot of financial support. He always knew that he could call us if he needed us in any way." (This may well have been the case, but those calls were not always entirely welcome, especially during the Seventies when their son was globally synonymous with self-destructive excess. Iggy: "I always kept in touch, yeah. I remember I rang them up from Germany in the middle of the fuckin' night once, rambling incoherently. I was practically an alcoholic. Awful . . . my dad just went, 'You're boring,' and slammed the phone down.")

Sam Treacy (Ann Arbor Sixties political activist): "The Osterbergs were very well regarded folks, blameless people. That their son turned out to be such a tearaway must have come as something of a seismic shock to them – especially to his dad – but Jim was hardly unique in that regard. It was the Fifties heading into the Sixties so the kids of respectable decent folks all over Middle America were turning on and dropping out. Or as my mom used to say, because there were lots of dope smoking sleepovers at our place, turning up and dropping in. One of my friends was taught by Jim's old man and reckoned that Jim had a tough, tough time of it. Mr Osterberg had great faith in the leather belt, but I don't mean to imply that he was an asshole . . . far from it . . . he was just entirely typical of his generation of American men. Jim's mother always had him turned out impeccably. I'm not remotely surprised that he's become something of a clothes horse or dandy in middle age. The Osterbergs were always a dapper family in their own quiet unassuming way."

Ron Asheton, subsequently the guitarist in The Stooges, remembers Jim Osterberg as just another kid at school. He would see Jim in the school hallway. "Today, he'd probably get his ass beat if he wore his hair like he wore it back then . . . it was like a regular haircut with little Betty Page bangs, like a teeny Beatle cut. That was pretty radical, but I was the guy who had to really try to hide my hair, 'cause I had like a Brian Jones haircut, all the way over my eyes, and sideburns. I had to sort of not wash it for a long time, so it didn't look like it was real long. But he'd see me in the hallway, and I'd be wearing leather vests and turtlenecks and looking way different than his cashmere sweater, chinos, and tasselled penny loafers. So he'd always give me a nod, and it was like, 'Yeah, this guy . . . I saw him play with that band at school, man. I wanna be in a band.' He played good drums, and he got to sing a song, and he's in the band and everyone was cheering."

Although Asheton mischievously assigns Jim Osterberg to the cashmere and chinos crowd, Iggy sees things differently and says that the rich kids at school used to put his trailer home down because he was unfortunate enough to fall into a school district where "all the sweater guys, ya know, all the cashmere guys" went. He reckons that mixing with the smoothies helped make a man out of him because their Hush Puppy hostility made him "a star", made him really brutal.

All the hip or weird Ann Arbor kids, including Jim Osterberg and the two nihilistic outsider Asheton brothers, Ron and Scott, hung out at the Michigan Union cafeteria, which was dubbed "The Jug". "Everyone was young enough," Ron Asheton says, "so we'd go in and sit down and we'd be there every afternoon. The security guards would come around once an hour and ask for ID if you didn't look right. We'd get kicked out. We'd just wait half an hour and we'd come back in, and stay until we were kicked out again. But he (Iggy) kinda started showing up, and that's how I kinda got to know him – just in the hallway, and then hangin' out at the Michigan Union cafeteria. He'd see me there, and by that time, he was in college, and was like, 'Hey, it's you, how's it goin', man?' "

When he was 15 Jim got involved with a band called The Iguanas after winning a local talent contest with school pal Jim McLoughlin.

Kids began to call Jim "Iggy" as The Iguanas – Iggy (drums/vocals), McLoughlin (guitar/vocals), Nick Kolokithas (guitar/vocals), Don Swickerath (bass), and Sam Swisher (sax/percussion/backing vocals) – grew in stature. Iggy subsequently denigrated The Iguanas as being the son of a realtor, the son of an insurance salesman, and the son of a clerk. The son of a teacher was trying to get his fellow bourgeois musicians to try out songs by The Kinks, England's most deviant R&B merchants, instead of semi-surf instrumentals such as The Ventures' 'Perfidia'. "I was the only one in the band who was really into music," he claims. "The rest of The Iguanas weren't so serious about it. There was a division in the band. They all liked Beatle songs; I liked the Stones, Kinks, and Them."

This notion that nobody involved in any given venture – other than Iggy – knew what they were doing runs like a river through all of Pop's pronouncements on important collaborators, with the notable exception of David Bowie who, as the whole world knows, knew exactly what *he* was doing. On the other hand Pop is the only one out of that provincial college band scene who went on to enjoy some level of global fame, the one who clearly had the Bunsen burner of harsh ambition up his ass from day one. You don't need to be an asshole to make it in music, but it sure helps.

He was – for sure – not terribly hot on the core inspiration behind The Iguanas; The Beatles' aesthetic of well-structured dippy songs and social activism. He rightly felt that their easy-going populist approach went against the spirit of the regular-guy, rugged-individualist blue-collar trailer park rock'n'roll which he favoured. "I enjoyed their early records. They lost me with *Sgt. Pepper's*, which I think is a really over-rated and depressing album. Once they got into the droopy moustaches, the whole thing kind of lost it for me . . . Basically, there was a move-ment by the sons and daughters of the middle class in America and England to take this greasy little lower-class phenomenon and claim it for themselves. We'll promote it. We'll lifestyle it. And in a lot of ways that's been convenient for me. I've made a better living at it. But it did take away a lot from the guts and flesh."

The Iguanas did pretty well locally, clean-cut boys with the somewhat bug-eyed Osterberg on drums. They played mainly frat houses and at various holiday resorts in the area. After graduating from high school in '65 Iggy managed to get the group a summer residency at the Ponytail Club in Harbor Springs, a resort in North Michigan. They had to work hard, playing five sets a day, six days a week. According to one biogra-pher, Iggy earned an impressive $55 a week from this gig. "Wow,

7

professional employment far away from home," he enthused. "Five 45-minute sets a night, 15-minute breaks, six nights a week. I plugged a phonograph into that socket and listened to *Out Of Our Heads* and *Bringing It All Back Home* all summer. Started getting wild, grew my hair to my shoulders and dyed it platinum, got arrested and took my first mug shot. Got fired from the Ponytail."

The Iguanas pressed up 1,000 copies of their own single and released it on their own Forte label. The 45 was sold on the door at their resort gigs. Girls were always good for buying these things, as were faggy guys and the occasionally intelligent one. The release featured a cover of 'Mona' by Bo Diddley backed with a Beatles-style original called 'I Don't Know Why' written by Kolokithas. (Iguanas' demos from this period – including 'Again And Again', the first instance of Iggy's words being put to music – were released on Norton Records in the mid-Nineties.) During the summer of '65 they spread their wings and played shows in Chicago, Toledo and Lansing.

When he was 16 Iggy switched from the Ypsilanti public school system to Ann Arbor Pioneer High School. Newall felt that his kid would benefit from the more intellectually competitive environment provided by the upper-middle class cashmere kids there. At Pioneer High he rubbed shoulders and crotches with the fit sons and daughters of lawyers, doctors, professors and the like. It can't have been easy going for a sensitive adolescent living amongst society's also-rans in a trailer park. Ann Arbor writer and friend Anne Wehrer, who subsequently wrote the autobiographical *I Need More* with Iggy, thought that Pop always felt a little embarrassed about the fact that he lived in a trailer. "The kids in Ann Arbor did look down on it," she recalled. "They were snotty about it." People who knew him then reckon that he has spent his entire life running away from his lowly roots towards the glamour of showbiz success with all the trimmings.

Iggy, an intrepid social climber from the outset, took note of how the other half lived, now that he was mixing with elite movers and shakers. "These rich kids had sweaters with V-necks made out of materials and things. I'd never seen anything like that before . . . I was burdened by the fact that whenever I tried to express myself I would be laughed at. I was considered weird. A weird kid. I was also very shy, very unhip, very unglib, and never wore the right clothes."

At the end of the summer of '65 The Iguanas broke up. Being the sons of straight bourgeois types, people who had a stake in society, their mutual attention now turned towards a future in the real world. Iggy, no different from the rest of them, applied for admission to the University of Michigan. Because of his good grades and track record he was accepted right away. After the breakup of The Iguanas he attended the university for one semester with the idea of studying anthropology. He fell in with a smart set who were a kind of cross between contemporary counterculture society and the geeky trenchcoat Mafias of more recent memory.

Anne Wehrer: "He wanted to study anthropology and he went to the University of Michigan but they were taking too long to get to the point. So he went and got the reading list and read all the books instead of taking the courses. He considers rock'n'roll a social anthropology."

Ron Asheton: "He was in college for a while, at the University of Michigan, then he'd go to the cafeteria and that's where I'd be hanging out with Dave Alexander and sometimes my brother or any of the other guys like Bill Cheatham – us who were 'the different ones', the ones with long hair. It was the only place you felt kind of OK. Out on the street, the frats, the jocks, they'd throw beer cans and shit at you, but you go to the Michigan Union, you'd find people like that. The beatnik people, some of the older professors with the goatees and stuff. 'Ah yes, young man, what is your philosophy of life?' And the guy'd be some weirdo fag – aaahhhh! That kinda stuff. But you met a lot of cool people that way. So that's kinda how our relationship . . . started to grow."

When he lost interest in his anthropology classes, Iggy got a regular job at Discount Records, an important Ann Arbor record store and subcultural hub, the cool place with the latest sounds. Robert Scheff, who subsequently toured with Iggy before changing his name to "Blue" Gene Tyranny, was a sales clerk at Discount Records, an outlet intimately involved in the evolution of the local band scene, a place where kids could hang out and have all the new releases played for them by compliant staff.

"Discount Records was one of those really interesting places to work," Tyranny says. "You could hear all the new music that was coming out, all the new singles, and all kinds of music. It was subsequently bought out by Columbia Records and became more of a conventional rack store. When I was working there, and when Iggy was working there, you could go in and order stuff. People used to just hang out because you could go there all the time and do that."

Iggy was in charge of the rock'n'roll section, a good sharp salesman. He was the sort of sharp guy you find in provincial record shops all over the world, the sort of guy who'd tell the kids, "We're getting in the first Stones album but not too many 'cause they don't want me to have them here."

Local big shot blues band – and Discount Records scenesters – The Prime Movers, founded in 1965, heard that Iggy was out of a gig and, since he was one of the most powerful little drummers in town, they set out to recruit him. The core of The Prime Movers was the Erlewine brothers, Michael and Daniel, along with "Blue" Gene Tyranny (still trading as Robert Scheff) and Jack Dawson. The thoughtful sophisticated Michael Erlewine had been hitchhiking with Bob Dylan in 1961. He'd already hung out at shrines associated with the Beat Generation such as Venice West, Greenwich Village, and San Francisco.

Iggy later denigrated them thus: "The Prime Movers was an effete, bohemian, intellectual, blues band of 25- and 26-year-olds. I was 18, which was a big difference at that time." On another occasion they were described as a "bunch of effete beatniks" playing "ersatz blues". The fact of the matter is that The Prime Movers were an impressive collection of individuals with strong track records behind them and, as it turned out, interesting lives ahead of them. It would be fair to say that, up until the time he got to know these effete intellectual types, Jim Osterberg was just another good-looking provincial Sixties kid messing around in a frat band on the fringes of real and interesting music. After The Prime Movers he was aware of things like art, politics, and experimentation.

Subsequent MC5 guitarist Wayne Kramer said that if you were black and grew up in Chicago, you knew all about blues bands, but that if you were a white suburban kid from Detroit, blues bands were pretty exotic. "The Prime Movers' drummer was this guy Iggy Osterberg," Kramer recalled. "He was really a great drummer; rock steady, no razzle dazzle, no flash, just pure power rock'n'roll beat. Their band was popular because they were so different. Everyone else tried choreography and had steps and did instrumentals, and just were like all the other bands of that era. Around 1965/66 when The Beatles broke, everyone had Beatle haircuts and learned to sing in harmony. The idea that Iggy, who was renowned as one of the best drummers on the scene, had joined this blues band was really exciting."

"We were influenced by The Paul Butterfield Band from Chicago," says Prime Movers leader Michael Erlewine. "They'd come to Detroit and we'd both play a place called The Living End. We were playing the music that the older black people liked, and I think they laughed a lot at us too. It really wasn't much of a scene, we were the first new kind of band that were counterculture, that wasn't a crappy frat band. When we knew Iggy he was very shy, especially around girls. He had long eyelashes, he was very effeminate in his appearance, the way he carried himself. Not in a bad way . . . women went to him."

Sam Treacy says that it's hardly surprising that women went for the young drummer, who was known as Horse Dick at school. "Iggy was a very shy guy. A pal of mine was a room-mate with him and he told me that Iggy had a huge dick. Iggy couldn't get over it. He didn't know precisely what to do with it. He was not aggressive to women. Women would come and get him and he liked them. But he was not what you would call a regular guy in terms of reaching out and making conquests of any kind. It had to be absolutely safe, they had to be subservient to him, like telling him that they loved him."

Iggy: "I was working with older, sorta older Beats. We still had Beats left over at that time. It was like 1966 and you have the leftover of the Beats, the beginnings of the people starting to grow their hair but make it clean. In those days if you had long hair it was dirty. That was being a beatnik. They were more interested in, like, shooting up or taking bennies than marijuana. Tea wasn't that popular. They called it tea, and kinda sneered at it."

Michael Erlewine: "We studied black music like other people study in college. That is all we did. Our band did not play anything else, and we were content to study the Chicago blues and try to play it . . . Our band travelled to San Francisco in the Summer of Love where we played at all the main clubs."

"Blue" Gene Tyranny: "I was always involved in avant-garde music as well as rock'n'roll since I was a young kid. A friend of mine who was a composer went up to Ann Arbor because he got a position in the University of Michigan Music Department. While he was there he met up with these fascinating people who were doing the ground-breaking ONCE Festival. The ONCE group of composers became one of the most generic New Music scenes in the Sixties. There are a number of books being written about ONCE right now, and there are a lot of articles in journals, etc. My pal got in touch with me and told me that I should come to Ann Arbor. I won a BMI Student Composer's Award that year which gave me enough money to be able to leave Texas, where there was a lot going on that I wanted to leave. I was offered a scholarship to Julliard while I was briefly in New York but I just got on a bus and came to Ann Arbor. I never went to college there but I worked in various places.

"While I was there I started playing in The Prime Movers blues band. We were one of the first white boy blues bands in the style of The Paul Butterfield Blues Band. We did Chicago and Delta blues. We used to play the black club in the small . . . what might be called the ghetto of Ann Arbor. A couple of streets long! I think we were appreciated by lots of people there. The bar guy liked us because we brought in the college crowd. Iggy was an excellent drummer. Very clean and not obtrusive at all, really tasteful. Also he was pursuing drumming very seriously indeed. Michael Erlewine, who was the leader of The Prime Movers, was actually sort of a mentor for Iggy at that time, really helping him making his decisions and stuff, because he was a younger kid. I think we were all older than him but it was at that time of life when a few years makes all the difference. Although he was the first kid to dye his hair silver at school and things like this, he was very shy, embarrassed to talk about sex around the other guys in the band. Oh, yeah."

Iggy: "Michigan's a funny place, and it's one of the few places where the racism works in a different way. Michigan's different than most of the other states filled with hillbillies. In Michigan, the hillbillies kind of always dug black people in a weird way; even though they didn't want to live next door to 'em, there was always an admiration for them, and for a lot of forms of black music. They were just trying to strut their stuff in a certain way. I don't know of anywhere else that that took place. What it did, that free jazz, it loosened up the music in bands and we all got more crazier."

The entire Asheton family – by all accounts an idiosyncratic collection of individuals, very much a part of their epoch – were on the fringes of the more collegiate and prosperous scene on which Iggy was now thriving. Garage band refugees Scott and Ron plus sister Kathy who fancied herself as a singer were wannabes on a thriving local band battleground where the main players were The Up, The Prime Movers, and the infamous MC5. As White Panther founder and MC5 manager John Sinclair saw it, the Asheton brothers were "just two dead end kids. Rock 'n'roll kids without a thought in their minds. Watching goofy shit on TV."

The Asheton boys were assiduously hanging out, but as yet they'd not placed themselves at the very core of the action. They lived at home with their parents in a part of Ann Arbor called the Division. Their father, a Marine Corps pilot, died when Ron was 15. There was a lot of wacky American Gothic musical hinterland buried deep within the Asheton family. More than a little of the raucous shrill eccentricity of The Stooges came from within the zany family background of the brothers. At one stage it looked like Ron might become a psychedelic accordion player, something along the lines of James Ellroy's Dick Contino character, rather than an undisputed inventor of punk rock guitar playing.

Ron Asheton: "My great-aunt Ruthie and my great-uncle Dick-Dick were vaudevillian performers . . . the whole family would get together in the summer and have big ol' clam bakes and get all sorts of crabs and oysters. Dick-Dick would always sit at the piano and play the accordion and violin along with a pair of trained parakeets. He'd play for me and be drinking his whiskey. While everyone was partying, I'd sit there and was just fascinated. Ruthie would come in and they'd put on a little show. It was just too cool to listen to her live music when you were five years old. She'd play the banjo and then she gave me her old violin, one of the old crummy ones. I started sawing away on it until my ma took it away from me and turned it into a planter. She asked me if I wanted to be involved in music. I said I wanted an accordion 'cause that's what Ruthie played so I started taking lessons. I went from a tiny one to a full-sized accordion. I actually ended up doing recitals because my teacher was good and I was anxious to learn. So here's this little kid playing this huge accordion. I wasn't really rocking out but I was playing well for a year's worth of lessons. They had to parade me out for the music schools. I'd play in ensembles and as a soloist. So I wanted to be a TV star instead of being a policeman or a fireman. Also my mother used to sing on Radio Detroit when I was a teenager."

In *I Need More* Iggy says: "Scott Asheton – he was the juvenile delinquent. He was this Elvis Presley looking character; a really quite handsome young lad, you know, somewhere between Elvis and Fabian, real rough dude, real badass, good fighter and shit like that. He used to always wear his sleeves rolled up."

Wayne Kramer thought that Scott Asheton was a pugilist worthy of respect. One night Kramer and MC5 guitarist Fred "Sonic" Smith went to Ann Arbor to check out The Prime Movers. Lanky and dapper Fred Smith had his hair reasonably long at this time so a bunch of local yokels started picking a fight with him and Kramer, slapping Smith across the back of the head and speculating as to whether he was a boy or a girl. Things were getting somewhat out of hand when Scott Asheton, who wanted to be a drummer, saw what was happening. Asheton picked up one of Smith's assailants and kicked him right across the dancefloor, ordering him to quit hassling the MC5 boys because they were his friends. Scott may have come to their assistance because at that stage Fred "Sonic" Smith was consorting with Scott's sister Kathy.

English rock writer Nick Kent confirms that the future Rock Action was a handful. When he got to know Scott in the early Seventies, Kent said that the drummer "resembled a hard-core biker type pondering his next act of imminent barbarism". These Asheton boys obviously existed in a universe on the other side of the tracks from Iggy's socially aspirant, arty avant-garde pals. The Ashetons' Marine father had groomed his sons for a life in the military. Ron was a Nazi obsessive. He subsequently wore Nazi gear onstage with The Stooges and in band photo shoots. "I didn't like what they stood for but I liked what they wore," he subsequently professed.

"These guys were the laziest, delinquent sort of pig slobs ever born," Iggy said of his pals. "Really spoiled rotten and babied by their mother. Scotty Asheton – he was a juvenile delinquent. His dad had died, his and Ron's, so they didn't have much discipline at home."

It was from within the Ashetons' milieu, and not from Iggy's posse, that the ground breaking outsider stance of The Stooges emerged. Bass player Dave Alexander was the Ashetons' young weirdo neighbour and their pal.

"David was kinda pink, because he had a really bad complexion," says Iggy in *I Need More*. "He used a whole lot of Clearasil, because Clearasil was advertised on Dick Clark for zits . . . Anyway, he had this orange hair, real long hair, and he used to carry a knife in his pocket. He was about 5' 7" and he would wear those stretch Levi's . . . they would always be coming down around his hips."

It was in the company of Dave Alexander that Ron skipped school before travelling, in his teens, all the way to Liverpool to check out the bands and to see the town that gave birth to The Beatles.

Ron Asheton: "The only reason I really got to go was I had a friend who I went to high school and junior high with. His father got a job in Southport, England, working for the Essex Wire Company. So I said, 'We're staying with them. They said it's OK.' But that wasn't true; we just showed up on their doorstep one night at 10 in the evening. His mother answered the door and almost had a heart attack. The next day they shipped us right the fuck out, man. The old man took us down to this bed and breakfast place, which wound up being really cool, 'cause we had total freedom.

"Dave and me had to share this one fuckin' room in this old house, this old couple, this old man and woman and these three giant dogs, but it was cool. At 11.15 every day, we caught the train to Liverpool, which is about a 45-minute train ride . . . we wanted to go to where The Beatles were; we actually went looking for The Cavern. And the Cavern's open, it's functioning every afternoon. So for 60, 50 pence, or 35 pence, you could go in and there'd be local bands playin'. And it was fucking unbelievably cool. Here we are going, 'Wow, this is it . . . we're in the fucking Cavern, and there's bands playing.' They're kind of on the level of bands that we're trying to start out; these guys playing the

Cavern are the dregs of Liverpool and the surrounding areas. They're the little guys that get paid 10 dollars to say they played in The Cavern. But we went every fuckin' day and it was so cool.

"We befriended these few guys. This guy Robert . . . at that time the Mods were really happening. 'My Generation' had just popped, so there were a lotta razor cuts. Little razor haircuts like Pete Townshend haircuts. This guy Robert, he was still in our vein; he had big Brian Jones . . . even longer . . . sheepdog bangs, and his hair was down to his shoulders. It was like, 'Wow, man!' and he took us to all the cool places where we could buy stuff with the little money we did have. I loved those big pinstripe pants, wide pinstripe black pants with little pinstripes like Brian Jones, 'cause I was deep into Brian Jones. Real Beatle boots with huge heels . . . they were actually flimsy and crummy as hell, but they were so cool, to get 'em. But the actual three-inch heels . . . Yes! We didn't have much money; we were basically living on one hamburger a day and a candy bar, but he took us everywhere. He took us to the Beatle houses.

"That trip to England was really a great thing. And when I came back, that was what totally changed my life. I could never look back again. Y'know, it's like, 'Nope, I'm never gonna go back to school.' I was a good student, even though I was kicked out – the first guy with long hair. Going back was like, 'This sucks. I don't belong here.' After that giant taste of freedom, to go to The Cavern every afternoon . . . now it's sitting in the classroom, listening to somebody try to teach me something that I don't give a damn about. 'Fuck this!' So that was the brace that was put on my backbone, to have the guts to go out and do the music thing."

When Alexander and Asheton finally got home from England they were kicked out of school because they had "superlong hair". They were sporting giant sideburns and had knee-high boots – the leather kind with Cuban heels, leather vests, and turtlenecks. Their school counsellor worked himself into a state of apoplexy and announced, 'This won't do!' Ron said, 'Fuck it!' and started hanging out again in front of Discount Records, while Iggy began to pay more attention to his school acquaintance.

Ron was now playing guitar in a band called The Dirty Shames, with Scott on drums, Dave Alexander on bass, and Billy Cheatham on drums. All these guys would later manifest themselves in The Stooges – indeed The Stooges were literally The Dirty Shames plus Jim Osterberg on vocals. The Dirty Shames were the very essence of what it was to be a garage band come from garageland. They never played any gigs in front

15

of an audience but practised away eccentrically for their own amusement and gratification. Their unique internalised fantasy of what music should amount to played a defining role in what subsequently became the "otherness" of The Stooges. Iggy described The Dirty Shames as a "one-note samba band".

Ron Asheton: "Me and Dave Alexander were super geeked on bands. We were always sitting around listening to records and talking about The Beatles or the Stones. We even had a band – well, sort of a band. We were called The Dirty Shames. We would play along to records and say, 'We're great!' Then we'd take the record off and say, 'Whaaa? Hey, maybe this isn't sounding too good.'"

The Dirty Shames built up a reputation for being "a great band" because they never played in public. They were eventually called down to Discount Records to meet up with the guy promoting a Rolling Stones show in Detroit, who wanted them to open for the Stones. "We were all excited," Ron says, "until we realised, 'Wow, we can't even play!' So we told the guy, 'I think we're going to be auditioning out in LA.'"

Despite ludicrous offers to open for the Stones, Ron was happy enough to jump ship when a real offer came his way. The Prime Movers were looking for a new bass player so Iggy suggested his old school pal Ron, who was a year younger than him. Ron, however, was sharp enough to realise, quickly enough, that he was as out of his league playing with The Prime Movers as he would have been supporting The Rolling Stones. "They were very serious," he reckoned. "I played with the group for a while. That's when I really learned how to play. I dug the blues, but I wanted to play more straight rock'n'roll."

Iggy and Ron grew close during their brief time together in The Prime Movers. Iggy took note of the dead end kid's ambition and sense of purpose. "He was really learning to play good," he felt. "They let him do it for a couple of weeks but he was really too rock'n'roll. So, as soon as they had a better chance to get somebody that was really experienced, they gave Ron the boot." Obviously determined to assist Ron, Iggy now got him a good gig with a Birmingham rock band, The Chosen Few. Iggy knew the group's pretty boy singer Scott Richardson, and the line-up also included an ambitious young guitarist dude called James Williamson.

Ron Asheton: "They fancied themselves as The Rolling Stones. James Williamson with his fair Keith Richards lookalike, and Scott Richardson deep into Jagger. I liked Scott because at the time there weren't many people around that wore white shoes and bell bottoms!

We hit it off right away and I went to Birmingham. I met James Williamson at the first practice."

"When I was in eighth grade," Williamson told Ken Shimamoto, chronicler of the Detroit scene, "I moved to Michigan and it turned out I moved next door to a family, the oldest son of which was in a folk music band, *a la* The Kingston Trio or whatever in those days. This was in the mid-Sixties. His younger brother was a good guitar player too, and we used to hang out and play a lot. He showed me a lot of stuff, so I rapidly got influenced by all the Detroit guys. In those days, that was a pretty broad brush in terms of music. In terms of songs I guess The Beach Boys, all the typical teenage song guys, The Ventures, and all them."

Ron ended up playing with Williamson for just a few weeks before James' dad sent his pesky son away to an upmarket reform school of sorts.

James Williamson: "I was incorrigible. Basically, I was kind of stupid, young. I wouldn't do what anybody told me to do. It was an interesting season. I was trying to grow my hair long, and they didn't like that at my school. I thought that Bob Dylan would never cut his hair, and they said you have to, and we didn't agree, so I got sent to 'juvie' and then they buzzed all of my hair off! I guess I found out a little bit about fighting city hall.

"The band kept on going, and it went through a few incarnations. Then finally when I was in 10th grade was when Ron played bass in the band. A lot of stuff up in Ann Arbor. The band was really based out of the Detroit area . . . It was mostly Stones, basically, and then we'd do a few other ones. On the side, I was writing songs, and that's how I actually met Iggy for the first time. One time when I was home from juvenile home, I went to New York, and lived there for a while. I sat in when the band (The Chosen Few) was playing in Ann Arbor at a frat house. Iggy came to the gig and on the side I was playing him some songs I was doing; we kind of hit it off. That was when he was playing in The Prime Movers."

Ron Asheton stayed with The Chosen Few for a year and a half until they broke up in the spring of '67. Meanwhile, Iggy continued his impressive apprenticeship in The Prime Movers, and became something of an ace face figure on the hopping, happening, local scene; a scene uniquely social and community-based. One photograph shows The Prime Movers playing in a trellis fenced suburban back garden, the other Prime Movers looking collegiate, clean cut, and of their time. Sexy young Iggy looks nothing like the rest of them, hunched over his drumkit like a demented diva while two little girls, about six or seven, look on indifferently. Another posed shot shows the Movers immaculately dressed in bebop suits, collars and ties, sitting upright (and perhaps uptight) around a small table. Iggy is slouched pensively over the same table looking studiously existential, louche, and disenchanted.

He learned his trade playing sessions with a remarkable range of passing-through superstars. He was a pick-up drummer for most of the Motown groups and learned a lot about stage presentation sitting behind those slick, uniformed, often female, acts. He backed up, and had plenty of time to study the ass movements of, The Velvelettes, The Marvelettes, The Shangri-Las, The Contours, The Four Tops, and The Crystals. He saw some great dancing that way. "I would play with anybody professionally coming through the area to learn," he later claimed. A contemporary from the Ann Arbor scene suggests, however, that his claims in this department are "somewhat exaggerated".

At one stage Tamla Motown – founded and based in Detroit – considered signing The Prime Movers to one of their white boy subsidiaries. They came to Ann Arbor and drove the band around town in black limousines, arranging a dinner between the Erlewine brothers and the Everly Brothers. The problem was Tamla wanted them to be a white pop band but The Prime Movers were too "black" for them.

When asked in the Nineties by feminist magazine *Bust* what Sixties women had influenced him, Iggy's response, betraying a sexism typical of his generation, wasn't exactly Jane Fonda or Simone de Beauvoir: "The Ronettes. Ronnie Ronette and also the blonde girl in The Shangri-Las. When I was a teenager I used to get pick-up gigs, to drum once in a while. I actually drummed behind them once. Man, she was so cute. She had a certain kind of complexion where the colour of her hair and the colour of her skin and the colour of her eyes were all about the same, this indeterminate sandy look, and it looked really cool, it really looked great. Girls like that. And basically what really used to influence me was girls that were at high school when I was in junior high; their look was like beehive hair, big pointy bras, wasp waists, and then you'd have a skirt, I don't know what the line was called, but it made their asses look really wide. This was very fantastic, you know, it was just like, 'Wow.' It kind of went with the cars . . . the Cadillacs and everything at the time. The big fins, big *chests*."

Ron Asheton's association with Iggy and The Prime Movers continued after he left the band and joined The Chosen Few. He kept in touch and roadied for them, while they let him sit in and play a couple of songs every time they rehearsed. This arrangement came to an end when Iggy finally quit the blues band. There were, in all, some 37 members who passed through The Prime Movers at one time or another.

After the Erlewines filled Iggy in on the shape and nature of the blues, his own direction changed. He checked out people like John Lee Hooker, Muddy Waters and, inevitably, Chuck Berry, taking note of the fact that all these guys were playing their own tunes. He felt, having enjoyed the real thing, that he couldn't go back and listen to The British Invasion. It was with The Prime Movers that he first went to Chicago to meet a variety of local blues figures. Later, slyly enough, he went back to socialise with those old men on his own. He did the occasional vocal turn with The Prime Movers, notably on Muddy Waters' 'I'm A Man'.

He decided that Sam Lay, a locally famous black blues drummer, was going to be his mentor so he quit his job at Discount Records and moved to Chicago. This musical pilgrimage represented a pivotal turning point in Pop's musical development and in his personal lifestyle. He left home for the first time, and got to sleep on people's floors and in their spare beds.

Lay was the drummer with the overestimated but influential Paul Butterfield Blues Band, famous for backing Bob Dylan when he "went electric" at the Newport Folk Festival in 1965. Lay had the reputation of being a man who might draw a knife on you, a somewhat forebidding presence to your average young white kid. "Sam Lay was a kind of rough guy, a big guy, very street," says Detroit producer and bass player Bill Laswell. "I think Iggy picked up a lot from him. About how to handle himself and about how to adopt the stance of a musician." Lay taught Iggy how to play the double shuffle. He wasn't the only Prime Mover to worship at Lay's altar – Dan Erlewine would subsequently play with him professionally.

Iggy: "I didn't play with Sam Lay. I got his number and address and went to Chicago and sought him out, as it were and said, 'Would you introduce me to some people who would get me some jobs?' That was after he left The Paul Butterfield Blues Band. He had a bad problem with his respirations, tuberculosis, and what's that other disease that's like it, it doesn't really matter, you know the type, you know these weird diseases, I can't remember the other one, it's one wet, pleurisy. He had to leave the road, so I can't remember who was playing, they got another guy. He was really nice, he was really nice, fed me some fried chicken as a matter of fact, when I got to town. He was a great guy, a really good man. From Birmingham, Alabama."

Big Walter Horton was one of the aging blues legends who gave Iggy a real chance to play in Chicago. One of the architects of modern blues harmonica, Willie Dixon said that Horton was the best harmonica player he'd ever heard, Horton gave his young disciple a baptism of fire by pulling a knife on Iggy in the car on the way to their first gig together. "Oh, now, if you can follow this," he sort of mumbled, knife in hand. Then he started blowing a rhythm through his mouth, supported by the tapping of his knife. Iggy was forced to tap it out with him. "Look, old man," he eventually cried, "I can do anything you can. Give me a break!"

What Iggy learned from the old blues masters was that the important thing about a sound was not *how* it sounded, but what it was. He learned that what was going on in a given environment was what made the music sound the way it did. Once a musician understood the component parts of that artistic process, which Iggy felt was always more important and fun than the final result, then the outer form could take any shape whatsoever. He started practising his singing in private but, a sometimes lonely or isolated figure, he kept this to himself. He drummed in public but he sang alone at night, walking the cold deserted streets of Chicago, smoking the occasional joint, thinking about going home to hook up with the Ashetons so they could get a band together.

CHAPTER 2

Birth Of The Stooges

"I thought, 'Why should I work for these spades, man, I'm going, I want to be in front, 'tis better to receive, let someone else play.' But I learned some things from them, I knew what I wanted to do."

– Iggy Pop (1980)

"I thought, my God, I'm free, white, and 19. I'm not a 40- or 50-year-old Chicago bluesman. I've got to take what I've learned here and apply it to my own experience. I'm gonna go home to Ann Arbor and find three or four guys who are not impressed with the music scene, who do not wanna imitate British bands and not do cover songs. I wanted to make songs about how we were living in the Midwest. What was this life about? Basically, it was no fun and nothing to do. So I wrote about that."

– Iggy Pop (1986)

AS soon as he got back to Ann Arbor, Iggy called round to the Ashetons' place because he reckoned that they were his only real friends in town. It was decided there and then that they'd put together a "regular band", whatever that was supposed to be.

There was another band idea doing the rounds right then. Pretty boy Scott Richardson, lead singer with the now-defunct Chosen Few, wanted to put together a band of his own, The Scott Richardson Case, with Scott Asheton and Iggy on drums and Ron on bass. This never happened – the nascent Stooges felt they should pursue their own hopes and beliefs – though the SRC went on to have a proper regional career in the years ahead.

The Stooges, the band put together by the dead end kids and the precocious social climber, began life as an instrumental trio and were often called The Psychedelic Stooges up until the time of their first album.

21

Iggy played a Hawaiian guitar and Fender piano, Ron Asheton was on bass, and his idiosyncratic brother Scott played homemade drums. Iggy occasionally played a vacuum cleaner, a blender, and something he called a "Jim-a-phone". The original idea had been to have Scott Asheton – the best looking of the three – as the singer with Iggy as the drummer.

There are two ways of looking at the early days of The Stooges. Either they were breaking down sonic and social barriers or they were in at the foundation of progressive rock, that most dubious and torturous of rock genres. While the first Stooges album was whipped into pretty serious punky shape by ex-Velvet Underground classicist John Cale, the second – *Fun House* – would reflect The Stooges' more free-form roots in – Oh Wow! – Rock.

Ron Asheton: "It did start out with Iggy getting a Farfisa organ, my brother coming up, using timbales and a snare drum and the 50-gallon oil drums. I would use the bass guitar that I was playing with fuzztone, and wah-wah pedal. We invented instruments; putting a contact mike on the 50-gallon oil drum; putting a mike against the lip of a blender with water, taking a washboard, putting a contact mike on it, and Iggy gettin' up on it with golf shoes with spikes and kinda doing rhythm things. We found that if you took a microphone and put it on the bass drum mike stand, take a funnel and you can lift it up and down and make different kinds of . . . almost like a bass synthesiser or something. Whirrrr . . . just different weird feedback through the PA. Or taking an old Kustom amp and crashing it, putting the reverb unit on high . . . 'Gee, it sounds like a thunderstorm or a rainstorm.' We got Dave Alexander to do that, and that's what he used to do . . . work all the weird instruments while Iggy played keyboards and I played the bass and my brother played this kinda bizarre drum set."

Just where all this wild experimentation came from is unclear. Iggy's own musical reputation was based on being a clean conservative player of frat rock and the blues. The Ashetons were out on a limb, socially and intellectually, but their knowledge of panic music was virtually nil. Through his bourgeois pals in The Prime Movers and at the University of Michigan, Iggy'd certainly rubbed up against avant-garde practitioners.

Most witnesses agree that the other Stooges *were* Iggy's stooges; that he told them what to play and when. It comes as no surprise, therefore, to find that the next big collective idea within the group was that Iggy should become their lead singer. The fledgling group banged away on their weird home-made instruments for months. "Then," says Iggy, hinting at the pure teenage decisiveness which governed his actions, "Ron and I decided we wanted a real band."

"You should just concentrate on singing," said Ron to Iggy one day. He suggested that they should let Dave Alexander take on the bass chores so that he could become the lead guitarist. He'd been conscientiously taking guitar lessons for three or four years. "That's what I wanted to do anyway," Ron admits. "We just sort of evolved . . . our sets were about half an hour to 18 minutes. Whenever we played, I think half an hour was the longest at that time. That's depending on how stoned we were. We'd get stoned out on marijuana and go up and sort of jam, and just see where it would go. And after a while, things started to develop. I'd come up with a little riff, and we'd have a foundation riff that we could start to jam, and then take it wherever."

The first thing the Psychedelic Stooges did on "getting serious" was to move into a band house. Everybody'd seen The Beatles movies and knew this was the way to forge a strong band identity. The four got a summer sublet at 1324 Forest Court, Ann Arbor – a small attractive two level house on a quiet sylvan back street. Forest Court was where they watched a Three Stooges TV marathon which caused them to pick their name. "We loved the one-for-all/all-for-one of The Three Stooges and the violence in their image," says Iggy. "We loved violence as a comedy. Besides sounding right, 'stooge' also had different levels of meaning: is calling yourself a stooge a self-insult?"

Scott Thurston, Stooge: "Great guys. But really they were all hillbillies out of their element. They had nothing going for them."

Throughout the summer of '67 the band practised and partied. 1324 Forest Court is where Ron Asheton heard Hendrix for the first time and where Iggy lost his virginity. It was a humble place, idyllic in its own minor way, with a back porch where Iggy used to shit. The turds were allowed to dry out at their own good speed. When he had women callers he tended to clean up the shit before they arrived.

In order to pay the rent Ron took a job in a local head shop while Iggy found employment as a waiter. Neither Scott Asheton nor Dave Alexander were willing to work, taking a sort of beer-guzzling, hillbilly, alternative society stance. Alexander stole money from his parents who also sometimes provided him with funds. It was an intense creative period for the band, who spent their time listening to all manner of music, such as Gregorian chants, Buddhist temple music, Ravi Shankar, and the left field Harry Partch.

Partch was a composer and inventor of musical instruments whose inspiration contributed a great deal to The Stooges' world of miked-up blenders and oil drums. Most of the music Partch wrote was designed to be played on instruments of his own invention such as "modified"

23

guitars or the "Bloboy", a powerful bellows which forced air through four old auto horns and three very small organ pipes. Partch also had strong theories on the relationship between audience and performer, and on the role of music in society. Ron Asheton and Iggy did a lot of talking to one another about this kind of stuff, and where their own music might go, Ron becoming intrigued by Pete Townshend's talk of rock operas. This tied in with his active interest in classical music. "We should do that, but we would really do it up," Ron said to Iggy, "so it literally will be one continuous piece of music that changes and changes, and gets like an hour's worth of music."

"After we left the house," says Ron, "we rehearsed here in my mother's basement or Dave Alexander's parents' basement. Of course, this was when the parents were gone 'cause at 5 o'clock, they'd be saying, 'You're going insane!' We were making sounds that to them, they would have called the mental institution to pick us up or something . . . My mother would come home and we'd just be blasting. She'd flick the switch to the basement light like a strobe light. She's had a stressful day at the office and she comes home to Wrrrang, Beeep, Zzzzz. I could tell that she was thinking, like, 'Is there something wrong with your equipment?' "

Iggy's father – who naturally understood a thing or two about good and bad schools – had envisaged that mixing with upper-middle-class kids would be good for his son's education. Things may not have panned out exactly as Newell hoped but his instincts proved to be essentially sound, for Iggy soon became pals with university families like the Wehrers; major players on the local intelligentsia scene. It was through Warhol collaborator Anne Wehrer that, as a teenager, Iggy met Andy Warhol, the ultra-cool guy with the silver hair who invented the concept of the underground superstar.

Andy Warhol in *Lou Reed* by Victor Bockris: "In March we left for Ann Arbor and the University of Michigan . . . Ann Arbor was crazy. At least the Velvets were a smash. I'd sit on the steps in the lobby during intermissions and people from the local papers would interview me, ask about my movies, what we were trying to do. If they can take it for 10 minutes, then we play it for 15, I'd explain. That's our policy – always leave them wanting less."

Gerard Malanga (Velvet Underground dancer, Warhol superstar, photographer, poet): "I first met Iggy in Ann Arbor in 1966. Andy Warhol and the Velvets and I were doing a performance at the University of Michigan. We rented a van and drove all the way out there. Iggy was a young kid at that point. He was friends with Anne Wehrer and we were all staying at her place. She threw this party for us and he was at that party. Anne was connected, I guess indirectly, with the Fluxus people. She and another Ann Arbor woman subsequently did Iggy's book *I Need More* together. I forget the other woman's name. Anne had lost a leg a long time before, and she had a wooden leg. Her husband at the time was a professor at the University of Michigan."

Andy Warhol (from his introduction to *I Need More*): "Anne Wehrer introduced me to Iggy Pop at a party at her house. It was after a performance of the Exploding Plastic Inevitable at the Ann Arbor Film Festival in 1966. He was just a kid in a band, still in high school. He was Jim Osterberg then. I thought he was cute. That's when he first met Nico and John Cale. It was the beginning of all that . . . his affair with Nico, a record produced by John Cale, a movie by François de Menil (with Iggy, Nico, Tom Wehrer, and Chris Daley); later Danny Fields became his manager. I don't know why he hasn't made it really big. He is so good."

Anne Wehrer: "He came to my house because everyone did. It was the 'George Washington Slept Here' house of contemporary culture in the Midwest during the Sixties and Seventies. It all started with the Dramatic Arts Center, an organisation that was producing professional avant-garde theatre and 16mm film screenings at that time. It also sponsored the ONCE Festival of Contemporary Music which was a week-long festival of multimedia before the term was used. The ONCE group was composed of architects, artists, composers, actors, and film-makers . . . We also started the Ann Arbor Film Festival of experimental 16mm films, the blues festival, and free concerts in the park. Artists who appeared included John Cage, Lusiano Berlo, Fluxus, Motown, The Grateful Dead, George Lucas, Andy Warhol, Claes Oldenberg, Stanton Kaye, Kenneth Anger, Merce Cunningham, Yvonne Rainer, and on and on, before they were discovered or they discovered Castelli, Cannes, Paris, Sao Paulo, Hollywood, or record jackets. Iggy was a part of this scene and a friend of my children, who went to the same high school. The house became his refuge. Once, during a Detroit performance, the flying glass from a beer bottle he smashed cut a teenage girl. She called her father, who in turn called the police. The Stooges, their roadies, and their manager, all spent the night at the house. When Iggy was down, he'd crash on the couch. When he was up, we'd design band costumes and fantasies."

Victor Bockris (Warhol, Blondie, Lou Reed biographer): "The Velvet Underground played Ann Arbor in March and they were staying with Anne Wehrer so Iggy got to sit down and see them perform. I think he was very, very impressed with the Velvets. Anne had arranged for the Velvets to visit and play at the Film Festival. She had known Warhol in NYC before that. Her husband was the head of the film unit at the University or something like that. She had a big house on campus. She and her husband were bigwigs at the university and she was a cosmopolitan woman in Ann Arbor who had the intelligence to recognise the importance of what Warhol was doing and give it a shot. That was rare in those days so I think he was impressed and he liked her a lot. I think he wrote about this visit to Ann Arbor in *Popism* and I think Anne Wehrer is mentioned in some detail."

When The Stooges first started rehearsing in earnest it was during an appalling Michigan winter. Iggy was back living with his folks because he was broke so each rehearsal involved a cold dispiriting tundra trek for him. He'd walk about half a mile through the snow to get to a bus stop. After a 40-minute bus ride, he'd get off and walk another 10 minutes before he got to the Ashetons' house.

Ron Asheton: "He'd take the bus into Ann Arbor to our house. I remember once, in order to get some money to buy an organ, his mother made him cut off all his hair. She said, 'I'll buy that organ for you if you'll cut your hair.' So he got this Raymond Burr haircut. Have you ever seen the movie where Raymond Burr plays the mentally retarded insane guy with Natalie Wood? He had these little teeny bangs, almost a crew cut kind of thing? Well, for some reason Iggy got a haircut like that, and he wound up wearing some baggy white pants. The cops stopped him because they thought he was an escaped mental patient."

Iggy, *I Need More*: "The trick would be to get Ronnie or Scotty to open the door, because they'd always sleep until noon. I'd ring, ring, ring, ring the bell, and sometimes they'd answer, sometimes they wouldn't. So I had to turn on the garden hose and spray their windows, throw rocks, yell weird things, throw snowballs. Finally I'd get in, and then I'd have to wake them up a couple more times. They were really moody guys – I'd spin a few records to get them in the mood. Later on Dave Alexander, who lived down the street, would pop over. Ronnie, Scotty and Dave were very good dreamers, which is mostly what my dusty Midwest is all about. The land that time forgot. Pete Townshend said something nice about that. He said it must be really difficult for a bright person in the Midwest because you don't have a London or a New York City that can provide you with fresh input, that can rub against you and rub off any illusions . . ."

Iggy had been, since birth, soaking up sounds from all around him. It was a noisy time with loud radios everywhere and TVs crackling from morning to night, trucks transporting and factories manufacturing. Looking back to the soundtrack of his youth in 1986, he hand-scrawled a list of his 11 favourite songs – all of which, tellingly, had been issued by 1966. Experimental jazz was represented by 'Upper & Lower Egypt' by Pharaoh Sanders and 'A Love Supreme' by John Coltrane. Intelligent cabaret tunes like 'Surabaya Johnny' by Lotte Lenya and 'Night And Day' and 'Under My Skin' by Frank Sinatra played a big part in his vision. More obvious influences came from within the broad R&B/ white boy blues territory occupied by the likes of '2120 South Michigan Avenue' by The Rolling Stones, 'Country Boy' by John Lee Hooker, 'Mystic Eyes' by Them, and 'Moanin' In The Moonlight' by Howlin' Wolf. Wailing warthog popular entertainers like Cab Calloway ('Minnie The Moocher') and Elvis Presley ('Mystery Train') completed his list of what was acceptable or desirable in a popular entertainer. Each and every genre played some part in unlocking the impetuses which had, by '86, driven Iggy's own long and varied career.

Iggy, *Spin*, '86: "Records that have influenced me are: the use of Jim Morrison's voice on the first Doors album, which was a unique way to use the voice at that time. He was the first person I'm aware of to sing rock'n'roll with a full baritone. Up until that time, if you didn't have a high voice, you would sing in a monotone, the way Mick Jagger did on *12x5* or Bo Diddley did – you'd kinda shout the song. Morrison sounded almost as if he was crooning, yet the background was not sedate. It had a beat, and I found out very quickly I could do that too; Bo Diddley was helpful in the call-and-response, the irresistibility of 'Hey, Bo Diddley, have you heard?' . . . 1-2-3-4 and second line, la-de-da. I used to use that format with great effect, without having any words planned, in the original Stooges shows . . . Chuck Berry was real helpful in the way he'd looked around the culture, find a catchphrase, like 'Sweet Little Sixteen', which is what everybody used to say referring to a girl's 16th birthday party, or 'No Particular Place To Go', where he talks about seat belts. Finding neat little things in the culture on which to hang a song. The girl in 'Little Queenie' hangs out by the record machine, 'looking like she's on the cover of a magazine'.

"Bob Dylan (*Bringing It All Back Home* and *Highway 61 Revisited*) and Lou Reed (the banana album) both influenced me by the way they'd used breathy vocals and very effortlessly ride a strong beat beneath it. To me that music sounded like a bunch of little Tartar tribesmen sweeping along the desert on their ponies, ready to bring savage visitation to all in their path, yet the vocal is almost floating over that. I used that technique on 'I Wanna Be Your Dog' and 'Real Cool Time'. *12x5* by The

Rolling Stones, for its understatement of any emotional content. There are emotions in the music, but they're kept in their place, so it isn't weeping all over the place. It sounds hard and tough, yet the beat is steady and nothing's overplayed. Frank Sinatra ('September Of My Years') above all others, for the ability to carry the emotions in a song and to get a rise out of me, as a listener, on an emotional level. I felt something strong when that man sang.

"Van Morrison (Them's first album) was a very powerful influence for the wedding of poetry and music and for the way he recycled blues clichés like on 'One-Two Brown Eyes' – 'Last night I went walkin'/ I heard someone talkin'/ Better stop staying out late at night and fly right' is an old shuffle blues phrase, but with Jimmy Page, who did those sessions, playing that strange guitar behind him, and with that hyper beat, it was a new way to use those clichés; that was poetry. Sun Ra, for his ability to use music to take you voyaging; also, Coltrane for that matter – those records opened me up. And Tina Turner, not musically, because I'm not a blues shouter, and I don't have a falsetto or a hot scream, but for her stage presentation, the way she never breaks form, almost like a Balinese dancer; the hands are up, palms are outward, the feet are always going, and the tension and posture are always maintained."

Ron Richardson, a trendy local schoolteacher, was doing some part-time but diligent bookings for heavy local acts like MC5 and Bob Seger. Through his MC5 connections, The Stooges came to his attention. "I recognised Iggy and the guys as having talent and charisma," he said, "or whatever it was. I really liked them and thought they were very good." Richardson supped from a poisoned chalice and became the band's first manager. The Stooges spent much of '67 struggling to turn their difficult and cumbersome vision into a solid form. They made their first public appearance at a private Halloween party thrown by Richardson in his home. Those attending the bash included the MC5 and John Sinclair, the infamous political and cultural activist. This first Stooges appearance took place, therefore, in the presence of two of the outstanding participants in the then-emergent global counterculture.

These were exceptionally stirring times; for Ann Arbor, and for America. On that Halloween '67 night the infamous Detroit scene was entirely nascent. The MC5 had just met up with John Sinclair, a free-form jazz enthusiast, boho sax player, poet, and music critic with *Down-beat* magazine. They were interested in him because he was the closest local approximation to what a Beat Generation anti-hero should be. Sinclair, for his part, was interested in rock music for several reasons. He saw it as a means to getting across a radical political agenda via the most popular musical form of the era – he would later talk about a Guitar Army. He was also a reasonably sharp local entrepreneur who fancied himself as a band manager.

John Sinclair: "It wasn't like anything else I'd ever been to. It was Halloween 1967 . . . it was just something that Ron Richardson was doing, and they just wanted to unveil The Stooges to people in Ann Arbor. Ron was a hip schoolteacher like Russ Gibb. Ron was a little hipper, a nice guy. It was really extreme, only I was terrified. It was so loud and it was in such a residential area, a state road. I was really blasted because the guy I went with had rolled up, like, a pound of weed into joints. He was just passing them around. He'd come to my house first to pick me up and he had this big bag with him. I asked him what was in it and he said, 'Joints.' I said, 'What?!' He opened up his bag and it was just full of joints. He said that he wanted to get everybody high. I said, 'Well, that's a noble aim.' Then when we got there I remember there being this freon in the kitchen. I think you extracted it from those whipped cream canisters. You got a big rush from it. You'd take it and everything would just grind to a halt. And then everything would start all over again, only slowly. Then everything would become entirely crystalline. And then The Stooges started playing! I don't know if there were 20 people there. It certainly wasn't a big house and there wasn't a big crowd. I can't imagine what the neighbours made of it but me, I got the fuck out of there! I was terrified! I just thought, 'Jesus, they can hear this all the way downtown.' Of course my senses were enhanced, it was loud anyway and I was probably hearing it two or three times louder than it actually was. I just thought, 'We're looking for trouble here. They're just going to come here and shut this down.' Which didn't actually happen, so far as I know. I was just paranoiac, like you get sometimes. It was all very exciting. Not rock'n'roll in any sense."

Wayne Kramer: "Iggy was sitting on the floor and he had a steel guitar with some kind of modal tuning and he was bashing away on it. He had this vacuum cleaner too. He held it in front of the mike and made different noises with it. The whole thing was tremendously abstract and avant-garde. People didn't know what to make of it. They didn't know to laugh and they didn't know to take it serious."

John Sinclair: "It was more like a Laurie Anderson show, performance art. Iggy would give these guys the parts and they would just play the parts they were given. The drum would go boom ba ba boom, boom boom boom, whatever the part was and he'd tell the bass player to just play this. It was drone-like, trance music, it didn't rock, it didn't roll.

But it was very powerful and loud trance music. From what I can remember at the first gig, Iggy wasn't dancing, it was all music. He was playing a theramin and an amplified food blender. They were really out there! We all knew about things other than pop music but for a pop music person who didn't have any exposure to jazz, art music, improvisation, or drone or noise or any of those concepts, it must have been, huh, stunning in its impact. It was always part of his sonic concept that you must submit, I think."

Sam Treacy: "They created quite a stir that night. They were not exactly the talk of the town after Ron Richardson's party but, as always with Iggy, the strategy was astute. Local freaks, beatnik leftovers, closet faggot arty types, guys from other bands, suave teachers and lecturers, chic students, middle–class babes, one or two local music scene gangsters, talked about little else for a while. And by the time they ceased talking about the first gig it was time to start talking about the second one, and then how they got signed. And then how they did an album with John Cale. And on and on. While the MC5, who were a very big deal, floundered."

The Stooges stood perfectly poised. The only people to have seen them play live were an influential cross–section of local intelligentsia. A few months after his trendy Halloween party Ron Richardson decided that things were becoming a little too strange for him out in the wild world of punk. "I was managing The Stooges and teaching school at the same time. It was just like being in debt and deeper in debt. There were promises from various promoters, but it was not happening as fast as you should think it should happen. Then we went our separate ways. I liked some of what they were doing but it was getting too crazy for me. They had the energy that they needed to get off in some way. It was hard being around that energy."

Richardson passed them on to a pal of his who was known locally as Jimmy Silver. The glamorous Silver looked like a sexy long-haired rock'n'roll kid himself. He seemed better suited to band membership than to band management but proved to be astute enough about business. He became The Stooges' first real manager in early '68. He'd been one of the local movers and shakers present at the band's debut Halloween show: "It was just the most bizarre music you'd ever heard and I thought it was terrific. Iggy was playing a little modified Hawaiian guitar. It made this incredible sound. It sounded like an airplane was landing in the room."

Jimmy's real name was Jimmy Silverman; a brainy Jewish kid working on a Ph.D. at the University of Michigan's School of Public Health. "I was supposedly getting my Ph.D. in a field called Clinical Care Organisation," he said. "However, the drug revolution had struck, and I used to sit around and argue with my professors. I was really getting 'out there'. My interests were moving in other directions. I wanted to spend all my time hanging out around music."

Danny Fields (manager, The Stooges, The Ramones): "Jimmy Silver was very nice and gentle and smart. I liked and respected him a great deal. I think he really wanted to be a hippie and not a manager. He didn't have the heart for it. He left soon after I got involved and went off to do organic foods. Just a sweet guy, a sweet, nice, bright guy."

John Sinclair: "Jimmy Silver and I were very close friends. He was a very Sixties kind of guy, a rock'n'roll hippie intellectual like myself. I guess the way Jimmy got involved was that I was looking after the MC5, my brother worked for The Up. We were all in the same social circle. Me, I was inspired by the guy who managed The Grateful Dead. I said to myself, 'Jesus, if he can do it, I can do it.' Jimmy probably thought along the same lines. 'Gee, if Sinclair can do this, I really like these guys, maybe I can do something for them.' We were friends before Jimmy got involved with The Stooges, when Ron Richardson was still responsible for The Stooges' watch."

Around the same time that Silver took control, in February '68, the Asheton's neighbour Dave Alexander officially joined on bass. Iggy's relationship with Alexander was stormy from the start. Speaking in 1996, Alexander long dead and dead young, he felt the need to denigrate his old associate. "Dave came later. It was the three of us and what happened was Ron was playing bass and I was playing the lead instruments and at one point I realised I wasn't gifted enough at that sort of thing to do that. It would be better if I sang. At that point I gave Ron the guitar one day, I said, 'You play this.' That was after that first gig. And Dave had come along that first gig just to operate the weird machines that I made up from parts from the junkyard. He was a totally neurotic individual but he was Ron and Scott's friend and he had a car and he could afford a bass amp." In *I Need More*, Iggy's early foray into autobiography, Alexander is dismissed as having been "just too drunk to live."

Ron formally switched over to guitar, and Iggy emerged from his arty muso cocoon to become that most artless and egotistical of creatures, the lead singer. "You really need the freedom, don't you, Iggy?" Ron inquired sympathetically. "Yeah, I do," said the freedom-loving punk.

Iggy managed to sneak a peak at The Doors during their University of Michigan show. What he saw Jim Morrison doing endorsed his decision to be the frontman in The Stooges. "It was after I saw Jim Morrison that

I decided I'd be a singer, no matter how much I laughed, cried or died." The Doors were enjoying phenomenal chart success with 'Light My Fire' but Iggy was taken aback by Morrison's disregard for the rules of showmanship. He took that studied carelessness very much on board and forged an onstage persona of his own, one half slut and one half tough guy. He also managed to screw a girl in the crowd during the show.

Iggy, 2003: "He [Morrison] had a great sense of occasion. And the first night I saw him, his sense of occasion was totally out of hand and he had no sense of anything else. He was just LSD'd out of his mind and reeling like a drunk, singing like Betty Boop and refusing to be correct, basically. And I thought, 'This is great. This is really great.'"

Iggy, *Bust*, '95: "The Stooges did not have the balls to get out and do it. There were two things that made us do it; one was seeing that Doors show, we saw that show. I just thought, "Well, this is so brazen, there is no excuse for us not to do it anymore." And the other thing was we went to New York. We had gone to New York a couple of months before that just to check out the scene, and we had never been in a place like New York. I was loaded out of my mind, and we went down around 8th Street there, where all the young tourists hang out, and we met these girls from New Jersey, from Princeton. They had a band called The Untouchables. We're like, 'Oh, you've got a band. Ha, ha, ha.' They said, 'Well, come to our house and see us play.' And we didn't have anywhere to crash. They played for us, and they completely rocked, and we were really ashamed. We were like, 'Ah, fuck!' Other than that, I had a teacher, who was most probably gay – I didn't think about that at the time – and he was from New Orleans, he had a doctorate, and he was my 11th grade creative writing teacher. He encouraged me. He was like, 'You can do this,' you know, and he really made me feel like what I wrote was of interest, like I had talent."

It was time, in the established Sixties tradition, to get it together in the country. With Jimmy Silver and his wife paying the bills, The Stooges moved into a farm house outside Ann Arbor. They gave their rural retreat various witty "head" names: The Old Bear's House, Loon Hotel, and Stooge Manor. Iggy got a room in the attic. Ron had a big apartment all to himself which he filled with his Nazi memorabilia; coats, flags and medals.

Jimmy Silver remembered that the various Stooges were really into watching TV. They had grown up with TV, and they knew everything that was on TV every night of the week, including every late night B-movie. "And in Detroit," he commented wryly, "they had a really bizarre selection of late night movies in those days."

"To tell you the truth we lead a very strange life," Iggy told a journalist. "It's only recently that anybody has even bothered to consider us part of any community. I sleep a lot. I watch TV a whole lot. I sit in my room a whole lot, and hang around the yard. I don't really have any friends outside the band. I don't really have any fun finding out what's happening in the world. I really don't know what's happening to people outside the band."

Silver and Iggy would leave the farm to walk around the back roads near the commune, talking for hours out in the fog. Although Silver had been to a lot of schools and known a lot of people who might be classed as intellectuals, he reckoned that Iggy was one of the most intelligent characters he'd ever met. Silver saw, from the start, that his charges didn't resemble a normal rock band. "They were always pretty far out and that was their premise. It was pretty clear to me that Iggy was trying to do something different.

"Iggy and I are a lot alike. One of the ways in which we're alike is that we retain almost everything that we ever see or hear. I felt a strong bond of commonality with Jim. He did things that intrigued and excited me . . . he has a good sense of humour although it's more biting and vindictive than most people in his position are supposed to have. He had a 'fuck you' sense of humour . . . In terms of intelligence I think Jim's got a tremendous amount."

Before the move to Stooge Manor, The Stooges – give or take a bit of grass now and then – were more or less a clean-living bunch of guys. All of this began to change. The drug thing crept in gradually. "When I first met Iggy he was one of the straightest guys I knew," says Ron Asheton. "In fact he was super straight! When he first came into The Stooges, he was still that way. I can't really say that we corrupted him, but I believe we brought out a craziness that had been hiding inside him all the time. The rest of us smoked and we started fooling around with marijuana and such. I think Iggy was a victim of peer group pressure."

The Silvers were serving up healthy macrobiotic food which countered the band members' earliest dalliances with drug consumption. It is worth remembering that while Iggy had a burgeoning reputation as a local cocksman and hellraiser, there was a profoundly quiet and withdrawn aspect to him before all hell broke loose. When asked by a contemporary journalist what he had been like before The Stooges, his response was sombre. He said he'd been very unhappy, a very self-conscious type, a very schizoid kid when he was young. He said he had a full fantasy life at all times, and that when he was about 18 he got into a series of serious car accidents, unbelievable ones, where everybody else risked death while he never got a scratch. He began to perceive himself as being, in certain ways, indestructible. "That was the first time in my life I ever felt anything like it," he said. "It was like drugs." The urbane eloquence which characterised his press interviews left journalists in no doubt that he was telling them the truth, that his claims to be a quiet and thoughtful fellow were borne out by his cool demeanour when sitting down opposite them. Iggy Pop the interviewee was gently spoken, provocative, self-deprecating, realistic. He was even honest – up to a point.

Jimmy Silver: "Iggy's asthma used to act up in the autumn. It was really bad sometimes. It used to lead him to be incapacitated and he wouldn't be able to breathe too well. Sometimes he would stop smoking cigarettes and dope and eat with us for a couple of days. We'd feed him brown rice and vegetables. It would take maybe a day or two until he would be completely cured."

The MC5 and John Sinclair's counterculture organisation, Trans-Love Energies, had abandoned Detroit after the riots of 1967. They relocated to Ann Arbor and took over two sizable Hill Street houses on Fraternity Row. These houses became the epicentre for radical and cultural activities in Ann Arbor in the late Sixties and also became the target of the local authorities. 1510 Hill Street, an impressively large place with a wooden porch and big grounds, was home to the MC5 and Sinclair. 1520 Hill Street, the second of their two residences, was home to prominent local band, The Up, managed by Sinclair's brother, and to various White Panthers. It was also a safe haven for the runaway teens in search of a place to stay who would show up for the free meals on offer. It hosted White Panther meetings and printing presses as well as having a Panthers' target range out back. The Stooges hung out in both houses. A large number of commune women took care of the cooking, sewing, comforting, and cleaning. As with their Black Panther brothers, it seems that Sinclair's Guitar Army reckoned that women's contribution to the revolution would take the form of pussy power. The entire Detroit music scene had a controversial reputation for sexism and misogyny.

Sam Treacy: "This was before the days of Women's Liberation. There was an awful lot of house cleaning and meal preparation going on. It's well known that the MC5 had a bad reputation on a personal politics basis, no matter how far left their politics were. You could always get fed on Hill Street, there was always something in the pot, you could get your clothes mended too and if you got lucky you'd get laid. Trans-Love Energies would have ground to an immediate halt without the hard work being done by a number of rather strange women, some of them rich girls, some of them rather dumb and unfortunate. Even though feminism was just a nascent idea which hadn't quite reached Ann Arbor, a lot of women were outraged by the scene there. My girlfriend at the time used to give me a lot of shit for hanging out there because of the way women were treated. She heard stories about women being beaten, she thought the girls were being treated like slaves. I think the other Stooges hung out there a lot more than Iggy. They were more pally with Sinclair and with the 5. Iggy liked to keep a distance."

Gary Rasmussen (bass player, The Up, Iggy Pop Band): "The Hill Street Estates houses were kind of a unique thing . . . They were kind of famous at the time. We always had people coming by . . . Abbie Hoffman came there, Jane Fonda came and stayed there at the houses. The Hog Farm, they all came and they were hanging out there. At one point Sun Ra and his band lived there at the houses for, I think, a week or two."

John Sinclair: "Ann Arbor was a hotbed of art school type stuff. People were emerging out of their regular lives through smoking weed and taking acid, hanging out, listening to everything from Ravi Shankar and Albert Ayler through to The Rolling Stones and The Beatles. There was a lot of crossbreeding going on; you'd have some guy doing a degree to become a bimolecular scientist who'd then take acid and become a different guy. He'd still be a scientist but one checking out The Rolling Stones. Robert Ashley was there in residence at the University of Michigan, very powerful culturally. George Manupelli, the 8 and 16mm film maker – he had a whole group of people around him who were involved in the Film Festival. Anne Wehrer was an art person, you had so many of these art people that in many ways the city was like New York. You had people around like Anne Wehrer and Danny Fields who were not rock'n'roll people *per se* but who were attracted by the energy and the beauty of the performers. It was all happening in this little town, centred around the campus. Commander Cody came out of that art school scene, and his brother Chris Frame who was an artist. Cody had a band going called The Fantastic Floating Beavers. They would play fraternity parties and just totally wreck the place. Just a lot of genuinely wild characters."

"Blue" Gene Tyranny: "The attitude in Ann Arbor was that freedom was freedom. When the cops came and prevented Kenneth Anger's *Scorpio Rising* from being shown, we were all there. Or there was a peace march or whatever. It is hard to describe what Ann Arbor was like right then, it was a really fiery town. There was SDS politics, John Sinclair, the Ann Arbor independent Film Festival which started out as part of an early ONCE Festival and then separated off. A lot of the arts organisations were raising funds for various progressive causes and for artistic things also. All these older and younger people, academics and non-academics, were supporting all of this varied activity. Nobody knew where it was going to lead. There were a lot of great parties. Artists from all disciplines were continually showing up in town, especially a lot of New York people. Bob Rauschenberg, the Fluxus guys from New York and New Jersey. The Independent Film Festival screened about 250/300 films during each festival after looking at about 600 submissions. I was a juror one time so I know!"

John Sinclair: "Trans-Love Energies were hippies on LSD! We got the name from 'Fat Angel', a Donovan record covered by Jefferson Airplane. 'Fly Trans Love Airways, gets you there on time.' I thought that was quite . . . mystical. That was our slogan. We didn't have anything to do with no political groups. The Stooges didn't know anything about politics. They had no political ideas. When I would be around their house The Three Stooges, which is what we called the other Stooges, they'd be sitting around watching television and sniffing glue. They were closer to the MC5 than they were to me. They were all pals. And I was pally with MC5 but I just knew those guys in The Stooges to see around."

Lots of people had bad things to say about John Sinclair and his polarising cultural/political activities. Kathy Asheton, MC5 girlfriend and fringe scenester, regarded him as "a pig". Prime Movers' leader Michael Erlewine found Sinclair's musical protégés hard to take. "The MC5 were not indigenous and did not represent Ann Arbor," Erlewine says. "They came from Detroit and planted themselves in us and were very aggressive. What was a very pretty scene became a lot uglier with them."

Iggy, *I Need More*: "He (John Sinclair) thought he was going to build as a demi-politician. Midwest Rastafarian, fakir, master of ceremonies, producer of rabbits, owner of hats, i.e. a jerk. Yeah, the guy was and always will be a compulsive organiser, meaning a jerk. Was I going to be on the side of the people or was I going to be some kind of pop star, he wanted to know. But to join the side of the people meant simply working for John Sinclair, and I knew it. So fuck that, Jack. So he came to my manager's (Jimmy Silver) place and tried to put the squeeze on me. I was smoking some hash and he went into this song and dance. 'I'm the guy who handles any good gig in this area. I am the one who runs the underground here. Now, are you going to be with us or not? Because if you're not going to play ball, la de da, then what are you all about? I'm John Sinclair, you'd better not mess with me.' I never forgot it. I could not open my mouth in response to that question."

John Sinclair: "I was really hurt when I saw that thing in Anne Wehrer's book. I knew both of them – Iggy and Anne – and we were friends. He made up that ridiculous stuff about how I came in saying, 'You got to do this. You got to do that.' I'd come to see Jimmy Silver to tell him that I had some gigs for his band. When Iggy was doing that book he was totally out of it anyway. When I would see him at that point I would try to get to the other side of the street before he saw me. He would be surrounded by all these bogus sycophants. When he puked they thought that this was a thing of great beauty. I wasn't into all that . . . I was kind of an adult by then. I thought that that was really a cheap shot. In any case it was part of the mythology surrounding the MC5 that I was this kind of radical Svengali character which was bullshit. I wasn't any more radical than the band. I was at least as much influenced by Rob Tyner as he was by me. He was a brilliant guy. I've seen a photograph of him with a saxophone in one hand and an assault rifle in the other. I'm thinking, 'He didn't get that assault rifle from me.' Kathy Asheton, who says I'm the pig who brainwashed the MC5, is just an idiot. She was some kind of weird groupie. Black eye shadow, you know what I mean? She couldn't string two sentences together in a row. She didn't ever do anything in her whole fuckin' life. By which I mean if somebody created something and then felt that they had to say that there was something wrong with me, I might take it seriously. From some kind of hanging-around kind of person, I don't care. They don't have anything else to do."*

One thing linking The Up, The Stooges, and the MC5 – other than a tight knot of managers – to the leftist political activists was opposition to the Vietnam War. In the case of the bands, this opposition was often rooted in cowardly self-interest, rather than in any extraordinarily brave or principled political stance. The Draft Board was the ultimate enemy of both white and black males who were unwilling or unable to attend university. The type of guys who end up in bands are rarely the sort of people who want to go to war.

Ron Asheton: "We all did the homosexual thing – nervous drug-addicted homosexuals! Each of us went through the whole thing with

---

* In an oral history of New York punk, *Please Kill Me*, Kathy Asheton was substantially interviewed. What she has to say for herself in that book tends to confirm Sinclair's assessment of her. Most of her quotes put her within some sort of sexual context or other. She remained somehow involved with natty Fred "Sonic" Smith – whom she imagined was her boyfriend – until 1975 when Patti Smith swooped down from Heaven onto the Ann Arbor scene and zapped her out of that position.

each other, preparing each other. Iggy was first. We got as high as he did and stayed with him right up to the moment of going. The same for all of us. Then we matched notes. Through the four of us, we learnt all the different aspects of going through it. Later on, through John Sinclair, we advised people who were going before the draft board. We offered our services."

Iggy, *I Need More*: "The only way to get out was to fag out. They were taking guys with every sort of deformity, so I just forgot to wear any underwear and when I had to take off my pants to get in line, I went and I just beat my meat until it was over a foot long, then I walked out . . . So I went to the shrink, and he asked me questions like, 'What does gay mean? What's a queen?' things like that. By this time, I was really into it, and he bought it and took me downstairs to the captain. I was almost in tears. I was so wrapped up in my role – lots of convulsion and tears . . . It wasn't too much of a problem, really."

The first proper public show by The Stooges took place on March 3, 1968. They opened for Blood, Sweat & Tears at the Grande (pronounced Grandee) Ballroom in Detroit. A very big deal for many years, Blood, Sweat & Tears were rock'n'roll's worst nightmare; a bloated and jazzed-up white vision of blues and soul fronted by one of the leading rock warthogs, David Clayton-Thomas. In their earliest incarnation they featured then-legendary Dylan sidekick Al Kooper. A large, psychedelic poster for the show proudly announces the Detroit appearance of Columbia Records' pride and joy, Blood, Sweat & Tears. At the foot of the poster two other bands are mentioned, Carousel and The Psychedelic Stooges.

John Sinclair: "We put them on at the Grande Ballroom opening for Blood, Sweat & Tears because BS&T were refusing to have the MC5 to open for them. It was a $125 gig and we didn't want to let it pass. We didn't give a fuck about Al Kooper and them, we thought they were pretty corny. But they'd heard about the MC5 in New York. They were told, when you go to Detroit, be careful of this band the MC5 because they'll just rip you from limb to limb. Leaving your audience in a very ho hum frame of mind! So they told Russ Gibb or whoever it was who booked them in that they didn't want the MC5. So I said to them, 'There's this new group in Ann Arbor. You'll really like them. The Psychedelic Stooges.' So it was, 'Oh, wow, man! Psychedelic Stooges! Let's do it!'

"Man, oh, man! A show like that on a big stage like that . . . Iggy was like a force of nature. Just incredibly forceful and impressive. He didn't sing. Not doing rock'n'roll in any way. That's what I thought was so funny later. That he turned into a rock hack, and has been a rock hack for so many years now. I never would have predicted that about him as an entertainer. That he would get together with Soupy Sales' sons and start playing toons. I think it was John Cale who knocked the tunes into shape for them. They'd just come out and play for twenty minutes. The show would last 20 minutes. People didn't want any more than that because in those 20 minutes they could make such a dynamic impression and that was enough."

"Iggy really started developing his charismatic stage presence at the Grande Ballroom," Wayne Kramer told Dorothy Sherman in 1982. "In those days, he had a lot more of a rhythmic sense of dance than he does now. It was like tribal dancing which to me was very exciting to watch. He was really, really good. It was mystifying and magnetic. He was just stunning."

Ron Asheton: "We were lucky enough to have the Grande in full swing, and that was a good venue for us. There'd be sympathetic people there. The people that came there were supposedly, most of them, hip, so that's where the old Psychedelic Stooges really learned how to play and came forward, playing the Grande Ballroom, or we wouldn't have worked."

"There was every kind of scene going on in Detroit right then," remembers producer/bass player and Detroit native Bill Laswell. "I was a kid going around to gigs. It was an exciting, energetic place to be a music fan. You had all this different music, Ted Nugent, The Up, MC5, and The Stooges. On top of that you had places where bands could play, like the Grande Ballroom. John Sinclair was incredibly active around that time with Trans-Love and the White Panthers. I saw The Stooges several times. I was at the famous peanut butter gig. What The Stooges were doing was very simple in a sense. They weren't untogether but what they were trying to achieve meant that they would drift in and out of time with one another. There wasn't a set beat or rhythm. At the beginning they were beating on stuff and didn't have a lot of songs. What they achieved was an almost orchestral drone or trance-like sound which was totally unique, valid, and impressive." Laswell's youthful immersion in The Stooges came in handy many years later when, in an altered universe, he produced one of Iggy's pivotal crossover Eighties albums, *Instinct*.

The Grande Ballroom, the great 2,000–capacity facilitator of the Detroit rock explosion, was *the* place to play in Michigan. Between 1967 and 1970 the likes of Led Zeppelin, Cream, Janis Joplin, The Who, Frank Zappa, and Jefferson Airplane – the roll call of *Rolling Stone*-approved rock – played there. The owner, canny idiosyncratic local DJ Russ Gibb, booked the touring national headliners while the Michigan-based support bands were booked in by "Jeep" Holland, who displayed a firm grasp of the indigenous scene.

Jeep – described as a "lovable asshole" by Michael Erlewine – was involved in managing both The Rationals and The Prime Movers at one time or another. Local heroes that he helped out at the Grande Ballroom such as the MC5, The Stooges, The Frost (featuring guitarist Dick Wagner who eventually worked with Alice Cooper and Lou Reed), and The Amboy Dukes (lead by Ted "Wang Dang, Sweet Poontang" Nugent) regularly wiped out the visiting acts. The local bands grew to be a popular and venue-stuffing scene in their own right.

It is hardly surprising that Jeep Holland knew what he was doing. He managed Discount Records during its salad days and was responsible for both its musical policy and its role as a social/musical melting pot in Ann Arbor. A charismatic man with a huge collection of singles and albums, enthusiastic to the point of obsession about the then-innocent rock revolution, he was a consistent booster and educator of young musicians hungry for experience and inspiration. It was Holland who employed the likes of Iggy and "Blue" Gene Tyranny.

It is hardly surprising that cautious but knowledgeable Russ Gibb knew what he was doing either. A listened-to founder of so-called underground radio, which sounded much like the rock radio we know today blended with nascent shock jock strategy, he got his break when the rules regulating radio were changed. The changes ensured that his station, WKNR, could no longer broadcast the same stuff on their AM and FM bands all day every day. A decision was taken to make their FM programming the opposite to the snappy in-your-face style on the main AM strand.

The already popular Gibb was transferred onto FM where he started playing longer album tracks and what was ironically styled as progressive rock. This was how FM radio got going. Gibb's contribution to the evolution of modern radio was substantial. He was also at the root of the "Paul is Dead" rumours which flew around the world in the late Sixties optimistically suggesting that Beatle Paul McCartney was dead. Gibb was one of the first people to introduce cable television into an American community, having seen an early version of the technology called CATV at Mick Jagger's place in England when he was visiting the midnight rambler.

Russ Gibb: "I had several venues; the most popular was the Grande Ballroom which I opened in 1966. I booked in lots of bands that were popular with the underground audience and worked out an arrangement with the station to promote my shows on the air. It was a win–win situation . . . Iggy Pop was an interesting guy. He grew up in Ann Arbor and had a day job as a camp counsellor at the YMCA while he was playing this music that came to be called 'punk' at night. He had just changed the name of his band to The Stooges. One time he came to see me with a toilet. He had modified the thing so that there was a microphone in the bowl that could amplify the flush. Another time he wore a tin-foil suit on stage. His mom made it for his act and during the course of the show he would slowly rip pieces of tin foil off of himself until it was in shreds . . . One day I saw someone in a band's entourage had brought a gun to the old Michigan Theater, where we were playing the New York Dolls. I began to realise that the drug thing had gotten out of control."

Ron Asheton: "With The Chosen Few I had played the very first night of the Grande Ballroom, the very first show ever when it opened (in October 1966). The Chosen Few opened for the MC5, and we did a little medley from the Stones *Got Live If You Want It* EP where they do 'Everybody Needs Somebody Like Somebody', 'Pain In My Heart' and 'Route 66' . . . I played the first notes ever at the Grande, and that was the place that we used to play, and that's the first time I ever saw the MC5."

Gary Rasmussen: "It wasn't a bar. It wasn't really a teen club. It was more like a counterculture kind of scene, like the Fillmore. I think the MC5 probably played the first show there. Russ Gibb had been around, and he was an older guy, and he'd seen the things going on in San Francisco and Chicago and other places, with the posters and the art. Really, the whole culture at that point was really something. A lot of it, too, was the war in Vietnam polarised people. When you're getting a draft card and thinking about going to Vietnam, it's pretty easy to start making decisions about what side of this you're on."

Jimmy Silver: "It was when Russ Gibb started up the Grande Ballroom on a full-time basis that there began to be an opportunity for a kid's scene. Previously there was a club scene, but the clubs weren't big enough to have enormous amounts of kids attend them. There was a whole bunch of clubs, in Ann Arbor, Birmingham, Leonard, etc. But it really wasn't until the Grande Ballroom opened and the ballroom scene got big that you could get a couple of thousand kids in one place in one night."

John Sinclair: "Iggy was a guy who had a brain, who was aware of things beyond the rock'n'roll horizons. They'd be up there thumping away and droning away while he made up these songs. He would be in white face. He would dance. He had a theremin, not the kind with the little tower, the little antenna like the one Rob Tyner had. His was like a flat surface. He would place his hands over it, moving them up and down, that would alter the sound. And he would do this in a very shamanistic way . . . the ritual summoning of The Stooges!! You know, we were on acid. Who knows what really happened? That was what it felt like. You couldn't take your eyes off Iggy for 20 minutes. He was riveting."

Jimmy Silver: "They had me play this crazy instrument that they had designed. We took an oil tank that people put outside their houses – not an oil drum – an oil tank that is used to store oil in. We spray painted it white and as a finale to The Stooges' act we dropped a microphone in this 55 gallon oil barrel and I got to play it with an automobile repair body mallet. It made a noise like it was inside you or you were locked inside the oil drum because it was going through a PA system."

The Psychedelic Stooges performed two songs on that first ground-breaking Grande Ballroom extravaganza, 'Asthma Attack' (relating to the asthma which afflicted Iggy as a kid) and the misogynistic master-piece, 'I'm Sick'. Iggy subsequently claimed that people fled his first appearance as a singer in droves; so embarrassed were they by the unpro-fessional aural mess with which they were assaulted. "Afterwards my friends came up," he said, "and put their arms round me and asked me if I had mental problems." The reviewer present from the local student paper praised The Stooges' thrust and intensity, commenting on the originality of the lead singer.

Ron Asheton: "People didn't know what to think about us. We had our own instruments. For example we poured water in a blender and put a mike on top of it. We got this really weird bubbling water sound which we put through the PA. And Iggy danced on a washboard with his golf shoes!"

Iggy: "A reviewer from the student paper at the University of Michi-gan, instead of reviewing Blood, Sweat & Tears, devoted almost the entire review to The Stooges, saying Blood, Sweat & Tears are a pack-aged act who have passed their prime, and the real story tonight came from a local band, The Stooges, fronted by vocalist 'Iggy Osterberg'. The article mentioned our use of innovative instruments that I built in a junkyard, our stage set and costumes, the thrust of our music, and partic-ularly Iggy's dancing. I took great note of that piece at the time, because in the Ann Arbor area alone there were at least 20 full-time, more-than-competent bands, all busting their balls for the same few gigs in the area . . . I saw an opportunity there and never looked back. This name's catchy. People now knew me by this name, so I stuck with it. Then I thought I'd tag a good last name onto it, and because this sounded like show business, I came up with Pop."

Scott Asheton: "Iggy had shaved off his eyebrows. We had a friend named Jim Pop who had a nervous condition and had lost all his hair, including his eyebrows. So when Iggy shaved his eyebrows we started calling him Pop. It was real hot in the ballroom that night, and Iggy started sweating, and then he realised what you need eyebrows for. By the end of the set, his eyes were totally swollen because of all the oil and glitter."

Lenny Kaye (Patti Smith Group, rock writer, *Nuggets* compiler): "Where Detroit was bland, its music was vibrant and exciting. Where Detroit tried to smooth over interior violence, its rock was consciously and defiantly brutal; where Detroit emphasised middle-class virtues and restraint, its rock promoted running wild in the streets, drugs, any former taboo. What could be turned about was simply subverted. Shying away from technical excellence, the music was raw, performed with intensity and total belief . . . the Motor City audience sensed this upsurge, breaking ranks to add encouragement at a time when other cities' crowds were beginning to passively sit and nod. In true communal spirit, they felt the bands were of themselves, thrown up from their own number to serve notice of awakening."

Deniz Tek, founder member of Stooges-inspired Australian/American punk band Radio Birdman, points out that when local guys like The Up, The Stooges, and the MC5 played New York or San Francisco it was common for them to blow away all opposition. He says they blew away both bands and audiences. He attributes the virile quality of those bands to local Michigan radio. Tek says that when FM radio got going, "All these little local independent stations started up. There were some great ones out of Detroit. The greatest was WABX, transmitting from high atop the David Stott Building. The DJs were rebel outlaws, they played anything, there was revolution in the air. Again, a fantastic time for listening . . . The local version of psychedelic rock'n'roll was way harder, faster and more blue-collar influenced, while being much further out than the West Coast stuff. The possible exception is Blue Cheer who should've been a Detroit band. Our local bands could and did bury anything coming out of SF, LA, or NYC at that time."

John Sinclair: "Iggy was so unpredictable – you never knew what he would do. It got to where he would recklessly jump off the stage into a bunch of people on the premise that he would land on them. He'd go out in the audience until he made eye contact with a girl. He would lock eyes with someone, zero in on them, pick them out and go over and throw them over his shoulder or get down on the floor and kiss them. Just do something outrageous out in the middle of the crowd. I'd think, 'I wonder if he's going to make it back alive?' Seriously, that's the feeling I got sometimes!"

The emergent Stooges were championed by the likewise emergent alternative rock magazine, *Creem*, which initially developed out of the Detroit scene before becoming a lesser national force. *Creem* declared that, "The Detroit/Ann Arbor community is first and foremost a rock'n' roll culture. Whatever movement we have here grew out of rock'n'roll. It was rock'n'roll music which first drew us out of our intellectual covens and suburban shells. It is around the music that the community has grown and it is the music which holds the community together."

The first time that The Stooges music got used in a commercial was when Detroit Dragway used the band on a TV ad. Iggy was so excited that he didn't find out if they'd paid to use it or not. His attitude has changed somewhat since then. They didn't get paid.

Lester Bangs, one of the first knight-errant journalists to defend The Stooges, and one of many to rise to prominence on the back of this defence – for The Stooges were always a writer's band and a musician's band – ranted and blathered about them in *Creem* and elsewhere. His well regarded, under-edited, indulgent critiques of rock in general, and his strong feelings about Iggy in particular, maybe betrayed an unacknowledged homosexuality common amongst intelligent rock writers who champion pretty boy singers like Iggy.

"The Stooges are one band that does have the strength to meet any audience on its own terms," Bangs wrote, "no matter what manner of devilish bullshit that audience might think up. Iggy is like a matador baiting the vast dark hydra sitting afront him – he enters the audience to see what's what and even from the stage his eyes reach out searingly, sweeping the joint and singling out startled strangers who're seldom able to stare him down. It's your stage as well as his and if you can take it away from him, why, welcome to it. But the King of the Mountain must maintain the pace and authority, and few can. In this sense, Ig is a true star of the most incredible kind – he has won the stage, and nothing but the force of his own presence entitles him to it."*

---

* Nick Kent subsequently wrote that what Bangs really wanted to do in life was to connect on an equal footing with the intelligent artistic rock guys whom he championed so compellingly, many of whom regarded him with "baleful contempt". "I went with Bangs to his interview with Lou Reed, his ultimate hero, in the spring of 1973,"

John Sinclair: "Iggy had gone beyond performance – to the point where it really was some kind of psychodrama. It exceeded conventional theatre. He might do anything. That was his act. He didn't know what he was going to do when he got up there on the stage. It was exciting. I'd just watch him and I'd say, 'Wow, this guy will stop at nothing. This isn't just a show – he's out of his mind!' Sometimes it was getting too weird. I remember when he started taunting the crowd with broken bottles. He did this as early as 1969. He'd get this audience response. I think he got to where he didn't really have any respect for the audience. So he'd do things to see what would get a response. He was doing something different."

The creativity surging through their community was reflected in The Stooges increasingly eccentric live manifestations. They started playing out a lot, building up a good following and reputation. Live sets would start off with a riff from a tune like 'Little Doll'. Dave Alexander would come in on bass, playing fast. Big slashing power chords would announce Ron's arrival. Then, according to Ron, "It would just erupt into total John Coltrane chaos, where the saxophone was screaming, but just imagine everyone's screaming. My brother's doing his very poor Elvin Jones imitation. I got way into feedback, and I'd just go back there and try to yank these sounds out of this guitar, while Dave'd be holding down some kind of riff, and it'd just go.

"We'd start off on this riff, and I'm goin', 'OK, we've gotta hold it down long enough so Iggy can start doin' his little antics,' y'know, let him work the crowd. We didn't even have to tell each other that, we were still so much (at that time) of one thought with one another that we'd let him go out and do his thing, and the show would just sorta build. As he got a little bit more frantic, the music got a little more frantic. Or if we got a little more frantic, he got a little more frantic, and then it would wind up just total power and chaos, where it's the exact opposite of 'We Will Fall' . . . that was more Dave Alexander's contribution to the first record, because he was into chants and into the spiritual stuff, and he was always looking for a new way to get high, and this was . . . 'If you keep doing this chant, you're gonna get high.' So I'd go to his house, and after a while, I'd think, 'Gee, I guess if I said anything over and over for half an hour, it might make me a little dizzy.' It did make us feel relaxed, so we thought, 'Cool. It's something different.'

Kent says. "Reed could hardly bear to sit in the same room as him. Shortly afterwards his beloved Iggy Pop called him a fool to his face and told him to shut up on their first meeting."

That was the total opposite of what we were back then, 'cause that was chaos, total chaos."

Asheton felt that, after these initial periods of total sonic mayhem and chaos, The Stooges were getting more accomplished on their instruments. Iggy was intelligent enough to take on board what was happening around him and to use the onstage confusion to his advantage. He played up his own peculiar sexual gyrations and his athletic ability. Asheton was not entirely sure that Iggy's stage dives served any good purpose. He believed that it was more of a stage show when Iggy focused the audience's attention on what was happening onstage, as opposed to his penchant for heading off into the audience all the time to "start trouble".

There were band discussions about this, with Ron expressing his disquiet, but Iggy kept on inventing modern punk and metal stagecraft despite the objections of his portly, nonchalant guitarist. "All the little things he did to them like climbing on their faces and making the swan dives off the stage, I used to laugh so hard," Ron says. "This sounds weird but he used to swan dive and the audience knew he was going to dive. 'When's he gonna dive?' In the beginning they were surprised – they'd either be flattened by him or they'd catch him. The next thing was, 'When he dives, move!' I'd see a huge crowd and he starts his run and by the time he hits the area it's completely vacant – he'd swan dive into folding chairs and no one's there."

The Stooges soon had a Michigan-wide reputation for being trouble with a capital T. They liked to do beastly things with the local women. They enjoyed drugs, confrontation, noise, and subversion. Word of the sexual and social outrages that went hand in hand with booking The Stooges spread wide and far. When they played the Delta Pop Festival at Delta College in Ohio, a contractual obligation stated that Iggy could have no physical contact with the audience. "I walked onto the floor and started digging this chick who looked really frightened by our music," said Iggy. "We tried to play nice songs and establish a sort of dream meeting between the audience and ourselves. I became carried away, obsessed with this chick and I scooped her from her seat. She screamed and scratched me, so I bit her and dropped her to the floor. I still have scars from her. The school threatened not to pay us, but the people dug it so much that we got paid and asked back."

The band were arrested in Romeo, Michigan on August 11, 1968 after Iggy allegedly committed an indecent exposure onstage at a club called Mother's. They'd been booked to do the show after Jeep Holland cajoled the reluctant student promoters into thinking that it'd be a good idea. "A show you will not forget!" announced the prophetic psyche-delic poster. "Iggy was wearing his super-killer low-leather pants and the crotch ripped during the middle of our set," says Scott Asheton. "The girls went bananas. They had never seen anyone dressed up in 'hobo' clothes before. Iggy got a towel to cover the rip, but it fell off. One chick got bummed out and split the joint screaming. It turned out that her old man was a cop, so 25 pigs came back to close the place."

Ron Asheton: "There was a girl in the audience whose father was a policeman and it just happened that the post was right around the corner or something. And she went runnin' out and said, 'There's a naked man at the show!' And so the old dude who was the security guard – must have been in his sixties or whatever – was saying, 'I'm telling you fellas right now, the state police are on their way.' And we were, 'Huh?'"

The Stooges were in their dressing room when Iggy heard that the cops were on their way so he just disappeared. The rest of the band, who took a relaxed approach to the matter since they'd done nothing wrong, were sitting in their room when troopers invaded the backstage, all crew cuts and hands on guns, demanding to know, "Where's that Iggy?" When informed that he was gone they told the rest of the band, "You're all under arrest until we get that Iggy guy."

At 10.45 pm Iggy was discovered trying to move from the boot of one car, where he'd been hiding, to another vehicle which was going to take him home to Ann Arbor. He was arrested, jailed, and early the next morning when his parents came to rescue him he was fined $41 plus costs. The charge was reduced from indecent exposure to one of being a disorderly person. "Everyone was so wired after the event," says Ron. "We stayed up all night 'til he came home. We knew his parents went up there and got him out, and I think he got home at six or seven in the morning."

The next day the Mother's promoters were out of business. Their lease was cancelled due to pressure from the landlord. The venue subsequently re-opened under new management but the building was torn down in the autumn of 1971. A branch of the Northern Bank now occupies the site, but the alleyway where Iggy hid in the boot of a car is still there.

As with his earlier band enterprises, things were going well for Iggy Osterberg/Stooge/Pop with The Stooges, still mostly referred to as The Psychedelic Stooges. They were weird but they were weird on a weird but supportive scene. They may have been part avant-garde and part-hillbilly, both cool and uncool, but they were filling 300–500 capacity clubs all over Michigan. Promoters in dives like Pop Patrick's in Saginaw, Fifth Dimension and Hullabaloo in Ann Arbor, and The Loft in Leonard were happy to give them repeat bookings. They also played in clubs owned by entrepreneur "Punch" Andrews, a Detroit business-man who had a string of teen clubs called Hideouts and who would go on to manage Bob Seger.

Inevitably, the unorthodox Harry Partch-style instruments gradually gave way to more conventional equipment. The Stooges became closer to a rock'n'roll band with songs and set-lists but the sense of extreme blood-drenched Mishima-like theatre was retained from the earliest days. Audiences got an awful lot of pleasure out of witnessing a little onstage gore and injury.

MC5 bass player Michael Davis understood The Stooges gorehound appeal. "At first Iggy had a white face on. It was shocking to see some-body so white – he looked ghostlike. Iggy gyrated around the stage and usually made a crazy fool out of himself to everyone's pleasure. Every-body liked it. Everyone who was at those gigs was shocked in a pleasant way – not in a negative way. They weren't turning people off. They were just weird and different and didn't play songs like everybody else."

MC5 drummer, Dennis Thompson, didn't share his bandmate's sym-pathy for the young devils. "The reason The Stooges were unique was 'cos they couldn't play, man," Thompson said. "That's why they started to come out with all this other shit, to get a reaction because no one gave a fuck about them. They just weren't good enough."

Iggy eventually admitted that there was something to this. The second show that he ever did, opening for The Mothers Of Invention at the Grande Ballroom in 1968, was the scene of his first audience invasion. "I couldn't think of another way to get attention and I did this thing," he recalled in 2003. "Ever seen how little boys sometimes when they want attention, they'll make themselves perfectly still and then they'll fall face-flat on the floor? I did that, except off a five foot stage."

Although The Stooges were getting out on the road to play lots of venues and to see new towns, meeting loads of new people along the way, they were still based in Ann Arbor. Iggy was frustrated by its small-town nature. "There's a whole lot that goes through Ann Arbor. Living there is like it must have been once to live on a trade route to the East. There's nothing of note there except the people themselves. It's not really any particular scene. For me, it's the place I was born and lived for 20 years, so the whole thing takes on a whole colour. Because I walk along the street, and I don't see the street of that day, I see the street for the last 20 years. All the years are crowded together . . . I might be in Ann Arbor for a month and go into town twice. And I don't go out at night, you know, except when we play."

On April 21, 1968 – Iggy's 21st birthday – The Stooges opened for Cream, the English supergroup featuring Eric Clapton, at the Grande Ballroom. Cream, perhaps the worst band that ever existed, were the antithesis of every aesthetic value that The Stooges stood for. Iggy spent the day leading up to the gig transporting a two-hundred gallon oil drum from Ann Arbor to Detroit so they could put a contact mike on it for Jimmy Silver to hit it on the one beat during their best song. He got it up the three flights of stairs into the Grande Ballroom by himself but when the band walked on stage they discovered that their amps didn't work, and were met with a barrage of "We want Cream! We want Cream! Get off, we want Cream!"

Iggy: "I'm standing there, having taken two hits of orange acid, going, 'Fuck you!' It was one of our worst gigs ever. I went back to Dave Alexander's house with him. I was heartbroken. I thought, 'My God, this is 21.' This is it. Things are just not going well. Dave's mom served me a cheeseburger with a candle in the middle of it. The idea was to keep going and things would get better. Don't give up."

CHAPTER 3

Getting Signed And Getting Married

"The Detroit-Ann Arbor area at that time was hot with talent, and distant enough geographically and culturally from England and California to shield it from the pretentiousness that had seeped into the music of both places since the 'golden year' of 1966. Most visible of the Michigan bands was the MC5, the only group in the world that had gone to Chicago to play at the festivities held in conjunction with the Democratic convention which gave us the presidency of Richard Nixon. The MC5 were looking for a record deal."

– Danny Fields

DANNY Fields, street intellectual and paradigm of cool, was the "company freak" (official title Publicity Director) at Elektra Records. A brilliant young homosexual, already a respected member of the Warhol scene, Fields was connected on any number of Up There Manhattan scenes. He threw a party in the Chelsea Hotel the day of John F. Kennedy's funeral. He could get people on the phone.

He assumed a sedate perspective on music, and was obsessed with the ideas behind sound itself. Like his pal and sometime employer at *16* magazine, Gloria Stavers, Fields knew a pretty boy when he saw one. John Sinclair, a sharp observer of human foibles, reckoned that Fields would like Iggy, would fall for the well-hung singer in a big way. It would be unfair, however, to suggest that Fields allowed his carnal aesthetics to cloud his aural aesthetics. Over the next decade he would involve himself in many important punk developments, and not all of them were so pretty to behold.

"Company freak" was an acknowledged position within record labels at a time when those in control of the industry were middle-aged bourgeoisie who had no feel for the countercultural end of the rock spectrum. "They hired someone at a low level who wore bell-bottoms and smoked dope and took LSD in the office," Fields said. "And I really would take LSD in the office. I would sit around and just lick it. My hands would be all orange."

Sinclair, in the process of hustling his MC5, initially connected with Fields via two New York print media hacks, Dennis Frawley and Bob Rudenick, who were hot under the collar about his radical rock'n'roll gang. John Sinclair: "I started barraging them with press releases and other types of propaganda material. They used to run a whole story about the MC5 as their column for the week . . . Even before there was any record, we did national publicity ourselves. Part of my strategy in trying to break the MC5 on a national level and get a record contract was to say that there was this whole scene out here in Ann Arbor/ Detroit."

Freewheeling Frawley and Rocking Rudenick also worked as disc jockeys (as practitioners of the wheels of steel were known back then) for WFMU, a New Jersey progressive station. Fields, as luck would have it, did his own show for the same station immediately before the Frawley/Rudenick programme. When Sinclair visited the pair at the station's studio, he also met up with Fields. When he discovered that Fields was influential at Elektra Records – home to The Doors, Love, and Nico – Sinclair persuaded him to make the trip to Ann Arbor to see the MC5 on their home turf.

On the bill for a community school benefit that Fields saw when he reached Ann Arbor were, surprise surprise, The Stooges, MC5 and The Up. Sinclair had a finger in each of these pies; his brother looked after The Up while close pal Jimmy Silver was minding The Stooges; Fields got to view the whole deal on offer. He could see that the MC5 were powerful and popular but he also noted that they were very much the conventional rock band. He had never seen a performer like Iggy before – he says that he has never seen anything quite like him to this day. Of the music that The Stooges were churning up, the young aesthete could only gasp, 'At last!' "

Iggy: "I was playing a free gig, one of my few. It got to the end of our show. I was just letting the amps play and shooed the band off. So I was just wandering around. I had this maternity dress and a white face and I was doing unattractive things, spitting on people, things like that . . . I wander off the stage and this guy says, 'You're a star!' Just like in the movies. I believed he was an office boy, who just wanted to meet me and impress me. He didn't look like what I thought a record company executive should look like. He was dressed like us, in jeans and leather jacket."

Danny Fields, *The Stooges* sleevenotes: "When Iggy came off the stage, I went over to him, gushing about the show, telling him I was from Elektra Records and was eager to get them a contract. 'Speak to my manager,' he said, still walking toward the dressing room, not even looking at me. His abruptness was not generated by his getting so many such offers that he was jaded, but by his disbelief – he'd never had *any* and didn't think it possible that I was for real. 'Yeah, sure, you're from Elektra Records,' he said to himself (as he told me later). 'And I'm Mr Ed.'"

Fields did as he was told and got Sinclair to introduce him to Jimmy Silver. The next day he rang Elektra CEO Jac Holzman from Ann Arbor and told him that he'd secured handshake signings with not one but two bands, both of whom, he assured Holzman, would make history, and lots of money for Elektra into the bargain. Fields had to offer the two managers some "hello money" and needed Holzman's guidance in that regard.

He explained that the MC5 were popular, while he reckoned that The Stooges had something new going for them and that their lead singer was in a league all of his own. Having been advised by his boss, the MC5 were offered $20,000 and The Stooges $5,000, subsequently upped to $20,000. "It was more money by far than either band or manager had ever seen," recalled Fields, who got together with Jimmy Silver and John Sinclair in the kitchen at 1510 Hill Street, the Trans-Love HQ, and repeated both, at the time, astronomical offers. The two bands said yes. They couldn't believe what was happening.

Danny Fields: "I consulted with Jac Holzman on musical things and he trusted me. He was not a suit and tie person, but a guy who was very sophisticated about music. He was a very adventurous individual who suddenly possessed a record company that struck it rich with The Doors, who were unique in their own atrocious way. People at the label were eager to break new ground. The troubles came afterwards when the suits around Jac rebelled. The MC5 were smoking marijuana in the office, The Stooges had no songs. But the initial ignition spark was not a problem, the problems came very soon thereafter."

Early in October 1968 Holzman, the man who'd popularised West Coast soft rock when he signed The Doors and Love to his one-time folk label, accompanied Elektra Vice President Bill Harvey, John Cale (recently escaped from the Velvet Underground and employed by Elektra as in-house producer) and Danny Fields on a field trip to Ann

Arbor to catch both the MC5 and The Stooges at the Fifth Dimension club. The night of that show Iggy was extremely ill with a temperature of 104 degrees. There were bruises on his head because he'd had a "kind of a fit" before the show. To top it all off his one good ear was acting up. Just before he went on he was to be seen backstage sitting in a blanket, shivering. It sounds more like drugs than illness but this all happened before the serious drugs really kicked in. When The Stooges finally performed he kept falling down and recalled being in unbelievable pain during his performance. He reckoned that Holzman *et al* were so freaked out by his condition that they decided that he must be the real thing.

Iggy: "These guys are sophisticated useless people with money and things . . . they had perhaps a bit of a broader understanding of the spectrum of man and all that shit than I did. I'm a simple guy, from the sticks, I'm a hick from the sticks, that just happens to be a genius and overflowing with talent, but other than my utterly superior grasp of my art and its implications, other than that, I'm just a hick from the sticks. So I don't know what they were thinking of me, because it all passed over my head. I think, looking back on it, it was something like having a wonderful toy to them. They didn't realise that a person like this ever existed and they didn't know . . . they weren't scared of me, it was great. They didn't know what to make of me."

John Cale, *What's Welsh for Zen*: "Iggy's a strange one. When I went to see him out in Michigan he was as thin as a rake, his icebox was full of cases of Bud. I don't know what his metabolism was like, but he ate chips and drank beer and that was it. His apartment was piled up with beer cans and the remains of old pizzas."

The formal signing of two of the most extreme bands in America, in the presence of various out-of-town corporate record label types, was such a big deal that it was captured in a photograph taken at the Trans-Love HQ on Hill Street by John Sinclair's wife Leni. In her visual document Danny Fields looks mysterious with his long hair and hipster sunglasses. John Sinclair, who on that day achieved a very great deal for two hard-to-market acts, seems distracted. MC5 guitarist Fred Smith appears young, arrogant and confident. Jimmy Silver and his wife Susan look beautiful and proud to be part of this great occasion. Bill Harvey, Elektra VP and the man who would eventually pronounce a death sentence over The Stooges' time at the label, seems uncomfortable; in the wrong room with the wrong people. Sitting on the ground in front of the standing men (and Susan Silver) are three attractive looking young women, each of whom was deemed to be an MC5 "designer/seamstress". The sewing machines, weapons of liberation like saxophones and shotguns, were obviously working overtime on the revolution.

In early 1969 Dave Marsh reviewed an appearance by the newly signed Stooges at Henry Ford College near Detroit. "As a pot-bellied junior college specimen walked out of the auditorium with his acned mistress, Iggy called out the soul-frying insult, 'Goodbye . . . (long pause) . . . you fat mothuh!' sending half the audience to its feet in repulsion, half in response to what they knew had happened – a strong occurrence of truth-telling from the platform for liars and sophists. Later Iggy was to hop atop a girl and become slightly too violent, lacerating her or something. Which wouldn't have been so bad if it hadn't been that she was the Dean's daughter!"

Iggy: "I'd like to strip some chicks naked and just start to grab anything. That's why I liked Saturday night. People were shouting and screaming at the end, and that's beautiful music to me. I can't really say that I care what they do – what the audience does – it's their business what they do and really none of mine . . . I just want to meet them and do things – I just want to see what develops in a large meeting. It's just what it is, it's a large meeting, and that's what characterises our band – that when we play it's a meeting, and not a performance. And, you know, it's a very broad meeting."

1969 saw Iggy sign another contract, one which held his attention for a matter of weeks. He married a rich girl called Wendy Weisberg whom he'd met through a college friend back when he was 19. At that time he still had a fear of women but he liked Wendy, a nice Jewish girl from a wealthy part of Cleveland. After that initial introduction they went their separate ways until, two years later, Wendy showed up at a Stooges show in Ohio with her boyfriend. She put up a magnificent struggle but Iggy eventually managed to come between them. The weekend after the Ohio gig he hired a car and romantically drove 400 miles to woo her and, having eventually disposed of her virginity, he started seeing her regularly. She had things going for her other than her beauty, most notably her prosperous family. Iggy said that her father owned a chain of cut-price farmer stores – The Giant Tiger – and that he was a self-made, tough, steak eating guy with attitude. Wendy also owned a record player and had good taste. The first time he heard 'Heroin' by The Velvet Underground was on Wendy's hi-fi. They also played Sinatra's 'The Shadow Of Your Smile', a romantic tune that'd serve Iggy well over the years.

Iggy, *I Need More*: "Then we got married. Her parents didn't come. My parents came. We had the wedding on the front lawn of The Stooges farmhouse. It was beautiful. It was a warm summer day. The bride wore white and long black hair. All in all it was an interesting affair. First of all Danny Fields, my publicist at Elektra – the 'architect' of my career – flew down. I had called him up the night before and told him. He just about swallowed his tongue."

It was a zany affair. Fields advised Iggy, "Jim, what *are* you doing? Think about your image." Russ Gibb rang the house while the wedding was in progress to find out if the rumours of nuptials were true. Iggy went to the phone and chatted with Gibb about the wedding, unaware that their conversation was going out live on WABX. Jimmy Silver – who conducted the service – was heard to mutter, "Hey, reality, truth – that's where Jim's at," to which Danny Fields replied, Manhattan-style, "Fuck reality! Who cares about reality?" Ron Asheton – who dubbed Wendy the Potato Girl – was the best man. He proudly boasted that he wore his Luftwaffe fighter pilot's jacket, a Nazi Knight's Cross, an Iron Cross first class, and a Russian Front Iron Cross second class.

Jimmy Silver: "I was a minister of the Universal Life Church. They asked me to get this ordination so I could marry them. The other Stooges called Wendy the Potato Girl. They called her that because she had a lumpy complexion and was sort of suntanned. They lived in the attic in the farm house. She was an absolutely beautiful girl, but it lasted only a few months; they got it annulled. She couldn't stand Iggy smoking pot and the behaviour of The Stooges guys."

The lousy behaviour started on day one. The band sat on the front porch drinking beer and flipping coins, taking bets on how long the marriage was going to last.

"Hey! I'll give you five to four on two months . . ." opined one.

"No, one day, I say. I know Pop!" chipped in another helpfully.

Bill Cheatham, a Stooges roadie who subsequently, and briefly, replaced Dave Alexander as bass player, said that he and Alexander went out and bought new tennis shoes for the occasion. At the wedding Alexander turned to Cheatham and quipped, "Bet you those tennis shoes last longer than Iggy's marriage." Unless they were really bad sneakers, he was on the nail.

Wendy Weisberg the Potato Girl didn't last long. When the divorce papers came through The Stooges hung them up on the wall because they found them so amusing, these large thick legal documents which said that there was no consummation of the marriage and that Iggy was a homosexual. The Potato Girl was allegedly 14 years old at the time of the wedding. Like other Iggy myths this seems unlikely. Poor Wendy got mixed up in history with her replacement, Betsy, who *was* 14.

Far from being traumatised by his divorce, Iggy quickly went back to his usual routines. He would bring home girls after a gig, they'd go upstairs, and after a while the girls would come downstairs crying, because Iggy had just banged them and then said, "Get out!"

Iggy, *I Need More*: "I was free again. I could roam the streets looking like I used to. I walked into a hamburger joint where the kids went after school. It's actually where I wrote the first Stooges record. I'd just observe their social patterns, which became material for my songs. So I went there and saw Betsy. I never saw anything like that. She was very cute. She was the exact opposite of my wife – blonde, white as snow. She was 13 and she looked at me penetratingly. So I guess you can figure out what happened next."

Betsy obviously won herself a semi-permanent place in Pop's cold, cold heart. Eleven years later his album *Soldier* contained the song, 'Dog Food', in which she is immortalised: "My girlfriend Betsy, she's just 14/ There's nothing better for me to do/ I'm living on dog food."

CHAPTER 4

Anarcho/Crazy Youths –
The Stooges

"The incendiary teen revolt of '1969' and the lust-for-abasement of 'I Wanna Be Your Dog' dwindle into the lapidary lassitude of 'We Will Fall', a 10-minute mantra that equates nirvana with numbness. Iggy Pop's nihilistic aggression curdles into void worship. The song is a rock mausoleum marbled with Indian raga drones that hark back to The Doors' 'The End'. But where Jim Morrison imagined cataclysm as a prelude to some kind of spiritual rebirth (a la T.S. Eliot's The Waste Land*), 'We Will Fall' is terminal, the triumph of death drive over Eros, a return to the womb-tomb."*

– The Sex Revolts

"I'll do it with music. I'll do it if I have to cut myself, if I have to kill myself, if I have to go barefoot, I don't know what, but whatever I have to do at any time, I'll do it. It had made my behaviour, over the last couple of years, more and more erratic, because that's what I feel – I just feel that it's a deadly struggle for me. I have to be able to feed my own self completely before I can be very happy about anything."

– Iggy Pop (1970)

RON Asheton visited New York with Iggy a few times before the whole band went there to record their first album, *The Stooges*. It was during one of those early trips, before getting signed to Elektra, that Iggy took STP for the first time. "He didn't know it was a three-day trip, so guess who got to watch him? Me," says Honest Ron, who tied a rope around Iggy's waist, leading him around town like a dog on a leash. About 200 times more powerful than mescaline, STP stands for serenity, tranquillity and peace (though it didn't necessarily deliver these attributes). Not a drug that exists in nature, it is generally reckoned that the effects last no more than 18 hours.

In June '69 the whole band headed for the Big Apple where, during two days in the Hit Factory, they recorded their first album with John Cale as their producer. They brought with them a tape of the five songs they had worked up for the record and played that tape for Jac Holzman. He enjoyed what he heard but felt that a few more tunes were needed if they wanted to make a full album.

"You guys got enough material to do an album, right?" he asked.

"Yes, of course we do," they replied.

The fact of the matter was that, despite all their free-form redneck experimentation, they only had three real songs plus a handful of inspirational jams.

"OK, guys, I'll give you two days to prepare for the recording sessions," said Holzman.

With Ron in the driving seat, they brainstormed back at their hotel. Asheton locked himself up in his room and came up with the simplest emergency tunes he could think of, like subsequent *The Stooges* tracks 'Not Right', a forgotten ace, and the less immortal 'Real Cool Time'. He got hold of Iggy and said, "Come in here, check out these tunes." Iggy wrote his quick lyrics and the two of them put some arrangements together. The following day the band rehearsed the new material. "Then," says Ron, "it was recording time." While they were in the studio another Velvets exile, the ice maiden Nico, sat haughtily alongside Cale, caught up in her private world, busy knitting while baiting her next prey.

Ron Asheton: "I'd never been in a recording studio, and I knew that Iggy had only been in a recording studio a few times. The Iguanas had made a couple of 45s. I don't think Iggy had much of a handle on the studio. But I think we did a pretty good job and that's why we wound up with John Cale, because that was his first job working as a producer . . . he made it much easier . . . Being that he had been in The Velvet Underground and had become a staff producer, that was his first job for Elektra. That's why he was chosen. 'You can handle this shit! Look at all the crap that you did – you handle this, this is a bunch of shit!' "

John Cale, *What's Welsh for Zen*: "Jac Holzman at Elektra had been happy and impressed by (Nico's) *The Marble Index*. He said, 'It's very European.' Then Danny Fields and I went to see the MC5 in Detroit, and the opening act was The Stooges. Both acts were already signed to Elektra. I met James (Iggy), and he was a nice guy and still seems to be. When I first saw him he was so much fun up there, with a really bouncy sense of humour, contrasting with the Nuremberg rally that was going on with the MC5.

"I fell in love with The Stooges, and so I produced them. I'd say that The Stooges and Patti Smith were the two biggest challenges I've ever had as a producer. With Patti, I wanted to capture her visionary perspective; with Iggy I wanted to retain the live shows' electricity. He had this impish quality – he'd be threatening you one minute and hugging you the next – and that was what I wanted to get across. It was incredible seeing him in the studio; he'd be climbing all over the amps and the desks like a mad animal, while the band just played as if nothing out of the ordinary was happening."

"I just took the band into the studio," said Cale in 1977, "and we did it as quickly as I would do anything with a young punk band today." Iggy was at his arrogant best, unimpressed by being in the studio with a distinguished former Velvet Underground member. He admired the Velvets but was determined that *The Stooges* would sound like nothing other than The Stooges. "We weren't interested in anything like writing a song or making a chord change," he said. "I didn't bother with anything like that until I had a recording contract. Once I had a contract I decided I'd better really learn how to write some songs."

Cale ended up playing viola on the epic 'We Will Fall', a 10-minute trance-inducing dirge which best displays a spiritual affinity with The Velvet Underground while also showcasing The Stooges' own left-field roots. Elsewhere, despite amp/voltage mayhem, Cale injected an admirable restraint into proceedings, allowing tunes like 'I Wanna Be Your Dog' and '1969' to emerge as perfect street anthems dealing with boredom and alienation, songs that say important things about their era and circumstances in much the same way that better known works of art like The Byrds' 'Mr Tambourine Man' or 'White Light White Heat' by The Velvet Underground are reflective of their very different times or places. The interesting thing about this achievement is that, whereas stuff like 'Mr Tambourine Man' seems redolent of a long forgotten epoch or golden age, the handful of real classics on *The Stooges* remain a contemporary reference point, reliable as the Northern Star, comfortable to the White Stripes/Green Day/Beck-listening ear.

Back in Ann Arbor, after the New York recordings, The Stooges played occasional gigs at the Grande Ballroom. Jimmy Silver kept a firm business hand on the tiller. "I had them play as infrequently as possible. There was a point when I could have had gigs for them virtually every night, but they told me not to. They said they didn't want to overexpose themselves. Really, it was because they did the same thing every night.

They didn't have a lot of musical breadth to what they could do. They had one show that they did wherever they went. I couldn't book them in the same area night after night. They had to be very widely spread out. It was pop festivals, clubs, ballrooms on weekends mostly."

John Sinclair, a cunning operator but less of a businessman than the subsequent macrobiotics millionaire Silver, employed the opposite approach with the MC5. "My strategy for the MC5," says Sinclair, "was to play as often as possible. Even if you had to create your own gigs. If people saw it, heard it, they became fans." The net result of this strategy was that the MC5 were eventually regarded as being a Big So What?, one boogie on down production too many, whereas, during their lifetime, The Stooges came to be regarded as the very essence of experimental cool, cutting-edge phunsters at the disposal of the ladies and the avant-garde alike.

Given the extent to which Iggy's own misbehaviour subsequently railroaded his career towards oblivion (Bowie famously said that he rescued defeat from the jaws of victory), it is well worth noting how crossover The Stooges looked like being during those Jimmy Silver-controlled days. They had big-shot industry people putting their money where their mouths were, and it was no mean feat to have the likes of Andy Warhol, Danny Fields, Jac Holzman and John Cale (not to mention subsequent fans such as Miles Davis and David Bowie) sitting up and paying attention to their somewhat ragged and tattered wares. The Stooges had the bit between their teeth for quite a while and it was Iggy, self-proclaimed convenor and leader of the gang, who took his eye off the prize.

The Stooges were invited to perform at the Saugatuck Pop Festival, in July 1969, sharing the bill with the MC5, Procul Harum, The Amboy Dukes, and Bob Seger. With Iggy still a fit and healthy frontman capable of commanding the attention of a mainstream crowd, they appeared formidable. An article in a local paper by one W. Rexford Benoit subtly commented on the emerging difference between the nascent cock rock and boogie rhetoric of the MC5 and the blitzkrieg bop which The Stooges were gradually honing to a fine art. "Now, today, the MC5 are more nationally famous than The Stooges, but look at Saugatuck for a comparison. Listening to The Stooges there was like watching a TV set with a finger in an electric light outlet. The MC5 invited free-form audience participation in Saugatuck, as they always do, and the cluster of bikers around the stage were moved to stomp co-promoter Pete Andrews. Andrews went down right in front of me, so I asked if he was hurt. 'No, dammit, I'm only resting,' he said. Since the two-day festival, the MC5 have been working on a new record with Jon Landau and The Stooges album has been released and is doing well. What does it all mean? Saugatuck froze 'the Detroit sound' over two days, and put it all in perspective, and here's how it came out: The Stooges and MC5 are the essence. Their distinctive sounds make them unlike any other bands and will undoubtedly make them both famous. Yeah, good."

The Stooges appeared with Eric Burdon and the MC5 at the Mt. Clemens Pop Festival and at another concert at the Michigan State Fairgrounds. Iggy's parents came and saw what he was up to for the first time. "My father tried to appear cool after the concert, but my mother told me that he had actually climbed a girder to the grandstand to see what I was doing onstage."

With perfect contradictory timing, *The Stooges* came out in August 1969 – the same week as the original Woodstock Festival. Both events, in their very different ways, marked the end of the Sixties. In the context of that upstate New York collegiate feelgood factor – future dentists and lawyers of America wallowing naked in the mud – The Stooges first album was a welcome antidote to the burgeoning mediocrity of FM rock.

Creem, who'd effectively championed The Stooges from day one, were naturally enthusiastic in their review of local boys making a national splash, noting that Iggy was less of an adolescent than he seemed to be (a trait which remains with him to this day), while arguing that this was every bit as much Ron Asheton's album as it was Iggy's. "The dangerous Psychedelic Stooges manage to quickly get down to the nitty-gritty of sensual frustration for all the neo-American adolescent malehood . . . '1969', the lead song on the disc, is the perfect expression of the oldest complaint of rebellious anarcho/crazy youth. Iggy sounds a lot younger than 22 for the horny American youth whose fantasies he summarises. 'I Wanna Be Your Dog' is reminiscent of early Velvet Underground music carrying it into even more bizarre levels. 'No Fun' features some physically abusive guitar playing by Stooges guitarist Ron Asheton. Throughout the album Asheton reveals himself as an insane master of the power The Stooges channel into their music. This is probably the guitar style of the future."

The luxuriant praise directed at Asheton is somewhat over the top. In the cold light of hindsight his playing betrays a certain amount of Hendrix-by-numbers and a more than passing nod in the direction of nauseating psychedelic/progressive convention. He was clearly a devotee of what Lester Bangs once called Far Out Rock. No doubt he was a proper guitarist in the making and *Creem* were terribly perceptive in their suggestion that he was creating the guitar sound of the future. His playing, particularly on 'No Fun', helped write the book on punk's no-trimmings staccato riff assault. Within the context of the long-playing vinyl album – the then-dominant format for the dispersal of recorded music – the record was like several other good early rock albums in one important regard – Side One was a seamless classic, Side Two contains the obvious filler dreamed up in the hotel while Jac Holzman waited patiently to hear a whole album.

Circus magazine reported that, "Nobody ever claimed they were superb musicians, especially they; they just do it as best they know how, not caring much about criticism and less about the people not equipped to dig what they're doing. The album is long and rangy, musically average, but emotionally as intense as, well . . . why don't you supply the analogy?" *Rolling Stone*, home of socially responsible collegiate commentary, very much caught up in the singer-songwriter and progressive rock end of things, was disgusted with this little slice of acned small town nastiness. They gave it a big thumbs down. "In 1957, it was conclusively proven that there exists a causal relationship between rock'n'roll and juvenile delinquency. This record is just another document in support of this thesis." Never has the aesthetic clash between punk sensibility and rock's flaccid underbelly been so perfectly framed. The review went on to call The Stooges "stoned sloths making boring, repressed music, which I suspect appeals to boring, repressed people."

English critic Nick Kent, who made an international reputation for himself by championing junk rock, assessed the album retrospectively in 1974 for London's *New Musical Express*. "While everyone else was all duped up, dousing themselves in patchouli oil and 'getting themselves back to the garden', The Stooges had the collective ear right down on the beat of the street like some thoroughly realistic *Clockwork Orange* manifestation."

Corporate Elektra decided that *The Stooges* was a very strange piece of business. The people working at headquarters shared *Rolling Stone*'s middle-class doubts about Danny Field's protégés. "Oh, this isn't The Doors, this isn't Love, this isn't Judy Collins, this isn't Tom Paxton, what the hell is this? This is a bunch of noise!" seemed to be the consensus up in the marketing department. "But it's going somewhere," insisted Elektra executive Steve Harris. "It's saleable. You don't understand – what he's doing is rock & roll!"

Iggy, too, was bemused by the frantic efforts of Elektra, effectively a classy folk label accidentally thriving in the lucrative but nasty world of rock'n'roll, to make a sow's ear out of the silk purse they'd been handed on a plate. There is nothing too over the top or aurally offensive about *The Stooges*. The company let the band down badly by not releasing '1969' or 'I Wanna Be Your Dog' as a single; possibly turning one of those tracks into, at the very least, an airplay hit. Iggy himself said of '1969': "It's a good type of song to put on after President Nixon gives a speech – it says a lot. Well, it's got to be that way, just because when you play music, most artists transmit their unhappiness or their happiness – and we're somewhere in the middle."

Iggy: "They were taking me over and whoring me to Gloria Stavers at *16* magazine. I was on the cover, I used to be on the cover, they didn't know where to put me! Should they make me a teen idol or should we make him a collegiate rebellion figure? I didn't want to be any of these things! I just thought, 'Well, gosh, they want me to meet this nice lady who is going to help my career, can I play some more music?'"

Stavers, a free-spirited former beauty queen, believed it was all about the singer not the song. (She allegedly once had a fling with Jim Morrison.) She dragged her teen magazine kicking and screaming away from the Fabians and Ricky Nelsons of this world in the direction of the more compelling tight-trousered rock gods whose "cute-n-cuddly pix" adorned many an adolescent bedroom wall. Stavers liked a pretty boy and surrounded herself with – and paid attention to – men such as Danny Fields and the exotic Leee Black Childers who liked pretty boys too.

Leee Black Childers (photographer, Stooges minder, David Bowie road manager): "I worked under Gloria Stavers at *16* magazine, with Danny Fields. She was right on the ball, and could spot talent right out. She broke Elton John, Bowie, Alice Cooper. And she was very much aware of what Iggy had going for him. A lot of people denigrate *16* magazine but those denigrators have no idea how influential the magazine was, and what a lot of good it would do for your career if it backed you."

In August 1969, The Stooges undertook their first US national tour to promote the album. The first show, with the MC5, was at the New York State Pavilion, Queens, on September 3. The Queens show was promoted by Howard Stein who, rather famously, claimed that his wife had a miscarriage after seeing The Stooges. He allegedly swore that he'd never put them on again. But he did subsequently promote Iggy as a solo act.

Cash Box: "The earth will shake as never before as Elektra recording artists The Stooges make their first New York appearance. Led by dynamite singer Iggy, The Stooges are sure to upset a few heads with their basic, gutsy, intensely passionate rock. Heavy, hard, hard, hard, The

Stooges should have the United States of New York dancing in the aisles before it's over. The wizard of Ig is upon us."

Karin Berg, *Rock* magazine: "Iggy is jumping up and down, writhing, hanging onto the stand-up mike, putting it between his legs, rubbing up and down against it . . . he leans forward, the mike breaks. He's on the floor on the stage, he moans, he yells, 'Now I wanna be your dog, now I wanna be your dog, well c'mon!' The fantasies the Ig is conjuring up, this crowd will not admit to. The Stooges can be a little terrifying – they put on a great show, but the show is not a put-on. The audience is coldly quiet, as if saying 'so show me' and Iggy is showing them!"

Rolling Stone: "As the hot summer breeze blew across the stage, and the deranged, forceful music hammered us, Iggy clawed his chest until it bled. He threw himself headlong into the audience. It was spontaneous, not calculated, theatre. Trash showered onto the stage."

Fred Kirby, *Billboard*: "Iggy Stooge (That's his billing!) has an act that is geared to appeal to all sexes . . . Iggy, clad only in cut-away blue jeans, swayed and gyrated, caressed and licked his mike stand, flung it into the audience, scratched his bare chest to the point of bleeding, rolled on the floor with lead guitarist Ron Asheton, among other things. In the long finale, '1969', Asheton and bass guitarist Dave Alexander joined in the erotic display. The stage activity took precedence over the quartet's music, which may be good."

Karin Berg: "Everyone is scrambling to see what he's doing, but no one is saying a word. There is only loud whining feedback. Iggy dawdles over to the drums, plays with them a bit, idly musing, he slowly ambles down to the centre of stage, holding sticks, looks at the audience, looks down, pauses, grasps both drumsticks firmly, holding ends out, and slowly cuts long welts into his chest with the tips of the drumsticks. He watches himself and what he is doing to himself, fascinated, fascinating. Then he walks offstage. A few people limply clap."

Karin Berg, all hot and bothered after the sex show she'd seen on the Pavilion stage, went back to the dressing room to interview Iggy. "I am a little stunned and agog and now I'm supposed to go backstage and I'm dreading it," she gushed. "I have been cowed. In the dressing room Iggy is putting some cold water on the welts on his chest, the rest of the group is there, things are rather quiet. I walk over to Iggy . . . 'What do you feel when you perform? Do you know what you're doing all the time – what you're going to do?' He smiled. 'Does it look as though I'm in control?' 'No it doesn't.' 'I'm not. I don't take charge. I don't like professionals, they take charge. I don't like to do that. I want to tap energy. I get this feeling, this area of concentration here, the genital area. It starts out that way, I can feel it, I just let go, and then it moves up my body through here, to the back of my neck, to my head, and it just kind of explodes. That's similar to what happens to people in religious dancing or rituals, the trance-like thing.'"

After giving New York a baptism of fire, The Stooges moved out into the less sympathetic hinterland, opening for Woodstock-conquering guitar heroes Ten Years After at the Boston Tea Party. Three-thousand responsible citizens – future trendy geography teachers of America all het up after seeing Woodstock reported on the news – were naturally there to see blues bores Ten Years After, not the demented Stooges.

Ron Asheton: "There was complete silence after every tune. The only person who was applauding for the first song was the president of our fan club, and she actually got her life threatened, so she didn't applaud. 'Pretty bad vibes in here tonight.' Of course, they were crazy for Ten Years After. It must have been hard for all of those people not to react to us when they were all flying on speed . . . you could see their faces when Ten Years After was playing, and those people had dropped so much speed, man; they were grinding their teeth and they're in fuckin' heaven, but they didn't like The Stooges."

Iggy: "It was strange to see that many people quiet. I just started the second tune, and beginning with the second tune . . . I began flinging myself at them! Flinging myself on the floor, drawing blood, cutting myself, taunting, but never direct – taunting them and mimicking them, walking amongst them. Finally, after the third song, there was an outburst of applause."

One attendee told Eric Erhmann from *Rolling Stone*, "He has more moves than James Brown, and you can see that he feels every move that he makes. The vibes bounce off the audience. Iggy picks them right back up and, before you know it, the whole place is flipping out with him."

Not everybody at the Boston Tea Party was there to catch Ten Years After. One kid told Erhmann, "A whole bunch of us drove down just to see Iggy. I had heard about him jumping into the audience and taking his clothes off but I didn't believe it until I saw it happen. His body animations are hypnotising, and when he was lying down with the guitars playing by themselves, it looked like he was going to die."

"I'm surprised they didn't need a stretcher to carry him off after he collapsed," said one exhausted and ready-for-bed Ten Years After fan. "How long can a guy like that last?" he asked. At least 30 years longer than Ten Years After, as it happened.

Maggie Bell, the emphatic singer with rootsy Brits Stone The Crows, a believer in traditional hard-working showbiz values, was horrified by what had crawled out on Ann Arbor. "Those bloody Stooges," she complained. "We worked with them in the States and they were terrible. The singer is absurd, he swears at the audience, and then throws himself into them. You know, this sort of thing really annoys me. I work my guts out, and we all do to put over the best we've got, and then we share a bill with somebody like this."

Iggy: "I'm at the supreme disadvantage, and you know, like Friday night there were thousands of people sitting there. They could see every move I made, and I couldn't see any of them. So they had a beautiful anonymity, they're like thieves – the audience is like thieves – they just sit there and steal from you . . . I want them to steal from me. I want to think that there's some huge mass of souls out there, that are having their lives changed when they listen to us.

"It's not ever important to me if a thousand people know that I changed their lives, because I know I did, and so I don't care because I know that there have got to be a couple of little tickers out there that just go crazy. There have got to be a couple of little brains that just go into high gear. It has to be, because I know I used to go to lots of concerts to watch the bands do the exact same thing, and I used to feel so good."

After the Boston Tea Party gig Eric Erhmann from *Rolling Stone* accompanied The Stooges back to their hotel. The band were ready to crash but Iggy was bouncing up and down on his bed, doing his pre-bedtime aerobics as if he were onstage, pointing a scornful finger at the ground. He said he used to do these particular moves back home with ? & The Mysterians when they'd come through town. "They were a bunch of Puerto Rican dudes from Saginaw, and a killer group," he said as he leaped into the air. "They were being what they really were, but nobody stopped to figure them out. They were 'out kids' just like us. After '96 Tears', everything was a drag for them. That's what happens when your music gets misunderstood."

CHAPTER 5

The Desert Shore – Nico

"I like the Velvet Underground and I'm one of those very few people who really, really like Nico's music. I love her last album and when I come into New York I make it a point to try to see her."

– Iggy Pop, *Jazz & Pop*, 1969

"I took John Cale to see the MC5, but he was more impressed by The Stooges, and wanted to produce them, which was fine. When Nico said she wanted to go along, I should have seen it coming. I mean, she and Iggy were so totally opposite, so different, yet perfectly suited . . . I'm sure he satisfied her. She loved the brilliant, the insane and the addicted . . . it was perfect. I just thought, 'Ho hum, another day, another poet,' but Iggy and Nico became a big deal."

– Danny Fields, *Punk*, 1977

WHILE The Stooges were in New York working on their first album, Danny Fields took them down to Andy Warhol's Factory where they got acquainted with the bizarre circus animals and freak show surrounding the painter. According to Billy Name, the Factory was full of "perfect-faced people" whom Warhol collected. Al Hansen, the Fluxus-founding grandfather of Beck, said it was full of jet-setters and people discovered in Times Square toilets. The rest of The Stooges found it all too queer for their Midwestern sensibilities but Iggy took to it like a duck to water. He was the Edmund Hillary of social climbers. It was there that he got properly acquainted with Nico, the exiled Velvet Underground diva who was trying to work out what she wanted to do with the rest of her life. She was older than most of the wild crowd she hung out with; she and Iggy hit it off right away.

The Stooges were staying at the Chelsea Hotel, the approved hangout for Warhol superstars like Edie Sedgwick and Nico. Soon Nico and Iggy were to be seen holding hands at Steve Paul's West 49th Street basement club, The Scene. They made an odd looking couple, him short and her tall, her just past her prime and him the very essence of virile young manhood. She was quite something just then. Gerard Malanga said of her, "If there exists beauty so universal as to be unquestionable, Nico possesses it." Leonard Cohen thought she was "the most beautiful woman I'd ever seen up to that moment."

Nico'd been living in New York since 1959, having appeared in Fellini's *La Dolce Vita* before abandoning Europe. She used to work as a model in New York, taking acting classes with Marilyn Monroe at Lee Strasberg's Actor's Studio. She was introduced to Warhol by Bob Dylan and Warhol foisted her onto The Velvet Underground. Credited with having broken Lou Reed's ice-cold heart, her sexual conquests read like a 1967 Top 10 for she had bedded Rolling Stone Brian Jones, Dylan, and Jim Morrison. She claimed Turkish, Russian and German blood, spoke five languages, and said she was a pagan. According to rumour, she walked into a Velvet Underground rehearsal one day and announced, "I cannot make love to Jews any more," by which she meant that she was done with Lou Reed. Shortly after this pronouncement, the legend has it, she left the Velvets and started her liaison with Iggy.

"Jimmy, you have one big problem," she explained to her young conquest, "you are not full of the poison! This is not correct. This is not right. How can you perform when you are not full of the poison? Me, I will help you just enough to fill you with the poison, otherwise you have nothing. We do not want to see a person on the stage, no, no, no, we want to see a performance, and the poison is the essence of the performer."

"She meant I had too much humanity," Iggy reckoned in *I Need More*. "Then she'd feed me red wines with French names I never heard of. That's how I learned all that bullshit; that's how I learned to modulate my voice . . . wear light blue suits and speak to record company executives."

Danny Fields: "Warhol's sexuality was quite complex. For example, one of the reasons he put Nico in front of The Velvet Underground was that he saw himself in Nico. A part of him wanted to be a rock star, he literally couldn't have been a rock star, but he would have loved to have had that kind of adulation and fame. Therefore he was also interested in the guys Nico got involved with, so on a certain level he would have found Iggy attractive, not literally that he wanted to go to bed with him but he would have seen him as a hunk on a certain level."

When work on the album was completed The Stooges wanted to go home to Michigan. "Jimmy, I go with you," Nico announced, and she did just that, eventually persuading some of her obliging New York pals to join her for an Ann Arbor film project. François de Menil, whose parents were influential art patrons and collectors, and who was himself very close to Warhol, wanted to make a movie with Nico. She insisted that she would only do this if it were made in Ann Arbor and if it also featured Iggy. When de Menil arrived in town he made *An Evening Of Light*, which also featured the other Stooges staring out through a window.

John Cale, *What's Welsh for Zen*: "She saw him as a naïf, and through Iggy she discovered that there were parts of America that reminded her of the more desolate landscapes of Europe. She even made a film with the art patron François de Menil in Iggy's back yard. The story that affected my view of him most at the time was the nights he told me he spent alone in the farmhouse, up until all hours of the morning, tuning each string on his lap-steel guitar to the same note, turning it up and immersing himself in the noise. That was vision to me."

Iggy, *Punk* magazine: "We ran around and around this potato field and mimed with plastic limbs. I never made much sense of it. It was jive. But I needed dinner that day. What had happened was that François de Menil of Texas money wanted to do a film with Nico and she said, 'If you wanna do a film, you gotta come out to Michigan and put Jimmy in it.' So he said, 'Well, OK.'"

François de Menil (architect, friend of Andy Warhol): "*An Evening Of Light* was initiated by myself and Nico as a sort of pre-MTV promotional item for an album she had out at the time. An early pop promo. It was her idea to involve Iggy, which I thought was OK. She decided on Ann Arbor as a location. It's about six minutes long and much of it can be seen in the documentary movie on Nico, *Nico Icon*. Indeed, they used more of it than I imagined they would. We sort of improvised it . . . I don't really remember how it developed exactly. I came up with the idea of using mannequins and it could be that Nico thought of using the cross. I travelled to Ann Arbor with my assistant, the camera equipment, and I think we brought all those mannequins with us."

Iggy to Nick Kent: "She was the one who took me when I was a skinny little naive brat and taught me how to eat pussy and all about the best German wines and French champagnes . . . I saw her later though, after things were starting to get bad for her. It was in Paris and . . . oh, forget the state she was in . . . she just wanted desperately to get in touch with me. Maybe with Bowie more, but, hell, I'd suffice and she had me followed. Had radio monitors scanning my every move. Taxi drivers were bribed – just everything. Anyway, when I found her I just rejected her immediately. I just said, 'You're not good enough for me to expend time on anymore,' and the first thing she said was, 'Jimmy you are strong!' and she got that look that Deutsche get when they're about to bite into a pig. She got that vampirism in her eyes. But she wasn't going to be defeated outright, or so she thought. Because her next number was to slyly offer me a snort of heroin. She laid out a line, figuring that heroin would get me into her little web. But, just as the enticing line came close to my nostril, I blew it off the mirror all over the floor, got up and said, 'So long baby! Nyah, nyah – fooled you!' And that's the last I've seen of Nico since."

Iggy, *Bust*, 1995: "She was wonderful. She was the first girl who told me, 'You know, there's something very nice you can do for me.' I was like, 'Oh, yeah. What's that?' 'Oh, let me show you.' (Indicates pushing imaginary head down towards crotch.) I thought this was pretty funny, pretty hilarious. Hanging out with her was like fucking your older brother. She was about 10 years older than me; she was 31 and I was 21. It was like somebody older and a lot hipper and very strong in her opinions and also incredibly fucking talented. The album she had just made at that time (*The Marble Index*) was just a phenomenal piece of work.

"So she had that, and then she was highly eccentric and also dangerous, and at the same time, where the danger came in too, was that she was very vulnerable. She was wild, she was a boheme. She was serious about her art, and I just welcomed the chance. I hung out with her day and night for about a month, a couple of weeks here and a couple of weeks there. And then, inevitably, the strain. There's a certain strain when you're trying to create with your mind, especially when you're very young, it comes with a lot of serendipity. It's difficult to have someone around, and so there was turbulence there. The band of course really wanted her out, they were jealous, and they would walk around the house imitating her accent and stuff. She would come to our rehearsals and she'd tell me what she thought of the shows, my haircut, and every other damn thing. It was highly provocative, one of my most destructive periods was right around that time. A lot of people, other people besides me were getting hurt. She taught me how to drink. She was like, 'Don't drink that Ripple!' I mean, I thought Ripple was like a good wine, you know? I got, like, 'Beaujolais! This is great!'

"She had cut someone with a broken glass about that time. Someone who she thought provoked her, someone very socially correct. She gave him a little slice. It was not as litigious a country at that time, so, I don't know, maybe there wasn't serious scarring, but there was this other side

of her, you know, a 'you-better-not-fuck-with-me' although I never
. . . I mean, she was bigger than me. She didn't do any drugs then.
Neither of us did. I would smoke my grass, she would drink her wine.
That's probably why she was with me, because I didn't do that stuff, and
I didn't realise it. She was probably running away from something.
That's pretty possible. But she knew how to dress, and she was one cool
chick. After that I came back to New York to do some gigs – we had
progressed and we were starting to play more like we played on *Fun
House*, a harder sound and a little time had gone by. I came to stay at the
Chelsea. She was staying there, and she always had a cute man around –
she had some new man, a French guy, and I was kind of like, 'Who is
this French guy, anyway? What are you doing with some French guy?
Let's have a look at him,' and I went to visit her in her room.

"I was really excited to see her, and she was sitting there, she had a
harmonium. I'd never seen her play her harmonium, it was just a little
thing, about three feet long and three and a half feet high, and she was
playing on it, and she played this song 'Janitor Of Lunacy', which is on
one of her records, and she sang the words, 'Janitor of Lunacy, paralyse
my infancy.' Just like, you know, very good poetry, just kind of like
hearing her doing that right there, complete, in the Chelsea, and that
was the way it was gonna go on the record. I was very impressed with
that . . . I saw her later, and we had our differences. I got stoned with her
many years later on some heroin and it was not pleasant, she did not look
well, and I did not react well. I wasn't much of a gent about that and so
there's some regrets there."

CHAPTER 6

We're Dirt, We Don't Care – *Fun House*

"The war, the riots, the demonstrations and everything else that co-ed students nationwide were involving themselves in at the time were the other side of the coin to this raging, violent attack of music. These guys were pissed off at the entire world when they recorded this. Pissed off during the years of peace and flowers. Galluci's production is super-fine, catching every bit of anger the boys translated into music."

– *Punk* magazine on *Fun House* (1977)

"Things are much different in Michigan now. Young girls, the same young girls that hated us, that had things to throw at us, they love us now, you know, because we're the bad boys. That's the only reason. I don't even care if they love us, but it's easy for us now. We're considered a successful band, but no more successful than a hundred other bands. I don't care. There's a tremendous amount of push when we play, but it's not a push to succeed. It's a push for something else. I don't know what it is. A strange type of life. You have to give a lot of yourself and then lose a lot of yourself also."

– Iggy, July '69

IN *From The Velvets To The Voidoids*, a history of seminal American punk rock, Clinton Heylin suggests that as the MC5, seduced by the baubles and bangles of the commercial rock industry, lost the plot after 1969's *Kick Out The Jams*, The Stooges stepped forward to become the heart and soul of the mutinous Detroit sound. As the MC5 turned their backs on the politics of John Sinclair and his hipster jazz sensibilities, The Stooges embraced that jazz vision by, amongst other things, recruiting Steve Mackay on sax.

Sinclair warned his band that they were making a mistake chasing after the big time but found, like Andy Warhol, that nobody listens to anything you tell them. The way Heylin sees it, the MC5 were already imploding when they signed with Elektra, all caught up in dated concepts to do with what constituted a kickass live show. The Stooges, conversely, had only been gigging for six months when they came to Elektra, but their far more interesting cultural ideas involved the concept of audience *plus* band, as opposed to the MC5's audience *versus* band insistence that the audience sit up and pay attention to what they had to say or play. The Stooges blossomed into true Rust Belt rebels who grew within a record deal, their playing improving in leaps and bounds. They were always writing new material to meet recording schedules or to impress John Cale, Andy Warhol or Jac Holzman and not in order to entertain crowds of provincial rock fans at the Grande Ballroom.

"Part of the difference between the vinyl legacies of The Stooges and the MC5," Heylin argues, "may be due to the former being signed to Elektra at a point when they were still experimenting with their music. They were thus able to sustain their brand of garage rock long enough to record two of rock'n'roll's most powerful collections of 'raw wails from the bottom of the guts', before they too imploded under the intolerable burden of a public demand for excess in its many malignant forms."

While The Stooges were rehearsing for what became their second album, *Fun House*, Iggy discovered jazz saxophonist and drummer Steve Mackay in Detroit. "I thought there was something missing," he explained. "I heard Steven play one night and I thought, 'Fucking A! This vision and imagination!'" Mackay, in many ways a semi-forgotten Stooge only getting his laurels right now, was originally a sax player with a school marching band before he got converted to weird rock'n'roll. John Sinclair introduced him to the wilder shores of experimentation at a time when Mackay already had his own Detroit bands, the unfortunately named Carnal Kitchen and the still more unfortunately styled Charging Rhinoceros Of Soul, on the boil.

Steven Mackay: "John Sinclair turned me on to a lot of stuff like that – Archie Shepp, Coltrane, everything. We (Carnal Kitchen) had adopted that pretty much early on. Iggy heard us play our first gig in '69 sometime. He came up to me one day and just says, 'We're gonna jam on Thursday night. You wanna come by and jam with us?' I'd been out to The Stooges house before, so I drove out there on Thursday night, and he pretty much already had *Fun House* figured out and how he wanted it to sound."

Sinclair's politics may not have turned The Stooges into Little Red Book-toting Commies but his musical vision was having the same effect on Ron Asheton that it was having on Mackay. "Through Sinclair we were indoctrinated into John Coltrane, Archie Shepp, Sun Ra, Pharaoh Sanders," Asheton says. "I especially liked Sanders' long suite, 'Upper Egypt And Lower Egypt'."

Dave Marsh, then a young *Creem* reporter, and subsequently Bruce Springsteen hagiographer, caught the band's last gig before they headed for California to record *Fun House*. "Mackay was playing with them on a couple of tunes," Marsh remembers. "The combination ended up as a really stunning and visceral sound."

Some of the putative producers for the second album – called *Fun House* because that's what The Stooges called their collective home at that time – were truly bizarre. Jac Holzman, providing ample evidence that he was as hit-hungry as any other record label boss, suggested Steve Miller's former keyboard player (now Elektra staffer) Jim Peterman, and a character called Madeira who'd produced Chubby Checker's 'Lets Twist Again' plus hits for risk-free popsters like Danny & The Juniors. Danny Fields, when he was consulted, was closer to the mark. He suggested Eddie Kramer, now famous for his association with Jimi Hendrix, but also involved with Led Zeppelin and The Rolling Stones. The man who eventually undertook the challenging task was Don Gallucci.

Gallucci was covertly flown to New York by Holzman to see The Stooges perform. "They were playing in some little club," Gallucci remembered. "Someone announced over the PA: 'And here they are, Iggy & The Stooges!' This terminally skinny guy comes out dancing and writhing in front of this loud three-piece band, and he's wearing nothing but Levi's, boots, and evening-length silver lamé gloves. That's it. I think maybe he had a dog collar around his neck. He immediately starts jumping up on tables and grabs the fishnet candle lamps, pouring hot wax all over his chest. Jac asks me the next day, 'What do you think?' I said, 'Well, it's a real interesting act, but I don't think you can get this feeling on tape. It's definitely a performance kind of situation.' Jac responded, 'Well, I really believe in them. I'm flying them out to the West Coast and you'll record them.'"

Gallucci, a dapper, straight looking guy, had solid roots in trashy sonic situations having started his music biz career in 1963 when, as a 15-year-old, he provided garage bands everywhere with the C-F-G electric piano chord progression on The Kingsmen's big hit version of 'Louie Louie'. (Amongst the thousands of other artists who've covered 'Louie Louie' is Iggy Pop, who did a vintage reworking of it on '93's *American Caesar*.) When The Kingsmen folded Gallucci formed a backing band called Don & The Goodtimes. Weirdly enough, Gallucci was the right guy for The Stooges job.

Ron Asheton: "He was Little Donnie Gallucci of Don & The Goodtimes. He was on this Dick Clark show every afternoon at four o'clock. They had all the big bands, but it was more a surfer-based, California thing. They'd have English bands and heavier bands. He was the house band so he'd do a couple of songs every afternoon. Then he went on to be a producer and it was really cool. They picked him, and we didn't even know that he was coming to a lot of shows in the beginning, and seeing us play, and then we kinda met him, and knew he was gonna be there, and 'He's gonna be your producer,' and we're like, 'Huhh? Don Gallucci? Why does that sound familiar? It's Little Donnie!' And don't call him Little Donnie, boy, does he hate that."

In May 1970 the band flew out to Los Angeles to meet up with their producer and to do the album. Gallucci pleased them when he said that what he wanted to do was to capture their live sound in the studio. Though he came from a straight part of the music business, his basic ideas dovetailed perfectly with theirs.

Ron Asheton: "He (Gallucci) was a short guy, he was always impeccably dressed in a really nice suit. I'm going, 'How is this guy, who is dressed in this really nice suit, gonna relate to The Stooges?' But he did an excellent job. He wanted to capture the show. I think he only changed the order of the set; he switched two songs, I can't even remember. What was even more amazing is when we first met him, we met the engineer, Ross Meyer – he was pretty quiet, probably in his fifties by then – and I thought, 'Oh boy, we're in trouble.' Little did we know we had very competent people in the control room. He finally started talking a little bit, and he goes, 'Yeah, this stuff's all right. It's a big change from Barbra Streisand.' He just got done doing Barbra Streisand's record."

This was The Stooges first trip to California. They holed up at the Tropicana Motel in Hollywood. Their fellow guests were such a powerful and motley crew that their mutual presence in this motel at that one moment in time is indicative of the countercultural ferment then in full swing in America. Paul Morrissey, Andy Warhol and the entire cast of Warhol's movie, *Heat*, were fellow guests. One day Iggy was swimming in the hotel's small pool. A strong swimmer, he'd just done three or four laps underwater when he realised that somebody was watching him. He came up for air to see Andy Warhol staring down. "My, you swim very well," Warhol said. After some brief chitchat Warhol departed, saying, "Come and see me sometime."

"I was very nervous," Iggy subsequently admitted. "He was in room

15 and I was in 9; somewhat kitty-corner from him on the top balcony on the fancy side of the Tropicana . . . he'd always leave his door ajar, just to see if I'd come in. I was very shy. I finally did come over one time and we managed to talk a lot."

The Stooges and the Warhol gang weren't the only fringe characters hanging around the Tropicana. A vaguely subliminal presence was Beat writer and Fug Ed Sanders, whose Tropicana room was adjacent to Iggy's. Sanders was midway through researching his classic Charles Manson book, *The Family*, and enjoyed impeccable counterculture credentials, being close to Allen Ginsberg, musicologist Harry Smith, *et al*. He was nicely positioned to win the trust of the many scattered-to-the-winds Manson lieutenants then drifting all over California. The Tate/LaBianca murders were recent events which had left a sour after-taste in LA. The Stooges were doing *Fun House* as members of the Manson family visited Sanders' Tropicana rooms on a regular basis. Still more synergy was provided by the presence of various youngish country rock musicians who would later form The Eagles.

Just prior to the *Fun House* sessions the band did two shows at San Francisco's Fillmore West, topping the bill over The Flamin' Groovies and Alice Cooper. In the audience were Jac Holzman, who flew in to catch The Stooges act, and future *Punk* magazine photographer Roberta Bayley.

Roberta Bayley: "Iggy & The Stooges played at the original Fillmore venue after Bill Graham abandoned it. It was being run by The Flamin' Groovies at the time and they were seriously committed to rock'n'roll. That 1970 show was Alice Cooper, The Stooges, and The Flamin' Groovies. Two dollars admission and the place was empty. Maybe a couple of hundred people. The Flamin' Groovies were the outcasts of the San Francisco scene. Bill Graham hated them. I don't know if in their entire career they ever got above third on the bill. When that show happened there was Alice Cooper wearing make-up like a bunch of fags and Iggy was wearing the silver gloves, shirt off and lots of feedback. It was different! I never bought into that peace and love stuff. I thought Iggy was amazing. I remember most clearly, at the end of the show, that they racked up their guitars and just left them on the stage so that there was this incredible feedback. Iggy just stood there in the middle of that stage with his back to the audience. I asked him about the show when we interviewed him for *Punk* magazine, and I think he was on acid the whole time he was in San Francisco. He was staying in a commune type situation and ended up with six different types of crabs and every STD on the planet."

Iggy, *Punk*: "I remember every minute of that. In fact I'm writing this book called *Dedicated User* and that night and the next three days are all in there. By the time I left town I had lice, crabs, two kinds of VD I'd never heard of. And numerous other things I don't know of. Yet at the time that show was a good show. I had my Cuban Beatle boots on, slimline jeans, silver gloves, and I was ON! I could feel it in my jaws."

Ron Asheton: "We were up in our dressing room and there is Jac Holzman with shades and a T-shirt and jeans. He's trying to be cool – getting close to the guys. We were smoking dope and we brought three black kids with us to the dressing room. They were about 11–12 years old, stoned out of their minds on marijuana. The next thing I hear is a girl screaming. We went out and there are these kids – they have knives and they have a girl up against a wall. Eleven-year-old kids! And here is Holzman. He is so insulted from all this. He had his limousine brought by and he disappeared as quickly as he could!"

It was a hard, nasty show, advocating everything that the ritzy San Francisco rock establishment avoided and rejected. "They're one hell of a rock'n'roll band," one member of the audience told *Rolling Stone*, "but I tell you, something awful must've happened to those guys when they were little kids." In the small crowd were the Cockettes, an early gay drag theatre troupe. They invited the boys back to their house for a party after the gig. "I remember how penetrating and strange the house felt," Iggy says, "and how three of them were peering at me – very strange. I had never been exposed to either homosexuality or opiate behaviour."

Back in LA with his exotic collection of San Francisco STDs, Iggy marched his men into the Elektra recording studio located just around the corner from the Tropicana, two blocks away on Santa Monica Boulevard. Whereas John Cale had attempted to record *The Stooges* formally – i.e. cutting a track with all the instruments, and then adding Iggy's vocals, tambourine, or whatever else was needed – Gallucci sought to capture the whole thing live in one visceral take. Back in 1970 recording live to mono was still OK studio practice and Gallucci was a veteran expert on this type of deal. He set about turning the state-of-the-art California studio that Elektra had created – perfect for Judy Collins – into a traditional Fifties rock'n'roll environment.

Don Gallucci: "Jac had one of the first transistor board studios on the West Coast, and he worked diligently to get rid of any room sound. The studio itself had infinite soundproof baffling – all kinds of movable panels, wavy walls – all the latest technology of that day to get perfectly clean, crisp recordings. He was also one of the first people to push

Dolby, so he could get this great voice and guitar stuff. So now we're in this superclean studio that is the total antithesis of how you'd want to record The Stooges. There's no edge to it. There's no grunge. There's no warmth of the old tube amps. So we basically just ended up tearing the studio down. We took out all the baffles, all the carpets. We did everything we could to make it a live environment. And then we broke all the rules. We didn't even baffle or separate them from each other. We just put mikes in front of their amps, and Iggy sang live with a hand-held mike. All of this muddied the sound and made it sound more live, even though you could still listen to it and think, 'Gee, it still sounds sorta clean.'"

Ron Asheton: "We were totally prepared because Gallucci wanted to capture the live show. That was the cool thing. We just set up in the studio and did our live show. There were really no overdubs. I maybe went back after I did my leads with the three-piece and added a little bit of rhythm guitar stuff here and there. But mostly everything was live."

Asheton reckons that Iggy took an astute approach to the recording process. He set himself up in the studio with his own vocal PA so that he was being recorded from an amplifier, just like the bass and guitar. "He liked that PA sound," Ron says. "We never even questioned it." Iggy says he did this because he didn't want anybody to fuck with his voice or with the sound of the band. His idea was to make music that was as "uncorrectable" as possible. Like Asheton he feels they were very fortunate that Elektra maintained such high standards of recording quality.

The *Fun House* sessions ran from May 11 to May 24, with two days of mixing afterwards. In the middle of the job, to get away from the studio and the Manson Family and the fledgling Eagles, The Stooges did a weekend gig at the Whisky A Go-Go.

Gay Power magazine: "Iggy wasn't there for the audience's benefit; the audience was there for his benefit and he told them so – when the audience didn't come to Iggy, Iggy went to the audience, knocking plates down, glasses, standing on tables, and telling people to get up and if they didn't get up, he pulled them up and out of their seats, spilling drinks as well as girls pocketbooks across the floor . . . And then, when he'd taken complete command of the audience, he turned his back on them. He then proceeded to add insult to injury by simply standing there for 15 minutes while people in the club just stared, their eyes glued to Iggy. They were enthralled by his torso, his silver lamé gloves and his ripped jeans . . . The only thing Jim Morrison is into is displaying his cock so he can prove he still has one. When Iggy is on stage, there is never any doubt."

The closing track on *Fun House* – 'LA Blues' (the band were homesick for Michigan) – was edited down from a 17-minute free-form piece known as 'Freak'. The decision to cut 'Freak' down was taken by Gallucci. "He was the producer, so nobody argued with him about it," says Steve Mackay. "We just said, 'OK, that's cool.' But it was really interesting trying to get that energy coming cold out of nowhere. That particular session was pretty far out. I guess I decided I was going to be 'psychedelic' for that session. And so I was, chemically, if you know what I mean. I don't know if anyone else in the studio was, but I certainly was."

Ron Asheton: "That was our tribute to ourselves, our original roots . . . it was our freak-out! Our whole set was a freak-out. We'd say, 'Now it's time to freak out.' So we'd end the set, we'd be playing a tune. Unlike the record, where they made it a separate thing, it would just digress or progress into the total free-form . . .

"But they wanted to make 'LA Blues' separate and it was way sterile compared to how we usually do it. There was my brother going, 'Uh, I don't know, what do we do?' I'm saying, 'Well, just pretend! Freak out, man!' He'd just be going diddle-liddle-liddle. I guess that day he just didn't want to freak out. It's way sterile compared to how we really did it. I got a couple of good things in there. But it was much more violent in person because it was the culmination of the show . . . I went to the ol' Brian Jones school – you just stand there and look a little glamorous. That was just the chance for me to pour out all of my frustrations and move my body. It was some kind of cosmic aerobics with some piece of wood and metal. These stacks of Marshall amps that would do anything I wanted them to do! I would make all these incredible sounds. It was much tamer on record. That's the one thing that Don didn't capture. They should have just segued. They thought, as record company people do, 'No. Cuts. There has to be dividing lines between the songs for radio airplay.' That's still the same today, the same stupid rip-off. So we said fuck it and they made a separate thing. My brother's attitude was 'fuck 'em.'"

Don Gallucci: "It's funny. I eventually grew to love it because I loved their rawness. There were no apologies in the music. But it wasn't just simple music; it was almost Zen-like. They had pared everything down, not because they were necessarily bad musicians or because they were dumb. They actually got rid of all the fey stuff that started to pop up in rock right about then. They eliminated all the artsy stuff and went back to just pure to the bone, to the studs, rock. At the same time, I knew that nobody would get it in 1970. But pioneers always get the arrows and slings. Eventually they were recognised and I think that's great. But back in 1970, they were on a mission."

Ron Asheton said that Gallucci was a fun guy to work with. "We'd always try to get him stoned," he boasted. "He wouldn't. He did his job, but even when it was over, he was straight. He was real smooth and it worked really well." Shortly after recording *Fun House* Gallucci produced Crabby Appleton, whose 'Go Back' single became a minor Top 40 hit in June '70. He eventually abandoned the music biz to work in real estate.

Fun House was released in August 1970. Lester Bangs, writing in *Creem*, was suitably impressed, initiating the critical applause which surrounds this OK timepiece. "It is as loose and raw an album as we've ever had, but every song possesses a built-in sense of intuitive taste which gives them an immediacy and propriety that most heavy groups lack. Everything is flying frenziedly around, but as you begin to pick up the specific lines and often buried riffs from the furious torrent, you also notice that no sore thumbs stick out, no gestures half-realised, or blatantly ill-conceived . . . *Fun House* is one of those rare albums that never sits still long enough to actually solidify into what it previously seemed. Not always immediately accessible, it might take some getting into, but the time spent is well repaid. Because properly conceived and handled noise is not noise at all but music whose textures just happen to be a little thicker and more involved than usual, so that you may not hear much but obscurity the first time, but various subsequent playings can open up whole sonic vistas you never dreamed were there."

NME, not yet partial to anything in a black leather jacket with a needle problem, missed the boat on The Stooges' progression towards terminal hipness: "The gross Iggy Stooge is said to be a sexy little devil on stage, but not having seen the band perform, and going only on their records, it is hard to see their appeal. Pimply rubbish rock is how one reviewer has described them in an article. If you can make a virtue out of reasonably played rock tunes, sung by a tortured non-voice over repetitive riffs, then *Fun House* is for you."

Perry Farrell, of Jane's Addiction, was sufficiently impressed to contribute her thoughts on *Fun House* to a *Q* magazine special in 1995:

> "Just such an inescapable sound. You could tell they were being spontaneous, which was what made me realise it would be cool to make records. It was the sound of the record, too. Devastating. You followed the guitar as it snaked through all this noise and it really led you somewhere. At the same time, it was romantic – definitely as wild as youth gets."

CHAPTER 7

TV Eye

"I turned on the TV and sat down to watch some rock'n'roll show that I heard was to be on, and there before my very eyes was a crazed wild man covering himself with peanut butter and screeching out, 'She's got a TV eye on me, she's got a TV eye.' I couldn't believe it. The fucking Stooges, man! No one had to announce it. I fucking knew who it was, even though I had never heard them before. It was a broadcast of the Cincinnati Pop Festival and The Stooges were there and on my television set! Somehow it seemed only right that I should see The Stooges for the first time in my living room. It was real electric music seen on the technological advancement of the twentieth century. The Stooges on the tube was the strangest yet the most logical thing I'd ever seen."

— Back Door Man (1977)

ON June 13, 1970, at Cincinnati's Crosley Field, a legendary base-ball stadium, The Stooges made such a big national impression that *Fun House* almost charted! The Cincinnati Pop Festival featured the likes of Traffic, Mountain, Grand Funk Railroad and Alice Cooper but it was Iggy, surprise surprise, who stole the show. He was fortunate that, for the first time, his antics were documented on film for posterity and for imminent nationwide consumption. Post-Woodstock, open-air rock festivals were the In Thing and a big deal with the media, so Crosley Field was filmed by NBC to be broadcast later as *Midsummer Rock*. It got good ratings when it was aired in late August 1970, perfectly timed to tie in with the release of *Fun House*. The TV special featured only two Stooges tracks, 'TV Eye' and '1970'. But that was enough.

Hindsight has tempered the shock or novelty value of much that rock'n'roll has to offer by way of outrage or excess but time has done nothing to diminish the visual effect of Iggy's TV debut. The blurred colour film of the young Stooges at Cincinnati remains right up there in the genre's iconography with the Stones at Hyde Park or Jimi burning his guitar at Monterey. A filmic representation of where rock music was coming from and going to, it caused a big splash which led to bigger waves. Who knows what the Vietnam-era television audience made of the salaciously pouting Pop, the two tabs of particularly good LSD that he took before going onstage kicking in, as he stood on the edge of the stage singing 'TV Eye'? Entering into a criminal conversation with the crowd he looks cracked, sharp, knowing, wanton.

Rock magazine: "The Stooges are halfway through 'TV Eye'. Iggy jumps into the crowd, lies down, you can hear one sweet girl's voice ask with soft concern, 'Are you all right?' Camera and sound split for a commercial. When we come back to The Stooges, Iggy is back onstage. Les Coulie (the announcer) is saying, 'Iggy has been in the audience and back onstage two or three times. The audience seems to be enjoying it and so does he, heh, heh. There he goes again . . .' And he did indeed. The kids hoisted him up and there are a few great moments for TV film, with lights on Iggy's back, Iggy standing, one leg forward, on the kids' shoulders. Iggy is staring straight ahead, raises his arm. The kids are all laughing with joy because they helped pull that great minute off."

Ron Asheton: "I think I'm in one of the pieces for like one second. All I remember from that was the big video camera guy didn't care about anyone onstage. I had to follow him . . . his wires were hooked up to my lead cords; he's dragging my fuzztone and wah all across the stage. 'Stop it!' as he tried to follow the antics of Iggy. For me that was a pain in the ass, pulling my stuff all over the stage. Luckily the roadies were smart enough to always tape the cords into the . . . lotta duct tape, electrician's tape, so there's no way the plugs can be pulled out."

As the camera tries to keep up with the singer he vanishes into the crowd, swallowed up by a tightly packed group of excited women and men while still singing. Then the singing stops and the TV announcer explains that they're trying to get some lights on the spot where Iggy was last seen. All the viewer can make out is a blurred shot of the audience; all that can be heard is the other Stooges banging away primitively on their instruments while middle-class girls close to Iggy's mike whimper gleefully. What had happened to the missing-in-action singer?

Like a primitive life form emerging out of the cosmic slime, Iggy wriggles to the surface, in control of the mike and of his performance. He is covered in peanut butter and raw meat. With great poise, looking like a particularly nimble skateboarder or a young man in the throes of sex, he hoists himself up from the ground, out of the crowd, and up on top of them, balanced on their hands, arms and shoulders.

He later said that at that moment he possibly imagined that he was Jesus Christ. Cut to another camera, and he seems, with great assurance while perched on their shoulders, to be walking over his audience like Jesus walking on the water. Stills from this bravura performance were distributed by Elektra and remain, to this day, amongst the defining images of Iggy.

The way Scott Asheton remembers it Iggy brought two jars of peanut butter and a couple of pounds of hamburger onstage with him so that, when he inevitably plunged into the audience, he could cover himself and the crowd in the grungy peanut butter and the bloody minced-up meat. Another version of the peanut butter conspiracy came from Stiv Bators, the reckless self-destructive leader of Seventies Stooges wannabes, The Dead Boys. He always claimed that he was the kid in the crowd that day who handed Pop a jar of peanut butter.*

The line-up now began to chop and change. With *Fun House* going into the shops and the Cincinnati triumph under their belt, The Stooges were nicely poised but bad attitude problems which dogged the band for the rest of their days, and Pop himself for the next 20 years, manifested themselves for the first time. He had never been entirely comfortable with heavy drinking bass player Dave Alexander, a band member very firmly located in the Asheton camp.

When The Stooges played the Saginaw Festival in August, things finally came to a head between irritated Iggy and dysfunctional Dave, a boozer since childhood with various drug and personality problems. "Iggy didn't dig Dave's attitude, his lack of interest or whatever," says

---

* Bators got his chance to play definite cameo roles or bit parts in the Iggy saga much later. When The Dead Boys and Iggy toured together, Iggy stole Bators drugs while Stiv was conked out in his hotel room. Another year Pop made up for this violation. He was doing a gig somewhere and, as was his mid-period touring style, he decided to catch another punk rock show after he'd finished his own work. Somebody told him that Devo and The Dead Boys were playing the other side of town so he headed there. Looking a little like Brian Jones *in extremis*, feathered boa and girlie-style huge sunglasses akimbo, Iggy joined The Dead Boys onstage unannounced, prancing up towards Bators from behind. They agreed to do 'Search And Destroy' together, a nihilistic blitz of a version which ended up with the two singers chanting "Destroy! Destroy! Destroy!" as they reversed up towards the back wall of the stage, sliding down the wall until they were sitting on the ground with a white spotlight focused on them, still groaning "Destroy! Destroy!" at one another. Then Pop turned to Bators and said, "Ya know Stiv, I wouldn't give a shit if all these people here died in their sleep," to which the Dead Boy replied, "Me neither." A young fan wanted to talk to Stiv backstage but couldn't think of anything to say so he asked him the time. "Punk rockers don't wear watches," replied the impeccably debauched and doomed drug fiend.

Ron Asheton. "He moved out of the band house and was late for practice. At Saginaw, Dave got really drunk and smoked dope, and he sort of freezed on stage and forgot all the tunes. After the gig Iggy said, 'Hey, you're fired. We don't want to play with you anymore.'"

"I love to fire people," Iggy said in *I Need More*. "Oh, it's the greatest feeling in the world . . . You're fired! Fuck you! You don't work for you. You work for me, cocksucker!"

Alexander was immediately replaced by Zeke Zettner, a Stooges roadie well liked by Iggy who described him as "about 6′ 4″, somewhat quick tempered but really sweet. A very beautiful boy. Very beautiful."

"Zeke had never played before," remembered Ron. "His attitude was cool, but he couldn't cut it as a bass player. I wanted someone who really could play the bass, but we couldn't find anyone. Zeke was one of the boys so we took him. But he couldn't really play the bass and he learnt slowly."

Next into the ring was old pal Billy Cheatham who joined in August as second guitarist to allow Ron to do more soloing. Starting August 18, 1970, shortly after the *Midsummer Rock* broadcast of the Cincinnati show, a new six-piece Stooges line-up, including two guitarists and a sax player, started a ground breaking four night residency at Ungano's, a small New York club on West 70th Street. Just before the well attended first show Iggy met a guy offering to sell him a decent quantity of high quality cocaine, then an expensive and slightly exotic drug. Iggy didn't have enough money for a substantial purchase so he made the eventually fatal mistake of approaching Bill Harvey, ultra-straight Elektra Vice President, looking for funds. He carefully explained that it was cool for him to take cocaine before going onstage, that he wouldn't dare to do to his body what his body wasn't accustomed to and that he really needed the drug in order to get through the entire gig.

"I'm sorry to have to ask you for this, but you're going to have to give me $400 for a one-quarter ounce of cocaine," he said to Harvey, who flipped out at the sheer neck involved. Harvey couldn't believe his corporate ears; Ungano's was a showcase gig organised by Elektra to get The Stooges some good media.

"That's impossible. Who do you think we are?" Harvey spluttered. "We don't give out . . . that's impossible!"

Iggy: "I was just leaping around the room. There was no question about this. We gotta have it . . . I took so much coke through those four nights. If you look at pictures of those gigs, I look like a Biafran or something; skinny isn't the word."

Circus magazine: "It's a club called Ungano's in New York, one of the last small rock clubs. The occasion is a press party thrown by Elektra Records in honour of *Fun House*, the new LP by The Stooges. Almost everybody is there. The air is expectant. The Stooges are on the verge of breaking through . . . The Stooges are almost an hour late. Nothing happens. Finally, 15 minutes later, the band strides out. As the equipment is readied, Iggy stands shirtless at the mike waiting, eyes self-contained but piercing as he stares around the room. Suddenly the silence is shattered by the loud electronic blast of Stooge-rock. Iggy contracts as though punched in the stomach, his arms flailing. The music pounds on as he dances like an angular snake. He slams the mike against his lips and whoops, then sings in a yelled growl. Iggy bolts into action, stalking out into the audience; people scatter like pigeons in Central Park. Those in the back are standing on their chairs as he goes down on the floor; the audience gathers in a circle around him. 'Did he cut himself? Is he bleeding?' Then he's up again dancing through the audience like old Egyptian tomb paintings. The band stand stolidly on stage, pouring out the sounds, all energy focused on Iggy . . . What does it all mean? Is it just a hype, an exercise in theatric weirdness? Is it an act, designed to draw attention that the music alone wouldn't? Or is it a 'real' stage madness designed to make the audience ask questions about themselves and the nature of what they want from rock groups?"

There followed a period of long months on the road. Iggy seemed to fall in love with his roadies whom he described as "all very beautiful – cute boys". He said that Eric Haddix was "very narrow at the hips, maybe a size 26, and enormous at the shoulders; very, very lean, quite muscular, sort of lantern jaw, almost oriental eyes, from a farm community". Leo Beatty was a "narcissistic, long-haired, wiry, tall, kick ass, beautiful boy, all grace and tiptoes". Roadies are not normally renowned for their thinness or pulchritude; The Stooges, and Iggy, seemed to have been unusually lucky in this department.

CHAPTER 8

Faggy Little Leather Boy – Max's Kansas City

"To the best of my recollection, I was only up there (Max's) twice – that's only what I remember anyway. Once is when I gigged myself – the best way I could put it is trying to do a rock'n'roll show in front of your first-grade class with the teacher present, except all of the students have morphed into your critics . . . it was a very stark and static and strange vibe, but it did bring out such an intensity. It was a room that operated from the neck up. It was not good clean American fun. It was not the room for Aerosmith to play. I found it a strange place to play."

– Iggy Pop

IT was time for The Stooges to get to know the queers, the leather boys, the painters, and the demi-monde. Danny Fields had dragged the Warhol crowd down to Ungano's to see the spectacle. Iggy was feted by the likes of Gerard Malanga, Brigid Polk, and Donald Lyons, professor of literature at Rutgers.

Leee Black Childers: "It wasn't even a stage. It was a band on the floor type of thing. Various people – most of whom Danny Fields had called – some of whom Lenny Kaye had collected in – were there and here was this person who was astounding! His sexuality then was totally available and yet totally scary. He had a brain. There were so many people in the rock'n'roll scene at that time who didn't have a brain, like Eric Emerson who was so gorgeous – everyone who wanted him got him. Nothing was going to happen with him other than fucking him."

Flesh superstar Geri Miller went to Ungano's with her TV eye firmly focused on Iggy's crotch.

Leee Black Childers: "She was sitting in front, and during one song,

Iggy stalked down to her. She was grinning up at him and he grabbed her by the face. His whole hand covered her face. He dragged her by the face, and when he took his hand off her, she was still grinning. She became a big fan. She had originally gone just to become a groupie . . . Iggy was so sexual. This was around the time of the famous Gerard Malanga nude photograph. In those days a full frontal naked picture was an astounding thing for a man to do."

Gerard Malanga: "Although I'd met him in '66 in Ann Arbor, I didn't really get to know him until 1971 when he showed up in New York one weekend. Danny Fields arranged it so that he would stay in this apartment where I was staying with Terry Ork who later managed Television. It was at that time that I did the full frontal nude. I shot off about three or four rolls of black and white film. I may have seen him in concert once before that weekend but there was no real contact. I liked, and still like, what he does an awful lot. To me he was a real performer/conceptualist. He really did kind of conceptualise his show. He took rock'n'roll, became the lead singer in a group, sang, but he made this decision to push the envelope and take it all a few steps further along to see what he could do with it on stage. There was a lot of in-depth thinking involved in finding out what he could do to go beyond the singing voice as it were.

"When he came to stay with us I was not at all aware of his drug taking. I knew nothing about that. To me his limbering up, warming up in the morning, seemed to be quite a natural situation. I guess he has to do that kind of thing to stay in shape as a professional performer. I was crashing on the couch one morning. My camera was on the ground by my side, and he was doing knee-bend exercises. I think he may even have had a shirt on. Then he took his shirt off. I picked up the camera and I started photographing him. He was very much aware of this. I just kind of worked around him while he was moving around. Then I don't know what happened or what possessed me. I think I said something to him like, 'Oh, well, maybe you should take your trousers off.' And he said, 'OK,' he was quite willing. That was the first time I ever photographed anyone nude, except for myself in a mirror."

Leee Black Childers: "You knew that if you were actually going to do it with Iggy he was actually going to want to talk to you afterwards. A big talker. Did you actually want to do that? Do you actually want to get involved with him or not? Was it worth it? He had this big thing a couple of nights I was talking with him. Apparently if the iris of your eyes did not reach your lower eyelid it meant that there was something wrong with you. That you're floating spiritually. So he was examining my eyes which go all over the place. He was going on explaining all about this to me until 9 am while we sat in front of the fire. I think he liked talking as much as he liked anything except rock'n'roll. If you just regarded him as a sex object you were in for a jolt. He would probably want to talk afterwards. And a lot of people then didn't want to do that. He always treated the girls with great respect and girls weren't used to that. They got a lot of abuse which they were ready for. That was part of the game they were playing."

The opening night of the Ungano's residency was such a crotch and cocaine-fuelled triumph that Fields, then Manhattan's leading barometer of rock'n'roll cool, invited The Stooges to Max's Kansas City, vibrant home of all things cheap and nasty in New York, a notorious stalking ground for predatorial up-there gays. Sometimes it seemed that there was hardly a heterosexual in sight. When you applied for a job at Max's, one of the questions you were likely to be asked during the job interview was, "Do you carry Vaseline?" Originally a hang-out dominated by happening painters, hence the Warhol connection, the social action concentrated on the notorious downstairs back room until 1969 when live music – nascent punk and art rock – started upstairs. This historic mix gave rise to vast swathes of art/rock crossover. The Velvet Underground's posthumous sanctioned bootleg, *Live At Max's Kansas City*, immortalised the venue and wrote the book – along with The Stooges' *Metallic KO* – on what was aurally acceptable by way of a punk rock statement.

Leee Black Childers: "Iggy very much exploited the whole gay part of things. I don't have any first-hand experience of what he actually did to fulfil things although we all know a million brilliant stories about people. A cock is only a cock and a mouth is only a mouth until you do the things you do. I'm not saying he did it. He certainly played up to the gay end of the market a lot. When I lived with him later in Los Angeles, and I lived with him for about nine months, he would sit on the bed in a loose kind of Japanese robe thing with nothing else on, and put his legs apart so that his cock would be right there. The only reason I didn't just dive for it was because – which I don't think he had taken into account – I was a little scared-to-death hick from Kentucky. I didn't know what would happen. Now I would dive for it because I would know what would happen. In those days I would just look at his cock and never ever touch it. Who sits there with their legs widespread, with their penis dangling between their legs in plain view? For what reason? Just because they're relaxing? Maybe. OK, fine. But I don't think so."

Danny Fields: "Max's Kansas City waitresses were wearing skirts

"Thirty years experience making rock'n'roll, singing rock'n'roll, drumming five years before that, helluva lot of experience, in the prime of my life, at the top of my game." (*Derek Santini/Camera Press*)

Introverted trailer park kid.

Regular guy, high school graduate. (*Ann Arbor Yearbook*)

Iggy rises above the rest of The Iguanas, 1965. (*Norton Records*)

With The Prime Movers, 1966; left to right: Robert Sheff, Iggy, Michael Erlewine, Jack Dawson, Daniel Erlewine. (*Andrew Sacks*)

"He was really a great drummer," said Wayne Kramer, "rock steady, no razzle dazzle, no flash, just pure power rock'n'roll beat." (*Andrew Sacks*)

Iggy gets with the Sixties' vibe. (*Leni Sinclair*)

The Stooges and MC5 sign to Elektra, 1968; left to right: Jac Holzman, Danny Fields, John Sinclair, Fred 'Sonic' Smith, Ron Asheton, (unknown), Iggy, Dave Alexander (behind Iggy), Scott Asheton, (sitting middle), Michael Davis, Dennis Thompson, Rob Tyner, Wayne Kramer (standing behind Tyner), and Bill Harvey (far right). (*Leni Sinclair*)

The original Stooges line-up, 1969; left to right: Scott Asheton, Ron Asheton, Dave Alexander, Iggy. (*Elektra/Warners*)

Fun House sessions, Elektra studios, L.A., May 1970. (*Elektra/Warners*)

The Stooges attend weight watchers, summer 1971; left to right: Ron, Jimmy Recca, James Williamson, Scott, Iggy. (*Photographer unknown*)

Raw Power rehearsals, London, 1972; left to right: James, Iggy, Scott, Ron. (*Mick Rock/Star File*)

Silver painted Pop, The Electric Circus, NYC, 1971. (*Bob Gruen/Star File*)

The Stooges only non-US show, King's Cross Scala, London, July 1972. (*Mick Rock/Star File*)

A street walkin' cheetah - Iggy displays his assets, *Raw Power* rehearsals, London 1972. (*Mick Rock/Star File*)

Open Up And Bleed, Whisky a Go Go, Hollywood, September, 1973. (James Fortune/WireImage.com)

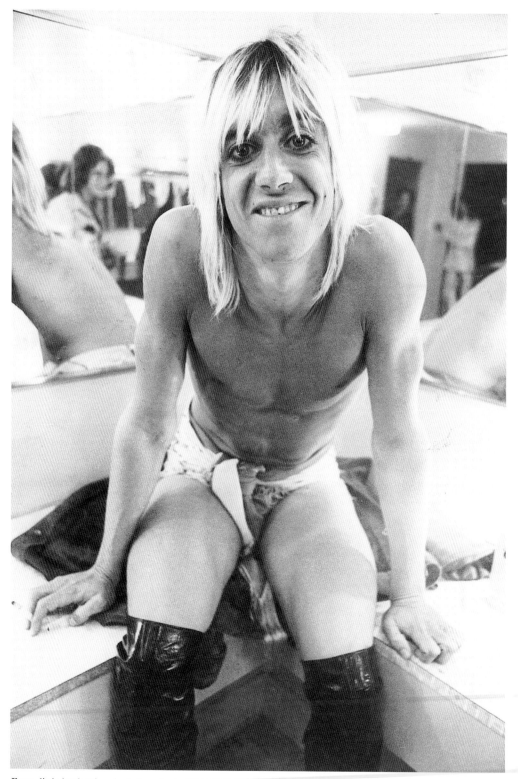

Faggy little leather boy, backstage Santa Monica Civic, 1973. (*Andrew Kent*)

shorter than anyone had worn them in history. A lot of the girls had been to see Swinging London and wore miniskirts that didn't cover their asses. Max's had a reputation for great-looking waitresses sporting skirts so short that, when they leaned over the tables, their bums showed. Iggy used to go there a lot in the afternoons with Nico, when nobody else was there. 'That was our little place to go have a private lunch,' he says."

Iggy: "For me there were two Max's. The first Max's was the back room, behavioural New York, gay intellectual Andy Warhol credited Max's. And then there was the other Max's which was the rock'n'roll venue. I was a kid from the Midwest who had some exposure, mostly through books and records, to both the outrageous and the arts. Coming into that room was kind of like a University of Dementia. I'm sure I came in the first time with Danny Fields who was my mentor and my Addison DeWitt in showing me around town.

"The people I gravitated to most were people like Donald Lyons. It was the first time I met older educated people who had some sort of straight positions, who looked very straight, who I could talk to as if they were still kids. Some of them looked like my parents on the outside but yet it was like talking to kids but not kids from the Midwest, interesting kids, and I felt a kinship with these kids. And then there were these other people like Taylor Mead and I just liked to watch him act out and, I thought, what a witty and strange kind of twisting and turning individual. He had a very serpentine quality to him. Then Jackie Curtis who was basically a Warhol actor. She was doing some of the plays and was in the Tony Ingrassia scene."

Alice Cooper (Seventies Glam Rock superstar): "I was like a social vampire. I'd get up around 7 pm, watch TV, leave at around midnight and stay at Max's until the sun came up. I probably lived on chick peas and Black Russians. We were pretty much established at the time. I liked it there because all my friends were there. Iggy was there, Bowie was there, and the Dolls. We were all in the same place so that was the place to be."

Leee Black Childers: "Iggy was very much the focus of the back room. I remember because I never got to get near to him. Jackie Curtis, Wayne County, Holly Woodlawn, all these people were in a room trying to get near to Iggy. When Iggy walked in the back room, everyone paid attention. The whole room was centred on where he was, who he was talking to and who he might leave with. He mostly left with Danny Fields."

Iggy: "Jackie Curtis, Leee Black Childers and Glenn O'Brien were three younger people. Maybe in another era these people would have

89

been young preppies perhaps working as interns at the White House or they would have been Senate pages. They would be doing their internships in this kind of twisted place and wearing dresses every other day. They had a certain Wasp-ish good sense behind it all and a very youthful sensibility. And then there were the rock people – Lou and Bowie and myself – that tended to come in less and be more musicianly. Probably in Lou's and my case, a little more peaks and valleys."

By the time Iggy hit the Max's scene with a vengeance in 1971, Leee Black Childers – the Scarlet O'Hara of punk and Glam Rock, a Southern belle in red rock'n'roll shoes sporting a black leather jacket – and Cherry Vanilla, an Irish-Catholic deviationist, were effectively the New York emissaries for a musical phenomenon about to change the face of rock history, and the life and career of Jim Osterberg from Hicksville, USA.

The pair worked for the Mainman organisation, a murky London band management company obsessed with breaking David Bowie in America. Cherry Vanilla, Leee Black Childers and Tony Zanetta (aka Zee) were young Warhol-connected faggy theatrical types who were meeting regularly with Bowie's English manager, Tony De Fries. De Fries, a sharp entrepreneur with legal training, was coming to New York more and more to check out the possibilities for his "product" in America. In keeping with traditional London showbiz methods, De Fries encouraged his young Manhattan thespians to run up big expense accounts and to drive around town in limousines, their flamboyance implying to all and sundry that Mainman had bottomless resources. This aspect of the Mainman School of Rock Management would subsequently enrage Iggy when he convinced himself that the bottomless resources came out of his back pocket.

Leee Black Childers: "Mainman behaved a lot like the Mafia. On purpose. Tony De Fries used to refer to himself in that way. Not as the Mafia, but certainly Mafia in their approach. You know the way the Mafia think of themselves as being kindly but firm. That's exactly the way that Tony saw himself as being, making reference to the word Mafia. He'd say to me, 'I've taken the decision, and now it has to be done.' By which he meant that I would have to do it. Tony never did it. Even when I eventually got fired, it was somebody else who made the phone call to me."

Bowie methodically absorbed the entire Manhattan/Warhol/queer scene but he focused in on the two most terminally cool bands America ever threw up, the Velvets and The Stooges. Within a couple of years, by which time he'd become a genuine superstar, Bowie had successfully wrapped the essence of both bands around his vampiric persona. In the back room of Max's, he set about seducing both Lou Reed and Iggy Pop at the same time.

UK born, Cambridge-educated Mick Rock photographed the sleeves of Lou Reed's *Transformer* and The Stooges' *Raw Power*. "Lou Reed, though he was all underground and wasn't selling any records, was nevertheless the darling of the Warhol set and the Max's Kansas City set," he says. "When Iggy showed up, I'm extrapolating, he had a big sexual vibe. Everybody knew he had a big chopper on him, an incredible body, everybody wanted to fuck him, girls and boys. I'm sure Lou was a little pissed off. Lou is more overtly cerebral in his lyrics, though in reality they're not that different."

Leee Black Childers: "David Bowie was very entranced and intrigued with the idea of Max's and the back-room scene. He never felt that he fit into it. A lot of times he got completely out of his mind, either drunk or something, because he couldn't understand the way the back-room scene was."

David Bowie's wife Angie wrote, in her memoir *Backstage Passes*: "David, you see, was very clever. Since his first trip to the States – before that, actually – he'd been evaluating the market for his work. Calculating his moves, and monitoring his competition. And the only really serious competition in his market niche, he'd concluded, consisted of Lou Reed and (maybe) Iggy Pop. So what did David do? He co-opted them. He brought them into his circle. He talked them up in interviews, spreading their legend in Britain, and then, in the summer of '72, he personally chaperoned their introduction to British audiences."

Leee Black Childers: "Like Claudette Colbert said, 'If you got to fuck somebody, fuck somebody who'll get you into the movies.' I think Iggy was not bothered by that. I think he must have fucked a lot of people in those days. He was so desirable. Danny Fields had made him so desirable, had thrown him into our laps. Danny had already had the experience of dealing with Jim Morrison. Danny actually physically taught Morrison how to put his penis down inside his pants so that it would show. Jim Morrison didn't know. He used to tuck it away like a drag queen. By the time Iggy came along, Danny had figured out how it all worked. Danny didn't need to teach Iggy as much as he needed to teach Jim. Iggy had an instinct about his body because he always exposed his body a lot on stage. He wasn't as sexual as Jim Morrison because that was not his deal. He was more forceful but his shirt was always off. He knew his sexuality. Danny only had to teach him that he could do it, that he could get away with it. God knows, he got away with it! His sexuality offstage was very available. Onstage totally not available. The very opposite of Jim Morrison, who was a difficult person to talk to in reality – to men or women. He was very hard to deal with whereas Iggy offstage would just talk and talk and talk. I can't tell you how many times I saw Nico with her hand down his pants in the back room of Max's Kansas City with everyone looking. He didn't care about that. Jim Morrison would never have tolerated that."

CHAPTER 9

Big Juicy Flies/Drugs – James Williamson

"In April or May of 1970, we returned to Detroit from doing the album in California, and things were changing. Suddenly unemployment was driving people out of Detroit. The whole atmosphere had changed, and we started sliding into hard drugs."

– Iggy Pop, *I Need More*

"These guys weren't sitting around injecting themselves with heroin. They were doing drugs that I thought were reasonable; things that could be psychologically or intellectually construed as mind-expanding. I'm talking about smoking dope and the psychedelic drugs: acid, DMT, etc. These things were taken in a casual atmosphere and with an amount of care and respect. The idea was that you would emerge from all this as a better person and with a better perspective. Amphetamines were something that people just didn't get involved with. John Sinclair and I used to have discussions about what drugs were OK and what weren't."

– Jimmy Silver

IN 1970 slick guitarist James Williamson, the savvy Stooge, came back from reform school in New York and moved to Ann Arbor. He started sitting in on Stooges rehearsals. As usual, things were in ongoing flux within a band that thrived on a state of permanent revolution. No doubt Williamson could work out the internal band politics – who was strong/important and who was weak/disposable.

Ron Asheton, perhaps unwisely, asked Williamson to take Billy Cheatham's place on guitar. At the same time sax player Steve Mackay went back to Detroit. Aspirations within the band now began to focus around a brilliant but conventional American rock vision, albeit a vision blurred by the chronic onslaught of manic drug consumption which eventually ripped to shreds dreams of world domination shared by Jimmy Silver and the individual members of the band. It would be fair to say that while Williamson was a guitarist of originality, he was not in the same league as the original Stooge triumvirate of Iggy and the Asheton brothers in terms of intellectual eccentricity, musical vision, or plain old human charm. One lady with personal knowledge of most of The Stooges said that Williamson didn't come from the same litter as Iggy and the Ashetons.

Leee Black Childers: "James Williamson was a monster. There is not a good word to be said about him. He was just a total user. I have nothing good to say about him at all. I'm sorry, I wish I could. I lived with him for six months and all I can say about him on a positive level is that he didn't sneak into my room and cut my throat. Very charmless, and for some reason, because he was so self-assertive, he had Iggy around his little finger."

James Williamson: "I graduated high school and I went to New York that summer when they were finishing up on the first album, and I met up with those guys in New York and listened to some of the tunes. It was pretty cool . . . I had seen them at gigs and stuff . . . I didn't hang out with them that much. I was more in the Detroit area than Ann Arbor at that point, but I'd seen a few of their gigs, and they were down at the Grande and so forth. They had a very unique show that was different, really way different than anybody else. I thought they were cool. I not only knew 'em but I liked what they were doing.

"I ended up moving up into Ann Arbor and eventually I ended up moving in with a coupla' guys that were in the band and we ended up hanging out more and more together and started playing with each other, playing some jams and so forth. Then eventually that incarnation of The Stooges started falling apart. Bill Cheatham and those guys were never really musicians, they were just kinda buddies of the band, and they just kinda played with the band for a little while, but they never could pull it together. I sort of fell in with them because I could play guitar, and they needed somebody. We started playing and that was kinda the last couple of phases of that first wave of Stooges stuff . . . we were trying to pull it together but I think it was pretty disorganised at that point. I would not call it exactly a professional rock'n'roll band, let's put it that way."

Williamson told Ken Shimamoto that he formally joined the band "somewhere in the neighbourhood of late '71". When he joined, Iggy's handsome ex-roadie Zeke Zettner was still the bass player. Zettner eventually quit so that he could enlist in the US Army; he wanted to go to Vietnam where the heroin was way cheaper. His replacement, strategically enough, was a pal of James Williamson's called Jimmy Recca. "I got sick with hepatitis and so the whole thing just kinda fell apart," says Williamson. Hepatitis has long been the illness of choice for serial heroin users. Drugs were chewing up the brilliant future that The Stooges all dreamed of, the wonderful life that his parents had foreseen for Jim Osterberg, and the confidence that the band's vital support team (label, management, agency) had in them. Williamson claimed that by then Iggy was all screwed up.

John Adams, The Stooges' mature, prosperous, experienced road manager, was a former junkie who, according to Ron Asheton, "fell back into it and took Scotty and Iggy with him at the same time." One day Ron happened to be alone in Fun House with Adams who had come into a quanity of heroin and was admiring it in the basement. Before long Ron joined him there.

According to Asheton this was the first time that the band ever snorted scag, a procedure which eventually led to them injecting the brown sugar. Asheton is strongly of the opinion that the emergence of heroin as the main drug of choice within The Stooges played a major part in his own subsequent fall from grace, a fall which he says was engineered by junk buddies Pop and Williamson. He says that habitual use of heroin was introduced covertly into the band, behind his back, because he didn't approve of it. He says that this disapproval made him the outcast. To be a non-user in a circle of junkies is to be the puritan at an orgy.

"We had no backing, nothing, nobody," says Iggy. "One guy, John Adams, invested just enough to get amplifiers, he was the roadie who eventually turned the band into junkies. He was an ex-junkie, philosophy major, and card shark – a dangerous combination. He was also a rich kid. So he put up three grand for us."

John Sinclair: "There was a guy called John Adams, their road manager, who kind of perverted the guys. He may or may not have been a rich kid. You never know in a college situation who was rich or what kind of background people had. The guy who became a prominent member of the Weathermen, Bill Ayers, his dad was the head of Con Edison in Illinois. Bill was the wildest radical on the whole campus. MC5 were the sons of factory workers. That was our constituency. People were taking acid so it was like everything was everything . . . where you came from or what you had been doing was totally irrelevant.

It was all to do with what you were doing right now. That was the fun part."

Ron Asheton: "It was the bad junk time, because he (James Williamson) was a character prone to addiction also and these guys were into heroin, and they sucked James in. Iggy really turned away from me, 'cause I was the only person that didn't do junk. Luckily, I had a girlfriend, and we had a house that had separate apartments. I basically just sealed myself off from them. The only thing I would do was go patrolling at night, to make sure there were no lit cigarette butts. I'd smell smoke and the mattress would be on fire, and I'd come down and Iggy'd be nodded off on the couch with a Lucky Strike in his mouth about to burn his lips (it had no filter on it), weird stuff like that. I was no longer part of the band. It was like, 'Yeah, he's with her, man, he's not with us,' and I'm, like, 'Yeah, right, assholes, I wanna be filthy and covered in impetigo and having to spend two hundred dollars a day . . . yeah, you guys are really cool.'"

Sealing himself off from the rest of his band, heroin or no heroin, girlfriend or no girlfriend, was a dangerous strategy for a lead guitarist. The bond between those who do heroin together is one of the strongest bonds known to man; way stronger and more resilient than the bond which exists between sexual partners.

Ron Asheton: "When James came, it was . . . even though things were really in bad shape, once he came aboard, it was the total swan song. It was some of the worst times in my life, just to see everything you had done fall apart, only because of drugs."

Jimmy Silver: "Once they began to get popular and got more money at their disposal and we began travelling more, they had access to other kinds of people. They got into drugs that were beyond where they were at and what I thought was reasonable. They got into heroin and harder drugs. The whole atmosphere of the scene and what was available in it was deteriorating about that time. That was really the end of the Sixties and the whole high-minded thing. All the people who believed that drugs were mind-expansive were really going downhill."

John Sinclair: "Before the Summer of Love, there was hardly any speed around at all, and the kids who were just starting to smoke weed and drop acid had never heard of it for the most part. The Acid was truly dynamite, so the first step was to start cutting the LSD with amphetamine and market it as some kind of powerful new trip: STP! And within a couple of weeks STP was the hottest thing on the psychedelic market – it debuted in San Francisco and spread back across the country like white lightning. All these were acid or synthetic mescaline mixed with amphetamine, and the speed gradually replaced the acid almost entirely. By 1968 just about every hit of acid on the street was 80 or 90 per cent speed with just a tinge of LSD to make it seem weird and scary enough to pass as a psychedelic."

According to Ron Asheton, Pop was taking cheques from his parent's chequebook to his old employers at Discount Records and cashing them. He liberated several thousand dollars in this way before the police got on the case. When confronted with their boy's misdemeanours, the long-suffering Osterbergs honoured the dodgy cheques.

"The choice of drugs shifted. In the Sixties it was all marijuana and LSD, an occasional hit of speed," says Wayne Kramer. "When we got into the Seventies, that's when people discovered heroin and coke and every other kind of pill, valium, etc. There was also a difference in life-styles; whereas we could always afford some reefer, we had to get out on the streets and hustle to stay high on smack."

Kramer recalls that the whole scene had developed junk problems by 1970/71. He and Iggy had a big junkie-style falling out when they set up a little drug dealing business together and Iggy stiffed him. Iggy once collapsed on MC5 bass player Michael Davis' kitchen floor. Davis revived him with a cold shower and mouth-to-mouth resuscitation.

All this high drama was getting to be too much for the level-headed Jimmy Silver, who struck up new daytime friendships with guys from Boston. While the band slept or nodded off all day his new buddies kept telling Silver that he should go and work with them in the world of wholefoods. Silver made his decision. "We were moving off in different directions," he says, "and I told the guys that I wanted to go back to California. I wanted to leave the music business and be in natural foods."

Before heading off into a lucrative macrobiotic sunset, Silver turned the band's bank accounts over to Danny Fields who'd left Elektra amid considerable acrimony. His wild-night-of-rock'n'roll-epiphany signings from Ann Arbor had turned out to be a complete disaster for the label. The in-decline MC5 had already been dropped as a result of a self-inflicted media disaster. They decamped to Atlantic where not a whole lot happened for them either. The Stooges weren't working out either – units were not shifting. On top of that Fields gravely insulted touchy Elektra VP Bill Harvey by casting doubts on the moral probity of a member of Harvey's extended family. "Everything I said about her was absolutely true!" Fields says. His penchant for high grade office gossip – true or not – resulted in his leaving Elektra.

Fields now looked after The Stooges while earning his wages as the company freak at Atlantic: "From a professional point of view, I wasn't very much of a manager at all. I was really just a friend in the right place at the right time, but I didn't really do what a manager is supposed to do. I didn't go out there and tell them to shape up and put their affairs in order. I just did patchwork repairs." Fields soon got tired of being rung in the middle of the night to deal with serial crises. Somebody would get arrested. There'd be a shoot-out at Stooge Manor. They'd crash their van into a bridge. There were rumours that they were robbing gas stations at the weekend. The authorities were planning to knock down Stooge Manor to make way for a motorway. Everybody else had moved out but the demolition was going to render Ron homeless. A motor-cycle gang were hunting for Scott Asheton. Field's answer to these late night emergencies was as state of the art as everything else about him; he put it all on his credit card.

During June 1971 The Stooges played a notorious night at the Elec-tric Circus on New York's St Mark's Place. Once again, Warhol super-stars attended in abundance. The Electric Circus was at the centre of Manhattan's foppish art/rock universe, the perfect place to make a garish statement.

Iggy, *Punk*: "I was in there trying to find a vein and screaming, 'Get out! Get out!' to everybody, even my friends – and they were all think-ing, 'God, he's going to die, blah, blah, blah.' Finally I'm up there on the stage and as soon as I walked on that stage I could feel it. I knew I just had to puke. I wasn't going to leave the stage, though, because I felt that would have been considered 'deserting one's audience'. So I thought, 'I'll do a James Brown thing . . .' A kind of hip side-step move – grab the mike stand. And then I ended up doing this real elegant jack-back off the mike stand, then kind of 'Que pasa! Que pasa! Hit me! Hit me!' number, and then I heaved off. It was very professional. I don't think I hit anyone in the audience."

Bob Gruen (photographer of New York Dolls, John Lennon, Iggy): "I first saw him on 8th Street at The Electric Circus. I didn't know all that much about The Stooges at that stage – I didn't really know that scene so much. I was working on things like Ike & Tina Turner. They were kind of scary because it seemed like darker drugs than the hippie scene I was more familiar with. I wasn't really drawn into that scene, with all of its ramifications. That came later, about two years later, after I got to know The New York Dolls. I guess I didn't understand the grunginess of it, what The Stooges were saying. Too loud, too fast, too sloppy, not really the kind of music I might listen to at home.

"In the pictures one had seen of him at the Cincinnati Crosley Fields show he looked like a virtual God coming out over the crowd, but in

New York we were all just standing around the front of the stage like New Yorkers will. So when he steps off the stage we kind of jumped out of his way, like 'Hey! Don't step on me pal!' He landed flat on the floor and was kind of wiggling around. I thought it looked kind of dumb, like 'What the hell is he doing on the floor?' New Yorkers aren't about to pick him up and hold him in the air. People were not going to let him climb up on them or anything. It was like 'Look at him! What are you doing on the floor, pal? Get back up on stage and do the show.' He was covered with the oil and the glitter, it was one of the weirdest things I'd ever seen. All this silver stuff. Would you hold this guy up? It wasn't really all that crowded. People didn't really know who he was all that much. Later when I met the Dolls and the people who did know him, they were like big fans, talking about what a genius Iggy was. But I didn't really get it that first time I saw him."

Leee Black Childers: "Iggy had gotten an outrageous reputation for self-destruction and being a junkie onstage. Geri Miller was right down the front again. She had this horrible little voice and she's right down in the front screaming, 'Throw up! Throw up! When are you gonna throw up?' And he did! He threw up. Iggy always satisfied his audience."

At the end of the gig Iggy clawed frantically towards the microphone, quoting from an old Dracula movie, "Flies . . . big juicy flies . . . and spiders."

Now the whole of New York, including the entire Elektra team, knew for sure that he was a junkie.

CHAPTER 10

Dalla

Dropped

"James and Iggy formed that junkie relationship, and in James, Iggy saw he had a person he could kinda control, and they somehow hit it off, and then the band broke up, and he would end up taking James to England, and then just dissed me and my brother, just dumped us."

– Ron Asheton

THE jazz approach of *Fun House* was soon shelved – permanently – in favour of the simple rockist structures favoured by Williamson. He and Iggy began songwriting together in earnest. Like many an aspirant before and after them they were going to be the new Mick and Keith. It can't have escaped Iggy's sharply tuned commercial and image-conscious antennae that Williamson looked cool, thin and mean, a low-slung guitar hero. His old pal Ron Asheton, by way of contrast, was a benign backwoods anti-hero, stout but steadfast. Songs brewed up out of experimental jams and fraternal respect gave way to adventurously crafted melodies with good lyrics. The songwriting was now reminiscent, in ways, of the fare being served up by contemporary superstars like Led Zeppelin or the Stones. The inspired incompetence of the Asheton axis was pushed aside to make way for derivative but very good songs.

At the same time that they were forming a solid songwriting team, Williamson and Pop began to pull the band in separate directions. It would be fair to say that Iggy remained true to his roots, still concerned with pushing back the aural envelope and seeing where that took him. Williamson, for some dumb and hungry reason, saw The Stooges as a vehicle for world domination.

Danny Fields: "If somebody wants heroin, you can't really get them interested in anything else, can you? What he (Iggy) did while still having that dope priority in his life, you've got to hand it to him, how he could perform at all, do anything at all, get anywhere at all but he did. Still it was the great monster squashing everything else and every possibility. It was all falling apart, there was no money, the records weren't selling. It didn't help to be a critical sensation. It didn't help to be as talented as he was or as they were. It didn't help to be as nice as they were."

During late June 1971 Fields persuaded his nemesis (and Iggy's old coke sponsor) Bill Harvey, along with *Fun House* producer Don Gallucci, to fly out to Ann Arbor to sit in on a live session by The Stooges with a view to OK'ing a third album on Elektra. The band got together in their rehearsal room to play their new tunes – the material which turned up later, much altered, on *Raw Power* – for the corporate suits. Fields was thrilled by what he heard during the loud showcase. The group and their new tunes sounded great to his extremely attuned ears. "Well?" he asked the Elektra men. They told him that there was nothing there.

"How can you say that? It was fabulous," Fields enthused.

"There's nothing there," said Harvey. "I don't want to pick up on the option; it's not worth it."

The singed Harvey was, no doubt, recalling Iggy's malingering Puke Circus in New York. Neither Judy Collins nor Tom Paxton would've vomited on stage or talked about big juicy flies! Jim Morrison was unpleasant enough in his own penile way but The Doors were a Top 10 act and everything is forgiven when you're a hitmaker as opposed to being a shitmaker.

Ron Asheton: "They couldn't believe it, especially Bill. He was almost afraid, but Gallucci was cool. We took them into the practice room. They were expecting little amps – we had double Marshall stacks! They stood there. It was so hard to play, I was laughing so hard. Bill was in a suit. Gallucci was a little more casual, but still a sporty little Italian. What the hell do they think we are doing? They must think we are the weirdest bunch of guys!"

James Williamson: "We tried to get Elektra interested in what we were doing, and it was just way too soon for people. Our sound in those days, even with *Raw Power*, was so far out for the average A&R guy. It just blew their minds when we brought them to Ann Arbor and had them listen to what we were doing. They were appalled. Truly, it really was bad . . . I'm not saying that the music was bad, but they really could not relate to it at all."

"I don't think they were terribly surprised that no one at Elektra believed in their music any longer," Danny Fields concedes regretfully.

"They anticipated it. 'We expected that. What do they know?' That was the band's attitude. The axe fell."

"They realised what they really had on their hands," Iggy explained. "This S&M rock, or whatever you want to call it. They kicked me off because they said I had no sales potential."

Having absorbed the bad news, Fields approached RCA to see if they were interested in picking up the psychic tab. There were no takers there either. The Stooges were now effectively out of the music industry. No major would touch them and the independent sector had yet to evolve. Three members of the band were major league junkies and their personal behaviour, lifestyles, and nasty attitudes were way out there on the total wild side. Ron Asheton said that, at the end of the deal, The Stooges owed Elektra $80,000 and had to sign away their future royalties on the two Elektra releases. Danny Fields returned to Ann Arbor after the band got dropped and tried to staunch the junk situation by firing John Adams, a naïve attempt to solve a slippery, undependable, crisis situation. "And a little while after he fired John," Ron Asheton said in sorrow, "Danny said he couldn't do it anymore."

After a show in Detroit's Eastown Theater, the singer decided that he too couldn't do it any longer. His addiction won out over his ambition. "I never planned to stop," Iggy said. "I felt forced into it because I was in a position where larger and larger audiences were paying more and more money to see us and because at the same time I hit a point where I had a lot of professional problems. I was unhappy. I felt badly myself. We'd just show up somewhere and there would be all these people and I really wanted to do good for them . . . The disintegration of The Stooges at that point was also, at least in my mind, a reflection of the germinal growth of what I wanted to do with James. Because we knew we could do something better."

Pop told *Melody Maker* journalist Chris Charlesworth in 1973 that, towards the end, the whole thing went really strange. He had worked for two and a half years on a national scale and had got to the point where The Stooges were drawing bigger and bigger audiences for more and more money, while Pop was performing worse and worse because he was so scagged out. "This was common knowledge at the time," he admitted. "So I quit. I took the chance that if I stopped playing and tried to straighten myself out, I could start again."

And again and again and again.

CHAPTER 11

Smartass Bitches And
Raw Power

"When I play my tunes, I've played some of them a billion zillion times, it seems like I always hear them different because there aren't many notes to get in the way . . . I think about half of Raw Power is really good. There's four really good songs on it. There's 'Raw Power', there's 'Shake Appeal', there's 'Search And Destroy' . . . 'Gimme Danger' is fair. There's about four good songs on it, the rest is just filler."

– Iggy Pop

"This state of directionless aggression and unbridled velocity was what Iggy called Raw Power – a deadly rigour of being that is the very heart and soul of punk."

– The Sex Revolts

DURING August 1971 the retired Iggy Stooge was contacted by the entrepreneurial Steve Paul, a friend of Danny Fields and manager of Edgar and Johnny Winter, important blues-rockers. Paul, in thick with the Warhol gang, wanted Iggy to go down to Florida to jam and maybe start a band with ex-McCoys and former Edgar Winter sidekick, Rick Derringer. "Steve Paul was a carney," Iggy said. "He'd started selling blackhead removing pencils through the back pages of *Popular Mechanics*, so he was pretty much meat and potatoes. 'Let's get some fast bucks here.' A carney."

Iggy, sophisticated enough to enjoy the more zany aspects of the rock biz, knew the Florida jaunt might be a senseless and worthless trip, though he had little else on his agenda and Florida was nice. He went down there in whimsical spirit and took his golf clubs along for the ride.

Iggy: "He (Paul) wanted to sign me and see if I could put something together with Rick Derringer, who had been with The McCoys but wasn't doing anything. Basically work as a front man for a rock band within Steve's stable. I knew I didn't want to do anything like that but to be at least polite and not slight him I had a couple of meetings with Rick about it. I liked Rick as a person and respected him as a musician for what he did, and thought fair enough, check it out. We diddled for a few minutes over at his house and I could tell immediately that the chemistry wasn't right. This was a fine musician but his vision was somewhere else and my vision was my vision. So I declined."

Steve Paul told Iggy he'd be allowed to contribute the lyrics. "I felt like a puppet even listening to shit like that," he says, "so I wasn't buying any of it." Paul may not have been as wide of the mark as Pop then imagined. Most of the Iggy Pop songs that the world hears today – on ads or movie soundtracks – are ones where he provided lyrics while others (usually Ron Asheton, Williamson, or Bowie) did the music.

Despite the fact that The Stooges' albums were beginning to manifest themselves in the bargain bins, despite the much publicised drug problems, Iggy was still somebody. He looked like a pin-up boy with a heart full of napalm and his picture had graced many a magazine. He was well known and looked to be in good shape so the commercial courtship kept on happening.

He turned down a new offer from Elektra to do a solo album – backed by "real musicians" – of what he called "David Cassidy-type songs". This was perhaps a more solid and sensible idea than he ever gave it credit for. Iggy certainly wanted to be a star, but he rejected the idea of going pop out of hand. He still had something to say. By the Nineties, a shadow of his former self, he was more than happy to sing for his supper, regularly accused of whoring himself to corporate America for a buck.

Nimbly escaping from the clutches of "real" musicians, he was free but broke in New York. By the fall of '71 it was hard times in New York, nothing was happening, and he was seriously thinking of quitting the music biz completely. Salvation was just around the corner; his whorish behaviour as everybody's darling in the back room at Max's Kansas City was about to bear fruit.

Leee Black Childers: "We were doing underground theatre, what is now called off-Off Broadway. Very good theatre out of which came a million people like Patti Smith. I was stage managing these shows, huge shows with no budget. A show called *Island* had a scene in it where 30 people were on stage at one time, all eating breakfast on Fire Island. I had each day, as stage manager, to prepare these huge breakfasts with pies and everything. This had to be real food because the cast had to eat it onstage. That show had Patti Smith, Wayne County, and Cherry Vanilla. This was the show that Andy Warhol came to see, it seemed like every night. He was always there in the first row of this tiny theatre. He'd be sitting there watching. Then he asked the director Tony Ingrassia if he would put on a show based on his tapes because Andy was taping everything, everything, then. Every conversation, telephone call.

"Tony Ingrassia put together a show called *Pork* which eventually ended up in London. David Bowie came to see that show there. He became entranced with us, the cast and crew, more than with Andy Warhol. We were very flamboyant. We'd all been living for years in the drag queen world of New York which, right then, was beyond belief. They would put on seven or eight pairs of eyelids and when they would flap their eyes up and down it made a noise. They would sew wigs up together until there were eight wigs on top of one another. David grew very entranced with that world and wanted to be part of it. And one person who was very much a part of that world was Iggy. He was very much into this scene, he was wearing false eyelashes, a lot of eye make-up, very little clothes, and he was hanging out with Jackie Curtis, Holly Woodlawn, Candy Darling. He was learning from those girls the art of showmanship. He was just hanging around in New York after The Stooges, almost like a little rent boy, perfectly willing to be a part of that scene. They never thought that anybody in their right mind would think that they were women. They were just trying to be flaming creatures, something that no one had ever seen before. To their great credit, both Bowie and Iggy picked up on this scene and saw what was interesting about it. These drag queens were innovative and creative people, brilliant people, not just lowlife drag queens.

"Iggy was just nothing, hanging out in the back room of Max's Kansas City taking lots of drugs. David Bowie had no artistic direction at all happening for him. He was going nowhere artistically. Iggy's problem was that he had a million instincts but he had no money, basically, and no place to live. He was just bouncing off the walls. So the two of them came together and saved each other."

Tony Zanetta was a pal of Lou Reed's via the Warhol scene, and he'd got to know Bowie the previous August when he'd been in the London cast of *Pork*. "We met a few times and then we became friendly in my last week in London," he says. "He did a couple of small gigs while we were there. We went to them, in a place called the Hampstead Country Club. Then David and Angie came to see us in *Pork* a couple of times. We also went to their house in Beckenham."

While Pop was staying with Danny Fields, Tony De Fries came to town with Bowie. Iggy reckoned correctly that they were "looking to co-opt the American avant-garde. I was an interesting candidate to join that circus. Bowie knew about me and I think it was just a happy coincidence that I happened to be in town, or a freak coincidence!"

Danny Fields, wearing his rock PR hat, was hosting a big-shot Max's Kansas City bash for Bowie, paid for by RCA, with whom Bowie had just signed a major deal. The party was attended by the head of A&R at RCA, rock hacks Lisa and Richard Robinson, Tony Zanetta from Mainman, the recently solo Lou Reed, Bowie, his quintessential glam guitarist sidekick Mick Ronson, and Tony De Fries. At the dinner Bowie told Fields that he wanted to meet Iggy.

Nico said Bowie's subsequent behaviour was like a decadent *Great Expectations*, with an old roué taking an orphan from the streets with a view to improving him.

David Bowie: "I was at an RCA party at Max's Kansas City in New York and was introduced to Lou Reed. He immediately started telling me some story about a guy who injected smack through his forehead – that's typical Lou. Anyway, up comes this funny ragged, ragged little guy with a broken tooth and Lou says, 'Don't talk to him, he's a junkie' – that was Iggy. You couldn't help loving him, he's so vulnerable."

"I was sitting around Danny Fields' one night watching *Mr Smith Comes To Washington* and I was deep into it when Danny calls from Max's," Iggy told Lester Bangs in 1974. "He says, 'You remember that guy David Bowie?' A year ago he'd listed me as his favourite singer or something. So Danny says, 'Grab a cab down to Max's, he wants to meet you.' So I said, 'OK,' but I couldn't tear myself away from the movie, 'cause Jimmy Stewart was so sincere. Fields kept calling me, saying, 'Listen, man, do yourself a favour.' Finally, I made it down there. Bowie and De Fries saw I was hungry so they invited me to breakfast."

The three of them talked and talked; there was an immediate meeting of minds. Iggy could see right away that Bowie and De Fries were "nutters". He reckoned that the two were "British music hall, pure vaudeville". Iggy always had a good nose for the zeitgeist and a sharp sense of circus. To him, it was clear as daylight that there was a circus in town. His immediate instinct was to join that circus. "I thought this could be good for me right off," he admitted.

Iggy: "Here were all these people with money and everything, all waiting for this little scumbag that's got nothing. I finally stroll in, and there's Bowie and De Fries and a couple of company freaks. David and I got along, and his manager and I got along too."

"Well, you know what we could do," Bowie said to Iggy, "what would be a great idea, there's a wonderful band in England, Third World War, have you heard of them? They're very heavy in England and they could be a wonderful backup band for you."

Iggy: "To give them their due, Bowie, De Fries, all the Mainman management people he later hired, were all these out-of-work actors – these people had a real appreciation for the arts. It went very deep, and still does with Bowie. And De Fries is the same way. It's no accident he signed Bowie, then me, then later Mellencamp. When I'd talk to De Fries and told him my ideals and my mad theories about life and theatre and music, he would listen. He had an affection for that and tried to respect it."

He soon found out that Bowie actually knew his records and seemed to be intelligent, friendly, decent and smart. "This is pretty cool," he thought to himself. He could actually sit down and talk with Bowie. He reckoned that De Fries was a "character" that people on the scene would go for – this pushy English guy who had a big cigar, a big pointed nose, and a big Afro. De Fries had a smug look on his face, an English accent, a big fur coat, and a belly. To the people who were running the American industry it all just spelled "Hot Manager".

What Iggy decided to do was re-create The Stooges on Mainman's dime. He perceived – incorrectly as it turned out – that these Bowie people were "soft clay enough" for him to manipulate. His plan was that he could get his own dainty foot in the door first. Later he'd start The Stooges agenda rolling, simply pulling the carpet from under Mainman's feet. On September 8, 1971, the morning after the night before at Max's, he consumed six consecutive Warwick Hotel working breakfasts with Bowie and De Fries, signing himself to Mainman as the employee of a production company. After that he started hanging out with Bowie and De Fries.

Tony Zanetta: "De Fries and Bowie liked Iggy immediately. Tony De Fries really liked helping people out. He knew David and Angie were into Iggy. Iggy came up to the hotel and he started spending a lot of time with David. They made plans right then and there that they would bring Iggy to England. Tony would manage him."

Both Iggy and James Williamson were on lime green methadone at this stage, desperately trying to clean up their drug double act. While Iggy was rambling all over the East Coast, meeting anybody and everybody who might help relaunch his career, Williamson was back in Detroit sick with hepatitis. For six months he did very little. Though not in close contact, the two of them successfully managed to kick junk.

James Williamson: "Meanwhile Iggy was tooling around, trying to figure out what he was going to do with himself for the rest of his life. I heard all kinds of things. I wasn't even involved in this. I was sick, so I was out of commission. Maybe about six months into that, he started coming round every so often to visit me and started trying this and trying that. Eventually he went to New York, he ran into Bowie and hooked up with De Fries."

During December '71 De Fries returned to New York from London and magisterially summoned Iggy from Michigan. It was arranged, with typical Mainman flair, that Iggy would move into the Mainman hotel of choice, the Warwick. Tony Zanetta was appointed as Iggy's minder. Mainman was serious about keeping an eye on its new charge.

Tony Zanetta: "He was totally off drugs at that point. I went up to the Warwick every day; I was kind of baby-sitting. Tony De Fries gave me money to take Iggy shopping. We went to some shops off Madison Avenue. Tony gave me 400 to 500 dollars and we spent 400 in the first half hour on two pairs of pants! The way De Fries acted, we thought he had millions and millions of dollars. We spent the whole 400 to 500; that was a lot of money to both of us. We didn't know each other so well, so we were both pretending that it wasn't."

With De Fries holding his hand, Iggy went calling on both RCA and Columbia. Despite RCA's realisation that they needed something more than Elvis on their lists, and despite the fact that they'd recently signed Bowie, The Kinks, and Lou Reed, RCA passed on Iggy. Their turn would come later. Columbia's brilliant but soon-to-depart boss Clive Davis gave him a pretty good look-over and a pretty good deal.

Iggy, *I Need More*: "I sang 'The Shadow Of Your Smile' for Clive Davis and just did a little soft-shoe. And totally, just whatever he asked. He asked me if I'd do this or that or the other thing. I'd say no. 'Will you do Simon & Garfunkel?' 'No, I won't.' 'Will you be more melodic?' 'No I won't . . . but I can sing, ya wanna hear it?' And I just sang that, and he said, 'OK, enough, enough!' And just picked up the phone and said, 'Yeah, call the legal department.' And that was it."

Mainman sent him back to Detroit to cool his heels because he wasn't agreeable to working with a band of English musicians. Back in Michigan he started hanging out with Williamson so he contacted Mainman and said that he wanted his guitarist on board.

"Oh, you mean, there's two of you now?" snarled De Fries. "OK, here we go! Now we're gonna get down and dirty."

"Yeah," Iggy confirmed. "There's two of me now."

It was agreed that Mainman would pay for both Iggy and Williamson to fly to London. Ron Asheton got piqued when he heard that Iggy'd invited Williamson to join him abroad. Moving to London was a fresh concept in the early Seventies. Ron was even more annoyed when he found out that the two intended working together as The Stooges. He felt that, as the three of them had started the group together, The Stooges' name really belonged to Iggy, Scott and himself. "Iggy had more of a rapport with James," Ron says. "They got tight through drugs, they were junkies together. And James was a better songwriter and a more accomplished guitarist."

March 1972 saw Williamson and Pop, both still off junk, walking the dark streets of London but sleeping in the impressively upmarket Royal Garden Hotel, near Kensington Palace. Big juicy flies were but a distant memory. After a month living next door to cast-off members of the Royal Family, De Fries moved them to a house in cozy St John's Wood. "The more we got to know England," Williamson said, "the more we felt there wasn't anybody there we wanted to play with. Because Iggy and I knew what we wanted, but we were just really disappointed with the whole thing."

London in 1972 was a post-imperial city in crisis; ruined, washed up and on strike – but its record business was booming. With the Stones having split for France to dodge the taxman, The Who, Led Zeppelin and The Faces vied for the heavyweight title. Meanwhile, lower down the pecking order, Roxy Music, T. Rex, and Bowie were in their own way laying the foundations of punk and new wave every bit as methodically as The Stooges had done out in Michigan. Bands as varied as Pink Floyd, The Deviants, and Edgar Broughton were thriving within one of the strongest and most sophisticated countercultures operating in the West. Young men like John Lydon and Joe Strummer, barely out of school, were already crawling onto the bottom rungs of the ladder. Pop and Williamson's inability to find the players they needed on the London scene tells us more about them than it does about London. For all of their Up There New York socialising, they were still small town boys at heart, insecure in the zany cosmopolis. Iggy liked to have men from Michigan around him.

Iggy: "I used to walk around London, through the park and stuff, with this leopard jacket I had, a cheetah-skin jacket actually – it had a big cheetah on the back – and all the old men in London would drive by in their cars and they'd stop and try to cruise me. All I liked to do was walk around the streets with a heart full of napalm. I always thought 'Heart Full Of Soul' was a good song so I thought, what is my heart full of? I decided it was basically full of napalm."

James Williamson: "So we're sitting around, trying to figure out what we're doing, and we're being introduced into all these English rock circles that David Bowie's in, and basically, we don't like any of those guys, because we're Detroit guys, and it's just not our scene. The kind of music they play and the way they are is just not what we're into. So we look at each other one day and I think I was the one who brought it up, I just said, 'Hey, we know a couple of guys that know how to play,' and Ron, in my opinion – I know I've taken a lot of heat on this, and there's a lot of different opinions about this – but in my opinion, Ron was always one of the greatest bass players there was, and so I said, 'Hey, we'll get Ron over here and put him on bass, and get Scott over here, he knows how to play drums, and just do it.' "

Iggy: "We sat around for a while and got acclimated. It was suggested that maybe there were some English rhythm sections around we could've used, possibly some of Bowie's Spiders From Mars guys, possibly this guy Twink who used to be in Pink Fairies, or some of the folks who were in Mott The Hoople like Overend Watts – but they really weren't very aggressive musicians the more we thought about it. Williamson said, 'Let's get Scotty Asheton over here, he's such a powerful, violent drummer, there's nobody like him here.' And I thought, 'If we're gonna get Scotty, might as well just get his bloody brother Ron and bring the whole can of worms over here and open it up!' "

Nick Kent, who may have taken his role as confidant to the Seventies junkie elite that little bit too seriously for his own good – imagining that he was *entre nous* with a variety of limousine-travelling musical scumbags – commented on Pop and Williamson's inability to find Brit musicians who fitted their bill. "So there they were, these two black-hearted ominous-looking individuals from the Motor City, looking for some like-minded limeys to fill in on bass and drums so they could record The Stooges' third musical chapter."

Kent asked the two what sound they'd be going for on the planned third Stooges album: "Iggy pondered the question for a moment while dangling a wine glass he was sipping from rather daintily from his left hand. Then he drove the glass down hard onto a little table directly in front of him, noisily shattering its base. 'Something like that,' he then replied evenly."

Eventually the Ashetons were phoned in Ann Arbor. Only they, it seemed, would be capable of capturing the sound of breaking glass. The idea thrilled Scott. Like most great drummers, he just wanted to get in behind his kit and get trashing. Ron, predictably, had more mixed feelings.

Ron Asheton: "Next thing I know, we're in England in Bowieland, Mainman Boulevard. It went from Bumfuck, figuring out what I'm going to be doing, to going into deeper and heavier shit with political intrigue. We were treated good but different. Mainman wasn't about a band, it was about Iggy. He signed with them . . . he took it upon himself that he was the creator. We were the ugly side cast-offs of the monster he created."

By general agreement the bass job is the shit detail in a rock band. Bass players are often seen as frustrated guitarists, songwriters, or lead singers. In popular mythology the bassist is overweight, egomaniacal, and bottom of the pecking order when it comes to picking up groupies. "Iggy calls me up," Ron said, "and goes, 'We can't find any guys that are good enough on bass and drums.' And first I thought, 'Well, fuck, thanks a lot man! You're calling me out of desperation after you have tried out every limey that was available in England.'"

James Williamson remains unrepentant about the fact that he clearly elbowed Ron Asheton onto the sidelines of The Stooges, a project that Ron had conceived and realised with considerable artistic and critical success. "To this day," Williamson said in 2001, "I think he has negative things to say about that, but I think at the time he was happy to get the job, and so he didn't hesitate at the time."

Ron Asheton: "I felt it was a blow since I considered myself a guitarist. Iggy was saying things like, 'Eventually, you'll switch over to guitar, we'll get another bass player.' I wasn't thrilled but I wanted to go to England to do something. Just do something."

Nick Kent: "They were back in but neither was at all pleased about having to play second banana to guitarist Williamson's abrasive arrogance. Iggy called James Williamson his 'secret weapon' and that's exactly what he was, at least in the musical sense. He played his guitar so intensely hard both his hands were a constant blur. In fact, at his best, he played guitar just as fast and as loose as the way he lived his life. Which was always very fast and loose indeed. The Stooges were quite obsessive in their quest to constantly project an overtly delinquent persona, but Williamson was the only bona fide delinquent of the four . . . even Scott, who didn't give a fuck about anything or anyone, was frightened of him because James was the best fighter too."

It would be 30 long years before Ron got his revenge. When The Stooges reformed in 2003, finally noted and respected, neither Williamson nor the body of material which he wrote with Iggy played any part in the many gigs which the band undertook.

After arriving in London on June 6, 1972, Ron and Scott started rehearsing all over again with Pop and Williamson. They practised from midnight to six, Ron says, "Just like that great Pretty Things song, 'Midnight To Six Man'." Iggy was achieving his stated ambition of reconstructing The Stooges while Mainman footed the bill. This was a nimble enough piece of work, an early example of his ability to interface with the serious money guys and come up smelling of roses. But he had gone about it in the most Machiavellian way possible. He had served notice, not for the first or last time, that he was willing to treat shabbily those with whom he collaborated on music.

To many it seemed that he took two decent Hicksville eccentrics out of the very core of The Stooges so that he could replace them with a slick hustler on the make. This remains a common perception to this day. But sometimes the Devil has the best tunes for, without a doubt, *Raw Power* is by far and away the best of the three Stooges studio albums.

Iggy, *Trouser Press*, 1983: "We all went over to England, lived in a lovely place in London, and rehearsed and rehearsed and rehearsed. Every morning The Stooges would troop dutifully to this filthy basement to practise. After about two months they said, 'Iggy, what are we practising for?' It was *The Bridge Over The River Kwai*. I felt like Alec Guinness. Why are we building this bridge? To blow it up! De Fries didn't want us to gig because Bowie was hot then. If I had been on the road I would have been hot too. I bitched to Tony De Fries, 'We're a band, let us play!'"

Photographer Mick Rock was a cool young London hipster-photographer in '72. He'd already done covers for Syd Barrett, Lou Reed, and Bowie when he got a call from Tony De Fries. "Two or three publications needed recent Stooges pics *en groupe* and there were none," Rock recalls. "It wasn't a commission. Tony didn't believe in paying for photographs. But he understood my enthusiasm and my naïveté, and knew that I would jump at the opportunity (which I did). In those days I came very cheap . . . It took me a while to locate the trashed out basement rehearsal studio off the Fulham Road, but I was buzzed. I had tracked The Stooges to their lair, and they were to be mine for a whole hour! There was no brief . . . Just grab a fistful of frames and get out. But it was my nature to linger and probe around, to cram as much variety as I could into a few modest rolls of film. And in fact, The Stooges were glad to see me. They were bored with rehearsing for the upcoming *Raw Power* recording sessions, and I provided respite and distraction. It wasn't as if they were inundated by attention, or local photographers kicking down the door desperate to immortalise them! Those were very different times and there were few shutterbugs on the music scene. I was the only one who shot them on their *Raw Power* jaunt.

"I remember James Williamson was the most voluble while Scott Asheton hardly mumbled a note. I remember James explaining to me that The Stooges' attention could wander easily, and not to linger too long with one set-up; a hint I readily took. Certainly the location and circumstances were ideal for The Stooges. I worked with the available light (three or four bare light bulbs hanging from the ceiling) and a long exposure or a small flash on the camera.

"Iggy had actually taught them how to play. These guys were really whacked out. The people I was dealing with were The Stooges Mark II. I found James Williamson to be OK. He was very important to that album, he was the other great musical force. There are a lot of photographs of Jim and James together, you could see how tight they were with one another. They were definitely like Mick and Keith, there was definitely that vibe between them. Iggy had taught the Ashetons a lot of what they knew whereas Williamson came into his life fully formed, a fully fledged musician. He could play. Even though spiritually the Ashetons were an enormous contribution, James was a much more sophisticated individual. I gathered there was a bit of tension there but it was not a problem for me.

"Certainly *Raw Power* without him could not have been the same album. You just need to look at the photographs I took of them. You can see the way they bond. They wrote together and they were close. He (Williamson) seemed to be quite a bright lad to me. In many ways he was the most articulate of them all, the one who would be the most talkative. When all four of them were together, Iggy would let him do a lot more of the talking. They had been through a heavy drug thing and the whole idea of bringing them over to England . . . They didn't know where to go to get drugs. The idea was to clean them up. If they were going to get fucked up, De Fries wasn't prepared to deal with them. He just wanted to placate David. He was very interested in managing Lou Reed, which never panned out."

Ron Asheton: "We lifted off our salaries to buy us half an ounce of hash every week. My brother and I chipped in some each of our money every Monday to have this guy come to our house and bring the hash. We were just smoking hash – no one was into harder drugs."

Bowie's *Ziggy Stardust* album was released in June '72. The following month a gang of important American hacks were flown over to London to see Bowie and the Spiders From Mars at Aylesbury Friars on July 15. After the Bowie gig the journalists were bussed down to the Scala

Cinema in London's sleazy King's Cross (where Lou Reed had made his solo debut the previous day) to see The Stooges Mark II play a 40-minute set which turned out to be their only English performance and their only gig outside the States. The poster for the show, proudly promised an event that would run from "midnight to 6 am, featuring Iggy Pop, ex-Iggy and The Stooges with support from the Flamin' Groovies plus Film Happenings". The Scala was located on Pentonville Road, on a thoroughly disreputable street corner where it was possible to score heroin, get mugged, or find a whore.

Steve Peacock, *Sounds*: "Thin and teenage looking, he's like an animated Scarfe Jagger, only more so. Iggy pranced and pouted, muttered with exaggerated lip and tongue movements, shook his arse, flailed his arms and legs, threw himself around, leapt into the audience and groped people, ran up and down the aisles and cursed everything in sight."

Mick Rock: "The audience was stunned. There were stories of Iggy cutting himself up and, of course, the photographs existed to prove it all, him covering himself in peanut butter and walking on the crowd. He didn't do anything like that that night. It was a seated audience and mostly they just sat there stunned. The wild thing about that show is that it has gone down in the annals of rock'n'roll history as being one of the classic shows. It was like 45 minutes long. It was pretty well attended – there were about 1,000 people there. They were very much the aficionados, those in the know. I do remember being mesmerised. Up until then there was nothing else that sounded like the music they were making. They sounded like a total assault. You listen to *Raw Power* now and it sounds downright melodic compared with much of what it inspired. Then it was raw and extreme."

Nick Kent, *NME*: "Iggy started off demonstrating his own demented version of the boogaloo, progressing to some particularly impressive acrobatics and then into his audience assault numbers. Once he grabbed a chick and stared blankly into her face, almost beating up some poor wretch who dared to laugh at him . . . The total effect was more frightening than all the Alice Coopers and *Clockwork Orange*'s put together, simply because these guys weren't joking."

Iggy's old pal from Max's Kansas City, Glenn O'Brien, was one of the New York hacks in London to see Bowie. O'Brien, writing in *Andy Warhol's Interview*, used a credulous agitated erotic staccato to tell his readers what he saw and liked in the smelly old cinema near King's Cross: "Iggy was walking in a circle 10 feet in radius from the microphone . . . the ultimate rock'n'roll body clad only in silver lamé pants, bagging enough in back to show black bikini briefs, and black boots.

The upper torso is greased and silvered. The hair, chin length, is silver. The eyes are made up black, the lipstick is black, and the nails. Iggy stares like an amnesiac Hamlet into the audience. He glares, circles, but doesn't speak. Minutes pass. The audience begins to titter at the touch of his theatrically outraged stare. Iggy begins to insult the audience. He tells it that it doesn't inspire him. He sits down on the stage. After a minute he rolls over on his belly like a centrefold girl and continues to wonder at the mediocrity of half a theatre full of London hippies . . . Iggy does several things London has never seen. He swings his microphone around his head in a big circle just like Roger Daltrey, but when Iggy wants it back, he lets it wrap around his neck. Iggy likes to visit with the audience. He likes to sing a song to a particular girl in the audience. He likes to grab her by the hair and shake her head like a handful of dice when he sings to her . . . Iggy was gone. The battery of amplifiers screamed a dull but deafening scream which drowned out the calls for encore, the applause, conversation. Absolutely stunned kids of London went home."

When his mike gave out under all the pressure, Pop did an impromptu version of 'The Shadow Of Your Smile', the torch ballad which'd charmed the knickers and the wallet off Clive Davis back in New York's Columbia HQ. The London set featured nothing from the two Elektra albums. Iggy's verdict on the show was calm. "That was one sort of audience," he concluded. "They seemed a bit older. I'd like to sample a real teen audience. I saw a lotta nice girls in the audience. I see beautiful chicks walkin' around London, but I never seem to meet any."

The next day a celebrated press conference took place at London's Dorchester Hotel where the glittering stars of the Mainman organisation, Iggy, Bowie, and Lou Reed, the Mount Rushmore of fag rock, held court. Bowie instructed the gathered hacks that, "Iggy has natural theatre. It's very interesting because it doesn't conform to any standards or rules or structures of theatre. It's his own and it's just a Detroit theatre that he's brought with him. It's straight from the street."

Angie Bowie, *Backstage Passes*: "He (David) held a very amusing day of press interviews with them (Lou and Iggy) at the Dorchester Hotel ('Any society that allows people like Lou Reed and I to become rampant is pretty well lost,' quoth Bowie, most quotably), appearing as their ally and benefactor and getting at least as much attention as they, if not more. He connected Iggy and his group, The Stooges, with Tony De Fries and Mainman, and achieved a situation where he and Iggy had the same manager, but he'd had him first . . . Everybody came out pretty well in all this action, and everybody ended up beholden to David Bowie in one way or another. That was some smooth operating, I thought, admiring David's moves and helping out with counsel and logistic support."

Mick Rock says that there weren't all that many people at the Dorchester event, maybe a dozen. He says it was teatime at the hotel, that they had an expensive Dorchester room during daylight hours, and that the whole thing was for the benefit of the American media present. Iggy wore a T. Rex T-shirt and Rock snapped away wisely. He points out that having the three of them seated around the same table didn't seem such a big deal at the time – Reed and Iggy were club acts – but that he knew it was an opportunity he couldn't afford to miss.

Todd Haynes (Director, *Velvet Goldmine*): "Bowie changed costumes maybe four times, they served champagne and caviar and fresh strawberries, and everyone literally performed themselves. Iggy played the junkie on the floor; Lou Reed played the snide American who is smitten with Bowie; and Bowie played the duchess of the entire event. It was a completely constructed theatrical performance that took place in real life."

All through June and July the uncouth young American werewolves worked hard so there were new tunes like 'Nigger Man', 'I'm Sick Of You', 'Tight Pants', 'Scene Of The Crime', 'Gimme Some Skin' and 'Fresh Rag' (a reworking of a Joe Tex tune) to be demoed. Old live faves like 'I Got A Right' and 'I Need Somebody' were knocked into shape during a period of creativity. With Williamson on board there was suddenly no shortage of proper songs with verses, choruses, riffs, chords, beginnings, middles and ends. This was a totally new sort of Stooges.

James Williamson: "When we got over there we started practising our asses off, and it appears to be a little known fact that everybody was really straight over there. We were practising almost every day . . . not every day, every night, almost all night long, and then we'd sleep all day and practise again all night long. We were practising maybe five, six, seven days a week, and we were pretty tight as a band. We went in and did some demos early on with some of the tunes we already knew, trying some different things, so that's where all those tapes come from."

Included on these demo sessions was an early version of 'Search And Destroy' – named 'R.G. Jones At Wimbledon' in honour of the demo studio where it was recorded. These tapes were sent in to Tony De Fries to give him some idea of what was going on. According to Iggy, De Fries "just went completely apeshit". "I'm ashamed to release this stuff, James," De Fries told Pop, "You'll have to go in and just do something else."

"So that was the album before *Raw Power* which had . . . a bunch of other songs . . ." Iggy reckoned. " 'I Gotta Right' and 'Tight Pants' and 'Gimme Some Skin'. They've not been released properly, you can get them around on bootlegs and funny little anthologies."

To De Fries' ears the demos sounded even worse than *The Stooges*. "He didn't know what to do," says Iggy. "Bowie was producing the very successful Mott The Hoople album, *All The Young Dudes*, which is probably how ours would've gone. I'm sure. He would have written a big hit song for us, then we could've done our other songs and it would've been a certain sound, and that would've been fine. I have a feeling De Fries said, 'What should I do with this guy?' to which David probably told him, 'Listen, the best thing to do is just let him do what the fuck he wants to do and get it over with.' "

Mainman got the band unlimited time at CBS's new studios. Creative input from Bowie virtually guaranteed sales of some sort but Iggy was adamant that The Stooges didn't want Bowie to be in the studio every night. He correctly assumed that Bowie would try to gain artistic control while they were recording.

Iggy was the only Stooge actually signed up to Mainman. The rest of the band were on wages of $150 a week. One day Ron was talking with two of the Spiders From Mars. Being musicians, the conversation soon came around to the subject of money. "What are you getting each week?" one of the Spiders asked Asheton. Asheton told them he received $150 a week. The Spiders exploded. They were getting $75 a week each.

"I dug a little bit and I found out that Mick Ronson was getting something like $2,000 a week!" claims Ron. "Trevor and Woody (from the Spiders From Mars) got $75 a week and Bowie got a cut of the action. That's what De Fries tried to set up with The Stooges. Iggy would get a percentage of the action, and the rest of the guys would get a salary. They wanted to make James' salary bigger but Iggy, knowing my brother and myself, knew we wouldn't go for it, so we got the same amount every week."

Iggy: "One afternoon David, who I didn't see that often, came over and said, 'Look, would you like me to produce a record for you or not?' And I said, 'No thanks, because I got something I gotta do.' And that was the beginning and end of that conversation. There was never any pressure or anything like that. I got my way, got the band over to England, got a house and started doing demos, practising a lot."

When Bowie was rehearsing for his ground-breaking Ziggy Stardust show at the Rainbow on August 16, 1972, The Stooges dropped in on rehearsals. Those were exciting times within and without the Bowie camp. It looked like Bowie was well on his way to becoming the new Bob Dylan, the new Rolling Stones, or both. A generation of impressionable youth were being captivated by his strong message, somewhat similar to the passionate social assault that Marilyn Manson inflicted on society in the late Nineties.

The Stooges went to Bowie's Rainbow show, and got the best seats in the house, ones scalpers would die for, right down the front. The show had barely started when Ron, who'd had enough, turned to his brother and suggested that they go for a drink; they'd got the general idea of Bowie's repertoire at the rehearsals. While the rest of the audience was rapt in the performance of the orange-haired vision on stage, the brothers strolled nonchalantly down the centre aisle from their front row seats and went to the bar where they bumped into none other than Lou Reed who was very drunk and gobbling Mandrax. Uncharacteristically, he dispensed pills to each Stooge. Ron claims not to have taken his but Scotty sure did.

The next day Ron was summoned to Mainman HQ. When he arrived, De Fries chewed him out for getting up after the first three songs of Bowie's show. Mainman was furious that the brothers so publicly walked out. Asheton displayed a real Detroit punk attitude when he told De Fries, "Fuck you, man! Every seat was full. I just didn't wanna be there."

Iggy didn't turn down Bowie's production offer without thinking it over. He felt that Bowie was talented and could probably improve the tapes. He also understood that the Bowie connection was a good selling point; rock's greatest hustler had just bestowed a lost cause like Mott The Hoople with 'All The Young Dudes' – a Top Five hit in September '72. None of this had the slightest effect on Iggy. "I didn't want Bowie to produce my album," he insisted, "and I got my way." The compromise was that Iggy would produce the album while Bowie would be allowed to supervise the final mix. That way they could at least get his name on the all-important back cover.

Iggy: "So we went in the studio and did the record, one helluva motherfucking record. I don't recall if De Fries ever visited the studio while we were in there. I don't think anybody from Mainman ever came down to that studio, we just did it ourselves. It only took 10 or 12 days to make. Bowie was never in the studio. None of them were ever there in any shape or form. At this point it was pretty much like, 'Well, we've got this disaster and let's just let 'em do what they're gonna do.' That was the idea. 'We don't know what to do with them.'

"Why should they have been there? I wouldn't have wanted them there anyway. I was intent on what I was doing – we had nude vocals going on there, all kinds of things! I was absolutely intent only on what I was doing, never a girlfriend around that studio, never a dealer or anything like that, never any histrionics or emotional ups and downs or anything like that. There was drug use. And vermouth, too. I used to drink it to keep my voice on the highs. I smoked cigarettes at the time, two or three cigarettes, and vermouth is really smooth on the throat, so I'd drink little shots of vermouth."

'Search And Destroy' took its name from a heading in *Time* magazine concerning the Vietnam War. It was one of the first rock songs to take on board the cartoon-fantasy aspect of Vietnam, subject matter subsequently exploited by The Stooges-obsessed Ramones in songs written by Dee Dee Ramone. Iggy read the *Time* article one warm summer's day while doing a large Chinese rock of heroin sitting under an English oak tree in Kensington Gardens. He was in the habit of going there to write, wearing his leather cheetah jacket, leather pants, and wraparound shades. All the rich old London men used to drive by trying to cruise him.

There was one specific oak tree that he liked to relax under when songwriting. Getting a snappy title, like the one he found that day in Kensington, was the most important thing as far as he was concerned. Once he had a title, he knew what to do with it. 'Search And Destroy' was mostly recorded in one impressive vocal take, with Iggy singing right at the top of his range. James Williamson recycled his riff from the 'R.G. Jones' eight-track demo that'd horrified De Fries.

Iggy: "I had eight guys recording a sword-fight on 'Search And Destroy'. You can kind of hear it on the original mix, this funny metal sound behind the tom-tom drum on the basic line. I wanted sword fighting and boot-stomping, what I really wanted was to get a drill team in there and stomp! A wonderful sound, but I couldn't get it together so, 'Aw, hell, we'll just do it ourselves!' So we got some old sabers from an antique store and did sword-fighting."

The powerfully nasty 'Gimme Danger' is an autobiographical meditation on Iggy's attitude towards women – one of many in his canon. Delivered in a smokey baritone, the vocal is the closest Pop ever came to sounding like Jim Morrison, whom he then claimed as his hero. He'd sort of sworn off "chicks" at this point because he thought that if he didn't come up with a really great album and grow in his music, all was lost. He entertained classic misogynistic notions of woman as destructive seductress, a vulvic Bermuda Triangle. "Chicks could just get in the way," he thought, "and I'd developed an adversarial relationship with chicks. So the only ones I was really interested in were the ones that would give me trouble, so I wrote about that."

James Williamson: "On the album, for most of the stuff, I used a Vox AC30. I know that's a little known fact. A lot of guys think I used a Marshall CPS because I always used a Marshall onstage. On some of the lead stuff, I would use a Marshall, but most all of the rhythm stuff is the AC30. Some of the lead stuff was AC30. I love those amps! Those still are, as far as I'm concerned, some of the greatest amps there ever were."

Iggy: "Usually, Williamson would come up with a first riff, and I'd come up with a first riff, I'd hear something he'd play to get really excited, I'd come up with a line really quickly and then I'd suggest to him, 'Wait, I hear this, it could go here,' and he would take it there, and I'd say, 'OK, great, I've got it now, this should actually be part A, and then it should go to part 2, not to C yet, but back to A, and then double B, then to C,' and we'd construct it that way. That's how I've worked it ever since, with guitarists or pianists basically I hear some little thing they'd do that I like, and my job is to give it form and kind of make it into a building. That's how the stuff comes up."

All the songs on *Raw Power* were credited to Williamson and Pop. Ron Asheton claims that Williamson was arrogant right through the sessions, treating the brothers like session players. Which is exactly what they'd allowed themselves to become. "My brother and I put a lot of input into it," Ron insists. "James would structure tunes and we would help arrange. We never got any credit. It was this Jagger/Richards trip. James fought tooth and nail that all tunes were written by Iggy Pop/James Williamson."

The vociferous 'Your Pretty Face Is Going To Hell' was *Raw Power's* second cutting, resentful, misogynist anthem. It was Iggy's way of saying to a woman he was using for sex that, "You're pretty now but just wait, you're not gonna have that weapon all the time!" His private life was littered with examples of a ferocious and unrelenting cruelty when it came to women, particularly ageing women. He would later describe the attitude of 'Your Pretty Face . . .' as being "unusually prescient for a guy in his mid-twenties, because most people that age just don't think about that. They think beauty and youth will last forever. I thought, 'Well, wait a minute here, she's not gonna look like that in 10 years, then what? Har har har! Not gonna be whistling such a smartass tune, are ya bitch?!'"

Iggy attributes the subject matter of 'Penetration' to cut up sex material found in *The Ticket That Exploded* or *Soft Machine* by William Burroughs. 'Raw Power', 'Gimme Danger' and 'I Need Somebody' were written during the long period of rehearsal for the album, in one of those cheap rehearsal complexes where songwriters pay for four hours so they can sit around with a guitar, trying to see if they'll come up with anything. 'Death Trip', the last track on *Raw Power*, related to the bad vibes or indifference emanating from Mainman, from the sense that the entire London project was predestined for failure or shot in the foot before it ever got going.

Iggy: "The reason it's last on the album is that I'm singing about what I realise is happening here. I know this album's doomed. I know the relationship with the management company is doomed, I know I'm doomed for putting out music like this. I know nobody's gonna promote it. I know it's not gonna be on the radio, there's a lot of people who aren't gonna like it. But on the other hand, I'm totally convinced this is the best music so that's what I'm gonna do, that's what I'm singing about."

The Stooges did a rough mix of *Raw Power* when they finished their recording sessions in September. The version released afterwards was a subsequent mix undertaken by Iggy and Bowie without the others being consulted. Ron Asheton described that version as being "Bowie's and Iggy's cocaine 'artsy-fartsy' mix. It was mostly Bowie."

Iggy: "When you get the record done you're emotionally spent, physically frazzled, you've put a lot into your sessions. You've paid so much attention to the songs while you wrote them, conceived them, rehearsed them and recorded them that you've lost perspective in a lot of ways. Yet, you don't want anybody else to touch this baby, it's your baby. You can go off the deep end at this point. The best thing to do, I've learned since, is as soon as you've done making that record, put the thing away, get away for a few weeks, then go back and listen to it and start to do the next work on it.

"But what I did instead was start listening to it, thinking, 'No matter how much treble there is, it doesn't cut enough, no matter how much bass there is, it isn't low enough, no matter how fast it is, it isn't hard enough.' I turned in a couple of mixes which sounded very extreme, exactly like the kind of mixes you heard on the independent hardcore punk rock movement of the Eighties when people started doing it themselves, just extreme middle and treble and 'Aaaarrggh!' Very amateur sounding. I could understand at this point that De Fries wanted to take it away from me. I was sleeping with the tapes, listening to them again and again. 'Wait, I can still make it better. I can make it more crazy!'

"They shuffled me off to Los Angeles, where I didn't want to go, a real bad place to send me. They told me by phone later, 'We're not releasing it like that. David will remix it.' To which I said, 'OK', because the other choice was I wasn't going to get my album out. I think De Fries told me that CBS refused to release it like that, I don't know. Who knows what the real story is? David and I and one of his bodyguards/gofers at the time, Stewie, went to Western Studios in Hollywood. To the best of my recollection it was done in a day. I don't think it was two days. On a very, very old board, I mean this board was old! An Elvis type of board, old-tech, low-tech, in a poorly lit, cheap old studio, with very little time."

Bowie defended his work at the mixing desk, claiming, "He (Iggy) brought the 24-track tape in. He had the band on one track, lead guitar on another, and him on a third. Out of 24 tracks there were just three that were used. He said, 'See what you can do with this.' I said, 'Jim, there's nothing to mix.' So we just pushed the vocal up and down a lot."

Iggy: "To David's credit, he listened with his ear to each thing and talked it out with me. I gave him what I thought it should be, he put that in its perspective, added some touches. He's always liked the most recent technology, so there was something called a Time Cube you could feed a signal into – it looked like a bong, a big plastic tube with a couple of bends in it – and when the sound came out the other end, it sort of shot at you like an echo effect. He used that on the guitar on 'Gimme Danger', a beautiful guitar echo overload that's absolutely beautiful, and on the drums in 'Your Pretty Face Is Going To Hell'. His concept was 'You're so primitive, your drummer should sound like he's beating a log!' It's not a bad job that he did. Somebody's since put something out on Bomp, *Rough Power*, which were some of my original mixes, but I think what David and I came up with at these sessions was better than that. So I think he helped the thing. I'm very proud of the eccentric, odd little record that came out."

Mick Rock: "The first two Stooges albums had gone nowhere. Iggy and The Stooges were pretty much regarded as a wild bunch. De Fries wasn't really all that interested in them but as Bowie's own star began to rise, he acquired a certain amount of instant clout. Bowie has so many stories about how he came up with this Ziggy Stardust name but the first time I broached the subject with him he said it was an amalgam of Iggy and The Legendary Stardust Cowboy, a totally whacked out sideways thing that was typical of what David was into then. Lou Reed and Iggy Pop meant something to people who really knew their onions but they'd had no airplay and the music wasn't really known unless you were super hip. In the space of seven days it transpired, though not by design, that I shot Lou Reed one Friday night and Iggy the following Friday.

From the Lou Reed show came the cover of *Transformer* and the Iggy gig gave rise to the *Raw Power* cover. I got maybe $250 for *Raw Power* and a bit less for *Transformer*."

Having made their album, London's charms were fading fast for The Stooges, all of whom wanted to go back home. Bowie had grabbed Ron Asheton by the ass and kissed him! Locating good drugs was heavy going. The backbone of the Mainman team, including De Fries himself, were preoccupied with breaking Bowie in America. The Stooges ended up being left to their own devices in London — a recipe for disaster if ever there was one.

Leee Black Childers: "They wrecked the house and disrupted the neighbourhood totally until they were thrown out. That's why they ended up being brought back from England. They could find no place for them and they were afraid that Iggy was going to be deported any minute."

It was the stuff of weekly comment in the UK rock press that David Bowie was pure cultural blotting paper, absorbing each and every cutting edge phenomenon that came in front of his scanner-like eyes. The selling-your-soul-to-the-Devil-at-the-crossroads deal on offer was that the victim of Bowie's vampirism normally got a hit single or a career boost. Cabaret singers like Lulu and rootsy folk-rockers like Steeleye Span did well out of the covenant. Lou Reed put considerable distance between himself and Bowie once the Ziggy connection got him a hit album in *Transformer* and an improbable hit single in 'Walk On The Wild Side'. Iggy Pop got no immediate benefit from the association but he continued to work, off and on, with Bowie. Over the next 20 years, Bowie helped him build up a small but perfectly formed body of rock classics. Ironically, most of that work has helped ensure Iggy's longevity and credibility, whereas Bowie's own once-pristine reputation would undergo seismic shifts during the Eighties. Today only Lou Reed and Iggy, of all the Bowie protégés, stand tall. They did it before him and they're still doing it after him.

CHAPTER 12

She Creatures Of The Hollywood Hills

"Tony De Fries had grown weary of them for some reason (I suspect their chronic, incorrigible drug use) and had decided that while the very best place for Iggy was still London, The Stooges belonged elsewhere, preferably another country. I was dispatched to escort them to Heathrow, their plane tickets in my hand (to forestall their conversion into drug money), and then accompany them into the air and all the way back to Ann Arbor, Michigan, where they, the MC5, and many other practitioners of heavy, doped-out radical pre-punk/metal rock had made themselves a home.

"I'd heard so much about the scene there from Iggy and the lads that I wasn't displeased with my assignment. I had myself an interesting time too. I had a fling with James Williamson, the lead guitar Stooge, followed by a fling with Ron Asheton, the bass-playing Stooge, and then Ron introduced me to Scott Richardson, the owner of a magnificent white-blues voice who played bass and sang with SRC, a wonderful hard-rock-and-blues band who were heavy local heroes but never made it in the national or international scene, and I fell for him. He was bold and blond and very attractive, and besides, he wasn't a junkie . . . Being with him, therefore, wasn't the kind of Waiting For Godot *experience I'd had with James and Ron: lots of motel rooms with the TV on, lots of great slow sex, lots of interminable interludes while they disappeared into the bathroom to cook and shoot and nod and dream. Those were my first intimate experiences of Junkieworld, as a matter of fact, and I didn't really like it much . . . I think that's the big reason The Stooges weren't too upset about being sent back to Ann Arbor. Home was where the best dope and the most dealers were."*

– Angie Bowie, *Backstage Passes*

IN mid-October 1972 Iggy flew out to LA, clutching his insanity-inducing *Raw Power* master tapes, to meet up with Bowie and his posse who were holed up at the Beverly Hills Hotel. Bowie was gigging

124

in style at the Santa Monica Civic Auditorium and Winterland in San Francisco.

"We all had bungalows," Tony Zanetta says. "There were 30 of us. Everyone was in the Beverly Hills Hotel. Iggy was really healthy. He was eating only vegetables . . . No drugs. He was in a really good state of mind and he wanted to stay in California and bring his band over there."

In early November the other Stooges, quitting Ann Arbor and Angie Bowie, followed him to LA. Bowie kept on touring right through November and December while The Stooges stayed holed up at the Beverly Hills Hotel, running up big bills. Iggy was told that he was too well known to go out doing little gigs. "I fought this, but it didn't matter," he said. "I was told this by a man I looked up to (De Fries) and who helped me out, so I went along with it."

Eventually De Fries instructed Leee Black Childers, for the second time, to go find The Stooges a house: "I found them several houses, but Iggy wouldn't settle on any of them. By his choice, he was going out in Beverly Hills Hotel limousines to look at the houses. It all went on the hotel bill. He found a house on his own. It was an incredible, beautiful, magic house! Right on top of the Hollywood Hills. From one window you could see all of Burbank and from another you could see all of LA. It had a huge, huge swimming pool and absolute privacy. It was a gorgeous place. We rented the house for $900 a month."

Childers was The Stooge's official minder, and he reported back regularly to De Fries. His initial assistant in this onerous task was the beautiful Cyrinda Foxe, a denizen of Max's Kansas City's back room who was close to the New York Dolls' David Johansen and who subsequently married Steve Tyler. The various junk habits within the band blossomed again under the California sun while a never-ending parade of naked nymphets, experienced concubines, hopeful faggy boys, rich drug dealers, blow job queens, and life's most motley crew basked by the house's archetypal Hollywood swimming pool. A mid-teen girl, Sable Starr, appeared upon the scene and went with Iggy, Ron and Scott. She had an equally attractive sister named Corel who became, for quite a while, the most important of Iggy's kennel of bitches.

Leee Black Childers: "We always had the prime VIP booth at the Whisky because we were Mainman's representatives on earth. We'd just walk in and the booth would be right there. All the kids, especially the groupies and stuff like that, would be looking hopefully at that booth. Cyrinda Foxe was gorgeous and I looked pretty cool too at the time, so everybody would be flirting with us. You'd take your choice from the crowd because in those days there were no sexual problems. I picked up this one boy who was really gorgeous, so sweet, and so willing. I brought him back to the house. Basically, when I usually did that, the next morning I'd get him a taxi and that would be that. Just that I didn't really want this one to go away. I wanted him to hang out. Then we were all sitting around by the swimming pool, the boy was swimming, and I was thinking, 'I always make Iggy send the girls home.'

"At that time James Williamson was living with Cyrinda Foxe so she was living in the house. But Iggy would be bringing girls home or they would just show up out of nowhere. I would say it was OK but that they couldn't hang out, couldn't stay for breakfast. But now I had this boy and I didn't want to have to send him away. So I had to re-evaluate things. But I was still a real policeman there. I think I wasn't that cruel about it."

Tony De Fries' policy seemed to be: if in doubt, rehearse. Most days of the week The Stooges trooped off to a nearby studio to do just that. Part of the problem lay in the fact that, with Bowie happening big-time, Iggy and his Stooges were just not glitzy or showbiz enough for the aspirant but occasionally duplicitous fags and theatrical types who manned Mainman. Another part of the problem was that De Fries, with his background in the treacherous waters of the Sixties Soho music biz, was genuinely tough. Angie Bowie said he was a good door-kicker who always knew where you were going and who promised very well. He knew exactly what he was doing when he hired a pile of penniless queens to do his bidding. Nice people or not, they were profoundly intimidated and fawning yes-men. The Stooges were left to their own devices.

Tony Zanetta: "Tony De Fries wanted the band to be in demand. He had theories about that kind of stuff. He wanted to create a demand for the band and he didn't want Iggy to do small clubs, or as an opening act or any small gigs. He wanted everything to be just right; but none of us at Mainman had the time to make that happen."

Iggy: "To this day I do not understand. I cannot quite figure out why we were not allowed to do a tour. De Fries said, 'It's because there is no demand for you,' but when he started these Bowie and Mott The Hoople tours, I went to each of their opening gigs and there was nobody there, about a hundred-odd people and they built up as they went along. De Fries had received, for my services, $100,000 from CBS Records, payable to Mainman as a production company. I had an employee contract so I had no right to touch a penny of it, and that was huge money in 1972, big serious money. De Fries would play each of us against the other. Bowie would ask him, 'Well, where's my money?' and De Fries would say, 'Well, Iggy needed some dental work,' and Bowie'd get flipped out. Meanwhile, I'd wonder, 'Where's my money?' and I'd see Bowie on tour and Mott The Hoople on tour and I'd know they couldn't be making money on these tours, and I'd see five or six employees at the Mainman office and I'd think, 'There's my money.' Things were at an impasse."

There is something to this analysis but Bowie was generating money of his own by then. His first forays into the US may have had a faltering aspect to them, but he was already an interminable chart presence and filler of music venues back home in Europe. As if by way of a deliberate goad, Bowie's next tour opened on February 14, 1973 at the impressive Radio City Music Hall in New York. The frustration began to tell on the stranded-in-Hollywood Stooges.

Leee Black Childers: "They weren't working and Iggy was feeling second banana to Bowie. He was feeling left out and he was most insecure and upset. I guess I wasn't very good at receiving all the complaints. We were all so in awe of Tony De Fries. He was like a god. I just didn't want to disturb him. Iggy's complaints disappeared into me. Very few of them were communicated to De Fries in New York."

The band were suffering from poor management. They were a musically proficient popular live act with a strong identity. They really should have been out on the road all the time since live work was their major suit and since only live work could build up a hard rock band in that pre-MTV universe. The lack of action drove Pop off the deep end, back into the arms of drugs. "Iggy should have been out of control!" Leee Black Childers admits. "He should have burnt the house down and run screaming down Sunset Strip. It's understandable. He was driven so crazy because he was totally ignored until he went completely bananas."

Eventually, after much shoving and pushing, one paltry concert was organised for March 29, 1973 . . . in Detroit! This was hardly a show of strength because The Stooges were always popular in their hometown. Showcases in LA, New York, or San Francisco – towns where the band stood for something and where the national media were hip – would have indicated a more confident all-round approach. The Detroit gig was the band's first since the forceful King's Cross London show. It took place at a prestige venue, The Henry and Edsel Ford Auditorium, which was normally reserved for the local symphony orchestra. It was one of the strongest ever Stooge manifestations, preceded by Iggy's tour de force whirlwind performance on a Detroit radio station. The "interview" almost resulted in the station losing their licence.

Leee Black Childers: "He took off all his clothes and was jerking off on the radio! 'I've got my clothes off now. I'm playing with my balls.' " Later he locked himself in the radio station's elevator with Cherry Vanilla and tried to rape her! Tony De Fries was beside himself with anger. Iggy was totally out of control that whole time in Detroit. But when he got on stage, he did a brilliant show."

Glenn O'Brien, *Andy Warhol's Interview*: "Iggy is still the same. He projects danger like no other rock performer. He walks a line between entertainment and attack, bringing the violent roots of rock out in the open. He's still the best dancer in rock, out-stepping what James Brown and Mick Jagger were at their peaks and out-outraging prime-time Jim Morrison . . . The highlight of the show is when he enters the audience. It's the theatre of cruelty come alive. Iggy jumps off the stage. He grabs a girl in the first row and kisses her hard. He holds her and grinds into her while he sings. When he's finished he pushes her down to the floor. Then he goes chasing after a boy. The boy doesn't want any of what Iggy might be offering, but he gets grabbed anyway by the silver-haired black-lipsticked singer. But Iggy doesn't kiss this time, he shakes. Some kids run, afraid that they're next. Others watch in awe. Nobody's going to rush the stage. The stage has rushed the audience . . . What we saw in Detroit was one of the greatest rock'n'roll shows ever."

Under instructions from De Fries the band performed no encore. There were two big industry bashes afterwards; the first at the Ford Auditorium, and the second at the Detroit Hilton. "De Fries had laid out this gigantic spread of food and alcohol. But we weren't allowed to be seen after we had played," asserts Ron Asheton. "We said, 'All right, just some drinks.' They said, 'Out in the limousine. You guys aren't going to be seen. This is for the peons.' We were grabbing things off the table, into the limousine and back to the hotel."

After the gig, De Fries had a major disagreement with James William-son. "He figured he'd put me out of the way," Williamson claims, "and that way he could control Iggy. Drugs were involved, even though it was only a minimal kind of thing." According to Ron Asheton, De Fries was pissed off with Williamson's gross egotism. Asheton, understandably enough, was certainly pissed off with Williamson's ego. De Fries was old school management who had a big problem with drugs. He eventually issued an ultimatum to The Stooges. If they kept Williamson in the band, they'd be dropped by Mainman. Williamson agreed to go quietly.

"Mainman was never drug orientated. No one was into drugs," says Tony Zanetta sanguinely. "Later on people got involved with drugs, cocaine, etc. It was never the hip thing to do at Mainman. We drank too much. We were all so chic, sitting around in restaurants drinking white wine and brandy. Leee Black Childers and I used to fill up bathtubs with ice and we'd order bottles of white wine, keep them on ice, so that we'd have wine after we'd gotten back from gigs or whatever." Zanetta says at that time Bowie wasn't doing any drugs. He says the star didn't smoke pot, hardly even drank a glass of wine.

"Typical Tony De Fries production. It was limos and a lot of hype and so on, and it was a big gig," James Williamson recalled of Detroit to Ken Shimamoto. "We did well there, I think everybody enjoyed the gig and in order to get ready for that we played in Ann Arbor and we rehearsed. As a result, I started telling Iggy that I thought we needed keyboards. I remembered Bob Scheff ("Blue" Gene Tyranny) from The Prime Movers and we got in touch with him because Iggy knew him. We started using him on our subsequent tour. We didn't do anything for a long time after that first one gig in the US. I think, for whatever reasons, I can't speculate on what Tony De Fries' reasons were, but at that point the relationship soured, and we didn't play any more gigs with him. In fact, I wasn't even in the band for three months. In fact, for four months, there wasn't any band.

"We came back to Los Angeles and about six weeks later, we were informed that something had to give," continued Williamson. "Where it ended up was I had to leave the band, so I left the band, because I was supposedly a bad influence. They tried a couple of different guitar players. I think they did one job somewhere and then eventually they just said, 'Screw it, this isn't going to work,' and they all left De Fries. So everybody left and we changed management and that's where Bob Scheff came in."

"Blue" Gene Tyranny (aka Bob Scheff): "We'd more or less been out of touch with each other all through The Stooges period, after Iggy quit The Prime Movers. Up until then I'd really had no idea of what had been going on in his life. He phoned me out of the blue, mentioning *en passant* that there might be a short tour to do. I went down there a couple of times and stayed there for a couple of weeks each time. I think that both Iggy and David Bowie were trying to get away from Mainman, who were these real Mafia kind of guys. I met one of them in Detroit, thought he was a real asshole. I was aware that there was all this tension going around.

"Anyway, as a result of our phone conversation, Iggy sent me a plane ticket and 'summoned' me to LA. He said that he just wanted to talk with me. So I went to LA and stayed at the famous house on Mulholland Drive. Iggy took me outside and we sat in the driveway of this old house that Douglas Fairbanks used to own. We had this heart-to-heart talk during which he basically said that he wanted to reconnect with the good feeling that he used to have in Ann Arbor. He was saying that he wanted to get out from under the drugs, talked about all this pretty negative business stuff that was happening to do with Mainman, and I agreed to do this short tour. That was good, so far as I was concerned. We'd rehearse from midnight until five or six in the morning. I couldn't even conceive of doing such a thing today. I guess we must have had some hamburgers or something! When we did get out on the road, I was impressed by how well he was received and what high expectations people had of him. We did a couple of informal recording sessions but I've no idea what happened with those."

James Williamson: "Bob played a couple of gigs, but this was just too weird for him. In the meantime, while I had been gone from the band, I was playing with a couple of other local bands, not really playing, but sorta thinking about playing with them. One day I was over at Capitol Records and as I was going out, I was watching this guy recording, and it was Scott Thurston with this other band. He was cool. I could hear that he was a great piano player, so I got his contact info and I said, 'You wanna play with us?' When we put the band back together, I asked him if he wanted to play with us, and he said, 'Sure,' and the rest is history."

Leee Black Childers: "They had a lot of unauthorised parties. A lot of broken glass in the pool. A lot of fights with me. They brought in a bunch of junkie groupies and they were shooting up around the pool! All I ever said to Iggy was, 'Be discreet, just be discreet.' Therefore the one thing he couldn't do was to be discreet. It's the old 'I must break the rules' syndrome.' He did!"

Tony Zanetta: "He was all down the tubes again. It was drugs as far as I could tell. He began calling all the time. He was looking for attention and there wasn't anybody to give him that. He felt left out. Everybody at Mainman was really too busy to deal with that kind of behaviour. There were robberies, there were abortions, there was this and there was that. It was a new problem every day. No one had the energy to deal with Iggy any longer."

As the Bowie entourage made their way through Japan, word reached them of the endless chaos enveloping The Stooges. There were heated arguments. "Here is this problem," somebody said to Bowie, "and that problem and none of us have the time and you don't have the time, and we just feel . . ." Bowie was frustrated by the whole situation. "There was a helplessness about it," Zanetta says with reference to Bowie's attitude, "but he realised that he wasn't going to go in there and sort it out by himself. It would be best for Iggy to go his own way."

Leee Black Childers: "Tony just called me and said, 'Get them out of the house!' Lo and behold, they all did. No fuss. They didn't destroy things. They didn't pour cement down the toilet or sugar in the gas tank. They just packed up and left."

They pooled their money and found cheap accommodation. Iggy descended into a world of transient accommodation and mental confusion. The lowest point in his life happened around then. One morning he woke up alone in an abandoned building somewhere behind Hollywood Boulevard, puking weird green bile. "My only alternative," he says, "was to nail a well-known publicist who would put me up for a few days. That was pretty low."

Raw Power was belatedly released in May '73 almost a year after it was recorded, and with the band at a profoundly low point – homeless and without management. Amongst many other management offences Iggy wasn't consulted about the cover. At the time this only enhanced his outraged sense of violation.

"When I saw that 'Iggy' on there like that," he says, "looking like a take-off on Fifties monster film poster lettering I flipped right out. I could have screamed! The cover was just the shits. Elektra's were better." His opinion of the sleeve mellowed over the years. "You had this real culture clash going on. The cover was dictated to me, I never saw the cover before it came in. I hated it, thought they were taking the piss with the monster dripping letters and everything. Since then I realise that, taking the piss or not, they did me a favour, the photograph is beautiful, the lettering is memorable, and nobody would've had the guts – I was too serious about myself, too earnest – to put that cover out like that. So they did me a solid."

Mick Rock: "He didn't have any say in the *Raw Power* cover. De Fries was high-handed and we were all very high-handed. I remember being in New York and he said, 'Oh, Iggy won't care about it. We'll take care of this. He's not interested.' I was given the impression that Iggy was not interested. I always imagined this to be the case until much more recently. I remember I met with De Fries at the Mainman offices around the time of the first Bowie Ziggy Stardust tour of America, late November or early December. Just me and Tony De Fries. Originally he was looking for another shot. The irony of it was that he'd seen some other images of Iggy, I think of him covered in peanut butter, but he couldn't locate them. The record company wanted the thing immediately so he went with one of my sessions. I think there were two of my shots that it came down to, the one that was actually used and the one I used on the cover of my book, *Raw Power*, where the head is turned just slightly to the front. It was all down to circumstances. They wanted to get the record released. Who knows? What the fuck did I know? I was just some kid photographer. Just pleased to be around it all. So if Tony was telling me that Iggy wasn't interested, I was willing to believe him. Now I look at the pictures and think I just got lucky. My timing was perfect. He looked better then than he ever looked in his life."

Raw Power heralded the birth of a new age. With a vaguely homo-erotic cover, strong compelling songs, and Pop's ongoing arrogant strut, it spoke of music yet to come instead of bowing in respect to what had gone before. This was hegemonic stuff, an avatar of what youth would spend the next 30 years listening to.

Lenny Kaye wrote in *Rolling Stone*: "With *Raw Power* The Stooges return with a vengeance, exhibiting all the ferocity that characterised them at their livid best . . . There are no compromises, no attempts to soothe or play games in the hopes of expanding into a fabled wider audience . . . For the first time, The Stooges have used the recording studio as more than a recapturing of their live show, and with David Bowie helping out in the mix, there is an ongoing swirl of sound that virtually drags you into the speakers, guitars rising and falling, drums edging forward and then toppling back into the morass."

Dave Marsh was similarly impressed in *Creem*. He made the important point that, although Ron may have been peeved at being demoted to bass player, he made a great job of it: "Bassist Ron Asheton pulls down the sound, melding it into something almost earthly, just like a great jazz bass player does, while the rest of the band accelerates beyond anything that's been recorded, or played live or even dreamed of, in years, so hard and so fast that if Iggy wasn't the singer you'd wonder whose record it was."

During the autumn of '73 *Melody Maker*'s Chris Charlesworth got to see what life was like with Iggy: "I drove to Iggy's hotel on Sunset and he suggested that we go to the beach to do the interview, which was a great idea as it was a lovely sunny day. He had Corel Starr with him, an incredibly beautiful girl with hair down to her ass, spray on faded jeans and loose white shirt. So I drove the two of them to a deserted beach south of LA. Iggy brought with him a couple of golf clubs and some old balls and during the interview he stopped every now and then to hit balls into the sea. He had a fabulous swing . . . really professional, and he whacked these golf balls way out into the ocean, looking well pleased with himself. I was amazed that Iggy, wildman of rock, played golf which is a bit of a pedestrian sport, but he told me about his dad and how he was a sports freak and how he'd been brought up real healthy.

Meanwhile Corel was sunbathing next to us, looking unbelievably cute, and joining in the conversation every now and then."

Charlesworth had been to see Iggy's show the previous night at the Whisky on Sunset. "Weird shit happened around Iggy," he continues. "The Whisky had a car hop who wasn't around when I left so I went into the car park at the back and got into what I thought was my car – same make, same model, same colour, same rental company – and drove to my hotel. Next day I notice a pair of jeans that weren't mine in the back of the car, with a hotel room key in the pocket. So when I get to Iggy's hotel I ask him if I can use the phone in his room. 'No problem,' he says. I call the hotel, get put through to the room and ask this guy if he's lost his jeans. 'Yeah, and I lost my fucking car too!' It was only then I realised what I'd done. So with Iggy and Corel in the back I went to this guy's hotel and we swapped cars. He'd taken mine as it happened. Iggy just accepted this strange business as if it were commonplace."

Rodney Bingenheimer (influential rock DJ "Mayor of Sunset Boulevard"): "One day we were driving down Hollywood Boulevard in my GTO, me and Iggy and Corel Starr. It was a beautiful sunny day so I had the radio on and the roof down. We did this a lot, cruising and talking about music. I used to see him a bit then – we were pretty good friends. I was one of the few DJs playing The Stooges on my show. I still play Iggy's new records on the show and I'm still one of the few guys playing him! He was hanging out at the time at my English Disco and we did some live shows together. Anyway he was with Corel in the back seat and I told them I had to put the GTO into the carwash. Iggy said that was cool and so I pulled the roof up and we drove into the carwash. Soon as the carwash started working, making all that noise, Iggy started having sex with Corel in the back seat. I'd seen all kinds of things but I'd never seen that one before."

The afterglow of The Stooges life on Mulholland Drive kept the party going long after the band had meekly departed for less salubrious accommodations. Local music biz rumour had it – correctly – that Iggy was living on the streets but Leee Black Childers was still enjoying the rock'n'roll Hollywood swimming pool lifestyle.

Leee Black Childers: "The Stooges were long gone but, for reasons best known to Tony De Fries, I was still there. I said to Jayne/Wayne County, 'Come on back to LA with me. I've got this huge house. Swimming pool, etcetera.' So she agreed to come, she'd never been to LA before. We got on the plane, but there was some problem with the plane. We ended up stuck on the runway on the ground for four hours. Jayne was not an easy flyer and neither was I. She was starting to really

freak out but of course they wouldn't let us off. Eventually we got going and it was a really bad flight.

"By the time we got to LA it was 5 am. Susie Ha Ha, my secretary, who was supposed to meet me at the airport, had naturally enough given up and gone back home so we got a cab to Mulholland Drive. When we got out of the cab we could hear all these voices and the whole place was lit up, there was all this laughter. We discovered all these people in and around the swimming pool. The whole house was wide open and the gang were all there. I asked, 'How did you all get in?' and Sable Starr shrieks, 'Ooooh! Anybody can pick a lock! We just wanted to welcome Jayne to LA!'

"I said, 'Didn't it occur to you that there might be something wrong? It's 5 am now!' 'Ooooh,' she laughed, 'we just decided that we'd wait.' All the booze had been drunk. All the food had been eaten. Poor Jayne was in a complete frazzle. I said, 'OK. Everyone has to go now. This is not a party. We're both very tired. We've had a very bad flight, and a bad trip.' So Sable went off and cornered Jayne, tried to make moves on her. Jayne kind of swung both ways in those days, which is not all that much different from Jayne these days. She was still calling herself Wayne then, and that was more than enough for Sable to make her move. Jayne says, 'Please, no, I don't want to do anything.'

"So Sable, who was drunk as a monkey, of course, went off and cut her wrists and dived into the swimming pool naked. The blood was flowing out into the water. I was going, 'Oh, my God, let's get her out of there.' Jayne said, 'Why?' Corel wrapped her up in a blanket after I'd gotten her out. And everyone went home. The next morning, which was two hours later, the phone rang. It was the Fire Department. They're saying, 'Please go out and hose your roof down. The Hollywood Hills are on fire.' So there was Jayne County and me out on the lawn with our hoses, because the roofs were made of wood. Ashes were raining down on the two of us. We both looked like Amos and Andy. Jayne says to me, while she's busy hosing, 'Thanks a lot! Thanks for inviting me!' This was her welcome to LA. A crazy suicidal groupie and a complete forest fire, all in the course of four hours."

CHAPTER 13

Blood On The Loincloth –
Metallic KO

"Ironically, the exhortation 'riot, girls!' is one of the challenges Iggy threw at a crazed audience during the gig documented on The Stooges' live album Metallic KO *. . . Iggy turned self-mutilation and reciprocal abuse between audience and singer into a grisly theatre."*

– The Sex Revolts

"I can't accept this mythology surrounding The Stooges. You've got to look at things as they are: we were just guys playing rock'n'roll that wasn't accepted. And rightly so: it wasn't timely or commercial."

– James Williamson

THE Stooges were treated atrociously by Mainman. They'd worked their asses off to create *Raw Power* in the face of all manner of external and collateral negativity. It was the strongest of their three albums and, given the golden Bowie connection, 'Search And Destroy' or 'Raw Power' might've made it as minor hit singles somewhere in the Western world. As it panned out, by the time Lenny Kaye and others were lauding the album, The Stooges were deeply demoralised and virtually homeless. Their mutual solidarity had been torn apart by internal ambition and external management. Esprit de corps was non-existent.

As a result of the mainstream showbiz world they'd allowed themselves to be sucked into they were comprehensively out of touch with the first manifestations of punk rock, the major cultural movement which claimed them as founding fathers a few years later. Nevertheless they were about to commit the quality of men that they were to posterity. Held together by sheer self-belief, the band didn't just struggle on for a few years, licking their wounds after being dropped by Mainman. Instead a third distinctive Stooges epoch occurred; wonderfully chronicled in bootlegs, underground publications, and in the memories of emergent punk superstars like Dee Dee Ramone, Patti Smith, Debbie Harry and Alan Vega. When we think in the mind's eye of Iggy & The Stooges, we think of this final renegade band of drugged out desperadoes riding involuntarily into the pharmaceutical sunset.

After being dropped by Mainman, Williamson was brought back into the fold and, in order to survive, The Stooges went out on the road and toured. They hooked up with Jeff Wald, the powerful manager and husband of Helen 'I Am Woman' Reddy. Wald booked out a Stooges tour on a handshake agreement with Iggy. Danny Sugerman, Jim Morrison's former teenage protégé, became the band's publicist cum manager.

To ease their path into Helen Reddy-land, The Stooges began to smooth their sound down a little and to fill it out. This could've incorporated honouring an earlier commitment to return Ron Asheton to guitar duties while recruiting a new bass player. Instead Williamson's muso instincts were entertained and keyboard playing jack-of-all-trades Scott Thurston, whom Williamson discovered in LA, was recruited.

Starting on July 30, 1973, the new line-up began a four-night residency at Max's Kansas City. The now-usual array of fagged-out and junked-out demi-monde superstars were in attendance; Lou Reed, Alice Cooper, The New York Dolls, Todd Rundgren, Danny Fields and a plethora of Warhol sidekicks. Mainman agents Tony Zanetta and Leee Black Childers were not too ashamed to show their faces.

Lynn Edelson (musician): "When I was working for Led Zeppelin, one night I did not go to the concert. I'm in Percy's (Robert Plant's) room and he says: 'Do whatever you want, champagne, caviar, but don't let anybody in.' Well he'd gone like an hour and there's this banging and banging on the door and I look through the peephole and it's Iggy Pop. It was at the Drake Hotel. It was during the *Houses Of The Holy* tour. It was Iggy Pop, so I figure what the hell. So I let him in and he's beet red. He's as red as that paint you have in kindergarten. I hadn't met Iggy before. I could see him shaking all over and he was perspiring, and I felt his head and he must have had a 103 fever. I got really nervous. I said, 'What did you do?' He said, 'Well, I ran out of coke so I shot up niacin.' So I'm like, 'Oh shit, we've got to get your body temperature down. Take your clothes off.' So he takes off his clothes and he lies down on

Percy's bed. Now this is getting really bad, here he is lying naked on the bed. I wrapped him up in towels and could feel his temperature going down and he fell asleep.

"A couple hours later Percy comes back and he says, 'Who the bloody hell is in my bed?' He's freaking out. And I just laughed and I said, 'Go and look.' And there's Iggy totally fucked up with towels all over him. They really thanked me. The next night I think Iggy was playing at Max's and one of Zep's road guys called me at home and said, 'All of us want to come down to the show and you know everyone there, can you make sure we have a table in the performance area.' So I set the whole thing up and they all came. I think that was the night Iggy cut himself up."

After Dark reported that, in the middle of his set during the second evening at Max's, the singer could be seen standing stage centre with blood gushing out of a number of gaping wounds on his face and body. "Insiders," the magazine confided, "reported that Iggy, distressed about his attachment to a local beauty named Bebe Buell, announced, 'My heart is broken,' and went to work with some pieces of broken glass."

"When Iggy performed he collapsed in my arms, blood coming out of his loincloth," recollects Jeffrey Brendan, Max's doorman at the time. "The only thing he said was, 'Is there a professional photographer in the house?' The story goes that Jackie Curtis said, 'I want to see blood tonight.' I think Alice Cooper, who was in the audience at the time, wrapped him in a blanket and took him to the hospital."

In due course Buell and Pop became one of rock's legendary couplings. Buell – now best known as Liv Tyler's mother – was also intimate with Todd Rundgren, with whom she was sharing a home at the time of her dalliance with Iggy, Mick Jagger, Steve Tyler of Aerosmith, and countless other lasciviously lipped no-hips rockers.

"Bebe was naïve of course about the drugs and she didn't realise the extent to which he was using them," says Victor Bockris, co-author of Buell's autobiography. "There was this great scene where he gave her this heroin and she vomited and vomited for hours. He cleaned her up and took care of her. I heard more about Iggy from girls than from anybody else. Girls just really liked him a lot, you know? He was very playful. I never knew anybody who was involved with him in a way that got intense enough for there to be a problem. It was just fun. The cool girls in NYC he actually would have enjoyed talking to. The girls he was seeing, the ones that I knew, were discriminating, astute individuals. There was a long period when people put him in the slot of being a 'punk rock character', therefore not intelligent, and it was a great relief for him to be able to hang out with women he could have a decent exchange with."

Many years later, when asked to recollect one moment in her raucous life which she would like to revisit, Bebe Buell said she'd like to be back in Max's the time Iggy did those shows. "The anticipation in the air that night," she said, "the crowd that was there, the energy being just right, rock'n'roll doesn't get any better than that."

Lenny Kaye reported that he heard some catcaller advise Iggy that "My granny dances better than you do!" Iggy, who'd been crawling across the stage, rose to his feet dramatically. Everybody turned to look at him, wondering what he was going to do next. "Will someone please pick up this glass," he requested, referring to the broken glass littered everywhere. Nobody made any move to clear it up, so he started hitting himself across the chest, smeared himself with the ubiquitous crimson blood, wiped his stained fingers on Scott Asheton's denim shirt. "The next song of the evening is entitled . . ." he announced, and then collapsed, hitting the floor with a loud thud. Lou Reed had supplied him with a fistful of valium some hours before the show. Kaye reported "two deep gashes bubbling over their seams".

With these gashes Iggy was sent to hospital for treatment. The two remaining Max's shows were postponed for a few nights until his stitches had time to set. Later the same week, when The Stooges went out on the town to catch Mott The Hoople and The New York Dolls at the Felt Forum, Iggy had to get more medical treatment because he collided with a door during the backstage soiree. He spent the Dolls' set in the Felt Forum's emergency room, causing a member of the ill-starred Dolls to comment that that was all they needed, Iggy Pop conked out backstage.

Dolls guitarist Johnny Thunders started hanging out with Iggy and with Sable Starr, whose sister Corel was still Pop's girl at the time. His association with Pop commenced the process which eventually led to Thunder's heroin addiction and destruction. Surviving Dolls guitarist Sylvain Sylvain told Thunders' biographer Nina Antonia that, "Johnny was a big Iggy Pop fan and the four of them (the Starr sisters and their respective boyfriends) were always together and one thing led to another. Johnny's the kind of guy, you turn him on to one joint and the next day he got a whole pound, so they fix together and that's when that started. Johnny began using, not regularly at first, just a little bit here and a little bit there. It turned out to be the worst thing you could ever introduce Johnny to."

"Iggy set out to turn people on to heroin," Leee Black Childers told

Nina Antonia. "I don't know for sure what his reasons were but I lived with him for eight or nine months and I watched him do it . . . It gave him something in his head, it was like sex I guess. He'd tie them off and shoot 'em up, watch the blood bloom in the syringe. Watch them have their first high and that's what he got off on."

By August 6 Iggy and the boys were back on stage at Max's. His wounds had healed so battle was recommenced.

Lenny Kaye, *Creem*: "You can't slander The Stooges," Iggy said after a round of band introductions, followed by a cooling bath of beer borrowed from an adjacent table. It was then that the newly written encore 'Open Up And Bleed' abruptly assumed its final shape. The words had been changing all week, but suddenly mumbled passages became clear, the lyrics in flick-of-the-wrist focus, the music delivered with nary a falter or misstep. 'I've been burned . . .' he sang at one point. 'I've been pushed aside, sometimes I've even fixed and died . . .' Then, 'It ain't gonna be that way no more . . .' with the emphasis on the last word."

Speaking to *After Dark* after one of the shows, Iggy let off some hot steam about the manner in which he'd been treated by Bowie and the Mainman camp. He also took note of the fact that Alice Cooper, his one-time support act and fellow purveyor of Detroit weird shit, was now emitting hit singles with something like the frequency with which Iggy was emitting vomit.

Iggy: "Personally I think David's a fine fellow. There are so many who stole a lot of shit from me, but the way David did I minded! Look at the photographs of me taken in 1970 and then look at the way David Bowie looks. Check out my lyrics and see how David Bowie has re-written them. Alice Cooper is a hell of a man, he really is. We were working out in California and he saw us working and he said, 'Ummmm!' Then he turned up in Detroit a few months later to see us work again and pick up a few more points!"

Rock Scene devoted a page to some well orchestrated industry-friendly photographs taken by ever-loyal Danny Fields. One shows Iggy, for all his gashes and geysers, doing his corporate buddy-buddy bit, arms around an old Elektra buddy, Steve Harris, now working for Clive Davis at Columbia. The Runyonesque caption reads, "Columbia Records' Steve Harris is knocked out by the crowds who have come to see Iggy". Another features the caption, "Ron Asheton watches as Jackie Curtis poses over Iggy and Lou Reed". Jackie Curtis, one of the most famous of the Warhol drag queens, was the Jackie referred to in Lou Reed's 'Walk On The Wild Side' ("Jackie has just been away/ Thought she was

James Dean for a day"). Curtis was also a close associate of Iggy's and can be seen hovering vampirically over the then-young grandfathers of punk.

Perhaps it wasn't quite the label-friendly bash that *Rock Scene* implied. "We were doing a live show with Iggy and all these record people were supposed to show," Sam Hood, who booked the bands at Max's, recalled. "He was very fucked up. Here was Iggy laying on the floor in the dressing room asking Clive Davis to piss on him. Iggy completely lost it." Maybe Davis enjoyed this sort of thing. Certainly Max's was a strange gig to do, and a lot of intense people showed up with intense action on their minds.

The Jeff Wald-booked tour proceeded productively through August and September, taking in Canada, Philadelphia, Washington, and points in between. Punk rock was getting going on New York's Lower East Side but The Stooges were drifting off into a world of their own, one informed by Glam Rock and the New York deviant scene. They shocked many a one-horse town audience into a state of submission. "We used to play for the lowest common denominator, all the bone-heads and the most sexually aggressive girls in the town," Iggy says. "Behind them was anyone who was just interested in mental aberration. A lot of disaffected high school kids, mentally deranged people. Guys who had just come back from Vietnam really dug us." George Smith, writing in *Village Voice* in 2000, endorsed Pop's own assessment of The Stooges' followers: "Motorcycle gangsters, their floozies, and lovers of skank weed and roller derby, an audience of such presumed shallow pocket that advertisers ignored them."

Nick Kent: "It was on this tour, too, that Scott Asheton gradually began losing his mind. He started developing this interesting theory that man becomes automatically closer to God when he decides to wear the same set of clothes 24 hours a day, every day. Then he started developing a strange relationship with his towel, the towel he always used onstage to douse the sweat from his body while playing. Sometimes he'd wear it over his head throughout the entire gig. He later told the rest of The Stooges that hiding under it helped him ward off the negative forces forever preying on the band, but it probably had more to do with getting hit in the face with eggs and rotten fruit thrown by angry audiences night after night. Still, when Iggy took Scott, or "Rock" as he now called himself – it was short for "Rock Action" – out on a double-date with two extremely attractive and sophisticated young women in a high-class restaurant and watched speechless as the drummer commenced to pull out his old towel and drop it over his head before he'd even ordered the first course, he knew it was over for The Stooges."

When James Williamson spoke with Ken Shimamoto he had particularly strong recollections of a show in Philadelphia, a town which boasted a Stooges fan club: "This gig was one of the key ones for the band. Columbia was there to record us in an attempt to get some product out of The Stooges. By this time Iggy had completely lost it. He was just completely out of control, beyond anything remotely related to sanity. Anyway, he took these two lines of THC just before the gig. He'd never taken it before and had no real concept of how powerful the stuff is. I can still recall the promoter's reaction when he arrived. He was one of the biggest in the States too. We turned up about an hour late – and when he saw us he took out his gold watch and threw it against the wall in a mixture of blind rage and complete despair. By this time Iggy literally couldn't stand up and couldn't put two words together straight. So the band just had to go on and start playing while three roadies got a hold of Pop, two for his arms and one for his legs, and threw him on to the stage. Somehow he fell into the audience and someone stuck a peanut butter and jelly sandwich on his chest which made it look like he'd been stabbed. So they closed the show down after only three numbers."

Chris Ehring (Stooges road manager, '73/'74): "He walked away from the edge of the stage and fell off. Just stumbled off and wiggled his way into the audience. People were throwing him around, pushing him from side to side. He turns around and his whole chest is dripping red. I said, 'Someone has slashed him with a knife!' I got one of the equipment men from Mott The Hoople and we ran down and dragged Iggy back onstage, only to find out that it was a jelly sandwich smeared all over him."

In September '73 The Stooges showed that, despite everything, they were not a spent creative force. The band went into The Doors' LA studio, Workshop, with in-demand producer Todd Rundgren, Iggy's rival for the affections of Bebe Buell, at the controls. "Working where Jim Morrison worked is like being in heaven," Iggy enthused. "Jim Morrison was my idol – if he were alive today I'd die for him." But the idea was not to die heroically but to turn out a single. This didn't materialise. While in town the band undertook a five-night residency at Iggy's old stamping ground, the Whisky A Go-Go. Since LA was the global capital of sleazy drug-addled rock'n'roll values, the shows sold out.

Phonograph magazine: "It must be demanding having to live up to your legend, but Iggy did enough every night to keep his rep intact. Whether falling into the crowded dance floor, pouring pitchers of water on himself, doing his famous dive across the stage into the mike stand, or dry humping into the thin air, it was the Ig all the way."

Danny Fields: "At the Whisky in LA Iggy went around to each booth, to people like Warren Beatty and Jack Nicholson, because it was a big celebrity night. He went to the VIP booths and threatened the Hollywood stars that he was not going to perform unless they came up with some money so he could pay his dope dealer who was waiting backstage. So they did. They took a little collection and gave him the money and he went back and got straight. Finally the lights went down, the spotlight came up, and he stood there at the microphone and promptly passed out, had to be carried out. No two shows were the same."

Despite the usual intense theatricals on offer, *Phonograph* was not taken in by the high jinks aspect of the late-period Stooges. The magazine's critic, Mike Saunders, saw the fundamental creative cracks that were showing on the surface: "Most glaringly, they had only a few songs worked up, with the result that both sets every night were almost identical. Iggy's vocals, strangely enough, were the other weak part of the show. The PA was constantly screwed up, with his voice often inaudible as a result. And when it was working, Iggy simply didn't pay enough attention to his singing. His stage act is equally important, sure, but for someone who is as great a vocal stylist as Iggy is in the Dylan/Lou Reed monotone tradition, he should get down and get with it . . . he wasn't even doing dog barks any more! But that's pretty irrelevant. What's more important here is that The Stooges have come back from the dead to become one of the most powerful groups in the world today. They still have their prime asset: stark energy. Williamson's addition has made a potential super-group, and Ron Asheton has proven to be an equal dynamo on bass, playing it almost as if it were a rhythm guitar."

"After *Raw Power* I just went out and toured until I dropped," Iggy told the *LA Times* in 1977. "As soon as I was dismissed by my management firm, I knew I was playing a losing game. But I thought what I was doing was so good. I was so proud of it that I was determined to let people see it. So I tried to organise things myself. I went after any bookings I could get. It was crazy: five nights at the Whisky, four at Max's, then five in Atlanta, two in Vancouver. There was no pattern to it. I'd just do the shows and then stumble back to LA with a couple of hundred bucks and just flop for a week until I could go out again. Whatever I didn't spend on the motels, I'd spend on drugs."

In October the strolling minstrels did a show in Memphis with the equally doomed New York Dolls. The local rednecks spotted the fact that there were queers incoming so the hall was full of cops. The Memphis

Board of Review were in attendance to see for themselves if, as legend had it, the Dolls were a gang of female impersonators. Female impersonating was illegal in Memphis. The Dolls set was closed down after an hour with David Johansen being taken to the local jail for disorderly conduct. He had kissed an ardent male admirer who rushed the stage.

Fag rock was breaking out all over the States. At a Stooges show in Atlanta, Elton John showed up with his pop star retinue, commandeered The Stooges dressing room, and walked on stage wearing a gorilla suit. Iggy was in pretty bad shape when Elton chose to join him. He'd spent the previous night taking a mountain of downers and sleeping in the shrubbery. When he woke up in the bushes he couldn't speak a word. "A doctor had to shoot me full of methedrine just so I could talk," he said. "I was seeing triple and had to hold on to the microphone stand to support myself. Suddenly this gorilla walks out from backstage and holds me up in the air while I'm still singing. I was out of my mind with fear. I thought it was a real gorilla."

Chris Ehring: "I went back to the dressing room when someone tried to physically stop me. I said, 'This is our dressing room!' Someone from the club said, 'Elton John is in there.' 'Big fucking deal! What's he doing in there?' I go in and there's Elton John getting into a gorilla outfit. 'He's going to go up on stage and sing with Iggy.' I just laughed. 'Fine. Maybe I should warn the boys?' 'Oh, no, he wants it to be a surprise. He wants to come out on stage during 'Search And Destroy'. He was supposed to scare Iggy! Scare Iggy in this gorilla suit? 'You don't seem to understand what these guys are about. They are from Detroit. They're not going to let you up on their stage!' Moments later, out of the dressing room comes Elton dressed as a gorilla, and he goes up on the stage. The band all look at him. 'Who is this?' James looks at me and shrugs his shoulders. Iggy looks over and walks away. The gorilla starts chasing him, pushing him away. It's really bad."

"Elton's a swell guy," gushed Iggy after the incident. "Be nice to see this mutual admiration turn into something more concrete," said *Creem*.[*]

After the performance Elton told *Creem*: "I simply can't understand why he's not a huge star."

The next stop on the road-goes-on-forever tour was Washington, DC and the prestigious, conservative Kennedy Center for the Performing Arts. The Stooges were sharing the bill with fellow Bowie refugees Mott The Hoople.

[*] Davey Johnstone, Elton's guitarist, also expressed admiration for the power playing of Stooges guitarist James Williamson.

James Williamson: "We stayed at the Watergate Hotel, and Iggy and Ron had some chicks down from New York to stay, see the show and stuff. These chicks came in with this goddamn crystal THC. Crystal THC you don't fuck around with; a little bit goes a long way. Iggy probably thought it was cocaine, so he sticks his nose down there and does about six lines; he was so out of his mind that he was seeing green Martians, couldn't talk, couldn't do anything. We had to go on stage in like half an hour and it was really serious; he was so b-a-a-a-d he should have gone to hospital but we had a gig to do. We needed him!"

The end of '73 found the band back in New York for a variety of club shows. On New Year's Eve they played the Academy of Music. Blue Oyster Cult topped the bill, the newly formed Kiss were added on at the last minute and, a harbinger of things to come, The Stooges were billed as "Iggy Pop".

Anne Wehrer: "Andy Warhol called me, 'I hear Iggy's going to commit suicide on stage. You have to stop him.' The last act – designing his own death – could I interfere? I went as a *Penthouse* reporter with a bodyguard-photographer, Bob 'White Eagle' Hendrickson. Iggy sang with demonic energy, in his hot pink pants and high top black boots. But his body control was off: backbends collapsed, and he missed the ramp falling into the audience. He pleaded to be touched. He asked to be destroyed but with no intention of destroying himself. Backstage he was flat out on the red concrete floor, rolling in spilled beer, dead cigarettes and broken dreams."

Wehrer met up with Iggy again on New Year's Day 1974 to do her *Penthouse* interview and photo session. "Let's go somewhere I won't be noticed," he said. Wehrer says this wasn't easy since he had long blond hair and a white jacket brilliantly embroidered with peacocks. They talked about doing the book which in 1982 became *I Need More*, perhaps the best autobiography ever written by a rock star, albeit a ghost-written job not entirely obsessed with factual accuracy.

The New York non-suicide gig was recorded for a possible live album but by this time, amid unprecedented controversy, Iggy's backer at Columbia Clive Davis quit the company and went off to found Arista, a lucrative venture which, amongst other things, gave the world Patti Smith, the mid-period Kinks, Barry Manilow and Whitney Houston, along with two of Iggy Pop's best solo albums and one of his worst. Pop now had a serious downer habit and was drinking all the time. He talked about this period as being his vodka tour. With Clive Davis gone, the band no longer had a foothold at Columbia – they were dropped when their contract came up for review early in '74. This didn't stop them either.

Despite themselves and despite everything else, The Stooges remained contenders at that moment in time; still working hard, drawing impressive crowds to mainly 1,500–5,000 capacity venues and selling them out. The press continued to bend over backwards, forgiving them for their serial transgressions. Iggy was settling into a pretty solid and professional stage persona and the band had an identifiable act and image. Their drug adventures were in no way different from, or more extreme than, the excesses of far more successful contemporaneous acts, like Led Zeppelin or the Stones, who stalked the Seventies in a maelstrom of coke, heroin, pussy and Jack Daniel's. Like there was no tomorrow.

Road managers often have an opportunity to take a long cold look at how the bands they work for are faring out there on the isolated, unhealthy, claustrophobic road. Chris Ehring felt that The Stooges, hicks from the sticks themselves, did better when they played out of town, away from cosmopolitan watering holes like LA and New York. He reckoned that at important shows, when anyone and everyone was swanning around backstage, Iggy succumbed to stage fright. It seemed to Ehring that Beautiful People-style flotsam and jetsam were always in the metropolitan dressing rooms saying, 'I'm your friend Iggy. Take some of these drugs.' Ehring felt that fucking up on drugs always happened at the shows that really mattered. "At the 'nowhere' shows, he did brilliant shows. Just brilliant performances," he says.

"The reaction has been encouraging," Iggy told *MM*'s Chris Charlesworth. "I've spent a few nights sleeping in cars, and there have been a few problems, but all in all I'm much happier than when I was a recluse. I'm playing and that's the important thing. I think I've surprised the audiences who come to expect some kind of clown show. It's not that at all, it's a rock'n'roll band."

The band that refused to die kept on working hard, coming up with strongly argued songs like 'I Got Nothing', 'Cock In My Pocket' and 'She Creatures Of The Hollywood Hills'. Artistically, they kept firing on all cylinders, writing the bible on sparse elegant punk.

Ron Asheton: "We had nothing, no management, no record company. Or the management . . . we'd go through a couple of managers, but we didn't know anything. We were lost unless we were on the road. Basically, we were living in cheap hotels and weekly apartments. We just played. When your costume is so filthy that you literally stand it up in the corner at night, or go, 'Don't hang that there, it stinks so bad!' We had to hide our clothes in the bathroom or something, then had to put them on every night, never being any place long enough . . . it was a big thrill to do laundry."

Chris Ehring: "It was a disorganised tour. We didn't have any money at all. We'd just go out and play shows. No one wanted to touch a band that was somewhat unreliable in their attendance – not in their ability to draw people, but their ability to put on a show! When we showed up at a place to play we had to scrounge around to get our equipment. We had to really hustle here and there. We had to pull a lot of moves just to get ourselves staying in a hotel, to eat, to get rental cars, etc. It was very tough for a band of five guys to support themselves playing that kind of music on their own. It was a nickel and dime operation."

A three-way exchange between Danny Sugerman, Pop's pal Corel Starr, and Iggy appeared in the limited-circulation fanzine *Heavy Metal Digest* in 1974.

> Danny Sugerman: "What's the band been doing?"
> Iggy: "You know damn well what we're doing! I don't know what the band's been doing. Last night I fell down. I drank a buncha Boones Farm and got really drunk and fell down and cut my cheek open, see?"
> Danny Sugerman: "Did you get sick?"
> Iggy: "I never get sick on alcohol."
> Danny Sugerman: "You're leaving for 20 gigs this afternoon through February, are you looking forward to the tour?"
> Iggy: "Well, I better not be looking back! No, I'd rather go to the beach."
> Danny Sugerman: "Your next album, when and if . . ."
> Iggy: "See, I don't know about the next album 'cause there are all these different companies and I don't know who to deal with. We're off of Columbia due to, ummm, differences."
> Danny Sugerman: "Is there any truth in the rumour that The Stooges have gone musical?"
> Iggy: "Yeah, yeah! That's true! We've gone harmonies and the whole bit. Even some acoustic guitar."
> Danny Sugerman: "What's your relationship with Elton John?"
> Iggy (backbending on the floor): "I don't know."
> Corel: "He's hot for Jim's bod."
> Iggy: "He's not either! Well, maybe but I don't know. He's a nice man and so am I."
> Danny Sugerman: "You went on record as saying you never were a punk."
> Iggy: "Who did I tell that to?"

Danny Sugerman: "Gomper."

Iggy: "Who? Oh yeah, I get it, well I ain't. I never was a punk. It's just that I'm so smart that people just don't know, you know? I'm just way over other people's heads. You know what I mean. There are so many people who wanted so bad to be literate but I was literate when I was five years old so I got past that."

Corel (laughing): "Sure, Jim."

Iggy: "It's true. When I was five years old, man, I had a bigger vocabulary than you do today!"

Danny Sugerman: "It must be awfully difficult finding a female mate who can match your extra superior intelligence."

Iggy: "I figure any girl I really liked wouldn't like anything about me. You know. Because all those girls who like my music I don't like. I literally can't touch them . . ."

Danny Sugerman: "Some say you're bent on death."

Iggy: "Ah, what do they know. I'm going to see 80! Everybody is saying he's going to die in two days, but they're wrong! No, uh, uh, not this boy. I'm OK."

Corel: "If you were meant to die, you would've died a long time ago."

Iggy: "Yeah, that's right. I've come close but close is a lot, lot different than that same thing. It'll take a lot to kill me. A helluva lot . . . The music we used to play was like a cross between ELP and ELO. No kidding. Really, it was. The majesties, not the instruments. I was on organ. It's the truth. It was before we ever went on stage. It was after I went out and saw all these trashy bands that I said, 'Well, people like the trashy bands, they don't like the good bands, so I might as well be trashy.' I decided to outdo all those kinda guys I hated at their own game, and I did. And I won. And I liked it! I called a nigger a nigger in Mass. last week. That's pretty bold. You know what I mean? You just don't say that sort of stuff in front of 3,000 people. But he really was. I mean he was niggering. Niggering out, grabbing at my leg and microphone cord. I said, 'Stop that you damn nigger!' and that takes guts!"

In February '74 The Stooges did some heartland gigs back home in the Detroit region. One of these shows took place at the Rock and Roll Farm in Wayne. "It was a sleazy club – a biker beer bar. Sure to be a riot!" Chris Ehring recalls. "It was a very small club and we rolled in there with all these amps. Eric, our equipment man, said, 'We'll blow this place out. This is impossible.' I called our agent and said, 'We're not playing here. This is crazy.' They just said, 'It's a day off and you need the money.' So we played it. Of course a riot ensues. Bikers are pushing each other, slamming their heads on the floor. It was horrible."

The Scorpions, a notorious Detroit motorcycle gang, were there to initiate a new member into their ranks. These biker initiations are abnormally pent-up, seedy, and fetid affairs. This one included big fun such as throwing eggs at The Stooges and punching Iggy with knuckle gloves. The road couldn't really go on forever, not in this case anyway. The positive end of The Stooges was now very close at hand.

Iggy, *Punk*: "Eggs kept flying up on the stage, and as the set went on I was getting really sick of it. So I said, 'OK, stop the show right now!' I'm calling the fucker down, and everybody just clear out. So everybody clears out and here's this guy about six foot three, like 300 pounds, with a knuckle glove on up to his elbow, with little studs on it. So I said, 'Well, what the fuck.' I might as well get it over with. So I put down my mike and stepped out and it was just like seeing a train coming. Bam! He just got me, but he didn't deck me. He couldn't knock me down. It was real weird. I kept standing up but I couldn't hit him. Finally the blood got to be too much for him so he just stopped and said, 'OK, you're cool.' I didn't feel so cool. But we went back on and played 'Louie Louie'."

That night Iggy crashed with this girl he was "going out" with, who lived in what he called "a straight home in the suburbs". He didn't have any clothes other than the ballet costume he'd been wearing onstage when he got his battering. In the morning her mother had to come to terms with a man in a bloody ballet costume sitting down to breakfast and greeting her with a chipper "Hi!" "To add insult to injury," he said, "it was a chick that didn't even screw."

The next show was at the Michigan Palace in Detroit. Iggy made one of his cavalier promotional radio appearances on WABX – Russ Gibb's station – where he challenged the entire Scorpions gang to come down to The Stooges gig at the Palace. "The Scorpions sent this asshole down to egg me," he proclaimed in his now-familiar incendiary radio style. "So I say, come on down, Scorpions, any Scorpions, let's have it out and see if you're man enough to deal with the fucking Stooges!"

Security at the Michigan Palace was understandably tight and neurotic by showtime. The Stooges – they were on their home turf – summoned their own tooled-up posse front of stage but hostilities were expected and, in due course, manifested themselves. Iggy went looking for trouble and trouble found him.

Iggy: "It became 'the last ever Stooges gig' tape, *Metallic KO*, with a picture of me on the front of it, knocked out cold. And you can hear all sorts of things on the tape flying through the air – shovels, four-gallon jugs, M–80s, blah blah – but our lady fans in the front rows threw a lot of beautiful underwear, which I thought was sweet."

It seemed like the entire Scorpions gang came down to the Michigan Palace. They started their assault with beer, wine bottles, rotten fruit, and vegetables. The Stooges had their own arsenal backstage, with pals and roadies willing to defend their turf. The band did not, as expected, get destroyed. Their loyal defenders showed grace under pressure and The Scorpions didn't close down the gig.

"Who out there hates The Stooges?" Iggy asked the baying horde. "Hands up who hates The Stooges! We . . . we don't hate you. We don't even care."

The show was recorded on a four-track tape recorder and extracts from those tapes which were made into *Metallic KO* were eventually released in 1976, as punk rock exploded, by Skydog in France. Lester Bangs said that, while nobody got killed that night at the Michigan Palace, *Metallic KO* "is the only live album I know where you can actually hear hurled beer bottles breaking against guitar strings."

Ron Asheton: "That recording was made by my friend Michael Tipton who lives in Detroit. I said it was OK for him to set up his little four-track machine and record the gig for fun. He gave us each a copy. Iggy lost his. James lost his and my brother lost his. I had the only copy because I save everything. So I had the tape and James goes, 'I've got a class in engineering and I need a project. Can I borrow your tape that Tipton gave you? I lost mine.' I never got the tape back. The next thing I know, Iggy and James booted my tape to Skydog for $2,000. Michael Tipton was furious. He recorded it! They didn't give me a penny."

Iggy denies any involvement in the sale. He says that, without his knowledge, Williamson sold Marc Zermati of Skydog the rights to get some quick money and that Zermati then took off to France where he figured Iggy couldn't find him. After an initial French release in July 1976, Zermati sold the rights on the album to the US label Import Records. They released it in the US in the spring of 1977. Given to the world at a moment when people sought to understand and like punk rock, *Metallic KO* became an aural document of some significance.

The night of the Detroit *Metallic KO* gig Iggy and Williamson talked with Lester Bangs, Iggy's gullible Boswell. Williamson was in oddly upbeat form: "It's all finally worked out like we've always planned," he told Bangs. If the nihilistic dead end back alley he and Pop had backed themselves into was what they'd "always planned", their strategy was pretty weird. "We've worked more in the past few months than in the past two and a half years," he correctly pointed out. "We're doing it the hard way and the right way. I'm not gonna say it's all on the up and up, because it's not. We've got a lot of problems right now; we have a reputation to live down, and we still make mistakes. But our following is getting stronger."

Ron Asheton: "There were a lot of things. The Bowie-Iggy link for one thing. Iggy was always in the papers, they wrote about him as the new rock star who was heading for a fantastic solo career. He read about how great he was, and how he could do much better without The Stooges. The shows were often billed just as Iggy Pop. All this created a void between Iggy and the band . . . he was physically and mentally wrecked. He had driven himself too hard, and he was doing lots of downers. He became so nervous and tense that he had to take downers just to relax."

After Michigan Palace The Stooges decamped to Ann Arbor one last time. A few days before they were due to go back on the road Iggy phoned Ron at home. "We had a few days off," Ron says. "I was at home with my mother, and Iggy suddenly calls me one day and he goes, 'Look, I'm sorry Ron, but I have to quit. I can't go on any longer. I just can't handle it any longer.'"

Iggy: "We had another tour to go on and I just said, 'Stop! Time out!' Because I can't stand to go out on stage and not feel proper about what I'm doing . . . The shows were getting crummy. They were violent, nasty. Attendance, ironically, was picking up. But I thought I should quit. I didn't want to look back on all those shows and think that they had been bad. I thought it was better to take a break, even if it meant that I might never be able to get started again."

Jimmy Silver: "They were too undisciplined. They were too arrogant – in a nice way – a way that I admired. They were just too loose, really. They didn't have anything focused on success, the way you have to do it. There was no one whipping them into shape. No one could really control them and hold all the pieces together."

CHAPTER 14

Living In *Kill City* – Overdosed And On Your Knees

"The two brothers, they get some cheques from publishing and some small royalties and some other bootleg royalties. They have bands in Detroit, and one of the guys has a sideline in B-monster movies, but locally, I mean, infinitesimally low-budget monster movies. They're eccentric people, you know. One of the guys died, Dave Alexander, the original bass player. I kicked him out of the band because he couldn't fucking play, well, at one point he just wouldn't do the work basically, and then he made a lot of money on the stock market, and drank himself to death. He died of pneumonia, complicated by alcoholism. He died in his twenties. And James Williamson, the last guitar player, he's done well: he's doing something in Silicon Valley, with computers. He's like sort of a tennis-playing, BMW-driving, cappuccino-sniffing dude."

– Iggy

"Maybe the stuff I did with Iggy is legendary now, but at the time we were living like dogs – hardly ever eating, never sleeping, drugs like you wouldn't believe, burning ourselves out like maniacs. You can't live like that for very long."

– James Williamson, *Bomp* (1977)

IN February 1974 Iggy Pop quit Ann Arbor for LA where he sometimes crashed with Danny Sugerman, sometimes shared an apartment with James Williamson and was sometimes homeless. He went into freefall. By the early months of 1975 Williamson and Pop were living in a small apartment in a building on Sunset Strip that was, according to Nick Kent, inhabited almost exclusively by prostitutes and drug dealers.

"Iggy was in such bad odour with the rest of LA," Kent claimed, "that most of the dealers refused to let him into their apartments."

In line with his upwardly mobile aspirations, Williamson was playing around with a rhythm section made up of Tony and Hunt Sales, the sons of Michigan TV celebrity comedian Soupy Sales. The Sales boys, who'd worked with Todd Rundgren and Ray Manzarek from The Doors, had become pally with The Stooges while the band were living in LA between '72 and '73.

Their association with Williamson was the bedrock of the career they enjoyed together over the next decade. Becoming an integral part of the Bowie/Pop circus, they played on some of the iconic albums and tours of the era before their reputations were destroyed by Bowie's abortive Eighties attempt to become the lead singer in a regular rock group, Tin Machine. If Bowie hadn't pushed them out front in silly Eighties suits to share the blame for his folly, they might be more fondly remembered today.

Bob Gruen: "Soupy Sales had this silly kids show, so silly that folks would smoke pot and watch it. You know that kind of thing . . . a phenomenon that doesn't necessarily exist any more. The show was a big deal until he did a very silly routine about getting kids to go to their daddy's pocket, take out a dollar, and post it to Soupy. After that they fired him."

The 1965 stunt referred to by Gruen involved Sales telling young kids to take "green pieces of paper" featuring the images of dead presidents from their dad's pocket and mail the pieces of paper to Soupy. Popular mythology suggested that as much as $80,000 came in as a result of this appeal but Soupy said this was a huge exaggeration, that it was just a few dollars. Iggy was soon jamming with Williamson and the Sales brothers.

Ron Asheton also washed up in LA, jamming with one-time Stooge Jimmy Recca and Amboy Dukes drummer K.J. Knight. Iggy was jamming with both bands and drinking heavily. It was an amiable and cooperative situation; small town Michigan boys in LA with their dreams and aspirations in tatters. Both bands took turns rehearsing in the house of Ray Manzarek. Things were taking a distinctly odd turn and Pop's life was evolving into a big Doors-like situation. Danny Sugerman was managing both Iggy and Manzarek. People around Sugerman who were used to the big bucks world of The Doors were aghast to see him involving himself with Pop.

Danny Sugerman: "Friends in the business thought I was nuts for taking him on. Still others (like The Doors' business manager, Gabe Reynolds) said it was an insult to Morrison's memory. I owed him a

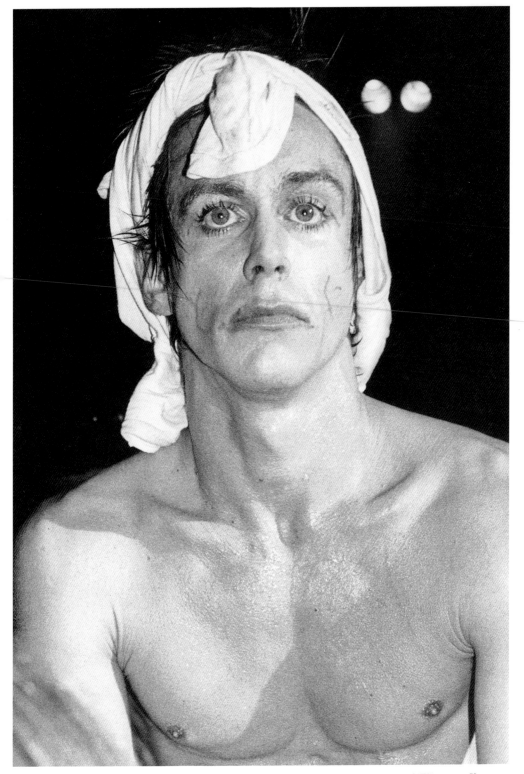

"Balls in place of brains. Brains in place of soul. Where is the soul? Where is the love? Where am I? Which mask are you?" (*Bob Gruen/Star File*)

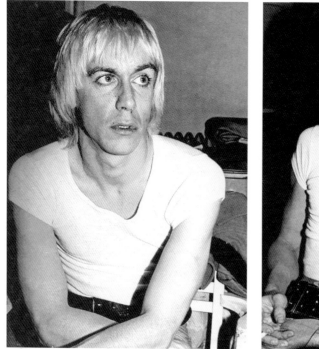

Talking to *Punk* magazine before heading for Berlin, 1976.
(*Roberta Bayley*)

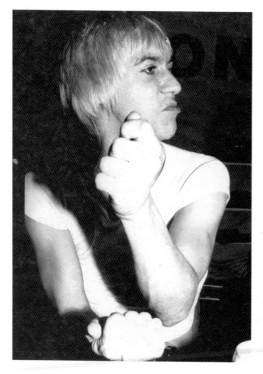

Iggy confronts the Blank generation, with Richard Hell (above) and the Ramones (below), 1976.
(*Roberta Bayley*)

With Bowie in Red Square, 1976. (*Andrew Kent*)

Bowie does his fair imitation of a bar pianist while Iggy works the crowd, Palladium, NYC, March 18, 1977. (*Bob Gruen/Star File*)

Party animals. Iggy and Bowie in Manhattan, 1977.
(*Bob Gruen/Star File*)

Iggy's first major TV exposure, with Dinah Shore,
April 1977. (*Andrew Kent*)

Iggy and son Eric defend the homelands, Detroit, 1977.
(*Andrew Kent*)

Lust For Life tour, 1977. (*Andrew Kent*)

Iggy takes some lickin', with Debbie Harry, 1977. (*Bob Gruen/Star File*)

Iggy backed by the Patti Smith Group, NYC, 1977; left to right: Ivan Kral, Jay Dee Daugherty, Lenny Kaye. Kral went on to join Iggy's band. (*Bob Gruen/Star File*)

On the road to god knows where. *New Values* tour, 1979, with ex-Pistol Glen Matlock (left). (*LFI*)

At breaking point. The Arista offices, Soho, London, 1979. (*Bruno Blum/Star File*)

An early example of Pop art. (*Mick Rock/Star File*)

better follow-up. Rock'n'roll had become big business in the past couple of years and Iggy wasn't considered a 'good investment'. He was an insult to the lawyers and accountants who were running the music industry."

July 3, 1974 was the third anniversary of Jim Morrison's death. At the Whisky A Go-Go there was a tribute show featuring Manzarek's band with Williamson on guitar and Iggy on vocals. Iggy did a set of Doors songs. During 'L.A. Woman' he improvised: "Jim Morrison died today, Jim Morrison was more beautiful than any girl in this town, and now he's dead, now I cry." There was even talk of an Iggy solo album to be produced by Manzarek. Pop was floating effortlessly into reactionary musical waters which would have horrified Stooges fans, while Williamson nurtured a musical vision of himself as a sort of New Wave Eric Clapton.

For one crazy season Pop was lead singer in the new band that Überhippy Ray Manzarek was putting together. "With the right backing," Manzarek told *Rolling Stone*, "Iggy could be really sensational. He's so dynamic on stage. Right now our friendship is at the bare bones beginning. After I produce his album, who knows what will happen? But I'd only add a singer to the band if it made the music better. I'd never get a singer to dance around or a lead dancer."

One morning Sugerman was woken by a phone call from a hysterical rich girl who was making no sense, emitting babble. He hung up and a few minutes later the phone rang again. This time the girl was almost coherent. She wanted to know if Sugerman handled Iggy Pop. He cautiously admitted that he tried to look after him.

"Well, you better get over here," she informed him, pleading. "He's at the bottom of the driveway chopping up daddy's Mercedes with the garden axe."

"What do you want me to do about it?" Sugerman demanded, starting to have a bad feeling about the conversation.

"You better come and get him before daddy gets home from the airport, or else my mom is going to call the police. He's totally crazy, please come and get him before we all get in trouble. I'm in enough already . . ."

Danny Sugerman: "As I pulled into the driveway, I passed a bright candy-apple red convertible Mercedes with wide gashes in the tyres and sides, windows splintered out, chopped up and gouged with some sort of large blade or a hatchet. Feeling a distinct invasion of dread, and not seeing Iggy, I raced up the driveway further, into a clearing before a six-car garage. A fleet of cars stood inside, a Jeep, a station wagon, a

Mercedes Benz sedan, and over in the corner by the lawn was a shining black customised Maserati. Standing on the hood was Iggy, axe swung over his head. He brought it down with a loud crash into the bumper, over and over again, ripping the shit out of the steel frame."

Another sunny California day Sugerman got a call from the president of the San Francisco branch of Iggy's gay fan club. He told Sugerman they were "sending him home".

"Be ready," the president warned.

Sugerman got a distinct feeling of apprehension. "Be ready for what?" he queried.

"He's a little out of it," the president said, as if that explained everything.

"What do you mean 'a little'? Define 'a little'."

"Well, maybe a lot," the fan club president chuckled before hanging up.

Sugerman had no idea what went on between Iggy and his gay buddies but suspected that it involved loads of brainwashing, orgies, and massive drug parties. It took the gays three days to get Pop to the airport and it took the star two more days to negotiate his way, by plane, from 'Frisco to LA. When Sugerman eventually went to the airport to pick up his charge he found that – not for the first time – the San Francisco boys had feminised their hero. His hair was dyed black and he actually thought that he was a woman, sporting a full-length white dress with a slit up the side, a "real cute" burgundy hat, a burgundy belt, burgundy pumps, and burgundy nail polish. There was a big bulge pushing up against the front of his rather tight dress.

Iggy: "I had a very intense and interesting bunch of male groupies. And I'm really perversely proud of it in a way, 'cause in the Seventies, when I was my baddest, it was just after *Raw Power* had been out, and it was down in the 30-cent bins, I was dropped by the record company, suspended by the management, and I had nowhere to live. I was also the most hardcore performer in America. These guys, these fags from San Francisco, decided, 'He's the one.' I mean, basically, they just wanted someone to party around with. They started this Iggy Pop fan club and they sent me this package with all these good drugs, which was really bad 'cause I would take them all. They were basically these San Francisco gay junkies who were living on ADT, which means they'd get a really big cheque from the government, and they were hustling.

"That was the first time I ever saw the word 'hardcore' applied to music, basically it was 'Iggy Pop Fanclub Hardcore'. They publicised in things like *Creem* magazine: 'Send in your money and you get a silver membership card.' These guys just basically liked to party and have a good time. They'd indulge me in whatever adventures I wanted to get into. Sometimes that would turn out really good. They'd do stuff like get me a photographer's roll, you know, like a big roll of that paper, and rent me the stand, and I'd paint for a week while they'd make me stuff. It would be really cool stuff and sometimes it would be really sordid. Once in a while, once in a while, if I was like really asleep and they didn't think I was watching or anything, they'd come and they'd try to pull my nuts. I'd go, 'No! Get off me! God, you boys.' But I liked them because I'd never been a big fan of butch America. It's just too fucking stupid, and they were culturally really aware and I dug that."

Things didn't go too well on the Manzarek rehearsal front either. Jim Morrison may well have been the Lizard King with a penchant for all manner of mojo-working antics, but his pampered hit single Hollywood lifestyle had been on a whole different level from Iggy's recent scuzzy history at the bottom of the barrel. Manzarek, a pretty mellow collegiate individual, was not entirely ready to go searching and destroying. A recent pop chart star, he had to visit Hollywood jail in person to rescue Iggy from the clutches of the police.

Danny Sugerman: "He'd wandered out of the house, down Laurel Canyon, over to Alice Cooper's house where he'd borrowed some clothes from Alice's girlfriend Cindy Laing and onto Hollywood Boulevard where they'd picked him up. 'What's the charge?' I asked him. 'Impersonating a female,' he said, as if they didn't know a real woman when they saw one."

Sugerman called Manzarek and said, "Man, your lead singer is in jail. We gotta go down and bail Iggy out of jail."

"Oh no, now what?" said Manzarek, who'd witnessed a fair amount of rock'n'roll Babylon in his time.

"Iggy's in the Hollywood jail," said Sugerman.

"What's he in jail for?" Manzarek asked patiently.

"I don't know," said Sugerman, "something about drunk and disorderly.

Manzarek, who eventually decided he didn't need to form a band with a kid like Iggy, said, "Lewd and disorderly was a more accurate description of the condition that got Iggy arrested."

One night, as part of his ongoing efforts to probe the depths of his psyche, Iggy showed up at his favourite LA stomping ground, Rodney Bingenheimer's English Disco. He got on stage and improvised a play of his own making called *Murder Of The Virgin*. With an ongoing Marlon Brando-like desire for public self-mutilation, he cut his chest with a knife. The show was considered to be a gross-out by all who saw it, but ace publicist Sugerman got on the phone to the media claiming that *Murder Of The Virgin* was his then-housemate's "most totally committed artistic statement ever."

Iggy's next major Hollywood appearance was at the New York Dolls' "Hollywood Street Revival and Trash Dance", also known as "The Death of Glitter". Men of integrity on the bill that night included the likes of Rodney Bingenheimer, master of ceremonies Kim Fowley, and Michael Des Barres. Iggy's band was a strong one, featuring Williamson, Manzarek, and Nigel Harrison who subsequently resurfaced in Blondie. Pushing back the boundaries of the place where noise, ideas and music collide remained strictly off the menu. Instead Pop opted for a covers set including shockingly obvious white boy blues-ish cabaret-rock standards like 'Route 66', 'Nadine', 'Subterranean Homesick Blues' and 'Everybody Needs Somebody To Love'.

And the good news just kept on coming. Original Stooges bass player Dave Alexander died on February 10, 1975 under somewhat mysterious circumstances. He was 28. Danny Fields was informed, probably incorrectly, that he died of malnutrition, possibly because of anorexia. Ron Asheton claims that his death was caused from an ulcer due to his excessive drinking. Jimmy Silver talked with Alexander shortly before his death. "I got a call from Dave. He said, 'My folks inherited some money and I've been playing the stock market with it.' I was later told that he made hundreds of thousands of dollars!"

Ron Asheton last met up with Dave early in '75, when Alexander drove him to an airport near Ann Arbor.

"I'll be back in town in two weeks. I'll see you then," Asheton said as they reached the terminal.

"No, this is goodbye," Alexander said.

"What do you mean?" asked a taken aback Asheton.

"No, this is really goodbye. I won't see you again," Alexander repeated.

"Well, that's ridiculous." Asheton said. "I'm going to be back here and you're not going anywhere." True to his word, Asheton was back in Ann Arbor two weeks later but, true to his word, Dave Alexander was dead. His mother had him cremated immediately.

There had always been fierce tension between Pop and Alexander. When Iggy and Williamson called around to Ron Asheton's place in LA to tell him the bad news about his old schoolfriend, Iggy announced, "Zander's dead and I don't care because he wasn't my friend anymore." But behind Iggy's feigned indifference, reality gradually sank in. Scott

Asheton reckoned that the death was the final straw, that Iggy was now comprehensively crushed and right in the middle of a real mental breakdown.

Having just turned 28 James Osterberg got in touch with the Neuropsychiatric Institute at UCLA* and told them he'd been addicted for a long time to very heavy drugs. Since then, from time to time, he'd come off them. "But now I'm a fool who uses pills and slobbers a lot. Would you help me? Would you lock me up here where none of my so-called friends can get at me? I want to learn self-discipline, self-protection and self-control, and try to get myself a direction again."

He had a health insurance policy that his parents had been subscribing to since he was young. "That was a good thing," Iggy now says, "because at that time there was no treatment for drug addiction like we have today." He went to his doctor and said, "I know that I'm not mentally ill and that my presence may be a problem here, but I've got to be put under control if I'm to quit drugs." The doctor finally agreed to help him out and wrote "hypomaniac" on his prescription sheet.

Iggy: "I found myself with all the usual loonies like the guy who thought he was in the FBI, he was pretending to have the CIA on his heels. There was a man who set the toilets on fire every morning. Above all, however, it proved to me that my analysis of America was accurate, with tons of housewives having nervous breakdowns. When they realised at 40 how they'd been used, given no love or gratitude, women who had not been kissed, who had not gotten a bunch of flowers for years. There were women to whom no one had ever said, 'You're pretty.' For whom no one had ever bought a nice dress."

During March and April 1975 Pop did some tracks with Williamson and the Sales brothers, featuring Scott Thurston on keyboards. Megabuck songwriter Jimmy Webb gave them the use of his home studio. LA rock writer Bob Edmonds, who held a torch for Iggy's talent, was impressed by the serious new tunes that Pop and Williamson were coming up with so he got involved both financially and creatively. "If we can make a good solid album, we're all right," James Williamson said in '74. "If we can't get record sales on this next album, then we're fucked. I think the material's gonna be a lot stronger, and our overall production sound's gonna be a lot better. It's gonna be a very clean album, very commercial album."

The resultant sessions were indeed much more commercial and

---

* Danny Sugerman recalls the situation in reverse.

melodic than anything that had gone before. Pop, often confused and tousled, had to be hauled out of the mental hospital to do his vocals so Williamson was in the driving seat. With Soupy Sales kids and slick Scott Thurston on board, this was a whole new ball game. The Ashetons were, for the first time, totally out of the picture and California's sunshine – as opposed to Michigan's desolation – was informing the sound. Williamson presented Pop with a contract guaranteeing that all new songs would be Williamson/Pop collaborations.

James Williamson: "I was taking him back and forth to the hospital while putting together the musicians and material and backup singers, etc., i.e. producing the record. I don't remember if there was a clause in the contract saying that only he and I could write songs but that's beside the point. The contract was simply a way to ensure that I wasn't wasting my time on this project. At that point, Iggy was progressively unstable, so I needed something to hang onto. I wasn't sure what was going to happen next. So, just as in any business relationship, I simply wanted something in writing saying that all this was going to be worth my while. After all, I'd been screwed in various activities involving Iggy in the past. In any case it was already an unwritten, but often mentioned, 'code' of that incarnation of The Stooges that only we wrote the tunes for The Stooges. In fact one time while in New York at Max's Kansas City (during the infamous Martini glass cutting gig), Lou Reed sat with us one evening and asked us if we'd like to record one of his songs. Both Iggy and I told him that we only did our own original material."

Bob Edmonds: "I saw that his new material was good and that his guitar player and piano player were both excellent. There was always a musical incompetence in Iggy's recordings, which meant that conceptually he was wonderful, but for people who couldn't get into things conceptually it didn't hold up very well. The idea for these tapes was to try to put him into a structured and disciplined framework to show what he could really do."

The tracks recorded during these sessions formed the bedrock for the subsequent Williamson/Pop collaborative album, *Kill City*, eventually released (by Bomp in the US, and Radar in the UK) in November 1977, and often regarded as being at the very top of Iggy Pop's list of achievements. It is an album whose cult popularity seems to perturb him, perhaps because of the fraught personal circumstances in which he did his vocals – on weekend leave from the Neuropsychiatic Institute. Of the songs from the Jimmy Webb studio sessions that eventually surfaced on *Kill City*, 'I Got Nothin'', with its cheeky 'Knockin' On Heaven's Door' rip-off, and the wildcat 'Johanna' were left over from

The Stooges days, while rough hoodlum classics like 'Beyond The Law', the arrogant 'Consolation Prizes' and the prescient 'Kill City' were new.

"He was . . . mentally not good. He ultimately went into the hospital for a while," Williamson recollected in 2001. "But right about that time, before then, he and I had been working up some demos for John Cale, to see if he actually would produce a new album for us. A lot of those songs were worked up from that demo. So we started doing that. Right in the middle of that Iggy went into hospital, so it was pretty rough . . . It was kind of a hardship thing, and the tapes don't really sound that good, honestly. I think there's some good material in there, but we never did work it up right. The riffs are good, that's for sure, but had there ever been a real record, I think we could have done a lot better."

Iggy: "Kinky Freidman paid me a visit but, hey, that's showbiz. People wanted to take advantage of my situation to do some work with me, or to become friendly with me, so that they might be my pal when I got out of hospital. One day Bowie came to see me with Dean Stockwell. I had told him that I was in this hospital. He was in the same building to pay a visit to Thelma Moss, a scientist who did research on astral beauty. She had a device which took pictures of the auras of animals and vegetables. So Bowie turned up in my room and immediately got me illegal substances although he knew that I was there to quit drugs. The nurses and doctors were so fascinated by Hollywood that they let him in straight away, they were so happy that Bowie was amongst them, that they could get near him."

Nick Kent: "The word was out on him (Iggy) in all the clubs anyway, and it wasn't just confined to the Sunset Strip and Santa Monica Boulevard. Open a music paper around that period and you'd often find some 'former acquaintance' running the Pop down in print. Lou Reed, who'd always treated Iggy with a kind of haughty disdain anyway, basically because he was jealous of his superior abilities as a live performer, had the gall to denigrate him during a drinking contest with Lester Bangs. 'Iggy is stupid. Very sweet, but very stupid. If he'd listened to David or me, if he'd asked questions every once in a while . . . He's just making a fool of himself, and it's just going to get worse and worse. He's not even a good imitation of a bad Jim Morrison and he was never any good anyway.'"

Another graduate of the Bowie charm school, Ian Hunter, who had just left Mott The Hoople, was next in with the dagger. "I think Iggy's the most overrated star ever. Iggy has all the attributes of stardom, except that he doesn't deliver on any level. He's the all-time 'should-have-but-didn't' and it's because he's just not quite good enough." Hunter's prognostication is ironic from a 21st-century perspective, where Iggy remains a star and Ian Hunter is now Ian Who?

The *Kill City* tapes were circulated to the usual LA label offices but nobody wanted to touch the risky Iggy Pop with a bargepole. In any case, by '75 the US rock establishment was, by and large, attempting to kill off punk rock before it even got started, recognising in it a potentially lethal threat to the increasingly lucrative and conservative FM world of Steely Dan, The Eagles, Jackson Browne, *et al*. The career of Iggy Pop, who'd led The Stooges like a demented stallion on steroids, was supposed to be over. But the man himself was just getting going.

"That was a time when there were tons of great bands about not getting signed," recalled Greg Shaw whose Bomp label eventually released *Kill City*. "So it was no surprise when a guy like Williamson walks in looking for a deal for Iggy, who couldn't get signed anywhere because of his reputation as a fuck-up. It was an opportunity to work with someone very important to me . . . I love The Stooges . . . We got robbed by our distributor on that record and never started earning money on the Iggy tapes until the Nineties."*

James Williamson: "I moved on. From an engineering degree I sort of moved into the electronics industry. I've been in Silicon Valley now for 20 years. I travel extensively and do a lot of things with electronics."

Alvin Gibbs (bass player, Iggy Pop Band, author *Neighborhood Threat*): "Iggy told me a story set in LA in the early Seventies . . . He'd been up all night in his Hollywood apartment popping pills, uppers followed by downers, in a vain attempt to achieve some kind of chemical balancing act. The sun was coming up and, feeling hungry, Iggy grabbed a couple of beefburgers out of the ice box and turned on the gas for the oven. As he knelt in front of the open oven door with a burger in each hand he suddenly realised that he needed matches to light the gas. At that moment Iggy experienced a complete and alarming physical seizure.

" 'I couldn't move a muscle,' he explained. 'Couldn't speak. Couldn't do anything but kneel there breathing in the gas with the meat slowly thawing in each hand.' Although he couldn't move, he could think, and

---

* Bomp subsequently made a fortune by releasing – with the blessing of the various band members – a series of albums known as *The Iguana Chronicles*, containing every grungy Stooges bootleg they could lay their hands on dressed up in deceptively well designed covers. Iggy didn't get actively involved in this cottage industry. "I hoped he'd cooperate on our series," Shaw said, "but he keeps his distance. But he's been positive; we send him a lot of money every year!"

the ramifications of the situation were obvious to him. In a short while he would be overcome by the gas. His head would fall into the oven and, sometime later, they would find his lifeless body and conclude that he had committed suicide. While he was resigning himself to being the next infamous rock'n'roll casualty, the next-door neighbours smelt the escaping gas and came to his rescue.

"They kicked down the door and dragged me outta there," Iggy told Gibbs. "If I had died, and they figured it was suicide, what the fuck would they have made of the beefburgers?"

CHAPTER 15

Here Comes The Zoo – *The Idiot*

"I'm more woman than any of 'em. I'm a real woman, because I have love, dependability, I'm good, kind, gentle, and I've the power to give real love. How else could you think that such a strong man as David Bowie would be close to me? He's a real man and I'm a real woman. Just like Catherine Deneuve."

– Iggy Pop to Nick Kent

"I've never had any kind of macho revulsion of fags, but Bowie and I . . . never, never, never, never. Everybody would think that but I never saw him be that way anyway. I'll tell you this. That guy got more p-u-s-s-y-y. I couldn't believe it. Talk about a bitch magnet. Damn! Actresses, heiresses, waitresses, skateresses. And me? I was just left holding my dick most of the time. I had this short haircut and I looked like a duck. But I got lucky sometimes. I got a good song out of a girl I was knocking off at the time, and it became 'China Girl'."

– Iggy, *Rolling Stone*, 2003

"He was given a second or third chance by Bowie. David helped him a lot, putting the records out, giving him confidence. They lived together in Berlin, a place Iggy really liked and felt was home. It was the first time he ever worked with anybody who made him do anything. He could be very, very lazy. David put him through some rough times – it was hard work. He learned a lot from David and he really enjoyed it."

– Anne Wehrer

DURING May 1975 David Bowie was at the ongoing height of his commercial powers. It seemed that, no matter how drug-addled he became, no matter how inclined he was to store his urine in his refriger-ator, he couldn't put a commercial foot wrong. Pop later recalled what it was like to be the constant companion of the Thin White Duke. One night they might be having dinner with The Crown Prince of Spain, with Iggy sitting there wondering what the fuck he was doing hanging out with suchlike, thinking to himself, "Dude, you're jealous!" He realised that Bowie was a man of affairs, with options and opportunities, whereas he had no options, choices, or opportunities of his own.

Rolling Stone writer Cameron Crowe – who initiated the *Almost Famous* movie wherein the Lester Bangs character slaps The Stooges onto his fevered turntable in the first reel – ended up at four in the morning in a cheap Hollywood demo studio, the four-track Oz Studios, in the company of Bowie, Iggy Pop, and various hangers-on. Crowe witnessed, and subsequently reported in *Rolling Stone*, the beginning of Pop's second career, which saw him climb back into the ring to roll with a few more heavy punches and notch up a few more rock anthems. Pop had reconnected with Bowie via a mutual drug buddy.

Crowe noted that Bowie was twitching with "energy", fidgeting, jabbing cigarettes in and out of his pursed lips, bouncing lightly on a stool behind the control board in the primitive studio, staring vacantly through the glass at Pop. Popular mythology has it that two of Bowie's more celebrated creations, Jean Genie and Ziggy Stardust, are homages to Iggy; Bowie certainly had some kind of magnificent obsession with Pop and remained the most loyal of friends.

Bowie had spent the last nine hours composing and producing Pop's backing track. Now it was time for Iggy to do his considerable bit. Bowie rolled the tape and the room was filled with what Crowe described as an "ominous dirge-like instrumental track". A stripped to the waist Iggy listened intently to the backing track for a moment, then approached the mike. As was his style, he had prepared no lyrics but, unabashed, he snarled out the lyrics to 'Moving On'.

Bowie clutched at his chest like a willowy creature from a Jane Austen novel and beamed like a proud father watching his kid in the school play. Crowe said that, when the superstar spoke, he could only whisper, and his whisper was "full of wonder". "They just don't appreciate Iggy," he told Crowe. "He's Lenny fucking Bruce and James Dean. When that ad-lib flow starts, there's nobody like him. It's verbal jazz, man!"

Pop listened only once to his effort before groggily proclaiming it "the best thing I've ever done." At this stage a female acquaintance showed up on the scene and the cultural agenda suddenly shifted. Her main aim was to drag Iggy away immediately; by a handful of his platinum hair if needs be. The two of them headed towards the door.

"Go and do what you will," Bowie called after them. "Just don't be too long. We have a lot more work to do tomorrow."

"Don't worry," Pop mumbled. "She never lets me kiss her anyway. Ever . . ."

"Good, good." David added as an afterthought, "Iggy, please keep healthy."

As he walked out of the door Pop mumbled to no one in particular, "I don't believe my patience. I just don't believe my patience. She won't even let me give her one little smooch . . ."

"He leaves Bowie laughing pertly at the soporific antiwit," wrote Crowe, "but mostly over a successful effort at producing the unproduce-able. Less than a minute later, Iggy Pop is the farthest thing from his mind. Bowie's blanched bony face has already fallen into furrows. 'I am very, very bored,' he says."

Bowie and Iggy never did make it back into that studio. Pop slept past the booked time, called up drunk several nights later, and when Bowie told him to go away, he did just that and disappeared without a trace. "I hope he's not dead," Bowie subsequently said. "He's got a good act." James Williamson later said that Bowie was at the height of his "stick insect paranoia" right then, while Iggy was on the booze. After the sessions collapsed with Iggy's disappearance, Bowie stayed on in the studio and improvised on the track with an acoustic guitar. Having finished it he is said to have remarked, "Another song; that's the last thing I need."

'Moving On', the tune recorded at that May '75 session, was part of an abortive process – Iggy was still trying to get a solo album together. In addition to 'Moving On', the sessions gave rise to early versions of 'Sell Your Love' (which later surfaced on *Kill City*) and two other songs 'Drink To Me' and 'Turn Blue' which, with a new lyric, featured on Iggy's 1977 solo tour and in much altered form on *Lust For Life*.

By late '75, still searching for new beginnings, Bowie became obsessed with the emergent German innovative electronica being created by Kraftwerk, and Neu! He took to cruising the California freeways with Kraftwerk's hugely innovative and melodic *Autobahn* as his permanent car stereo soundtrack. February 1976 saw him tour his cocaine-fuelled *Station To Station* album across the States. The tour was dubbed the White Light tour, a reference to a Velvet Underground song 'White Light White Heat' and to the Man Ray-inspired light-drenched *Station To Station* stage show. A tape of Kraftwerk was used as intro music before Bowie hit the stage each night.

After a show at the LA Forum Iggy went backstage, and ended up becoming Bowie's buddy, not just for the rest of the tour, but for the next year or two. Other White Light backstage luminaries in LA included exiled-to-California Brit artist David Hockney and, prophetically enough, the famous chronicler of the Berlin gay scene of the Twenties, veteran novelist Christopher Isherwood. There was lots going on – good and bad – in Bowie's life. While his tour was an ongoing sell-out, he was packing up his US home with a view to decamping to Clos des Mésanges in Blonay, Switzerland – a home chosen by wife Angie, from whom he was soon to be divorced. Iggy, fast becoming a permanent fixture in Bowie's life, made a mutual pact with Bowie to quit drugs. It didn't quite work out as planned.

The *New York Post* of March 22, 1976, reported that Bowie and three companions were ordered to appear in court in Rochester, NY that Thursday to answer possession of marijuana charges. Busted at the Flagship Americana Hotel in Rochester, Bowie and the others were charged with criminal possession when the police found eight ounces of marijuana in his entourage's rooms. The *Post* reported that "James Ousterberg [sic] and Duane Vaughns, both of 224 Jefferson Ave., Brooklyn, left Rochester last night for Springfield, Mass., for a concert". Bowie put up bail for all four persons of $2,000 each. The woman in the party, one Chiwah Soo, aged 20 from Rochester, did not travel on. State police said that the hotel had been under surveillance for several hours. "Rest assured, the stuff was not mine," Bowie insisted. "I can't say much more, but it did belong to the others in the room that we were busted in. Bloody potheads. What a dreadful irony – me popped for grass. The stuff sickens me. I haven't touched it in a decade."

It was at this time that Bowie and Iggy got to know each other pretty well. There was a lot of travelling and many endless nights. Bowie at long last got the other man's confidence because he seemed to be genuinely concerned that the two of them should do some work together. "And much to my credit I trusted him," Pop concluded, "which is to my everlasting benefit because he's a trustworthy person." Trustworthiness is a characteristic not always associated with Mr Bowie but he certainly showed his better side in his dealings with Pop.

Iggy: "I had never seen anybody work that hard! He was getting up at eight in the morning to travel by car – he didn't fly – to the gig. Gets to the town, does a couple of interviews, catches a half hour of sleep and he's onstage doing the show. Then, after the show, the guy won't stop! He's out checking out whatever band is in town. I was exhausted just watching him. He really knows what it is to work hard. No wonder he was doing so well and I was not."

The well-read Iggy proved his worth by bringing left-field ideas – for which he had a genuine understanding and sympathy – to the attention of Bowie who was essentially a middlebrow musician-type guy principally interested in the underground as a cool but cheap marketing device. One of the ideas talked about during those all-night hotel bedroom sessions was the Cut Up Method, a discipline developed out of painting by Brion Gysin for Beat novelist William Burroughs. The albums which Bowie made over the next few years were influenced directly by Gysin, Burroughs, and the Cut Up Method.

Iggy and Bowie got to know Gysin through the superb Paris minx/adventuress Susi Wyss Versa. Gysin called the socialite his "Open-gate girl" in one of his novels and she was associated with Karl Lagerfeld, the Stones, Paul Getty and the indulgence of exquisite vices. "I had made it possible for the Super Stars David Bowie and Iggy Pop to meet their much esteemed, venerable idol," boasted Susi.

Like so many other beautiful women Susi was immortalised in song by Pop. The song 'Girls' on '79's *New Values* was all about him hanging out with Susi, who was

> Somebody to talk to/And to tell my troubles to/
> She was somebody that's so fun/Worth my looking into.

Pop was fascinated by the polymath Gysin who was well in with The Rolling Stones' camp, particularly Keith Richards and Anita Pallenberg. It was Gysin, via the Moroccan national painter Hamri, who'd introduced errant Stone Brian Jones to the Master Musicians of Joujouka. In his cancer ridden sixties, when most people are slowing down, Gysin was determined to carve out a career in rock music. To this end he wrote rock songs, supported punk bands like Television, and put a great deal of energy into trying to persuade Iggy to record the song he'd written for, and about, him, 'Blue Baboon'.

No doubt, like Bowie, the wily Gysin felt he'd learn how to do this rock thing if he watched Pop carefully enough. No doubt Pop found this curious, mysterious man from nowhere whose apartment overlooked Paris' in-construction Pompidou Centre, who was deeply involved in the deconstruction of conventional musical and other forms, fascinating and spellbinding. In the Nineties Iggy would purchase several of Gysin's paintings at the last New York show staged by maverick downtown art dealer Guillaume Gallonzi.

Iggy contributed this text on Gysin to the 1992 *Here To Go Show*, a countercultural festival celebrating the three major members of the Tangier Beat Scene, Gysin, Burroughs, and Hamri: "Brion Gysin – what a beautiful guy. I met him in Paris, he had red apple cheeks like Maurice

Chevalier, a head of wavy white hair and a cool blue blazer and eyes too. The eyes bubbled and danced and I had fun with this guy. He acted like a human being and never 'interviewed' me or pried into shit or talked creepy rubbish – tho' he was a good-time boheme sweetheart with plenty of rubbish he could talk. I dug his record, the one I heard, I really dug his book – *Let The Mice In* – and I think his painting is so beautiful. One time about four or so in the morning I wanted to sleep and he walked off down the dark Rue saying something like, 'Oh shucks, don't wanna go home alone.' He was a real human being."

Brion Gysin, 1977: "Iggy the djinn who escaped from the bottle to make our every wish come true. When he staggered into my life I'd spent a long time immersed in the music and magic of Morocco. I had involvements with experimental music as practised by Steve Lacy, Henri Chopin, Joujouka, Ornette Coleman . . . experiments with Uhers . . . the atonal as much as Bo Diddley or the Stones . . . so we had things to talk about. When punk came along with people like Richard Hell and Patti Smith I could see parallels between what those people were doing and the earliest manifestations of surrealism so I determined to get involved. Then I wrote this song for Iggy. He did talk about recording 'Blue Baboon' but as of right now nothing had come of it. Somebody whose judgment I very much trust made the point to me that he isn't as sexy or as attractive as people say but, in fact, somewhat creepy or small-time. I never saw that myself. He is a good talker, like a Moroccan he'll keep you up talking all through the night, a son of a gun, all-night riffing on nightmares and dreams and facts and figures and right and left and what are we here for?"

By now New York punk was up and running. Poets, painters and writers were putting bands together in dives, art galleries and squats. One unifying influence across this scene was respect for the myth and stance of Iggy Pop & The Stooges. Joey Ramone said that one of the reasons why The Ramones hired Danny Fields as their manager was because he'd signed up The Stooges, and that The Ramones "were big fans of The Stooges, so there was an instant click there".

Victor Bockris: "In 1977 I published with my room-mate a magazine called *Travellers Digest* which was a collection of punk writings by photographers, writers, etc. In that we had an interview with Iggy. What was interesting to me was the fact that he seemed to many people to be this godlike figure. An interview with him was regarded as being a Big Thing. The guy who did the interview was very uptight that we didn't change a word and all this kind of stuff. People were so impressed by Iggy – punk was really taking off – he hadn't been in New York that much around then so his appearance was sort of dramatic. He was playing the Palladium one night. I think that he must have opened for The Ramones and it was a big concert. Everyone was down from the punk world and we all went on from there to CBGBs to see Richard Hell. I was walking with Lenny Kaye from the Palladium to CBGBs and he was asking me how I liked the show and I was saying how I thought all the songs sounded the same and I was kinda disappointed. Lenny tore into me, saying all rock music sounded the same.

"I was backstage early on that night so I saw him arrive on his bus, I saw him get off his bus. I didn't recognise him because when he was off-stage, not being Iggy Pop, he really looked almost like a nerd. He had these sort of big glasses, he was a regular looking guy wearing very ordinary clothes. So he was a guy who did a lot with the theatre of rock. With bands like The Ramones the idea was that they were the same people offstage that they were onstage, the same clothes and the same attitudes. Iggy came before that, from the idea that the 'rock star' was an impossible person, was a god onstage."

Never entirely comfortable with the political ramifications of punk ideology – Iggy liked being signed to a major and having the occasional limousine on call – he was nevertheless enough of a rock diplomat to go check out the kids, and to give an interview to their bible, Legs McNeil and John Holstrom's *Punk* magazine.

Roberta Bayley: "Iggy came down to CBGBs to see The Ramones. I'm not sure who arranged that, maybe Danny Fields, but he came down and it was a very exciting thing. It was like a big celebrity visiting CBGBs. We did pictures of him with Richard Hell. Jim seemed to me very pleased to be getting the attention. He was very gracious and polite. He agreed to do an interview with *Punk* magazine – we'd only done two issues at that point; we weren't exactly a big magazine. He actually took John Holstrom and I out for a dinner. He took us to a little restaurant called Phoebe's up the Bowery. Jim picked up the cheque and we were really poor then. I think we had lobster and we were like, 'Wow! Iggy bought us dinner.' We were just really thrilled and he seemed very happy being interviewed. I think that was when he was coming out of the bad time in LA, coming out of the hospital. He seemed pretty healthy and happy. He was just leaving to go to Germany then to be with Bowie. He wasn't staying at Bowie's hotel, he was staying at this little place, the Hotel Seymour.

"Before he left, he gave me some gifts to mail to his son, they were things he'd bought in Times Square. It was like some toy handcuffs, and some other things I don't remember but he wrote out the address in

Ypsilanti for his son Eric, who I guess was six or seven then. Pretty young. Then he was off to Germany and when he came back, it was a whole turnaround; he did the tour with Bowie with Blondie opening and I was working for Blondie then. I travelled with them to Detroit to see the shows there. You know that was really exciting because the CBGBs bands like Blondie were just starting to get to tour and go outside New York.

"The New York musicians were in their early to mid-twenties and some were pushing 30 so there wasn't that much of an age gap between Iggy and them, it was just that The Stooges were legendary. When he came down to CBGBs, he still had platinum silver hair, he had big movie star kind of glasses, he had a suit, he had the look. He was sharp. Nobody was wearing a suit then. He came in like Mr Hollywood, he had the suntan and everything. Coming down to CBGBs where everyone's as pale as a snake. You know, it was very glamorous and we were just thrilled and we put him on the cover. To us it was the biggest thing. In '76 when we did that interview, I don't think The Ramones had their contract yet. It was kind of such a small thing it wasn't national at all. We were called *Punk* magazine but it might as well have been called anything. It was just this little scene of a bunch of little people. Iggy came over to Arturo Vega's loft when Joey Ramone was living there too. My friend Pam Brown, she did the interview and she was really 'girly-girl', she was thrilled to be meeting Iggy because it was just like Frank Sinatra for us. It was just a really big thing. I took pictures, you know, we weren't analysing anything. If anybody in punk rock had got rich, I could see how Iggy could have got resentful of it. Even later, everybody became more like The Ramones, a working entity the way Iggy himself was. It was only people like Blondie who went on to become really successful. You don't resent people when they're just as much of a failure as you."

In the course of the *Punk* interview, he claimed that the last book he'd read was *The Journal of Experimental Analysis Concurrent with Dosage Reinforcement of Cocaine and Rhesus Monkeys*. He said skinniness was a last attempt on the part of somebody who can't look, talk, walk or feel right to be cool. He also told them: "I believe very strongly in fascism . . . extremely strongly – not Nazism. I don't think fascism was ever done right. Fascism for me is when a person . . . like children are fascists . . . They're all fascist little buggers. They believe what they see immediately. Bam!"

The interview was the last thing Iggy did before going to join Bowie on tour in Europe. In April '76 the White Light tour made a longish stopover in Berlin. Bowie and Iggy hit the city's gay and transvestite club scene with a vengeance.

Andrew Kent (Bowie photographer): "We went through Checkpoint Charlie and drove around East Berlin in David's big limousine. It was the President of Sierra Leone's old Mercedes 600 and it had one of those windows where you could stand up and wave to the crowd. He had a great driver, Tony Mascia, and we went out a couple of times at night and drove round Berlin real fast. David and Iggy loved it, they were out all the time."

Following a show in Zurich on April 17 there was a week's break before the tour kicked off again. Train tickets were organised by Andrew Kent to take himself, Bowie, Bowie's indispensable sidekick Coco Schwab, Iggy, and a handful of other flunkies to Helsinki via Warsaw and Moscow. As the high-stepping gang made their way across the Polish border into Russia, books by Goebbels and Albert Speer were discovered in their luggage. Bowie claimed that the tomes were merely research material for a film script he was working on. "We didn't know what was going to happen," Andrew Kent recalled. "The train stops and an albino KGB man comes in! He takes us off the train, we go into this large Russian inspection place and an interpreter comes up and says, 'We weren't expecting you.' We were all separated. Iggy and David got strip searched. I think they took some books away, that was all. I don't know what they took from David but they took a *Playboy* from me."

The Communists said they'd have somebody meet the Bowie entourage in Moscow but when they showed up at Moscow train station there was nobody there. They were free to inspect the city unsupervised.

Andrew Kent: "So when we got off the train, we actually hired a military truck to take us to the Metropole Hotel. We went to Red Square and the GUM department store, then back to the Metropole for caviar, then we met the next train in a different train station and left. We were in Moscow for seven hours, that's where all those pictures came from. And then in Helsinki they thought we were lost, because the train schedules were wrong. There were headlines all over Scandinavia saying we were lost in Russia."

The beautiful Moscow photographs taken by Kent during that brief visit appeared all over the world, providing the visual meat and potatoes for a stark and influential feature in the *NME*. It seemed to all and sundry that Bowie and Pop, united by some unmentionable or undiscussed mutual attraction, passed long winter months in the Russian capital, chemically absorbing the bitter-sweetness of the crumbling Communist monolith. It was an exceptional example of Bowie's ability to control the media while nurturing his own image. The appearance in print of these photographs did everything to get rock types talking seriously about Iggy Pop for the first time. But for Bowie's untypically generous intervention, Iggy was, right then, in danger of joining the ranks of the Roky Ericksons and Alex Chiltons of this world.

Bowie's next major public appearance, after a few "misunderstood" remarks about Hitler, was at London's Victoria Station where he did his infamous "Heil and Farewell" number, complete with misunderstood Nazi salute. The youthful Gary Numan, subsequently a supporter of the political right himself, was present at Victoria that day and confirmed Bowie's contention that the alleged Hitler salute was nothing more than an opportunistic snap – all he was really doing was waving to the crowd.

Angie Bowie, *Backstage Passes*: "Berlin for him was the terminus of other obsessions of his: German Expressionist art, Nazism, and the mystical underpinnings of Master Race culture. I first heard him talking about the whole dark underworld of Nazism with Lou Reed and Iggy Pop when they came to London; it seemed to have held his imagination with growing power. He wasn't, as the English tabloid press suggested, infatuated with the more simple-minded, racist aspects of Nazi ideology, and indeed he was furious when one London newspaper ran a photo of him apparently giving the stiff-armed fascist salute after arriving at Victoria Station from Berlin. The photographer had caught him in mid-gesture, he explained, and he disavowed any embrace of Nazism in general and one recently attributed declaration in particular. 'I believe Britain could benefit from a fascist leader,' he was reported to have said. 'After all, fascism is really nationalism.'"

In the spring of 1976 Bowie and Iggy moved to Berlin together, accompanied by Coco Schwab whose job it was to organise everything for Bowie and to keep him in touch with his lucrative global career, no matter how far out on a limb he seemed to be. Edgar Froese from Tangerine Dream helped ease the demented duo into the frenetic Berlin scene. British paratrooper Stewart Mackenzie was recruited as the pair's "informal bodyguard". He witnessed Iggy snorting coke from a large vase while Bowie consumed vast quantities of alcohol. To Iggy, Berlin was a haven for "cult behaviour" or a "fairyland", a whole deserted city full of booze and drugs. Fairyland seemed to be the right word. In Berlin, Pop began to betray hitherto unnoticed gay tendencies and interests. Romy Haag, a Dutch-born transsexual, running the Lutzower Lampe cabaret, witnessed Iggy and Bowie stumbling into her club and her life "coked up and wasted".

"Walking into that place was like going back decades, to the Berlin of

Christopher Isherwood," was how Angie Bowie described Romy Haag's club, "the glory days of avant cabaret before Adolf, the Soviets, and the Americans turned underground Berlin into little more than an anything-goes meat rack. Romy was very wild and very sophisticated."

Today, reborn as some sort of macho rock star who gets his picture taken with reactionary heavy metal bands, Pop puts a profound distance between himself and suggestions that he has any kind of gay past. "The gayest it got is some guy approaching my scrotum with oral intent," he claims, perhaps referring to his San Francisco Fan Club or to the time he suggested that Television manager Terry Ork lick his balls. It certainly can't be a reference to the time he jumped up on top of a table and sang 'The Shadow Of Your Smile' for Clive Davis or the time he asked Mr Davis to piss all over him. Many people who knew him or worked with him, based on what they saw, find his recent hetero assertions hard to swallow. One band member refers to downright peculiar backstage behaviour involving Pop and Allen Ginsberg after a show. He certainly wallowed in drag queens in New York and in transvestites in Berlin.

Looking back on the times that he and Iggy enjoyed in the city, Bowie enthused: "Berlin was the first time in years that I felt a joy of life and a great feeling of release and healing." Bowie and Iggy haunted gay bars, discos, and bierkellers, drinking large amounts of Konig-Pilsener. According to *Uncut* magazine: "One night, Iggy went to a punk club where a model of the Berlin Wall was prophetically smashed to pieces. On another boozy occasion he stumbled onstage to deliver half an hour of Sinatra songs before a bewildered cabaret crowd hauled him off."

Initially the Bowie/Iggy/Schwab triumvirate stayed at the Hotel Gehrus but in the late summer of '76 Bowie and Schwab found an apartment in the Schoneberg district that Christopher Isherwood used to frequent back in the pre-Nazi *Cabaret* days. A dark wood-panelled hideaway in an anonymous tenement block, the Bowie home was a seven-room mansion flat with an office, its own studio, plus bedrooms for Iggy and Coco. Bowie slept under his own painting of Mishima, the S&M gay Japanese novelist and neo-fascist nationalist paramilitary. Speaking to *Uncut*, Bowie remembered his home as a simple place full of simple people: "155 Hauptstrasse, second floor. Knock hard because the bell sometimes doesn't work. Iggy eventually moved in with a bird next door."

This "bird" was Esther Freidmann, the striking blonde daughter of an American diplomat. A talented photographer, Freidman chronicled her affair with Pop in a series of photographs which portray a somewhat at ease Iggy perhaps knowingly living the life of the poetry-reading boheme. In Freidmann's Volkswagen the two drove into the flat, wooded lakelands around Berlin. Iggy waxed enthusiastic about the "rinky-dink villages full of strange old German people. We used to get lost. I like to go out and get lost and be in places made of wood, just to totally wash every shred of America off. Taking a walk was like taking a shower."

Iggy, *I Need More*: "I had a real home once. It was Berlin. I lived there for two years, well really just over that. I had a residence for two years with a girl named Esther. A lot of people don't know Berlin is a special city. There are just a few children and hardly any people in the middle ages. It is mostly young people and old people . . . Music movements have been springing from there. That was very nice."

David Bowie: "Some days the three of us would jump into the car and drive like crazy through East Germany and head down to the Black Forest, stopping off at any small village that caught our eye. Just go for days at a time. Or we'd take long, all-afternoon, lunches at the Wannsee on winter days. The place had a glass roof and was surrounded by trees and still exuded an atmosphere of the long-gone Berlin of the Twenties."

Iggy: "The first expensive thing I bought with my first big pay cheque, not counting drugs, was in Berlin, Germany, in 1977, after I had finished *The Idiot* album, and I had got a rather large advance for the *Lust For Life* album. David and I had determined that we would record that album very quickly, which we wrote, recorded, and mixed in eight days, and because we had done it so quickly, we had a lot of money left over from the advance, which we split. With my share I renovated my apartment, which was on the fourth floor in the back part of the building in which David had a fairly large, handsome place. My place rented for $80 a month – three rooms, a kitchen, bedroom, and something like a living room, all tiny, with a single hallway running down the side. A man who was too old to walk up the steps any more had lived there before me, and there were maybe six or seven layers of linoleum in the kitchen, which I peeled off one at a time. I decided I loved the place, and with the money bought nice rugs, wallpaper, and an oak table with the German eagle motif for the four legs and huge oaken chairs with leather backs that had an arcane symbol of some secret German clan. Those were actually the first things I bought, before the wallpaper and the rugs. I had this bare apartment, cold water, coal stove, the arcane chairs, and the eagle-motif oaken table. And I wrote *Lust For Life* there."

The manner in which Pop lapped up the sheer European-ness of Berlin – all strange old people, arcane chairs, and places made of wood – was pretty corny. Iggy felt he'd discovered a hitherto unknown civilisation, and he wallowed in that for several years. Blending traditional rock star bullshit with American tourist brochure prose, he announced: "I've always wanted to come to Germany. Even when I was a kid, I read everything about it. I always knew I wanted to come here, just like some guys always knew they wanted . . . to wear a dress! . . . Berlin is a green and pleasant city. I love the air, I love the streets, I love the people. I aspire to be German some day, quite completely."

Europeans, he said, had been twisting the social fabric much longer than the Americans, so they'd become better at it than Americans. "Americans," he said, "keep tripping over each other." Iggy claimed that living in Berlin was like living in a ghost town; that nobody cared about drugs or drug trafficking, that it was in action 24 hours a day, full of clubs that opened in the middle of the night when the first wave of clubs were closing down. A place with seven lakes, most of them connected by waterways.

After spending afternoons shopping for chocolates and other high-brow artist-like activities, Bowie says they passed their nights hanging out with "intellectuals and beats at the Exile restaurant in Kreuzberg. In the back they had this smokey room with a billiard table and it was sort of like another living room, except the company was always changing."

Angie Bowie, *Backstage Passes*: "He chose to live in a section of the city as bleak, anonymous, and culturally lost as possible: Schoneberg, populated largely by Turkish immigrants. He took an apartment above an auto parts store and ate at the local workingman's cafe. Talk about alienation."

Ricky Gardiner (Bowie/Iggy guitarist, co-writer, 'The Passenger'): "The autobahn was just as Hitler had built it. It had not had any repairs carried out. The broken concrete slabs had taken on a tectonic plate-like life of their own and we bounced from slab to slab. The autobahn was occasionally crossed by overhead walkways. Here, small numbers of people would gather to watch the affluent West exercising freedom they could only dream about. Their dress was drab and colourless. They had the demeanour of inmates of some restrictive institution."

After the White Light/Station to Station tour ended in Paris in May of 1976, Bowie had used his clout to land Iggy a three album deal with RCA, with an option to renew after that. Then Bowie and Iggy went to the Château d'Hérouville outside Paris to do some work on a potential Iggy album. 'Sister Midnight', with music by Bowie guitarist Carlos Alomar and lyrics by Bowie and Iggy, was the first product of this visit. Intended as a one-off single, it proved to have a long shelf life. Bowie never recorded the song himself but took the melody and had used it for 'Red Money' on his *Lodger* album. Bowie had been working on other tunes during the tour so they headed for his new Swiss home where the likes of 'Dum Dum Boys' and 'Tiny Girls' were thrashed out.

Right through June and July they kept working at the run–down honky Château complex until a prior booking meant that the studio became unavailable. Then they relocated to Munich's Musicland Studios where they met up with disco genius Giorgio Moroder. It was typically astute of Bowie to link up with the Munich sound; a cool ultra–modern urban fusion of Kraftwerk and disco spearheaded by Moroder. Bowie tried to persuade Tony Visconti to produce what became *The Idiot* but Visconti was too busy to do anything other than mix it later in Berlin.

It was Iggy, Bowie and Visconti who eventually worked together on the varied tapes at Hansa Studio in Berlin, right alongside the Berlin Wall. Visconti subsequently commented on the rough state of the tapes, describing the mixing as being "a salvage job". He said Bowie and Pop, "just totally inspired each other". Despite the drinking and repeated lapses into drug consumption, the two were seriously trying to clean up their acts. "They had some kind of pact or agreement to get themselves healthy," says Visconti.

The Idiot has originality going for it, albeit an overestimated originality. The music was mainly down to Bowie, with Iggy contributing strongly in the lyrics department. A lot of its attraction lies in the fact that we have Bowie's prissy little Brit pop melodies rubbing up against Pop's determinedly cranky, backwoodsman, masculine vocal attack. *The Idiot* is more unprecedented than it is enjoyable, spearheaded by a series of souped–up dirges.

The commercially long–life 'Nightclubbing', a celebration of hedonism, is a slowed down generic Berlin cabaret tune – in fact the backing track sounds like it's being played at the wrong speed. Built around a few slightly weird and dated Bowie sci-fi special effects, with lots of redundant guitar work thrown in for good measure, only Pop's hip lyric gives it any touch of the new.

'China Girl' links girls to drugs or drug addiction. File under "Females are trouble" in Pop's extensive body of politically dubious songs about women. Later, when Bowie and Pop made a fortune out of cleaning up 'China Girl' for the Eighties market, they insisted that it was a love song, not a paean in praise of heroin. It goes: "I could escape this feeling/ with my China Girl/ I'm just a wreck without/ my little China girl."

'Dum Dum Boys', which names and shames every member of The Stooges, was an exceptionally insensitive use of old colleagues for theatrical effect. Iggy tells the world that James has gone straight, Zeke is dead on a jones, Rock Action is living with his mother, and Dave

O'Ded on alcohol. He can't seem to speak their language any more but he admits that things have been tough without his dum dum boys. "Where are you now when I need your noise?" he pleads, surrounded in the mix by b-division rock hacks employed by his superstar pal. Pop says the song was Bowie's idea, not his, and this is probably true. "Then he added that guitar arpeggio that metal groups love today," says Iggy. "He played it and then he asked Phil Palmer to play the tune again because he didn't find his playing technically proficient enough."

Though none of Bowie's melodies on *The Idiot* are particularly memorable, except for 'China Girl' and 'Baby', they do demonstrate his sure hand when it came to hack songcraft. 'Baby', often incorrectly called 'Street Of Chance', is the best thing on *The Idiot* with a louche carousing refrain. Iggy carries off his vocal job with aplomb, fulfilling his alleged Frank Sinatra-on-smack aspirations to the max. Though self-evidently a Bowie song, Iggy possessed cock and balls in his rich baritone that Bowie could only have dreamed about. The nightmarish 'Mass Production' is like the soundtrack to some unwatchable Russian movie – perhaps the two collaborators wanted to show just how arty they could be

Iggy: "Bowie and I really just brought the best out of each other. 'Nightclubbing' was my comment on what it was like hanging out with him every night. 'Funtime' was originally sung more like the Boy George version. More rock'n'roll. And Bowie just said, 'Sing it more like Mae West.' 'Mass Production', he just said, 'I want you to write a song about mass production,' because I would always talk to him about how much I admired the beauty of the American industrial culture that was rotting away where I grew up. Like the beautiful smokestacks and factories, whole cities devoted to factories."

In another spin of how 'Funtime' came about, Bowie is alleged to have advised Pop to sing it "like a bitch who wants to make money". Something that Bowie knew all about, and which he eventually taught Pop how to do too.

Frank Black (guitarist/singer, The Pixies): "All those Berlin albums by Bowie and Iggy Pop, they're all kind of dark and brooding and also very arty and poetic. So many bands have used those references as influences and tried to go to Berlin themselves to capture that. The Pixies recorded a song there at Hansa Ton Studios. It's not there any more unfortunately but the main recording room used to be a Nazi headquarters and it had a lot of leftover orchestral instruments including a big timpani drum. The Pixies were tempted to use that on the recording – and I've since realised that on every record ever made at Hansa, you'll hear a timpani drum at some point."

Lisa Robinson, a reliable propagandist for the Pop cause, reported (in *NME* dated October 9): "Iggy Stooge phoned from Paris to say he's finished recording (with David Bowie producing), and that the album will be released in January. He says it's a cross between 'James Brown and Kraftwerk'. Iggy sounded in control, said that he looks '15' and admitted to yet another colour change . . . Asked whether Bowie had 'rescued him', Iggy replied, 'Well, not really . . . because I know what I'm worth. But David did take a chance on me when most other people in this business gave up.'

" 'Of course,' he added, 'you know what I think of this business . . . Although a lot of people made remarks, I wasn't surprised when David came to the US for his tour and took me on the road with him. I'm really at the point where I just don't give a damn what people think . . .' Iggy said he missed performing, and planned to go back out to do concerts in January. He'd been checking out musicians in New York and Detroit, and said it was 'possible' that he would continue to work with James Williamson again, but that they hadn't really talked about it yet. He had a lot of kind words for Carlos Alomar; saying a lot of people thought he just played in one funky style, but that he was quite versatile.

" 'I don't see any need to change the way I perform at all,' said Iggy when asked what he planned to do onstage. 'Surprised? Some of my friends have asked me, "What are you going to do onstage this time?" as if I would have a big spider come down from the ceiling.' "

His mention of spiders refers to his old nemesis Alice Cooper whose show, by this stage, had degenerated into a Las Vegas cabaret act replete with mock executions, guillotines, spider's webs and other Corman/ Hammer horror movie paraphernalia. Ironically, David Bowie would later, to universal derision, tour with just such a giant spider descending onto his stage from the ceiling.

The Idiot was released in March 1977. Iggy said it was his "album of freedom. I'm not saying that it's a great album or some fantastic work of art, but I love it and it means a lot to me." The cover photograph was allegedly taken by Bowie and fashioned after a painting, *Roquairol*, by German Expressionist Erich Heckel (1883–1970). Roquairol was an incurably insane character in *Titan*, a 19th-century German novel by Jean Paul. Bowie was hot under the collar about Expressionism, finding in it a "mood of melancholy or nostalgia as if they were painting something that was just disappearing". *The Idiot* sleevenotes credit Bowie's then-photographer-in-residence Andrew Kent with the shot, and it seems probable that, the claim having been made in print, Kent *did* shoot it. There are all manner of cracked rumours and wishful thinkings surrounding the Bowie/Iggy/Berlin period. The most substantial are those concerning the nature of the Bowie/Pop partnership and the notion that Brian Eno, not Tony Visconti, was the main producer on the various albums that came out of the liaison.

The Idiot went to number 30 in the UK and number 72 in the US – Iggy's first chart entries in either country. Along with its follow-up, *Lust For Life*, it had a profound effect on post-punk underground electronica. When mournful Ian Curtis from dippy Joy Division was found hanged in his Manchester apartment in 1980, *The Idiot* was supposedly on his turntable. Anyone would feel like committing suicide after listening to 'Mass Production'.

Alleged masterpieces like 'China Girl', 'Nightclubbing' and 'Sister Midnight', became part of the soundtrack of the age, the synthesised post-punk Eighties. Punk protagonists like Giovanni Damodo, Nick Kent and Lenny Kaye hammered home the legend of Iggy in print. *The Idiot* penetrated in Europe better than it did back home in the States where it was correctly deemed to lack a kick-ass guitar attitude.

Siouxsie Sioux (Siouxsie & The Banshees): "*The Idiot*, well after the demise of the legendary Stooges, was re-affirmation that our suspicions were true – the man was a genius and what a voice! The sound and production is so direct and uncompromised. Iggy on a good day, and this most definitely was a good day, is my favourite lyricist without a doubt. I still prefer his version of 'China Girl'."

Buoyed by some chart action, many good reviews, and the realisation that Bowie was now firmly on his side, the first Iggy Pop solo tour commenced in March 1977 with Bowie on keyboards, the Sales brothers for a rhythm section, and Ricky Gardiner on guitar. Like the Ashetons before him, James Williamson was now out of the picture. The band rehearsed in a screening room at Berlin's UFA film studios. "Fritz Lang worked there before the Nazis took over," Iggy waxed lyrical about UFA. "They still had all these wonderful German Expressionist films just sitting in cans rotting, because they still can't figure out the politics of who should get them."

The tour took in the UK and the US. Iggy knew exactly what was on the line – that he was making that most dreaded of showbiz things: a comeback. He announced that he would now give an interested punk generation an Iggy Pop who was "safe, professional, fast, dependable. A responsible entertainer who was going to give all the paying customers a good disciplined rock show, with a little extra that is uniquely mine." It wasn't just Pop who was playing safe. The whole thing was pretty safe, fileable under just about as far away from English pop as David Bowie was willing to stray, which was not very far at all. On the other hand, 10 more years of interesting fucked-up work awaited Iggy before he eventually succumbed to his anti-art, safe, professional, dependable, reactionary, responsible instincts.

The tour set list included many old Stooges songs — almost half the set had been co-written with the now-ditched Ron Asheton — plus tracks from *The Idiot* and the still unrecorded *Lust For Life*. Ricky Gardiner, a recent graduate from the progressive rock school, was not the right guitarist to play Ron Asheton's and James Williamson's angry punk rock riffs. Bowie's keyboards and backing vocals showed just how expert he was at both expanding upon and watering down the grungy nature of Iggy's "hits". Hunt Sales proved himself a notable thrasher on drums, though his brother Tony, like Gardiner, remained mired in the tasteful adult picking which represented everything that Iggy, up until then, had stood against.

The tangled interlinking of Bowie's career with Iggy's was now total. This was extraordinarily to Pop's advantage, but this didn't stop him from occasionally rebelling against the popular perception that he was Bowie's bitch. Speaking by phone to *NME* during March '77 Pop went all difficult and Lou Reed-like when asked about his relationship with Bowie.

"I think I've had enough," he said gruffly.

"Beg pardon?" said the *NME* hack, somewhat taken aback, since Iggy was never anything other than an enthusiastic yapper.

"The interview," Iggy made himself clear. "I don't want to do any more."

While *Low*, the album Bowie recorded immediately after *The Idiot*, was charting globally, Bowie was hiding behind the keyboards in Iggy's live band. As many commentators have pointed out, soaking up Iggy's enormous rebel credentials was sharp timing on Bowie's part. According to *The Complete David Bowie*: "It was a generous and at the same time a canny manoeuvre. Bowie's presence undoubtedly helped Iggy to sell some tickets, but at the same time it removed Bowie from centre stage at a time when any remotely mainstream artist was in danger of being rubbished by the cheerleaders of punk." *Uncut* said, "Bowie's association with Iggy probably helped him protect his reputation during the Stalinist purges of punk."

London's *Evening Standard* promised great things in advance of Iggy's Rainbow shows, talking of his "bizarre stage appearances that have included antics like vomiting over a member of the audience, smashing his teeth out with a microphone and smashing a broken glass against his chest." England's tabloid *Daily Mirror*, reviewing the first show on the tour, held out-of-town at the Vale Hall, Aylesbury, said: "His performance was interesting if not totally enjoyable. It was difficult to hear exactly what he was trying to sing at times although he managed to express himself perfectly in other ways – with his body. Without Bowie's presence the concert would have become boring. His musicianship managed to lift it above tedium."

The real point about Pop getting coverage in papers such as the *Evening Standard* and the *Daily Mirror* lay in the fact that these were two influential mainstream papers, part of the fabric of workaday life. That Iggy Pop, Clown Prince of the Boulevard of Broken Dreams, recently returned to Planet Earth from the bargain bins and the junked-out gutter where he'd been studying the stars, was getting adult coverage in such media illustrates the good that Bowie was now doing him.

David Bowie: "It was the first time I'd ever really put myself into a band since The Spiders. It was great not having the pressure of being the singer up front . . . Iggy would be preening himself before he went on and I'd be sitting there reading a book." *Sounds* reported that, "If you wanted David you also got the band. He barely looked at the audience."

Punk had, ironically enough, passed the two Berlin boys by. Iggy's immediate reaction on encountering The Ramones had been to imagine that they were, in a way, stealing his licks. According to Bowie, "The few punk bands that I saw in Berlin struck me as being sort of post-1969 Iggy and it seemed like he'd already done that."

Johnny Rotten and Sid Vicious from The Sex Pistols – the B-side of 'Pretty Vacant' would be a cover of The Stooges' 'No Fun' and the first that many punk kids ever heard of the band – came to check out the show in London. Iggy, who took a long hard look at the younger hellraisers, later speculated as to why Sid Vicious imploded while he survived. "He was from London, and maybe it's because he was urban. I was from a small town and after 18 years of being sheltered I was physically a strong little product – perfect, as it were. Things that would wreck others would only tend to slow me down. Maybe Sid wanted to die – and what's wrong with that? I've always deluded myself that I have a reason to live that's outside of myself, which is my music. I quit drugs for my music. It was the wrong reason to begin with, but I got to the right reason later."

"Iggy Pop?!?" Johnny Rotten spat out the name. "Musically he's so bad. I don't need to go and listen to a saw-mill all night." On the other hand, in his autobiography, *No Irish, No Blacks, No Dogs*, a slightly older

John Lydon admitted that, back when the Pistols were getting their sound together, he had *Fun House* in mind as something to aspire to.

Lester Bangs: "I'd just like to ask some of these spikedomed little assholes if they think when Iggy formed The Stooges he sat down and said, 'OK, boys, let's be punks: we'll get fucked up all the time and act like assholes and make a point of not knowing howta play our instruments! It'll make us famous!' . . ."

Bowie finally overcame his alleged fear of flying – Leee Black Childers says this fear was a scam aimed at getting RCA to send him everywhere on cruise liners and in limousines – to do the US leg of the tour. A minor riot occurred in New York during the show at the Palladium on March 18. On April 13 at the Berkeley Theater, San Francisco Bowie made his only venture stage centre, joining Iggy for a medley of Otis Redding's 'That's How Strong My Love Is' and his own 'Fame'. Two days later the band did *The Dinah Shore Show*, performing 'Sister Midnight' and 'Nightclubbing', with Iggy on his best behaviour being interviewed by the incredulous host, who'd clearly booked Iggy because she knew she'd be getting Bowie thrown in for free.

"Jimmy and I collaborated because I was intoxicated with what I thought he stood for," Bowie told Shore, "and I never want it to be thought that I'm some kind of hand manipulator or Svengali behind what Jimmy's doing now because he's getting popular now. It's only because he was six years too early with what he was doing with The Stooges."

Except for his brief front-of-stage singing during the San Francisco gig, Bowie, like a bar pianist, chain-smoked and smiled his way through the entire tour. The first leg ended in late April in LA when Bowie took to the town with Mick Jagger. "I kept wanting to leave the tour to keep off drugs," Bowie said later. "The drug use was unbelievable and I knew it was killing me, so that was the difficult side of it. But the playing was fun."

Nervous about or ignorant of punk rock he may have been but Bowie's impeccable sense of timing was still with him. He heard a young New York punk band called Blondie and arranged for them to be the support act on Iggy's US tour. While Bowie crossed America in the same limousine he'd used in Nicholas Roeg's *The Man Who Fell To Earth* movie and while Iggy flew from gig to gig, Blondie drove from show to show in a Winnebago. The package on offer at these gigs was a remarkable triple whammy, a zeitgeisty event of historic proportions for those who witnessed it and for the about-to-explode East Village punks, the Thin White Duke, and the Godfather of Punk.

Fred Schruers (author, *Blondie*): "The tour, after beginning in Montreal and Toronto, had stopped in Boston (Harvard Square Theater), New York (the Palladium), and Philadelphia (the Tower Theater) before heading through the Midwest, Northwest, and California. The tour, especially the Hollywood phase, is well captured in a series of photos Chris Stein took for publication in *Punk* magazine's 10th issue, which appeared shortly after the CBGBs benefit for the magazine on May 4–5, 1977."

Bob Gruen: "Iggy was much more on his game when I caught up with the tour where Bowie was playing with him and Blondie were supporting. The songs were better. I was impressed that Bowie was his piano player. It was a show, and he was putting on a show. Backstage I got the opportunity to hang out with him a bit more. I'd met him a few times before that but, in Toronto, he seemed to be a kind of fun, nice guy to hang out with. Certainly he and Debbie and Chris were getting along famously together. That's when I really started being a fan. Now he had a whole show and a real tour. He had some sort of hits in the show, or at least songs that people knew.

"Bowie was kind of dark in the background, not spotlighted, not highlighted. He was the piano player. It was kind of funny. People were going, 'Who is this guy Iggy Pop, who has Bowie as his piano player?' It suddenly gave him a lot of respect, a lot of attention. To see a really big star just backing up somebody else was pretty much unheard of. When George Harrison did the Bangla Desh concert he had Bob Dylan appear with him, but to have seen George Harrison as Bob's guitarist with no spotlight on him would have been bizarre. Seeing Iggy, who seemed in the context like some guy from a bar band, seeing David Bowie as his piano player . . .

"The joke doing the rounds was: the Pope is in New York and he has these different meetings all over town. One day, between meetings, it's just the driver and the Pope. They're a little ahead of schedule. They have an extra 20 minutes. The driver says, 'You know Pope, we got this little extra time. Is there something you want to do? Somewhere you'd like to stop and take a look before the next appointment.' And the Pope says, 'Well, you know, I've never been in America too much. This limousine of yours is such a big, beautiful American Cadillac car. I would like to drive this car.' So the limo driver says, 'Really? That's easy. I can pull over and let you drive for a few minutes.' So they do – they switch places and the driver crawls into the back and the Pope drives uptown on Fifth Avenue – which is one way, downtown. Immediately a cop pulls them over for driving the wrong way on Fifth. The cop sees the Pope in there, goes, 'Oh, my God! I don't know what to do!' So he calls his sergeant and says, 'Sarge, I got a problem here and I don't know what to do. I got this situation here. This limo I got here. It's a really awkward situation.' So the Sarge says, 'Well, what the hell is it? Who the hell is in the car? What's the big deal?' The cop goes, 'Well, I don't know who's in the car. But his chauffeur is the Pope!!'

"That was how it was with Iggy. There was something going on. You had to sit up and pay attention. Also, now, he was very good. He had a very emotional and interesting show that was well balanced. Bowie had done a good job on him. Some songs were really rocking. There were loud ones and quiet ones like there should be. And of course Debbie and Blondie would always put on a great show and warm up a crowd, they were coming together too at that time, so you got a whole, great evening."

Clem Burke, (Blondie drummer), *New Wave*: "We got word that we were gonna do the Iggy tour and we were totally floored. This was just coming from playing clubs twice a month in New York. David Bowie had heard our album while he was in Berlin and wanted us to do the tour. We stayed in California and played the Mabuhay Gardens in San Francisco. We met The Nuns and The Avengers and wound up staying there three weeks. Then we came back to New York and the tour began. That was another six or seven weeks. We got to know Iggy really well . . . we learned a lot from him, and David would help us, too. Like we'd be doing a soundcheck and he would prop his head on his elbows right in front of Debbie and take in the whole thing. He'd give us suggestions, too.

"The last gig we did with Iggy on the tour (San Diego Civic Auditorium on April 16), the last night was the culmination of everything that had happened to us from the first time we played in LA until then. We wound up having this big jam. We did 'Anarchy In The UK' with Joan Jett, and 'I Wanna Be Your Dog' with Rodney Bingenheimer doing keyboards. Joan played guitar and Tony and Hunt Sales were involved. I was singing lead and Debbie was my dog – I had her on a chain. It was total chaos."

Victor Bockris: "Debbie and Chris turned me onto Iggy because their first national tour was opening for Iggy – the tour where Bowie played piano. They told this story about how they had driven up from New York to Toronto to hook up on the tour and they had two grams of cocaine with them for the entire two week tour, that was their stash. Of course, the first night they met Iggy it was gone. Debbie told me this other story how one night after a gig in Toronto, some local kids came round the hotel and said they were having a party and did the band want to go? Debbie didn't want to go, but Chris went with someone else in the band and Iggy went with them. They went to the apartment of these teenagers who were having a regular teenage party and they went in and of course everyone was stunned. Iggy had a four hour jam session and had a wonderful time and everyone was really nice to everyone. He talked to all the kids and stuff.

"Chris and Debbie were telling me about him in that way, that he was just a great guy and nothing like the image of being so weird or distant or difficult. I think, at that point, David Bowie backing him was giving him a lot more confidence. I was hanging out with this girl group called The Erasers and they had a really nice loft downtown somewhere. I went there one night and Allen Ginsberg and Iggy were jamming with a couple of guitarists and a drummer. I was very drunk but in that sort of way where you're active. I picked up a tennis racket and used it as a per-cussive instrument and got involved. I think I really, really annoyed them because I was playing out of time and I was really being intrusive. I was impressed that they didn't say, 'Fuck you, get the fuck out of here,' or 'Get this guy out of here.' They just let me do this and I certainly wasn't adding anything in any great way. I jammed with them for about 10 minutes. Allen was very keen to jam with rock people in those days. I remember that James Grauerholz, William Burroughs' secretary, was at that session and the next morning he called me on the phone and kind of reprimanded me for being so fucked up. I was defending myself saying I had a wonderful time and he said, 'You know what Iggy said about you?' and I said, 'What?' and James said that Iggy remarked, 'Well, that's his investment.' "

CHAPTER 16

Here Comes Success? –
Lust For Life

*"The man who made it happen teamed up with the man who fell to earth to kick
the Eighties into gear 10 years ahead of schedule."*

– Iggy, *Creem*, 1989

AFTER a holiday in Japan, the two wonderboys returned to their safe
European home in Berlin to work on an immediate follow-up to
The Idiot – Lust For Life. This far superior stab at it was completed in
three arduous weeks at Hansa By The Wall, using the Iggy touring band,
plus Carlos Alomar on guitar. This time the principal intensity was
fuelled by Iggy, who had a lot more direct involvement than with *The
Idiot*. He now had the bit between his teeth; a well-received album and a
sold-out solo tour under his belt. As a result, the finished work sounds
more like an Iggy Pop album, and a lot less like a sophisticated piece of
Bowie manipulation. "The band and David would leave the studio to go
to sleep," Iggy said, "but not me." This intense input paid off hand-
somely. Tunes from these sessions like 'The Passenger', 'Lust For Life'
and 'Tonight' eventually helped turn Pop into a millionaire.

Iggy: "Three of the songs were written while we rehearsed for the last
tour but the best of the stuff was written in about one and a half days.
That was the way I wanted to work on this album. To achieve the
immediate effect that I wanted I had to work hard, much harder than
everybody else in the band. A six-to-eight-hour session involved 12
hours of work for me because I was taking the tapes home with me and
just kept on working."

The album's wounding, percussive title tune was written by Bowie on
a ukulele in front of the television at his Schoneberg apartment; its

driving rhythm inspired by the Morse code beat of the Allied/American Forces Network theme. Bowie said that the Network was "one of the few things that was in English on the telly, and it had this great pulsating riff at the beginning of the news." Iggy described that riff as being "a guy tapping out that beat on a Morse code key. Ever the sharp mimic, David picked up the nearest available instrument and started strumming." The intro also owed something to The Supremes' 1966 hit, 'You Can't Hurry Love'.

Ricky Gardiner on co-writing 'The Passenger': "At the time I was living in a house situated in the middle of a walled garden which had at one point been part of a large country estate. I was out walking with my guitar in a field near my house, one lovely morning in May. The apple trees were in bloom and I was doodling on the guitar as I gazed at the trees. I was not paying any attention to what I was playing. I was in a light dream enjoying the glorious spring morning. At a certain point my ear caught the chord sequence which became 'The Passenger'. The riff is exactly as I caught it that day.

"David, Iggy and myself convened at David's flat in Berlin to pool ideas for Iggy's next album. David asked me if I had anything. I did not realise they wanted material so I had nothing prepared. However, I remembered the chord sequence. I played it into Iggy's little cassette machine on my unplugged Strat. He returned the next day with the lyrics complete."

Iggy said the lyric to 'The Passenger' was based on a Jim Morrison poem "about modern life as a journey by car". There is speculation about almost everything to do with Bowie/Pop in Berlin and there is speculation that the lyric is Iggy's knowing commentary on Bowie's cultural vampirism. A B-side at the time, it later became a hit when featured in a car commercial and covered by Siouxsie & The Banshees on their 1987 *Through The Looking Glass* album of cover versions.

Stephen Morris (drummer Joy Division/New Order): "On *Lust For Life* the drums sound not huge but massive! The loudest cymbals known to man, that riff! I wanted to sound like that, still do. Definitely Iggy's best. *The Idiot* was good but *Lust For Life* was louder and better . . . The thing about all these Eno/Bowie/Iggy/Hansa albums was the mythology that went with their creation. Why was a studio overlooking the Berlin wall so important?"

"*Lust For Life* benefited from a lot of spontaneity," says Ricky Gardiner, who is partial to new age notions and whose wife Victoria was astrologer-in-residence on Pop's previous tour, "and was largely recorded as the moon was waxing towards full." This explains everything.

Gardiner also thinks that another of the songs he co-wrote on *Lust For Life*, 'Success', "epitomises the jubilant energies and the album as a whole shows imaginative qualities consistent with the rising lunar energy." Maybe.

Speaking to British journalist, Barney Hoskyns, around the time of the coming-of-middle-age *Avenue B* (1999) – no longer a poor runt on the fringes of society, but a man grown rich providing soundtrack material for movies (*Laurel Canyon*, *Almost Famous*, *Bedazzled*, *School Of Rock*) and commercials – Pop reflected: "When I made *Lust For Life*, I really thought America was gonna rock to this motherfucker. And it took 20 fuckin' years which is a really long time to wait. I guess what happened is that there was this system that wasn't gonna fuckin' give me a break, and I outlived the system. The movies and advertisers have subverted the stranglehold of radio in America, and there are now other ways for people to hear music. All of a sudden – a few years ago when *Trainspotting* came out – I was walkin' down the street and I'd heard *Raw Power* comin' out of the bars."

Lust For Life was released in September '77. Iggy resumed touring in the autumn, without the added attraction of Bowie on keyboards. With Bowie out of the way, this was a substantially rawer show. This time, there was scope for a proper tour of continental Europe. In Holland 'Lust For Life' became a hit single. Bowie was replaced on keyboards by former Stooge Scott Thurston, while Canadian guitarist Stacey Heydon, who worked on Bowie's *Station To Station* tours, replaced Ricky Gardiner. Maybe the planets were not in correct alignment for a Gardiner involvement.[*]

It seems extraordinary in retrospect, but relations between the punks and Pop remained tense, with the problems deriving partially from Pop's attitude. Instead of embracing a positive movement which saw him as a founding father, he seemed to misunderstand punk and to be wary of its aesthetic politics. His humourlessness about the biggest art-jest of the 20th century betrayed the fact that he was no kid, but a 30-year-old man

---

[*] Gardiner is now "raising potatoes in Wales", according to Iggy. "His wife is an artist and they send me giant art projects from time to time plus many thanks every time they get a royalty cheque for 'The Passenger'. This one song has allowed him to raise potatoes which is what he wanted to do." He also wanted to breed children with wife Victoria who obviously hovered over his career like a benign Starship Enterprise ready at any moment to beam him up from Planet Punk. He recently recorded his own versions of 'Neighborhood Threat' and 'The Passenger' because Victoria (artist, mystic, potato farmer *and* singer) wanted to sing them. Gardiner regards those days touring with Iggy as having been "an enjoyable holiday".

with 10 years of recording, drugging, fucking and gigging behind him. He betrayed his mindset when he looked at these young punks and decided that the whole lot of them were competition, merely stealing his tricks. His comments on politics were veering increasingly towards the right, and he had hitched his star to Bowie's at a time when, despite subsequent denials, Bowie seemed to be wittering on endlessly about fascism.

Something must have happened right then which informed Pop's career from that day right up to this. Fundamentally, and for the first time, he was no longer what he seemed to be. He was no longer an existential street corner Huckleberry Finn. As Roberta Bayley implies, he'd started becoming a "working entity". To punk commentators, with his bargain bin masterpieces, his essentially homo-erotic Genet-esque persona, and his debauched lifestyle, he seemed entirely iconic, indie, and praiseworthy. In fact this was the man who'd got used to expensive living, flunkies, plush hotels, the company (and money) of David Bowie, tours booked out by Mr Helen Reddy, corporate record deals, playing Jim Morrison songs with ex-members of The Doors, and much else that closer examination by the Punk Politburo would have found lamentable, if not downright treacherous. During a '78 San Francisco radio phone-in interview, a caller asked Sex Pistols' Steve Jones and Paul Cook if they thought "Iggy Pop was God." He was met with, "I think he's an old wanker," from Cook, while Jones said, "He wears a three-piece suit with glasses now."

Iggy: "Then capital P – Punk – happened, and I went out and did a gig and all of a sudden they were all doing what I do, they were all spitting and pogoing and doing all this stuff and it was a whole different ball game . . . I was shocked. I didn't like the spit all over me. I was like, 'ewww'. I played a gig in London and Rat Scabies was in the front row – I didn't know he was Rat Scabies then – and he could pogo really high enough so that he could get up and get a good aim and then he'd spit on me. I mean, I was just covered in gob. And it pissed me off, but after a while I'd just roll with it and go, 'Hey, I used to spit on people,' and I could be really assholey too if I got stoned enough. Anybody can. Especially when I got older and got in my 30s, 'cause 30, I think, is a horrible age for guys who do what I do. It's when you start losing your baby looks and so you go through this whole fucking number, and you have to shift and it's a hard shift."

Bob Gruen: "Around this time I went with Chris and Debbie to go visit Iggy. He was staying up in a hotel up on the East Side. This was the first time we talked sober in some place that wasn't some mad pressurised backstage scenario or whatever. It was the first time I met Jim rather than Iggy. He was very relaxed and it was almost a homely atmosphere. He was talking about how nerdy he always felt when he was growing up. He said that he felt surprised that people thought he was such a cool dude. Onstage he didn't think that what he was doing was all that cool. He thought it was kind of geeky, that he was basically jumping around, waving his ass, his hand up behind his head, just basically making faces. He was totally surprised that people found that to be cool. He was sort of saying, 'Isn't that great?' That people actually bought into this trip of his. He didn't really understand why.

"I used to see the kind of awe he inspired in people. Around that time I used to drive around the city a lot with David Johansen. We'd go to a lot of shows in different clubs. I remember one time this French guy I knew called me real early in the morning. I was half asleep and don't know what I said to him. Anyway, apparently I said that I was going to be in CBGBs that night and that I'd see him there. Instead, I ended up out on the town with Johansen and we went down to the Mudd Club where, inevitably, we ran into Iggy. We sort of hooked up with him and, eventually, we did head on to CBGBs. We just walked right in. The French guy, of course, was there waiting for me. He was a film maker and writer, an intelligent guy, but his two favourite people in the whole world right then were Johansen and Iggy. It was like God had walked into the room, not this insecure self-described geek I'd met in the hotel with Chris and Debbie."

Towards the end of the tour, in November 1977, Iggy ended up with three new albums on the market because *Kill City*, from the last abortive sessions in Jimmy Webb's studio with James Williamson, got released. Williamson had held onto the original tapes, remixed them, and flogged them some time before to Greg Shaw from Bomp.

Williamson, correctly, thought that *Kill City* was the best music that he and Pop had ever done. His erstwhile partner thought otherwise. "It wasn't a finished product, and I wished James would have waited. I wasn't happy with it; it should have been finished off. It's the closest I've come to mediocre work. I wouldn't advise anyone to buy it."

It's hard to fathom this contrary attitude. Iggy was about to sanction yet another new album, the live *TV Eye*, cobbled together from his last tours with and without Bowie. This would certainly turn out to be the closest he'd ever come – thus far – to mediocre work. *TV Eye* is overblown and Bowie-sounding. Great Stooges songs – 'I Wanna Be Your Dog' and 'TV Eye' – are badly mauled, while the new Bowie-related material is sold cheap and nasty. *Kill City* is, by way of contrast, full of elegant, luscious, and wicked tunes. Perhaps Iggy didn't like the fact that

Williamson was finally getting his name up in lights; the album gave equal billing to him and Williamson. Maybe he didn't want to see product over which he had scant control shifting units at a time when he had his own stuff out with RCA. He was expecting America, after all, to react to *Lust For Life* by "rocking to this motherfucker". Then again, *Kill City* went out on indie labels. Pop, no carefree punk, remained a major label guy; a long distance from the humbling experience, which eventually did envelop him, of having to go indie. Maybe he just didn't want to be reminded of that awful time in his life when he was living in a mental home. Whatever the case, he dissed *Kill City* and went on the road to promote *TV Eye*.

"I made that record because I was short a few bob," Iggy said about *TV Eye*, "and wanted to make as much money in as short a time as possible – bleed the record company like they bled me. The best thing about the record is that the budget was $75,000 and I spent $5,000 making it! I lived a while off the money, and I did it to get off RCA." He told *Creem* that his profession was "cultural sodom of the musical kind" and that he embodied the spirit of the "der Übermensch and Alfred E. Neuman, all in one wiggly package". He said his hobbies included extreme pectoral development, running away from Nico, pro-nuke benefits and phone calls to the dead.

The great pity is that he didn't issue an album of live tracks from the *TV Eye* promotional jaunt. In May 1978 he returned resolutely to his grungy Detroit roots, recruiting a new band – a band far removed from the top-drawer, somewhat AOR, aspirant session guys who'd peppered his last line-ups. Featuring Fred "Sonic" Smith from the MC5 on guitar, Gary Rasmussen from The Up on bass, Stooge Scott Thurston on keyboards, and the unsinkable Scott Asheton on drums, this was an exciting band. Pop went out fronting the triumphant best that Detroit had to offer. Smith, Rasmussen, and Asheton were at that time a working unit, members of Smith's Rendezvous Band. The Rendezvous Band made significantly ambitious music, and enjoyed critical if not commercial success.

"I think at that time he was having trouble with his record company," Gary Rasmussen told Ken Shimamoto, belying Pop's assertion that he was the one who wanted to leave RCA and not the other way around. "He'd been a mess, screwin' up, and he pretty much needed to prove to the record company that he could do a good tour with a good band – it had to be somethin' special – that he wasn't just a total junkie and all that stuff. He called up and was talking to Scott Asheton to start with, and then to Fred. We knew Iggy because he'd come through with his band

and we'd go see 'em. We'd be playing some awful place down in Detroit and Iggy would be playing the Masonic Temple; he'd come to our gig after, y'know, and come up onstage. We were all friends. So at that point, I think he needed something like that, and asked if we would do that – come and do a tour with him and be his band. Scott Thurston was already with Iggy, so he knew all the songs that Iggy was doing, he kinda knew what was going on, so I think Iggy wanted to keep Scott Thurston in on it . . . Fred had met Patti Smith already, and I think they were deep in love. Fred probably spent all the money we made over there on the telephone talkin' to Patti! He'd be on the phone for hours from somewhere. I don't think money really mattered that much to him.

"Iggy paid us well. RCA Records was covering everything, and we had a bus and equipment and the whole deal . . . Iggy was very popular at the time. He still is but in '78 Iggy was big in Europe. We were playing in theatres and outdoor venues. Nice shows, really. He was the headliner. 'The Godfather of Punk'."

Rasmussen recollected some odd anti-punk flak in Norway, where the band were attacked with fish: "I think there's a city called Orebro. I'm not exactly sure, at an outside festival, kind of sick situation. Iggy was the headliner, maybe 3,000 or 4,000 people there. Didn't know it at the time, but found out later that there was some kind of a Norwegian organisation of 'Fascists Against Punk Music' or something like that. They were organised, a small percentage of the crowd. It coulda been five or six people or something. We went up to start playing and right in the first song, these fish are coming up. Somebody's throwing fish, these herrings. They come up and smack you on the bass or something, these fucking herrings. And you look at each other going, 'What the hell is this?' And Iggy is like . . . it don't take much. He starts sticking his ass out at the audience. 'Hey, fuck you, man, fuck you,' sticking his ass out and then people are throwing . . . it started out fish, and then it turned into other stuff.

"I saw something coming through one of the big spotlights, you could see shit coming through the big beam of light, and I just caught it between my bass and my shirt. It was a broken bottle. It cut the button off my shirt. I said, 'I'm done!' and walked back. I turned my shit off and walked off. Finished! Not worth dyin' about. I think 99 per cent of the people there were there to see the music, and they were pissed off. They were finding the people that were throwin' stuff and beating the crap out of them. It was kinda people walking around with big hunks of wood and stuff. But we never did go back out and play. No way!"

Like Iggy, Rasmussen was interested in the quaint habits of Europeans living in houses made out of wood who attacked one another with dead fish. "We found out later that in that country, if somebody sends you fish like that, you got a herring on your doorstep, that's supposed to mean something." Maybe.

London's *Evening News*: "At the London gigs he (Iggy) wore a black leotard and fishnet stockings – an outfit that amazed even his most ardent followers. 'I wore that because it makes me look beautiful. I stare at myself in the mirror and I think, 'Wow, I'm really great looking.' I don't want to disappoint my fans who think of me as being superman. I want to live up to their ideals. Also . . . I think I'm the greatest anyway!' But he has dubbed himself 'The King of Failures'. 'I'd rather be a failure than a success because all the successes I know are such boring little cheeses. Once they're exposed to that dirty thing, otherwise known as the public, they become ignorant and inhuman.' "

The *Evening News* reporter then asked Iggy about his son Eric, the product of a brief liaison between Pop and Paulette Benson. "He's either eight or nine, I'm not sure. At the moment he lives in California and rides horses all day. I provide for him but I hardly ever see him. There's no way I want Eric to be a showbiz kid. That's no life for anyone." He didn't see much of Eric's mother either because he liked it that way. "I guess I'm a loner who loves moving around a lot," he said. "My parents are very important to me. They have a great deal of control over me. Everything I do, I do for them. It's funny, but most rock artists never mention their parents. That's because they're fighting the battles they should have fought at seven . . . better they be shocked by me than by a stranger."

When the tour ended, the guys from the Rendezvous Band turned down Iggy's offer to come to work permanently for him. "I think that was mostly Fred," Gary Rasmussen said. "At the time, while we were in Europe doing the tour, the Rendezvous Band's *City Slang* record was being pressed here in the States and Fred had met Patti and just the timing of everything . . . I think Fred wanted to come home and see Patti, because it was the beginning of their thing. We were all thinking really that we've got a record coming out . . . we kinda thought that this was gonna be something big for us, too."

Hard rockers from Michigan or not, touring with Iggy, who'd kept up a drug-fuelled lifestyle for 10 years now, wore down the boys from Detroit.

Gary Rasmussen: "After three months in Europe (the tour actually ran from May 10 through to June 13), doing that kind of thing, we were exhausted. Hadn't quite figured out yet that you couldn't drink and everything that was there and show up! It takes awhile before you realise, 'Hey, you know what? You can't do all of it!' So after three months of that, we were tired! I think everyone was ready to come home. It wasn't really 'til the end of it that Iggy started saying, 'You know what? This is a great thing, and it's a great band, and we could take over the world. We could go to Japan, and we could do this and that.' Actually, David Bowie was at the last couple of gigs that we did 'cause like the last gigs we did were in London (at the Music Machine). He came to the show and he seemed to think we were really quite a power-ful band. He invited us, instead of going home, to come with him to, I think he was playing in Glasgow or someplace. I think it was the timing of it, but at that time we were all thinking, 'God, it's time to go home.' Personally I was thinking, 'Yeah, let's go!' But I think the other guys were pretty whipped, and it didn't take too much for me to go, 'Yeah, OK, I'm ready to go home too.'"

The next five years were to see Pop fritter away the career achieve-ments of his Bowie years. He would be plagued by endless line-up changes in his band, alcohol, drugs, and by the fact that the Eighties, a no-nonsense time in the music industry, were around the corner. By the time he retired from that industry – in 1983 – he was playing small clubs in front of indifferent crowds, was willing to record disco singles under pressure from his record label, he had no deal, but he was on his way to becoming a very rich man.

America never rocked to *Lust For Life* in '77 but Royal Caribbean Cruise Lines sure rocked to the motherfucker when they used it on their advertising campaigns in the Nineties.

CHAPTER 17

Chairman Of The Bored –
New Values / Soldier / Party

"I got my guitar, stopped touring, disbanded all bands, got a new manager. I decided to go truly solo and hocked my Chinese rugs to stay alive. I lived like a pauper in Berlin all winter. I was very cold and very, very poor and very happy and made up all this music. I made up about three albums worth. 'I'm Bored' – that was written on the Hauptstraussen, across from Annie's Nuaghtchau, across from the naked show. I just wrote all this stuff and I just assumed my manager was in England. I said, 'I know you're going to get me a contract, you know, I'm not worried.' Course I was. And he did. And then I started putting out records on Arista."

– Iggy Pop

TIME was passing. White Panthers were on their way to being Grey Panthers. The contrary spirit of the Sixties – with all that that implied for music – was just a nostalgic memory and rock music was being bought up by the big boys; mainly because the financial rewards had grown so large. "It's been made into something like golf," the thirtyish Pop scowled, "just another American sport with an expensive set of apparatus you have to buy in order to play. Most of the music is just a sack of shit. It's ghoulish, creepy, and backward and is no part of the future at all. Right now rock stands for 'Come on, men! Let's go backwards!' I hardly ever hear anything I like on the radio." He had, nevertheless, developed a taste for the Yankee dollar himself. He saw money as something that could pay for trips to Bolivia, cars, auto accidents, drug habits, and a new stage to dance on.

After the exposure of the Bowie period, his parents liked what he was doing and were somewhat proud of him. "They're older now, around

60," he said, "and it gives them something to do. They get letters and stuff like that, and that's real good." He now liked to sit around and talk, to have an ordinary life that nobody knew about. "Nobody. And that's hard. All I get of that now is maybe a few 10 or 15 minute parts that nobody knows about – but, still, that's more than most people have. If you're ordinary it's hard to get people to treat you like you're a person because you're forced to hang out with a dumb class of people. That's why so many extraordinary people end up being famous. Getting others to recognise it is the problem. You can be very extraordinary, but the ordinary will always be trying to drag you down. When I get ordinary and common, and everyone does, it's usually because I'm tired, nervous, or tearful. Those feelings make me very base."

Returning from the European *TV Eye* tour, he spent most of the rest of '78 off the road working on new material. He'd done over 80 gigs and two substantial studio albums over a period of 15 months. During that same period he oversaw the release of *TV Eye* and witnessed the critical acclaim which greeted *Kill City*. He'd begun to develop a love/hate attitude towards his fans, and he was a tougher individual than he'd ever been. "I'm smarter now and physically I'm much stronger, which helps one think more clearly," he said. "I don't take drugs now to work, but I still do take them to have fun. Sometimes they're not so fun."

His feelings about being an entertainer were hardening up. While working on his next album, *New Values*, he told one LA writer, "I generally give what I get, just like any animal. I always had a certain honesty in my policy that made people come back, for some reason. The purpose of the violence was to protect my music because my music was not the conventional prattle. Most people didn't want to hear it because most people are washed out. I'm not a bacteriologist, but they must be taking something that kills what's natural in them. They're not dirty enough. A pop star is just a composite of the lowest garbage that's shared by the universal mind and playing with that garbage is simple once you learn how. Americans have a real sickness about 'Truth and the American Way'. Fuck the truth."

Jack Rabid (musician, music writer, editor *The Big Takeover*): "I saw him play more or less naked a bunch of times. Once he had nothing left but a jockstrap which I guess is not really naked but you could see everything anyway. I was with my girlfriend and she was just standing there going, 'Whoaaaa! OK. You don't see this every day.' That particular stage was kind of low so he'd be at crotch level, blowjob level with her eyes so I'm going to her, 'Look a little higher, will ya?' He'd come out in these pants that'd already been ripped. All the way up and down the seam of his thighs, and they'd rip more as he was going around. Some girls would rip them some more and he'd get hot, start taking this and that off. Around that time I heard that he did get a blowjob onstage in Philadelphia. I guess some girl said, 'Well, what are you waiting for? It's right there. I might as well help myself.' It's part of his art. I always thought Iggy Pop existed so that I didn't have to be that sort of creature. I was willing to do 60/70 per cent of what he did. The other 30 per cent, I didn't want to do that. I didn't want to stand on a stage wearing a jock-strap saying, 'Come here and have sex with me.' But you were sitting in the crowd, laughing your head off, going, 'God, this is great. The guy is just so unbelievable.'"

There was trouble brewing at RCA; Iggy was selling records but not all that many. His manager Peter Davies scouted around looking for a new deal. The UK division of Arista was interested, so in late '78 Iggy signed up. Clive Davis, who'd already found him a charming desktop dancer when he signed him to Columbia, was busy building up an immaculate rockist roster at Arista including punk poet Patti Smith (who delivered a proper hit single in 'Because The Night'), hippie icons The Grateful Dead, the ubiquitous Lou Reed, and the revived, stadium-conquering Kinks. It looked like a good home for Pop but when Clive Davis discovered that his London office had signed Iggy he wouldn't commit to putting out putative product in the States. Maybe he was pissed off, or just pissed out, but he didn't sanction any US releases until the autumn of '79.

Iggy wrote most of the music on *New Values* himself; something he hadn't done all that much of. After several important songwriting part-nerships, he now didn't want to rely on other people. He picked up a guitar, went out to get some diet pills, and sat for 10 hours a day learning how to play the guitar. When he'd learned how to play adequately, he wrote the songs. When asked what the songs were about he explained, "Boredom again, because I'm bored by things like the record industry that I'm part of. A lot of the songs are very sceptical, possibly because my work demands a certain amount of cynicism in order to bring it to a point of fruition. I need to maintain a spiky attitude. It's how I protect myself. I get angry very easily and although I can modulate it, I can't make it go away. I get angry with stupidity. I like a nice dull person – that can be great – but aggressive stupid people are intolerable."

Early in '79 he flew to LA to team up again with James Williamson, who was to produce the new work. Having grown comfortable under Bowie's considerable shadow and with the faux-artiness of the European scene, Iggy was none too happy to be back in an American studio. "I only went there because they're so good with costs," he said. "I felt it was important that every dollar spent on this album went directly into the studio and onto the record, rather than being spent on silly extras. America is the best place for getting something done very correctly." The new album would be his first official product – ignoring the unsanctioned *Kill City* – recorded in America since 1970's *Fun House*. Fifteen tracks were cut at Paramount Studios in LA, three of which never made it onto the album.

The *New Values* team was Scott Thurston on guitars and keyboards, Jackie Clarke on bass, and Tangerine Dream drummer Klaus Kruger, a Berlin acquaintance of Iggy's. Contrary to popular belief, James Williamson played one guitar solo on the whole album.

James Williamson: "I only played guitar on a couple of things, Scott Thurston played almost all the guitar, he's a very talented guy. He plays with Tom Petty's band now, and he plays guitar for those guys too . . . He was in our band. He knows how I used to play. He just kinda took that style and played it. I played on 'Don't Look Down' and a couple of other rhythm things, but those are all his things."

Williamson's abandonment of the guitar was strange – he was gifted in that department. He always claims – from the plausible perspective of his prosperous adult life – that he just kind of grew up and had other fish to fry. Certainly the advent of computerisation, something he was in on the ground floor of, caused many intelligent people to undergo fundamentally life-altering changes of direction. On the other hand, rumour has it that towards the end of The Stooges the bones in his right hand were crushed during an altercation with an Alice Cooper roadie, resulting in permanent damage which interfered with his ability to play.

James Williamson: "I was studying engineering by then, and I'd pretty much given up. I was doing recording studio stuff, so I had all the connections, but I had sorta given up that aspect and moved on to more technical stuff. One day I get a call from Iggy, saying that he wants me to produce his album for him. I think what had happened was he went over to Europe and recorded a couple of albums. I think he was very popular in Europe as a result of *Raw Power* and also *Kill City* was quite popular, despite his objections, 'cause he didn't want that album to be released at all, he fought it tooth and nail. So I think he was surprised by the reaction, 'cause he was off doing all these Bowie things and I think his real strength was in the earlier stuff, and in my guitar playing and so on and so forth. So he was sort of trying to exploit the connection . . . Honestly speaking, and that's fine with me. So he called me up, and I said I'd do it because I thought it would be kind of fun."

Iggy: "James Williamson, who knows me best except for one or two people in this world, had a lot to do with the lyrics. We started with my usual 'blurting' at the beginning of the process. Once a song was created, we stopped there. I took a long vacation in Mexico, came back to LA and James and I sat down with paper and pencil together and tried to refine the content of what I'd said so that the people would understand it. I tried to be very explicit on this album."

Iggy was an older and mellower individual than the wildcat who'd once terrorised LA; a vampiric denizen of Rodney's English Disco. Now a typical day might see him driving out to Malibu to eat some fish in a restaurant filled with old people. Then he might whimsically think about getting cigarettes and petrol before going for a drive in Topanga Canyon. One day he remembered an old house he'd lived in back in his lost years and went to have a look at it. He found that it was now condemned. "The sign had a great word on it – it said 'unfit building'," Iggy told a journalist, "and I thought about a secretary I know and decided I didn't want to go over to her house."

Nobody in Los Angeles seemed to share his enthusiasm for the things that he felt were interesting. He didn't want to hear bullshit about the City of Angels being the New Babylon because that was not an exciting thought to him. He was, after all, the world's expert on Babylonian practices. "All this crap about modern man and freeways changing the social structure is shit," he opined. "Newspapers and books are full of boring shit. I want to know about the little things."

Released in April '79, *New Values* was almost unanimously praised by the critics and the cool kids. It was a real new call to arms, living proof that Pop had moved on from both The Stooges and Bowie; this was a contemporary Iggy for changed times. After an appearance on the BBC's august TV show, *The Old Grey Whistle Test*, where Pop promoted the single 'I'm Bored', the album had impact in the UK. Encouraged by this businesslike state of affairs, Davis finally OKed a Stateside release. It went to number 180 in the *Billboard* charts, not exactly competing with Fleetwood Mac or Pink Floyd, but proving that Iggy Pop was now, at long last, a viable act without David Bowie there to sustain him.

New Values soon graced remainder bins internationally, but it is one of Pop's most powerful albums, seething with lyrical wit and rage while underpinned by complex but sharp melodies. Albums made over the next couple of years showed the world an increasingly pro-American Iggy, one whose reactionary stances were either a sophisticated joke or all too real. He was swiftly reverting, it seemed, to his small town Ann

Arbor persona – Jim Osterberg the rugged individualist and regular guy. His politics began to sink in, for the first time, with his fans. There was talk in lowlife circles (i.e. his fan base) about the fact that while he was a fine fellow, an anti-example to everyone else, a supreme presence, etc., he was also given to strange social and political views that his fans, such as they were, certainly didn't share. Like Dylan's damaging Born Again odyssey, this public drift to the right did imperceptible collateral damage to the next phase of his career.

Iggy: "Since I've been back in LA, I've been told lots of things about what this or that cult thinks of me and all that stuff frightens me. I want to make sure I don't get to know any of those people. I like regular people, and I'm no more impressed with the fine arts world than I am with the rock world. People who operate in what's known as the high echelons of rock are generally very unnatural people, because they spit on their own hand to do it in the first place. That's not the case with me. I find myself quite natural, and pretty savage at times. What I do is not contrived or unnatural, although it is unique. But I go out with shop girls. I like shop girls. They like me and we get along fine. We think the same in a lot of ways."

The politics he'd absorbed in Berlin, combined with the burgeoning right-wing thrust of American society, inspired him. He became an early member of that most exclusive of Eighties clubs, the Junkie Republicans. He said in an interview that now he had a little money, he could give some to his son Eric "and send him to school with white people, which is something his mother bitches about." When Ronald Reagan got elected president in '79, Pop was a strident supporter.

He was doing a radio interview on WHFS, Bethesda when Reagan's electoral success was mentioned by the host.

"I'm happy about that," Iggy said.

"Mr Reagan. You're happy about that?" asked his somewhat surprised interviewer, seeking clarification.

"Really, yeah, no more pussy," confirmed Iggy, before getting himself off the hook. "Yeah well, anyway, I'll see you later. I think I've talked enough."

"I moved back as soon as I thought Reagan would get elected," he told *Zigzag* magazine. "I've campaigned quietly for him, asking people at my gigs to vote . . . I've been waiting for someone who could communicate the joys of liberty as opposed to the joys of equality." Like Johnny Ramone he became known as one of a small coterie of doctrinaire reactionary punks.

Because of the situation with Arista in America, *New Values* was promoted at different times in Europe and the US. A two month European tour of mainly club and university gigs began in April '79, featuring Scott Thurston (keyboards/guitars), Jackie Clarke (guitar), Klaus Kruger (drums), and ex-Sex Pistol Glen Matlock on bass. On the tour the band did cover versions of the 'Batman Theme', Jackie Clarke dressed as Robin while Iggy played Batman, segued to a raunchy reading of 'Louie Louie'. This was a sort of self-referential joke. Don Gallucci had played on the hit version of 'Louie Louie' while the 'Batman Theme' was a hit for The Ventures, whose 'Perfidia' was once a part of The Iguana's set.

When the tour ended in June Iggy went into Rockfield Studios in Monmouth, Wales with Matlock and Kruger to record yet another album – *Soldier*. Thurston headed off to join The Motels so Pop's line-up was completed by Ivan Kral, borrowed from The Patti Smith Group, Steve New from The Rich Kids, and Barry Andrews from XTC filled out the New Wave, as opposed to punk rock, band. Kral was a good find and his initial input was useful. He'd moved to the US from Czechoslovakia as a teenager in the Sixties. After Patti Smith wound down her band to become Mrs Fred "Sonic" Smith, he joined Iggy and subsequently worked with John Cale. In his rant memoir *I Need More* Iggy described Kral as a dumb "ass-fuckin'-guitar-player-twit who just wants to make money and make it in America. He thinks to be big and rich and to be somebody is all he's got in him, and he's selling himself short. There's this wonderful, beautiful European music in his heart." Maybe the boss was sore because Kral, shortly after *Soldier*, played a big part in Pop's most compromised work.

Five songs on *Soldier* were written by Iggy solo while three were co-written with Matlock, the author of a handful of truly beautiful rock anthems. Guests on the album were Simple Minds (whose singer Jim Kerr was going through his Hamish Mac Bowie phase) and David Bowie, who had a violent altercation with Steve New after making a drunken move on New's girlfriend. Once more, James Williamson was pencilled in for production duties. This arrangement lasted only two weeks before Iggy fired him and continued with studio engineer Pat Moran at the controls. Another story is that Williamson and Bowie were originally supposed to produce *Soldier* but had a violent falling out.

Ivan Kral: "We were in the middle of the sessions when Iggy decided enough was enough with James. James wanted to go for the big production. He wanted to transfer the 24 tracks onto 48 tracks. Iggy didn't like many of James' new production ideas. 'What are you doing with my tape? Who are you, Phil Spector? This is my album.' That was the end of their collaboration."

James Williamson, 2001: "I was the original producer on that album. Bowie just showed up to check it out and visit. He ended up doing background vocals on one song, so he was never really involved other than to stir up Iggy. Jim and I had a falling out over the approach I was taking (very high tech, with 48 track recorders) and the control I was commanding in the sessions. I left after the basic tracks were done. That was the last time I really talked with Jim prior to around five years ago."

When *New Values* finally came out in America in October '79, Iggy toured the States extensively, replacing Jackie Clarke with Damned guitarist Brian James. Americans who'd fallen in love with the notion of Pop as the International Garbage Man, and who exercised a correctly standoffish caution towards any product involving David Bowie, breathed a sigh of relief. *New Values* saw their hero conquering nasty new territory via beautiful well-crafted songs.

Jack Rabid: "I remember when *New Values* came out . . . I remember them playing it on the radio, it got great reviews, people were saying, 'Iggy Pop is back. On a new label.' He sold out The Palladium with The Cramps at Halloween that year. A great fucking show. Great tour. That band was just smoking. Glen Matlock, great bass player who really had it. Brian James always wanted to be in The Stooges as far as I could tell. They were all just ripping it up. When Brian James was playing 'New Values' it was such a great shock because his hands looked like one of those counters in a hospital measuring heartbeats or something. He was so smooth. It looked like he was so much in tandem with that guitar. Iggy couldn't hold a band together because he was putting them together to go on the road and the next time I'd see him, say '81, he'd have a different line-up."

Iggy: "When I'm not performing, I needn't respect anyone unless I feel like it. Whether they're my fans or not, I couldn't give a shit. A lot of people I really like are definitely not fans of mine, and that doesn't bother me. But when I'm performing I respect my audience because they've put their money where their mouth is and so have I. I've always liked the people that come to my shows. I get a really spunky bunch of very intelligent people. A lot of smarties and sensualists come to my shows. My fans don't usually like other records."

Having relocated from Berlin, via LA to New York, Iggy finally established a base on Bleecker Street. Years before he'd told *Punk* that New York always made him feel hopeless. "It reminds me that combat is combat," he said then. "Reminds me to keep my hands in my pockets. Which is good." Now he was living in reasonable circumstances, within a community who knew exactly who he was, and what he was worth.

He can't have imagined it at the time, but the wandering was almost over. He based himself in New York for the next 20 years – when he eventually quit the hyperfunky Lower East Side he was a rich man in late middle age.

Jack Rabid: "I first saw him around 1979. Being 17 at the time he seemed like 4,000 feet tall to me. If you were nice to him he was so nice to you. He was just so nice to me. First time we met I was going, 'Hey Iggy! Hey Iggy!' and he says, 'Call me Jim.' Like we were friends. He doesn't say that anymore. Now it's just, 'Hey!' I guess he doesn't want to be Jim anymore with people. He was very approachable. He'd listen to your question, and give you a good answer back. You never felt like you were wasting his time like some of the bigger rock star kind of people who take this attitude. I was from the suburbs and everybody there was dead, chasing the same old dumb American dream that's been a crock for 200 years. For me to move here to the Lower East Side and meet people like Iggy was such a high. He'd be going, 'Oh, you bought my new album, that's really cool. Thanks for buying it.' It really didn't seem like a bullshit trip that he was on. If you said something else interesting to him, then you'd have a conversation going. It wasn't like, 'I'm here to suck your dick.' He had respect for you on your own level. I ran into him all over town. I'd see him at this gig or that gig or just walking down the street. When he was living on Bleecker Street, you'd see him around there coming back from the grocery store and I'd be like, 'Hey, Iggy!' and he'd give me a real cheery and hearty, 'Heaaaaay, Man!' He was always on in that regard. Big smile. Big toothy grin. The cover of *Lust For Life*! He was an icon walking the streets but, on the other hand, he wasn't, because he didn't act like one. He was a great . . . example. Of how you should be. Not like a God you went to worship in the temple. It was like, 'You should build your own temple. Get it going!' "

The touring in support of *New Values* had barely stopped when *Soldier* was released in January 1980. Every bit as impassioned, tormented, gratifying, and politically dubious as *New Values*, the touring that accompanied its release instigated the slow process of on-the-road disintegration which would bring Iggy's career to a grinding halt three years later.

Soldier represented a double whammy. This was Pop's second consecutive tour de force in a 12-month period. 'I'm A Conservative' says – perhaps ironically – that when you're conservative you get a better break; that you're always on the right side when you're conservative. 'Knocking 'Em Down In The City' speaks out for those seeking employment who are ready, willing and able. 'Loco Mosquito', a pumping triumphant Bo Diddley-esque gem, announced that he didn't "believe in fairies anymore", and was sick of hanging around with old transvestites who stare at his rubbers and make him uptight. On 'Play It Safe' (co-written with Bowie) he perceives in America the very same things that Eisenhower saw. 'I Need More' celebrates his need to lead a dissipate existence, playing scratchy records while enjoying his decline.

These first two Arista albums were amongst the best he'd done but there was something very wrong with the chemistry between artist and label. All the Arista albums failed commercially, Clive Davis remained reluctant to back Pop, and he slid into a sort of obscurity which didn't make him feel too good about himself. He didn't deserve the commercial indifference which greeted his best efforts; as a result of his Bowie years he *was* somebody. Arista didn't seem to be able to do for him what they'd done for The Kinks or Patti Smith.

Mick Rock: "I was doing this session with him. I think it was only the second proper session that we did. I got him to paint a clock on the wall. He did this very surreal looking dripping clock, Dali-esque. Andrew "Loog" Oldham showed up in the middle of the session, me and Andrew were big cocaine buddies at the time. I actually got six shots of Iggy and Andrew together. I don't know if there was any heroin involved in Iggy's life at that time but I was in full flight, cocaine-wise. Everyone was, Iggy was certainly doing it. He was physically tough. From what I can make out his heart stopped at least two or three times. He had the constitution to have weathered that. But obviously he was not a happy person. He seemed all right at that moment in time. That was before his current manager Art Collins was involved."

Ivan Kral: "Iggy would drink a lot. So would I. He would eat for three people, then he would go back to the hotel and sleep until the gig. Then, he wouldn't eat, just drink early in the morning. I saw people for the first time on tour with him. They would get sucked into that lifestyle, even though they had no experience on the road. They'd say, 'Oh, yeah, party time!' and after a week they would be dead. They couldn't keep up . . . A lot of times Iggy was like a baby or a little kid. Sometimes he would be very calm, gentle and intelligent. But other times there was total meanness in his eyes and he would say horrible things. I remember a lady who came backstage one time. She wasn't that young anymore. Iggy took one look at her and said, 'You're old. Look at you. Just look at you!' She started crying and screaming. Iggy just said, 'Get her out of here!' He would rip anybody apart."

The *Soldier* tour started in February '80. New boys on the road were ex-Heartbreakers' bassist Billy Rath and guitarist Rob DuPrey, a protégé discovered by Iggy in a New York club. Three shows into the US leg of the tour, Rath and drummer Klaus Kruger were fired; Rath because of his various dependency problems. For a man with his own exotic tastes and needs, Pop was demandingly puritanical when it came to the life-styles of those around him.

Ivan Kral: "The German drummer Klaus had just had it. He didn't like the rock'n'roll scene. He wanted to be by himself a lot and he would never go out with us. Also, he didn't like how Iggy treated women. I think he was depressed. He threw a chain against a wall and yelled, 'I can't stand it anymore!' Iggy just said, 'OK, you don't like it – you can split.' "

Kral, on whom Pop grew increasingly dependent as a general fixer, was sent back to New York to recruit a new drummer and bass player. "I hired Michael Page and Douglas Browne. I had seen Douglas on drums with John Cale and I thought he was tremendous. I auditioned several different bass players, including Kenny Aronson, who used to play with Wayne County, until I found Michael Page. I remembered him from the Dolls. He was a sweetheart. He was really incredible – a very nice and generous guy."

Michael Page had done sessions with one of the later reunited line-ups of The New York Dolls, and with Chuck Berry. This placed him halfway between Iggy's two favourite kinds of music, fag rock and rock'n'roll. Starting in Atlanta in September, the Nightclubbing tour – so named because most of the gigs were in small clubs – extensively toured North America and Europe; playing 110 concerts with little or no tour support from Arista. Most of the time Iggy was borrowing money upfront from the booking agencies in order to finance the band.

Iggy: "They're a bunch of creeps, no accounts. Michael Page on the bass, who used to play with Chubby Checker, 'Do The Hucklebuck' and all that stuff. He's the love interest in the band, he's a real big guy. And little Dougie Browne, who I kind of heisted from John Cale, and Doug's a very talented drummer actually. Ivan Kral and Robbie DuPrey on the guitars. Rob's from here, he's from DC. Ivan, he's not, he's from Czechoslovakia, you may have heard of him in The Patti Smith Group. Rob, he used to work with this kid, you know Lance Loud, is that the name, Loud, you know, *The American Family* (sic) . . . the creep with the lunchbox? Yeah, he worked with him in a band called The Mumps, and had done numerous other things as well."

DuPrey's previous band, The Mumps, was led by Lance Loud, who'd first come to public attention when his family were featured in an early fly-on-the-wall docusoap. A TV crew filmed an ordinary California family going about their business. During the course of the show – *An*

American Family – Lance announced to the world that he was gay, causing quite a sensation at the time, and headed for New York where The Mumps became a fixture on the club scene.

"Rock'n'roll to me is like a travelling carnival." enthused Rob DuPrey. "It's a shame to see it get so sophisticated. Groupie-ism is phenomenal. It's disposable. All the girls fuck the guys in the band and the next day you're gone. You don't have to deal with their crappy boyfriends." Or, of course, the sexually transmitted diseases, pregnancies, or abortions.

"I'm working with an American band," announced Pop, "and these guys are so fucking great they keep me laughing 24 hours a day, out of my mind. I haven't been so happy since the original edition of The Stooges." This was extraordinary hyperbole, presumably aimed at flogging tickets and making the session players feel good about themselves. In fact Pop felt, during the Arista years, that he was scraping the bottom of the barrel.

He knew he was working on a dead-end circuit but didn't know what else to do. He took note of what happened in a tiny club in some college town where some fans came backstage to talk with him after a show. He imagined that he'd done a good show and that this was what these fans were going to tell him. But they looked at him seriously, shook their heads, and one said, "Iggy, you deserve better than this. You shouldn't be here." He wasn't so stupid or so far gone that he didn't realise the implications of what they were saying. He had a drowning sensation, a sense that his job was no longer him, that he was knocking himself out of shape though he really wanted to work.

Arista wanted the next album to make much more of a commercial dent on the market. They made it clear that if the next release wasn't a hit, they'd be considering their options. Pop got together with Kral at the Iroquois Hotel in New York with a view to writing new material for the album that became *Party*.

Ivan Kral: "I loved it! Some days he'd feel really creative and we would work until five in the morning. Other times, he'd say, 'Fuck it. I can't even get up today. There's nothing there.' We were like stepping over each other trying to get ideas. He was making up words all the time. Sometimes I would suggest lines and he caught on to it."

The touring band went into the Record Plant in New York with Tom Petty engineer Tom Panunzio as producer. Panunzio was a big comedown from producer-facilitators of the calibre of John Cale, Don Gallucci, and David Bowie. And he was no James Williamson either. Twelve tracks were recorded during these sessions but Arista – who were now coldly determined to squeeze airplay and chart action out of the perpetually pissed and compromised Iggy – were not happy with the results. They sent for bubblegum/Monkees songwriter Tommy Boyce, an extraordinary choice and an extraordinary one for Iggy to go along with. His willingness to humour his label is indicative of how vulnerable his career had become. Boyce thought there was nothing wrong that a few good cover versions – the last resort of a floundering act – wouldn't cure. Kral played Boyce 'Bang Bang', a grim piece of New Wave punk pop co-written by himself and Iggy. 'Bang Bang' subsequently became a minor club hit, but is one of the saddest pieces of product Iggy Pop ever leant his voice to. Bowie later covered 'Bang Bang' on his 1987 fiasco, *Never Let Me Down*.

Ivan Kral: "We needed some commercial stuff and I started playing 'Bang Bang'. Boyce was immediately interested. 'What's that? Let's do it, it's danceable.' I gave Iggy my lyrics but he changed it to his own. Originally it was very non-Iggy – a song about the emancipation of women . . . Boyce really got the work done. He was excellent. I really like the sound he got on 'Bang Bang' and the covers."

Party is defined by poor singing, a miserable choice of material, and a mundane version of 'Sea Of Love' that Iggy could have happily performed at a White House soiree for his hero, Ronald Reagan. A record seemingly produced by A&R people and guys from the publicity department, *Party* didn't sell but did further damage to Pop's crumbling reputation, and betrayed his age for the first time. He was now in his mid-30s, and the lengthy, directionless guitar soloing he favoured was no longer acceptable popular music practice, either in what was left of punk or in the increasingly relevant part of the market dominated by dance music. Nick Kent talked of the "rah rah rah rockism" of *Party*, describing it as "a brain-addled celebration of the 'rock'n'roll band as gang' concept, instigated by a man who at the same time as he made the record was openly admitting to friends, 'I'll always be a solo act.' "

Party showed Pop to be totally out of kilter with both his own art and with his own time. For almost 10 years he had been a part of the daily zeitgeist of hip young street culture. Now he was drowning in cheesy synthesisers.

He had carefully nurtured his image throughout The Stooges and Bowie period, and had succeeded in presenting himself to his public as a sophisticated primitive with sharply attuned cultural antennae. By the Eighties things were losing focus and his life was becoming a remorseless downward spiral of low-level touring and recording. The touring continued right through 1981, and for this trek the band was joined by

Richard Sohl, from Patti Smith's group, on keyboards. The American wing of the tour kicked off with three nights at New York's Ritz club. For Kral those shows were the proverbial straw that broke the camel's back. "I felt like I couldn't grow as a human being anymore," he said. "I felt like I was trapped. I like parties and going out but there's a point . . . it's not the same as when you're 18 or 25 years old. I was simply tired of the entire rock scene."

Ron Asheton: "That one band he had with Ivan Kral and some of those guys, that was a good band, but once they got some recognition, he dumped 'em, or would treat them weird. I remember Ivan calling me up and going, 'What's up with him, man? We can't do any interviews or anything.' 'He's Iggy, he's the star, he wants to be the centrepiece.' So Ivan goes, 'What should I do?' I go, 'Quit.' So then he quit. He said he couldn't take it. Jim was getting weird."

Pop took this resignation very badly. "I guess nobody has ever left Iggy," says Kral. "He always fired people and he always had a new band. Maybe I was the first one to leave him and that's what got him. Later I ran into David Bowie and Iggy. David came up and said, 'You owe Jim one.' I was crushed. Anyway, I hope we'll work together again some day."

Gary Valentine, bassist with Blondie when they supported Iggy four years before, stood in. Iggy's old Ann Arbor pal Anne Wehrer showed up in his life again around the time of the Ritz gigs.

"Why are you in New York?" Pop asked her.

"I split from my husband," she explained.

"Did you love him?" Pop wanted to know.

"Yes," Wehrer claimed.

"No, you didn't," Pop insisted. "You don't love anybody. I'll take care of you. Let's do the book. I never forgot that you told me not to quit music."

The "book" was Pop's putative autobiography, something Wehrer and he had talked about doing for a long time. Work began in earnest with the first taping session on September 9, 1981. *I Need More* was published in 1982. While they worked on the project, Wehrer and Pop got to know each other all over again. They had a brief romance, and Wehrer attempted to reconnect Pop with the old Ann Arbor avant-garde.

"Blue" Gene Tyranny: "Anne Wehrer is one of the most fascinating women around, incredible. A brilliant conversationalist who can talk non-stop and it's always interesting, always original. She has just had the most incredible life, meeting just about everyone. She knew Kennedy and Frank Sinatra. The ONCE Festival in Ann Arbor did a piece called

The Trial Of Anne Opie Wehrer And Unknown Accomplices For Crimes Against Humanity. They staged this several times in '67 and '68. The show basically featured Anne being asked questions by an offstage voice, with all this "evidence" being shown of her life. The basic idea is that we all commit crimes against each other in different ways. For each question she would have these amazing stories. Around her there was no real separation between the political and the artistic."

During October 1981 Wehrer took Pop and his gang – including the groupie-loving Rob DuPrey and longtime road manager Henry McGroggan – to the Brooklyn Academy of Music for a show featuring the world premiere of Trisha Brown's *Song Of Gone Fishin'* (with sets by Robert Rauschenberg) and Robert Ashley's *Atalanta*. Ashley, an old pal of Wehrer's from her days as Ann Arbor's "Mrs. Robinson", had been in the Music Department of the University of Michigan, where he investigated cultural speech patterns. The *Village Voice* once said of Ashley that when the 21st century looked back on where the future of opera came from, he would be perceived as representing "a radical new beginning".

In the foyer of the Academy of Music Wehrer and Pop received polite kisses from composer John Cage and art gallery big shot Leo Castelli. Iggy pinched Castelli's ass, a gesture, Wehrer thought, "of punk recognition".

"Bob, this is Iggy Pop. Do you know his music?" Wehrer said to Robert Rauschenberg.

"No," the celebrated painter replied, "but if he's hanging out with you it must be good."

During the intermission Iggy, putting aside his onerous social duties, exited the building to piss on the Academy wall. Backstage, noting patrician civilities being exchanged in a smokey haze while accolades, champagne, and roses were being presented, he thought, "It's so beautiful and civilised. Why can't I do that? I am so rude and crude after a gig. They expect that of me. If I don't terrorise I'm not Pop, but I could change that."

Robert Ashley asked Iggy if he wanted to work with him on his new opera. Pop's part in *Atalanta* would be in the final dance, when he, Rauschenberg and Trisha Brown would be suspended on stage – hanging from long ropes. Ashley remembered seeing young Jim Osterberg hanging out in Ann Arbor 15 years earlier. "When I saw that chubby kid," he said, "in white shorts and T-shirt swinging around on top of a parking meter in front of Discount Records, smiling and waving at the world and singing, 'Hi, hi, hi – high!' I knew we'd know each other again."

Anne Wehrer gave a good account of life on the road with Iggy in her postscript to *I Need More*.* "He invited me to tour, to prove that rock is harder than art," Wehrer wrote. "We leave his love-struck Baltimore groupie, with a return ticket and $20 for a cab and tears. Headed for Three Guys Shopping Center in Charlotte, North Carolina, the fans demanded: 'Is it true that Iggy has fucked more women than anyone? Does he have the world's biggest cock?'

"Raleigh, North Carolina – another Holiday Inn. We pick up matches to confirm where we are. Jim carries two pieces of Indian cotton cloth to 'claim' his rooms – one over the screaming yellow bed-spreads, and one over a lamp to soften the glaring sameness. Add a few books and his acoustic guitar, and we are home. The worst part is facing the bags – pack, unpack, costumes, clean stuff, dirty . . . I don't know, always the bags. 'Anne, would you unpack? Figure it all out.' Neat piles, jeans, boots, T-shirts, bras, ear muffs, dresses, garter belts, socks, sweat-ers, lace bikinis, stockings, shoes – the monotonous ritual of touring. I am confused. Who am I – journalist, maid, sister, lover, mother or the 108-pound bodyguard to groupie-proof him? A woman he didn't have to fuck? An equal one-upmanship partner? A little of each? He felt my nervousness and in one quick motion the piles were off the bed and me on it.

"I wore his jeans and shirts, and he wore my reversible black and fuscia satin cape and my gold and black jacket. The image was so weird it worked. The groupies ranging from 14 to 35, from street kids to royalty, mostly female, didn't know what was going on. Imagine Mother at the backstage door. Some cursed, spit, and kicked; others gave me love letters, addresses, dope, jewellery, Jack Daniel's, and whatever to deliver to Iggy, hoping they'd get to see him. The major focus is on fucking the star. After he makes his selection, they go for the rest of the band – the adoration is fanatic."

Shortly after William Burroughs and his secretary James Grauerholz moved to Lawrence, Kansas, Grauerholz started promoting a few local rock shows. He ended up doing an Iggy Pop gig at the Opry House. Pop gave a powerful display of his skills, his baby blue eyes as big as the moon. The local yokels witnessed the totally untamed beast of legend in

---

* When the book was reprinted in '97 by hardcore entrepreneur Henry Rollins' pub-lishing firm, 2.13.61, Wehrer's text, along with her author credit, a photograph of herself, and a photograph of her home, disappeared. That's what you get for helping a guy out.

the flesh. He was professional, in complete control of his show, keeping the customers satisfied.

Victor Bockris: "Iggy looked up to William Burroughs a lot. He was very keen on Burroughs. They must have met up at some point because James Grauerholz was very involved with Iggy. James told me this wonderful story. At one point Iggy had come to James and said, 'Would you do for me what you did for Bill? I watched what you did and I was very impressed. I need somebody like that. My manager's no fucking good. James, why don't you manage me?'

"They were having this conversation in a redneck bar in Kansas. James had promoted an Iggy gig and they were hanging out afterwards, drinking quite a lot and doing various things. Later they were out in the parking lot and they were lying down on the ground talking to each other, having this very soulful 'I dig you man' type conversation, exchanging verbal intimacies. Iggy was telling James how existentially lonely he was. Then some redneck came out of the bar and got into his pickup truck and proceeded to back up over Iggy and James. James had to grab Iggy to rescue him from under the wheels of the truck. Iggy got up and made some sort of a 'Fuck you!' type remark to the redneck. 'Don't you know who I am?' he demanded. 'You could have finished off the history of rock'n'roll! You fucking pig!' James saw immediately that this was not going to lead to a very healthy conclusion – the trucker was this real lumberjack kind of guy. The redneck got out of his pickup and went for Iggy, calling him a faggot. Suddenly there was blood everywhere, that kind of scenario. James had to rescue him out of the situation. It was going to be a bad scene. The interesting point about the story is that Iggy had this sense of, 'Gee. I want a situation like what William Burroughs has.' You got this sense with him that he was always trying to get it together, he really wanted to get it together. He saw other people doing it and he reckoned, 'Why shouldn't I do it?'"

Back in New York at the Savoy Hotel, at the end of the *Party* tour, Douglas Browne, wearying of the party lifestyle, quit to go in a more jazzy direction. Then Iggy dumped Richard Sohl. "Iggy felt that Sohl didn't contribute enough in the way that was called for," Rob DuPrey explains. "He wanted a real kind of upfront, bash out, 'I got a boner' type of guy." In his major punk memoir, *New York Rocker*, Gary Valentine puts this a little differently. "Iggy fired Sohl because he didn't have the rock'n'roll persona he wanted in his group – taking lots of drugs and fucking lots of girls. Richard wasn't a stranger to drugs, but the fact that he was gay prevented him from meeting the second requirement."

Annie Vendor (New York clothes designer): "I was seeing one of the guys in the band. He was living with his girlfriend but when he'd come off the road he'd come to my place on the Lower East Side first to rest up. He used to say it was getting really fucking muddled out there. Iggy was still real good on a good night, but the booze, ironically, seemed to be doing to his skills what coke and smack had never done. He was drying up, fucking up. *Party* was shit, the whole band felt that. The guy I was seeing said some of the shows left a lot to be desired, dives with fucking heavy gangster bouncers, and Iggy . . . not indifferent . . . incapable, really."

Gary Valentine (Blondie, Iggy Pop Band, author *New York Rocker*): "Iggy had been taken up by the punk generation, but in most towns the punks didn't number more than a few hundred. Iggy had been punching it out in small venues in Europe and the States for the last couple of years and the strain was beginning to show. *Party* needed to be a hit; Arista had pretty much told him that if it wasn't, he'd have to look for another label. There was a sense of desperation, a feeling of last chance hovering around the tour . . . At one godforsaken place in Rochester, New York – really just a sleazy roadside bar – we didn't even have a dressing room. A door behind the stage just opened onto the parking lot."

He may have been haemorrhaging band members, but he was still able to recruit from the very top of the league. It was always going to be instructional to work for a while with one of the founding fathers of a genre. Next up for tour duties were old pal Carlos Alomar on guitars, and another Blondie alumnus, Clem Burke on drums. The subsequent tour was dubbed Follow The Sun, and Iggy started dressing like a woman onstage. "He had a collection of things that he'd been wearing at home," said tour lighting man Sal Lupo. "It had nothing to do with transsexuality. For him it was total comfort. He felt he was so comfortable in them that he started wearing them on stage. Some of them were skirts with tops – others were dresses."

The highlight of the Follow The Sun tour was two shows supporting The Rolling Stones at the Pontiac Silverdome, an 80,000 capacity stadium north of Detroit, on November 30 and December 1, 1981. Keith Richards was a big fan of Iggy and got him the gigs.

Iggy: "The first night I wore trousers and did a 23-minute set. The second night, I wore a miniskirt and apparently it was a bit revealing under the lights. I still have a lot of the stuff that was thrown at me that night. There was a definite mixed reaction that night. At least half the people liked what I did. The other half – fuck them. There was definite booing."

Concert promoter Bill Graham, in his memoirs *Bill Graham Presents*, wrote: "Never in the history of rock'n'roll have more material objects been thrown at any artist. Hair brushes, combs, lots of Bic lighters, shoes, sandals, bras, sweaters, hats. Tons of shit. I have never seen anything like it. I thought The Sex Pistols had set the record at Winterland. But now we were in the Silverdome. Eighty thousand people throwing shit."

Gary Valentine: "Objects appeared, hurtling at you out of thin air. It didn't stop. For the whole set. No applause, no cheers, just a constant shower of projectiles . . . Iggy was as provocative as he could be, lifting the skirt, spreading his legs, fondling his crotch, leaving nothing to the imagination . . . After our set, Bill Graham had someone collect all the stuff and itemise it. He came into our dressing room. 'Ig, I gotta tell you. You broke every fucking record in existence.' Then he had an idea. He told Iggy to go back on stage and instead of doing an encore, to read off the list. Item by item.

"Iggy did. He and Graham went back, and with Graham holding the box, Iggy went through the list. 'I want to thank you all for being so generous tonight.' And then he started. Twenty Bic lighters. Six sneakers. Ten combs. Five pairs of underwear. The audience didn't get it at first but then they twigged . . . Afterwards, Graham gave the box to Iggy as his tribute. Iggy brought it back to the dressing room and asked us each to take something as a momento. I took a bullet. Iggy kept a few things and chucked the rest. But what Graham didn't mention was the money. I don't know how many quarters hit the stage. Iggy asked for a couple bags, put them in and took them back to the hotel."

Due to the disappointing sales of *Party*, Pop's deal with Arista terminated. He would remain without a major label deal for the next four years.

CHAPTER 18

At Breaking Point – *I Need More/Zombie Birdhouse*

"Sometimes I believed I was going to hit the mainstream while being myself. That was the case with Lust For Life, *I thought I was gonna be a star in the US. But it didn't happen. When Arista also let me down after I did* Party, *Chris Stein proposed that I should do what I wanted to do. You've got to do something as close to your guts as possible. When you try to seduce the public they think you're pathetic."*

– Iggy

IGGY settled in Brooklyn where his path crossed again with Chris Stein from Blondie. Stein, using his clout as one half of the Blondie axis, had set up his own label, Animal, which was in the process of recruiting firebrand acts like complex, irascible Jeffrey Lee Pierce's Gun Club and seminal blues lizards, Tav Falco and Panther Burns. As with Blondie, Mr Stein was displaying impeccable good taste all round. "A rumour started that he (Stein) was forming Animal Records," says Pop, "and I was going to be on it. When I returned from my tour I saw Chris and he laid it on the line, 'Look, I'd like to record you. It's a rumour now anyway, we might as well go ahead.'" Things had turned around. The kids who'd trundled all over North America in a Winnebago to support Iggy and his superstar pal were now in the power position, while out–in–the–cold Iggy was about to do an indie album.

With Ivan Kral out of the picture, Rob DuPrey became Pop's major songwriting collaborator. The pair worked closely between January and May '82 on the songs which eventually became *Zombie Birdhouse*. "I just made recordings for the love of doing it," says DuPrey. "Not for any real direction or purpose. It wasn't particularly commercial, just quirky. I gave Iggy the tapes and he was very interested."

Stein gave DuPrey and Pop the money to buy a four-track recording machine, which they set up in DuPrey's spare bedroom, and the two worked at length on the album before going into the studio. Iggy felt that, particularly on *Soldier* and *Party*, he'd lost "the articulation of what I wanted to be saying". This time he was determined to return to the wild unfettered territory where he'd originally staked his claim. Though he now has mixed feelings about the slightly cracked *Zombie Birdhouse*, it's one of the greatest rock albums anybody has ever made.

Produced by Stein, *Zombie Birdhouse* was recorded on a 16-track machine at Blank Tapes Studio and cost $30,000. DuPrey contributed all the guitars and keyboards, Clem Burke played drums and Stein did a little bass. It was completed by June 1982.

Iggy: "I made the album and I recorded it in a room without heating in the Italian Brooklyn suburb of Bensonhurst, between retired old ladies and penniless couples. I took the B Train to get back to Manhattan, it took me 40 minutes. After the *Party* tour, I was broke and I didn't know how to get a room to live in. A roadie from that time, an Italiano-American, helped me to find a room. It was a gloomy neighbourhood and I felt very lonesome. No one knew I lived there. It was a simple life. I came down to buy some kosher hot dogs or a good Chinese dish or, on good days, I'd even get a big plate of pasta from the Italian restaurants, much better than those in Manhattan."

Victor Bockris: "I went to some of those sessions because Rob DuPrey was a friend of mine. Rob was a talented guitarist and songwriter. I remember Iggy saying he had to go out, take a walk around the block, to get some energy, some air. I was impressed because there didn't seem to be any coke around. I didn't see any on that particular session. He seemed to be trying to get healthy. He looked pretty healthy. I talked to Chris Stein a lot about it because we were working on that Blondie book together at the time and Chris was very enthusiastic about *Zombie Birdhouse*. He had a very high opinion of Iggy. I think Chris was drawn to people who were sensitive and crazy. Chris and Debbie had a big house on the Upper East Side on 72nd Street then and I saw Iggy a few times there, hanging out, sitting around in the afternoon talking. Whenever I saw him in those situations he seemed surprisingly normal and somewhat subdued."

With *Zombie Birdhouse* in the can, Iggy went to Haiti to shoot the cover with his old Berlin girlfriend Esther Friedmann and to continue work on *I Need More* with Anne Wehrer. Things were going bad for him but the art he was making was first rate.

Anne Wehrer: " 'Jim called, wants you to work on the book with him in Haiti.' Stepping off the plane Jim took me to a bar-whorehouse, where I was the whitest woman surrounded by sensuous women with black eyes, men with imaginary swords, and children stroking my hair. The stroll of the women, the pulse of the drums – one wild, open sensation . . . We work on the terrace, on the beach, in the bar, by candlelight, and in a Napoleonic villa. We brunch next to Baby Doc. Iggy parades nude, displaying his big cock, much to the maid's shock. He gives me words, worries, and Haiti."

He was thrown out of the local clubs because he was drunk all the time. He often got mad on the street and started screaming at people. Wehrer reckoned that Haiti was the wrong place for Iggy if he wanted to work because, in Haiti at that time, you could buy any drug you wanted from the drug store with a prescription. "Look, you're not working on the book," she said to him as she packed her bags. "I've got to get back or else I'm going to blow the publishing contract."

He was now an insomniac and, after a car crash, he ended up in hospital with broken ribs and pneumonia. Several benefit gigs in the summer of 1982 had to be cancelled because of poor health. He confided to Wehrer, "I'm getting older, I can't be a rock'n'roll star forever. I really have to expand and do other things like David does. Get into movies."

In October 1982 *I Need More* was published, complete with an Andy Warhol introduction and a not terribly competent back cover painting of Iggy by Bowie. The publishers were Karz-Cohl, a New York imprint who, according to Pop, specialised in promoting Polish poets. Ann Arbor poet Donald Hall commented that the text was "the poetry of a man in the world, responding to what he sees: with disgust, with pleasure, in rant and in meditation."

"In the end," Pop said, "I think the book became a kind of an autobiography, but what I wanted to show was that the most interesting things about rock'n'roll are the homemade things, before the band even gets its recording contract." It is one of the few authoritative autobiographies ever written by a rock singer, a real book as opposed to being some sort of self-serving showbiz memoir. Full of accurate and amusing descriptions of what getting a band together involves, about coming up against the realities of the music industry, *I Need More* is the real deal. Things may have changed a lot in the industry since the book first came out but any young musician thinking about getting a band together that is going to be arty, innovative, original, idealistic or badass would do well to read it.

215

Conveying the unpleasant, pungent, treacherous, dishonest, nature of the rock'n'roll life, there is nasty stuff about Nico, Dave Alexander, John Sinclair and the Ashetons. As with all interesting autobiography, it works because Pop makes consistently harsh judgments on himself, thereby excusing – or at least putting into context – his equally harsh treatment of those around him. Internal and external evidence suggests that he had little to do with overseeing the final text. Jimi Hendrix becomes "Jimmy" Hendrix, Elektra becomes "Electra", while Jac Holzman is "Jack" Holzman.

Scott Morgan (The Rationals, worked with the Asheton brothers and MC5 members): "I think that book was probably not very accurate . . . The story I heard on that was that he did an interview with her and he made a bunch of stuff up and what he didn't make up, she made up the rest . . . To tell you the truth, it may just be a step up from that to *Please Kill Me*. I'm sure that book is probably riddled with inaccuracies also, but I think that *I Need More* book is pretty much fiction."

William Burroughs, whom Pop got to know via Brion Gysin, endorsed it as being fresh, courageous, and evocative. He said it was "the story of a man who stands up to tell the truth in a house full of lies . . . bridging the schizophrenic gap between fact and public image." Bowie said it was, "a genuine rock action account of snatching defeat from the jaws of victory." Debbie Harry's back cover endorsement announced that Pop was, "one of my all-time heroes".

Wehrer calculated that Pop earned around $400,000 from his '80/'81 tours and still had nothing to show for it. The band for the next punishing swathe of shows on "The Breaking Point Tour" – thus named because the hero at the eye of the hurricane *was* at breaking point – featured DuPrey on guitar and keyboards, Michael Page on bass, Larry Mysliewicz on drums, and yet another Blondie member, Frank "the Freak" Infante on guitar.

Don Waller reviewed a November '82 show at Rissmiller's in LA for *Rolling Stone*: "The backup band was wretched. Half the crowd were spoiled, peroxided thrill-seekers who'd come to see the geek slice himself with a beer bottle, as he has in years past. And the star of the show, The Crown Prince of Bozos – Mr Iggy Pop himself – has proven himself capable of giving a far better performance than that with which he chose to grace his full house of faithful followers at Rissmiller's on Friday night. It was still a terrific show. By most objective critical criteria, it was nearly a shambles. It was also honest, authentic, funny, unpredictable and human in a way that you probably wouldn't associate with the redoubtable Ig, who seems to view himself as our own Global

Village Idiot these days. 'What do you want out of me?' he asked the audience, when it became clear that neither the Jim Morrison-joins-a-garage-band-that-owns-a-synthesiser material from his latest LP nor his current quartet's mauling of his old Stooges classics would satisfy the crowd's lust for lunacy."

Three months across America was followed by his first gigs in Japan and Australia. Twenty years later, on top of his game, Pop admitted that this tour represented one of the lowest points in his life. There was one show in Japan during June '83, attended by 7,000 respectful fans where he was so drunk that he couldn't remember the words of the songs. There he was in a beautiful theatre, with a lot of people really interested in what he could do, and he thought to himself, "Gee, you really let yourself down tonight." It was a night which made a big impression on him and which informed the fundamental sea change which he was about to undertake.

Something else happened in Japan which also played a part in permanently altering his life. After one of the Tokyo gigs he met a beautiful young Japanese writer, Suchi, who subsequently became his wife and helped him rise up from wilful obscurity and self-destruction. "I did a show in Tokyo," he said. "Saw her in the crowd from up on the stage and something just clicked, so I asked one of the road crew to invite her to the dressing room to talk and we got on so well that we've been together ever since."

This appears to be a somewhat romanticised version of what actually happened. In fact, the for-a-long-time love of his life emerged from a much more typical Iggy-like situation. The roadie who supposedly rescued the future Mrs Pop from the rock'n'roll crowd says that Iggy instructed him to bring backstage "the Japanese girl in the glasses". The roadie did what he was told and went out looking for her, but there were so many Japanese girls with glasses out front that he opted for the one closest at hand – who just happened to be Suchi.

It wasn't just his private life which was about to change fundamentally. He had reason to believe that he was about to lay his hands on a pretty hefty slice of money. For the fifth or sixth time, he had one last chance to get his act together. For the third time, David Bowie was about to save his ass. He disappeared for the next three years, and finally, in his forties, he *did* get his act together. Thus far his life had been a desperate squandering of opportunities and hopes. He was about to become the sort of steady rock industry star he'd always wanted to be, albeit at a considerable artistic cost.

Anne Wehrer: "He was very, very concerned. The whole thing about calling the tour 'The Breaking Point' was that he was either going to drop dead or he was going to go to other things. It was time to change. At one point he said to me that he didn't think he would make it into 1984!"

CHAPTER 19

Visions Of Swastikas – China Girl

"I grew increasingly curious as to what it would be like to be very sober. I thought, 'Christ, how would it feel? Could I do that? What would it be like to write a song without sort of conceding that moment of panic, when you say, oh hell, down a couple of quick beers and then it'll come out, or smoke this joint and my thoughts will expand.' I also found myself suspecting that my promiscuity, sexually, was getting in the way of my music, because it didn't allow me a home life. I thought that with a home life, perhaps I'd have a better foundation for harder and better work."

– Iggy Pop

IN 1983 David Bowie underwent yet another phenomenal musical shift, this one more fundamental than anything that'd gone before. He was no longer the Thin White Duke, he had a lucrative new record deal with EMI, and he recreated himself, once more, as a sort of singing Prince Charles. Now every bit as pompous, stiff and boring as the Prince of Wales, he was – for one last time – totally in step with the times – namely the right-wing, besuited Eighties. His new album – *Let's Dance* – was something of a throwback to the white funk of *Young Americans*, but with all the wit, balls and intelligence pushed aside. Now he dressed like an extra from *Miami Vice*, all pastel suits and frosted hair. He included 'China Girl' – up until then an obscure junk dirge he'd written with Iggy for *The Idiot* – on his new megabuck album, and issued it as the follow-up single to his global hit single, 'Let's Dance'.

Bowie had played keyboards on 'China Girl' throughout the 1977 Iggy tour. On *Let's Dance* he popped the tune up with synthesised guitar motifs and gung-ho backing vocals declaiming "oh oh oh oh, little

China girl" to tie in with his new anodyne role as The Man Who Bored The World. Chic supremo Nile Rodgers came up with the catchy guitar riff, and said it was "the most nervous moment I had in my entire career . . . I thought I was putting some bubblegum over some great artistic heavy record. I was terrified. I thought he (Bowie) was going to tell me that I'd blasphemed, that I didn't get the record, and that I'd be fired. But it was exactly the opposite. He said it was great!"

Accompanied by an attractive attention-grabbing video which featured a sultry reworking of Burt Lancaster/Deborah Kerr's memorable *From Here To Eternity* beach scene, 'China Girl' caused a serious stir. The lyric was cleverly camouflaged to hide the fact that this was yet another Iggy Pop heroin homage. Forebodings about cultural imperialism and despoliation sat uneasily with other lines which betrayed Bowie and Pop's forgotten dabblings in Nazi chic: "I stumble into town/ just like a sacred cow/ visions of swastikas in my head/ plans for everyone." Iggy was, naturally enough, happy to play along with the absurd idea that the song was about a girl, as opposed to being a hymn to heroin's dark pleasures. The money he made changed his life. In June '83 'China Girl' peaked at number 2 in the UK and 10 in America. Mr Pop, after 15 years of trying hard, had finally escaped from the Boulevard of Broken Dreams, never to return.

Iggy: "I couldn't go on playing music with idiots who play their hair-dryers more than their instruments to audiences who were only interested in the size of my dick. It was the end. Either I was going to kill myself and this time I wasn't fooling around. Or else . . . something had to drastically change in my life . . . Then David played me his 'China Girl' and that allowed me to breathe a little better, take more time."

Nick Kent: "Bowie's 1983 recording of Iggy's 'China Girl' – although $750,000 of publishing proceeds went immediately to the IRS – still provided the song's lyricist with enough ready cash to retire and reassess his career situation. Similarly Bowie's recording of five Iggy lyrics on *Tonight* helped deter US tax authorities from making the Mighty Pop's life a living poverty-stricken hell for many years to come."

Iggy retired from rock'n'roll and went into detox at an LA clinic; this time it worked – more or less permanently. "The first steps were just very basic." he said. "Let's see if we can manage getting up in the morning, getting through the day, starting to do basic things to set up a small household. I learned to keep books, learned to balance a cheque-book and a bank account, pay taxes, leased an apartment – first time for everything."

While detoxing in LA, he recorded – with Danny Sugerman and

former Sex Pistols guitarist Steve Jones – the title tune for Alex Cox's cult movie, *Repo Man*, a sort of post-punk remake of Robert Aldrich's *Kiss Me Deadly*. The soundtrack to the movie, featuring the cream of the new hardcore bands like Black Flag and Suicidal Tendencies, helped place Iggy in a healthy contemporary context. On release the movie became a must-see counterculture winner that changed the face of indie cinema. Pop's presence on the soundtrack reminded several generations of old and new fans that he was still a contender.

He went to check out the all-black speed-punk-metallers Bad Brains in New York. "What a scene that was at the A7 club," he told Jack Rabid. "That little club, just clandestine! They never advertised in the *Village Voice*. It was just word of mouth. Everything you could dream of . . . That one band were very accomplished, in a certain way. Really strong with really good rhythmics but at the same time totally out to lunch! That night I spent the night in the neighbourhood and then went back to Midtown at first light. I didn't know if I was going to get killed or eaten or what . . . Years later I was trying to get Martin Scorsese to put me in a movie (which he finally did). He told me, 'I collect lots of tapes and I have Bad Brains. Do you know about Bad Brains?' I said, 'Yeah, I saw them,' and he was saying, 'It's cool. Wow!' He kept saying the name. I think the name fascinated him, because he's pretty dark, you know."

Alvin Gibbs: "Suchi had a major role to play in the maintenance of the new career-orientated, chemically reformed and moderate Iggy Pop. By his own admission, Iggy had a quick temper . . . combined with his impatient nature . . . But on all occasions, Suchi was able to get through to him and stop the situations escalating by pleading for calm and pointing out his irrationality. Iggy, in turn, valued his wife's ability to change his reckless behaviour. As well as pouring cold water on his sometimes hot-headed conduct, Suchi also seemed to be an important and trusted source of advice for Iggy. She generally offered an opinion on his clothing decisions for stage and video shoots, and gave counsel on his performances and stage presentation."

Later in '83, Iggy and Suchi went with Bowie and Coco Schwab to Bali and Java. During the holiday, Bowie and Pop were sufficiently inspired by their surroundings to write the political 'Tumble And Twirl'. Buoyed by the unprecedented success of the whole *Let's Dance* project, Bowie spent the next few years making increasingly unlistenable sub-Bryan Ferry middle-of-the-road cocktail music before ditching that racket in favour of equally unsuccessful heavy metal noise with Tin Machine. At the end of this process Iggy had a solid career as a personality and as a live hard rock act on the fringes of nu metal. But Bowie was all but washed up.

It is to Pop's critical discredit that he played a major role in the creation of those albums which marked Bowie's unprecedented fall from grace. During the spring of '84 he worked closely on *Tonight*, the dismal follow-up to *Let's Dance*. *Tonight* includes several songs that Iggy co-wrote, including 'Neighborhood Threat' and 'Tonight' from *Lust For Life*, 'Don't Look Down' from *New Values*, and two new tunes.

'Don't Look Down' written with angry young James Williamson, started life as a heroic celebration of Golden Age demi-monde New York. Now revived to a white reggae Eighties beat, the song was struck dead by Bowie's newly discovered, unerring nose for the unpalatable. An instrumental version was used on the soundtrack to Julien Temple's *Jazzin' For Blue Jean* – a Bowie pop promo movie given a theatrical release. Bowie knew how to squeeze money out of every fold and orifice of the entertainment industry. Now Pop got the full advantage of such astuteness.

'Tumble And Twirl' emerged from the Bali and Java excursion at the end of '83, and related to the peculiar social – and unacceptable political – vision that the two men shared.

David Bowie: "The rich oil magnates of Java have these incredible colonial-style houses with sewage floating down the hills into the jungle. This stayed with me, and watching films out in the garden projected on sheets. It felt so bizarre to sit there in the jungle watching movies at the end of the garden through monsoon weather with rain pouring down. Images of Brooke Shields . . . it was quite absurd . . . I think it worked out around 50-50 lyrics on most of the songs, but Jimmy's work stands out most obviously on 'Tumble And Twirl'. I think that's obviously his line of humour. The lines about the T-shirts and the part about the sewage floating down the hill."

The song's "I like the free world" refrain is supposed to be a commentary on the repressive nature of Indonesian society.

David Bowie: "I guess those circumstances make one quite fond of the 'free world' because a country like Java or Singapore is most definitely not free. There's an extraordinary split between one class and another, far more exaggerated than any class system in the West. If I had the choice between Singapore or Java, I'd pick England! That's what I meant by that line, but when put in a musical structure these things take on a life of their own – as we know from past experience."

'Dancing With The Big Boys', dreamed up by Pop, Bowie and Carlos Alomar, was the last track on *Tonight*. It serves to remind people of the yawning gap which now existed between the Iggy Osterberg who'd once banged on oil drums while miking up food blenders and the newly prosperous Manhattan celebrity much concerned with buying antiques, domestic appliances, and pontificating. Mashed up by those most reactionary of rock instruments, trumpet and sax, 'Dancing With The Big Boys' was endorsed by an in-your-face backing vocal from Iggy. It got onto the B-side of the 'Blue Jean' single and was remixed by Arthur Baker.

Bowie said 'Dancing With The Big Boys' was a sound he'd sought to achieve for quite some time. "There's a particular sound I'm after that I haven't really got yet, and I probably won't drop that search until I get it. I'll either crack it on the next album or just retire from it. I think I got quite close to it with 'Dancing With The Big Boys'. That was quite an adventurous piece of writing in the sense that we didn't look for any standards. I got very musical over the last couple of years; I stayed away from experimentation . . . but in '. . . Big Boys' Iggy and I just broke away from all that for the one track."

"Iggy wasn't anything I imagined him to be," said Hugh Padgham, *Tonight*'s co-producer. "He was very quiet. I think most people's conception of him is being a complete lunatic who is just out to lunch and running around like a madman all the time. When he came in, he had these big glasses on and he just used to sit in the control room and read. My idea of Iggy now is that of an intellectual." Although *Tonight* failed to match the success of *Let's Dance*, it sold plenty of copies, resulting in more big bucks for Pop.

Now fat with funds, Iggy and Suchi could get a Manhattan penthouse apartment, overlooking Tompkins Square Park, on Avenue B in Alphabet City. Their building, the Christadora, was something of an architectural gem. It was originally built as a settlement house to help the poor but was converted into upmarket apartments in 1986. The conversion led to anti-gentrification protests in the area. Pop purchased a spacious penthouse which gave him panoramic views all over Manhattan, his proud display of affluence giving the finger to the local community's desire to keep their area real. He claimed that he and Suchi got married to get the US government off their backs. "We just had so much trouble getting through customs," he said, "that we thought we'd better. She's been very good to me and has repeatedly, at crucial moments, urged me to curb my anger.

"When some problem has peaked, and my thinking isn't getting me anywhere, I like to pull out the vacuum cleaner and vacuum the house. We've got a Singer, which we bought at the central Singer Sewing

Center of the United States, up at Rockefeller Center, in New York. We got a warranty. A nice, sweet little old lady sold it to us. We took pains to try each model. It was one of the first things Suchi and I bought together when we moved to New York. It was hard to get a cab so we dragged it home. I like stroking the floor with it. In fact, I especially like it because I'm really into rugs. I like buying little rugs. I don't buy really expensive ones, but I got one with a motif of an Indian (as from India), hunting deer and tigers. That's my favourite rug, and I vacuum it almost religiously. Besides helping me think, it also feels great at night. I got one chair in my home. Basically, all my seating is within 18 inches of the floor, so I use the rug a lot. It's almost as if it's my flying carpet. It's my thinking rug, it's my play rug, and a lot of times it's my kitchen table."

The apartment contained a work room complete with eight-track studio, guitars, and a microphone all permanently set up. Another room was set aside for the hanging and displaying of Iggy's paintings. The main room had ethnic furniture with African and South American native artifacts dotted around the place. The separating walls were made of glass giving an all-round view of the New York skyline. The overall effect was overly tasteful, arriviste and ostentatious.

Alvin Gibbs: "He had a bunch of his paintings hanging up in the apartment. He was light-hearted and humorous about them, he didn't take his paintings seriously or anything. There was one painting he showed us and it was like he was telling us the story behind it concerning him and David Bowie. They'd been on a boat with Michael Palin, they had a yacht somewhere in the South of France. They were all staying in this yacht vacationing. Iggy'd gotten out his easel one morning and was painting Bowie, Suchi and Palin drinking champagne on the deck. The actual figures in the painting in the apartment bore no resemblance whatsoever to the individuals aforementioned, you couldn't tell which was which. Iggy was saying, 'Yeah, well, as you can see, it all went a bit wrong.'"

A big consideration for Iggy was his son Eric Benson, now in his early twenties. He'd grown up in LA with his lesbian mother Paulette Benson who, in 1982, got in touch with Iggy, saying she was having difficulties with their son. She wanted to know if Iggy would take over responsibility for a while.

Iggy to Nick Kent: "He lives in Philadelphia where he's got his own apartment. He's studying accountancy, basically in order to find a way to make large sums of money. That's his thing currently. We get along well now, although there were big problems in the past. He was displaying some very disturbing traits which I feel were his mother's influence . . .

her lifestyle kind of messed up his thinking for a time. Now I can afford to support him financially in his efforts at self-improvement. I wanted most of all for him to have a person in his life, a paternal friend he could communicate with. When he moved to Philly I started corresponding with him and I've finally established a successful rapport with him. Him being the son of, y'know, 'the fucked up godfather of nihilistic horseshit, the monstrous Iggy Pop' was a big factor in my determination to live a responsible, organised lifestyle. I didn't want him to remember me, like, 'Papa Was A Rolling Stone'."

Iggy (*Interview* Joey Ramone obituary): "I used to live on Tompkins Square Park and I remember being out one night at dusk, walking to buy something at the liquor store, and seeing Joey in the twilight walking like a ghost or a wraith through the park. I remember he just had this certain hunch to him but this certain height, also. He wasn't dressed in a leather jacket or anything; he was very, very unobtrusive. I remember thinking then, 'Wow, this guy's a landmark.'"

Iggy took to leading the life of the East Village Manhattan intellectual, albeit an intellectual whose lifestyle was funded by another man's mediocre dance music. He wrote essays, poetry, and song lyrics, sometimes lugging a typewriter into Washington Square Park, looking for inspiration. He was also painting and talked about doing another book. This would be a graphic recollection of a series of sexual encounters and how they moved him. He started taking acting lessons and going to auditions for roles. "It was a good opportunity to take off my armour and perform in just a bare room for a few people who had no clippings on me . . . I admire the discipline of the people in the theatre. They work hard. It was a good way for me to stay on my toes. If you know that anytime the phone rings, you might get a call that says, 'There's a great script with a part for you coming over, you can't be stoned, out romancing or whatever. You have to be poised.' I couldn't be in a musician's mode where if I wasn't working I could just light up a spliff and stare at the sun."

Iggy got three small acting roles in worthwhile projects. He played a pool player that Tom Cruise comes across on the road in Martin Scorsese's *The Color Of Money*. In Alex Cox's *Sid And Nancy* he played a straight trying to book into a room at the Chelsea Hotel. In *Miami Vice* he played the manager of an S&M bar but his part got edited out and was never broadcast. He was not a very good actor. There was nothing wrong with his career that a hit single wouldn't cure.

CHAPTER 20

Mixing Business With Leather – *Blah Blah Blah/Instinct*

"I play a bit of golf, something I do on a yearly basis with my father. We're both kind of athletic outdoor people. If I was handicapped now, it would be high, around 15 or 16. I shoot in the nineties, which isn't bad for someone who plays a couple of weeks a year, but I still got a decent stroke. When I was about 17, I used to shoot in the low eighties, and I can still, on a very good day. I only took up golf when I was 16. My particular weakness in golf would probably be strategic. More than anything, I tend to go for the big shot when I should play it safe. I just can't resist the thrill of going for the very difficult shot. Like, let's say, I'm 200 yards from the green. It's a par four, 400 yards. I duff my drive and half duff my second shot . . . Now there's water in front of the green, sand on the left, and woods on the right. If I take out a three-iron and hit it really, really well, one shot in 15, I can hit that three-iron just far enough so it's going to go down at 190 yards, which is about the edge of the green, roll the extra yards, and then I can drop the putt and still save the par four. But, if I don't, I'm gonna end up in the trap, in the water, or in the woods, and I'm gonna be penalised, whereas if I would just take out the five-iron and lay it up 150 yards anywhere, basically, in front of the green and have a simple pitch over, I get down with my bogie. That's the kind of situation that would prove my weakness. The other thing I do wrong is that I swing from the heels. You don't swing hard in golf to hit the ball very far. You have to swing easy and have a good sense of timing. How this relates to the rest of my life, well I guess at times my work has tended to be spotty. Often, in the past, I would expect to go out and give an almost miraculous performance every night, and I really didn't care if the business was straight or I didn't make sure the set was going to be long enough. All I cared about was that when Iggy Pop got on that stage, something explosive had to happen."

– Iggy, Spin, (1986)

AS he planned his comeback, Pop got himself a new manager in Art Collins, a dapper and outwardly mellow operator with huge diplomatic and entrepreneurial skills. Collins, who used to work for Rolling Stones Records under influential art collector Earl McGrath, involved himself in the careers of such flamboyant and idiosyncratic individuals as Marianne Faithfull, Peter Tosh and Jim Carroll. He had a taste for mavericks and, as it turned out, an astute nose for turning one generation's rebellion into another's consumer durables. "Art Collins," says Mick Rock, "is basically a nursemaid and Iggy is mostly interested, and I don't blame him, in getting his money."

Alvin Gibbs: "He told me he had the choice of two managers. He said he was really lucky in the choice that he made. It was a really close thing, it seems. He didn't name the other person he was going to go with but subsequently he found out all these terrible things about this guy and that this guy would have really fucked him over. He was very pleased that he chose Art Collins when he did. It has worked for him, certainly on a professional level."

Iggy: "What I learned the past five years since *Party*, my previous last record on a major label is one – to do my work without being intoxicated. I used to think unless I've screwed five girls this week, I won't be sexy anymore, and maybe if I don't get high right now, I won't be able to write a song. Two – to work hard; I used to depend much more on my abilities to perform, but I didn't work that many hours a week or that hard, compared to what other people used to do in this world, and consequently, my work would suffer. Three – to take some time off, focus my mind, and clean up my body. Four – to control my temper, which used to get in my way all the time. Five – to not feel filthy about doing business; I always prided myself on being outside the world of organisation and thought of myself as someone who was never going to stand on a line, never going to fill in a blank. Now I can do all these things without losing passion."

By June 1985, despite the best efforts of the IRS, he'd saved $40,000 from publishing royalties. It was time to make some new music or, at least, some more music. He went to LA, rented a house with Sex Pistol Steve Jones, and spent four months doing demos on an eight-track machine in the house of photographer Olivier Ferrand. Eleven tracks, including covers of Hendrix's 'Purple Haze' and Sly Stone's 'Family Affair', as well as new tunes like 'Cry For Love', 'Winners And Losers' and 'Fire Girl', came from these sessions. He wisely used his own money to rent the recording studio and to cover Jones' expenses.

'Family Affair' takes on board the dark brown nature of Sly Stone's original and adds Pop's own sombre perspective to the brown sugar mix. Pop is at his most radio friendly here while sacrificing nothing by way of hip intelligent delivery. The track is, however, marred by a duet vocal from an anonymous lady who sounds like she was recruited in the local karaoke bar.

In October he returned to New York, where as luck would have it Bowie was in town doing his soundtrack for the Jim Henson movie *Labyrinth*. Iggy visited him at his hotel suite, and they played each other their new demoes.

Iggy: "He was sceptical at first; I think he didn't want to put the tapes on because he probably thought that I was out in California doing Stooges retreads. And he heard the tapes and his jaw dropped! I was really proud that he and Coco really liked them. I was able to show them that I had not been wasting my time, or wasting the money that I'd made off his records."

History does not record why Bowie's jaw dropped when he heard the rather hackneyed rock anthems that Jones and Pop had concocted out in LA. But the tracks did the trick because Bowie decided to get on board. Between November '85 and May '86 Bowie and Pop travelled to the Caribbean and Switzerland, swimming and skiing and meeting all the other beautiful people. They created the great 'Shades', the passionate 'Isolation', 'Blah Blah Blah' and 'Hideaway'. On top of all that Bowie wrote music for what became 'Baby It Can't Fall', offered to write still more material, and proposed that he should produce an album of the collective material at Montreux Studios. Iggy agreed and went back to New York to polish up his lyrics. Songs from the LA Steve Jones demo sessions which made their way onto the eventual *Blah Blah Blah* album – 'Cry For Love', 'Fire Girls' and 'Winners And Losers' – were decidedly weaker than the Bowie co-writes. Jones and Pop had concocted pretty much Old Guy tunes; the Bowie collaborations were marginally more contemporary.

Bowie: "We went to Gstaad with our respective women and had a skiing holiday which went on for three months. I took a four-track up there. We wrote in the evenings and skied all day, and then we went down to Montreux and recorded *Blah Blah Blah* there. It worked out so well that I thought I'd record my album (*Never Let Me Down*) the same way."

Spin described the routine for *Blah Blah Blah*. "The album was recorded at Mountain Studios, in Montreux. Every morning, around 10 o'clock, Iggy and David drove around the lake, listening to a bit of tape that was laid down the night before, or maybe just listening to the radio, then got to work, went all day, occasionally taking in some sun or walking around town, getting back to David's home around 9.30 at night, whereupon they'd eat dinner, watch a movie, and go to bed. There was a kind of rhythm to the session, from doing this routine day after day, that was tedious, perhaps, but not unhealthy."

Blah Blah Blah used Brit guitarist Kevin Armstrong – who'd been a part of Bowie's Live Aid band – plus Turkish multi-instrumentalist Erdal Kizilcay as the basic instrumental grid. Co-producing the album with Bowie was Queen's engineer David Richards. This team did 10 tracks in two weeks. Steve Jones was not featured because he was busy working on former Duran Duran guitarist Andy Taylor's solo album. At that moment in time, pretty boy Taylor was expected to be very big metal business, so it was understandable that Jones passed on the Iggy project.

To achieve the so-called state-of-the-art drum sound that permeates the record – the now discredited sound of the Eighties – Bowie and Richards combined drum chips borrowed from Queen drummer Roger Taylor with live percussion. For the snare drum effect, they scanned records by Prince, PIL and Bruce Springsteen to find the sound they were looking for. All those years of swimming were now paying off for Iggy. He was prepared to sink pretty low into mainstream, mundane and contemporary fare, and to hold his breath for a long time. 'Real Wild Child' – previously recorded in 1958 as a novelty rocker by Ivan (aka Jerry Allison from Buddy Holly's Crickets) – became his first proper hit single.

The best song on *Blah Blah Blah* was 'Shades', an elegant, lean essay on male narcissism and sunglasses. It is perhaps Iggy's best hymn to his own beauty, boasting a brutally human melody. 'Shades' rises up to a plateau of male intensity – reminiscent of the Berlin work Bowie once imposed on Pop – concerning the fact that a really fine pair of shades means everything to the narrator.

After the leisurely European recording process, Iggy and Art Collins started circulating tapes of *Blah Blah Blah* to the labels. Naturally, given the Bowie involvement, albeit a Bowie who was now devalued currency, the labels wanted to hear it. Iggy got a deal with A&M, a company associated with major league AOR/MOR acts like Peter Frampton, The Police, Chris De Burgh and The Carpenters.

Iggy: "When I begin a professional relationship with somebody, often I'm called Iggy. When I met Jerry Moss, chairman of A&M Records, he called me Iggy. The president, however, always calls me Jim. The credit card company calls me James. When my father's in a good mood, he calls me Iggy just to hassle me. Occasionally my father calls me Jimbo, and sometimes my wife does too. My audience calls me Iggy, but groupies always call me Jim, because Iggy's not a romantic name. It's a dangerous name. It's the kind of name that, when shouted across a room, makes nice people wince. It's a dangerous game being called Iggy, no question about it. I'm really proud to be Iggy Pop, but if anyone's more comfortable calling me Jim, that's fine too."

He now pursued a very typical Eighties trajectory, joining the club of previously fucked-up drug addicts and deviants from the norm, now reborn as preachy and occasionally humourless shadows of their former selves, hair implants and plastic surgery akimbo, anxious to spill it to the media while flogging demeaned product in the marketplace. As part of this commercial strategy, he seemed to relish denigrating his entire previous heroic stance as an outsider artist of some importance and integrity. If you wanted to get released on music industry parole in the Eighties, and Pop certainly wanted one more chance from the corporate industry, you had to admit your sins and express your regret.

Iggy: "I knew there was this perception of me as a flake that was making it difficult for me to be taken seriously. So I combed my hair, put on a suit and went and sat down with every company president who seemed suitable and talked to them until they were convinced that I was serious."

Pop felt that radio neglect in the past had hurt him more than anything else, and that if more people had heard his music back in the Sixties and Seventies, his life might have been different. He made a conscious decision to use Bowie as his producer because he knew the big shiny name would help sugar the bitter pill which was his reputation. "I realised it's very important that the record should sound as polished, as competitive as possible. I didn't want there to be any obvious reasons why it shouldn't get on the radio."

Released in October 1986, *Blah Blah Blah* had the desired effect. A&M invested a lot of money in promotion, with ads in all the right rock papers featuring the stark black and white photographs of Michael Halsband. In these honest shots Iggy looks older and worn, his face noticeably sagging. The ad copy announced: "Get home. Kick back. Tough and steady. Better with age." The times were certainly changing; now Iggy Pop was going to make music for kicking back to. "I have no desire to continue being a failure," he admitted. "I have achieved failure so I want success. I want badly to be a very, very good artist and I don't think I'm all that great. So I've got a lot of work to do to be as good as I want, which is why I've never given up."

In *Rolling Stone*, David Fricke took the album at face value. "There is a vital edginess to Iggy's singing that elevates *Blah Blah Blah* way above recent Bowie ham like 1984's *Tonight*. In fact, although he doesn't sing or play a note here, this is one of Bowie's most dynamic outings – in terms of content, spirit and sheer cracking energy – since *Heroes*." *Creem*, no longer quite the minute bastion of underground credibility it once was, got closer to the mark. "It comes across as something of an Iggy-flavoured Bowie album. Ig's vocals are as lean and mean as his body in the cover photo, and his lyrics do their usual provocative-and-remote-as-a-trailer job. But what the public will take to heart from *Blah Blah Blah* are the swelling, booming, orchestral, fatally Bowie-esque choruses which distinguish each song." Jon Wilde of *Sounds* seemed to have either listened to a different record or to the accompanying press release. "These are Iggy's wanton instincts gathered up, back to his narcissistic, real gone best. These are ominous, boundless rhythms thundering outside your front door and yup, Iggy Pop is back with a slam. The last hero."

'Real Wild Child' did the job that cover versions are supposed to do; it went to number 10 in the UK and there were impressive chart placings all over the world for both the album and single. He appeared on *Late Night With David Letterman*, won front covers from style bibles on both sides of the Atlantic like *Spin* and *The Face*. He got his first gold record for Canadian album sales. There was lots of video airplay on MTV, especially for 'Shades', the video for which showed Pop at his best, soaking up the camera as the camera absorbs him. *Blah Blah Blah* was his biggest selling album ever. It's not much of an album, but it represents an unprecedented escape from the Last Chance Saloon.

John Cale: "A cult figure is a guy who hasn't got the musical ability to make the charts."

"I did a kid's show once . . ." Iggy chortled, delighting in his new-found media-friendly image. "There was a giant teddy bear in the corner and you had to do it at eight in the morning. I was in a bad mood, so early, and said, 'Let's rock this place!' I took this teddy bear to dance with it and during the thing I danced with it like I was having anal sex with it, and they got a lot of calls." The programme, *No. 73*, was transmitted live on December 20, '86 on the British station, ITV. They *did* get loads of complaints – so many that Iggy received a lifetime ban from that mainstream commercial channel – a lifetime achievement award of sorts. Similarly, he wasn't invited back to the BBC's flagship *Top Of The Pops* after damaging a studio piano while dancing wildly on it.

Doors that had been locked and sealed for 20 years began to open wide; Pop had finally joined the ranks of the remote rich and famous. Now he got some juicy career opportunities, including one to do a long-distance collaboration with aural manipulator and former Yellow Magic Orchestra member Ryuichi Sakamoto. This new artistic friendship – facilitated by big shot Manhattan producer Bill Laswell (who was about to play a major role in Pop's upward career trajectory) – subsequently collapsed in somewhat amusing and humiliating circumstances on a Tokyo street corner. The Sakamoto collaboration gave Pop his first real taste of what it was like to be featured on a corporate advertising campaign. By the late Nineties, the provision of his songs and Iggy Pop himself for mainstream advertising would be the most significant aspect of his career. The Sakamoto/Iggy track, 'Risky', is another great example of Iggy-as-demented-Frank-Sinatra-freak.

Bill Laswell: "No one knows this, but when we first did 'Risky' in Japan for Sakamoto they told me that I had to get Peter Gabriel to do the vocal so I said, 'Yes, of course, no problem!' I came back to New York and even talked to Peter. I said: 'They got this Ryuichi Sakamoto track they want you to do the vocal on. There would be no problems with it.' But somehow it didn't happen and I just thought of Iggy because he has that voice of his. When they finally called me from Japan I said, 'Well, don't worry. I don't have Peter Gabriel but I've got Iggy Pop.' They said, 'What?' Sakamoto was into it but nobody else got it. When we finally agreed to do it I had the tape and I went to Hawaii to do Iggy's vocal. We did it there in George Benson's recording studio, which is located in a shopping mall. We did it really quick. In Japan the track was used on a commercial for a motorcycle. A big company. Yamaha or somebody. Sakamoto was the one who got the deal on that, the track got a lot of airplay because the song was the central theme for a whole campaign."

How ironic that Iggy's lyric on 'Risky', concerning being born in a corporate dungeon, the futility of careerism, the senseless acquisition of material goods, ended up at the centre of a piece of corporate whoring. Born to a trailer park, he was about to lock himself up voluntarily within the corporate dungeon, wherein he got paid for denouncing his employers. The ironies would come rolling in as the next few years went by.

Arriving in the UK to recruit a new touring band, Iggy gushed a Niagara Falls-like amount of label-pleasing bullshit. The man, who in 1972 couldn't find a Brit rhythm section to do *Raw Power*, had changed his mind about Brit musicians. Apparently the problem with American musicians was that they were only interested in fucking women and taking drugs. "Again and again I find myself working with

"Being a survivor, that's one kind of accomplishment, but I also want to be appreciated for the work I'm doing now. I need to prove to myself that I can achieve this transition from 'God's garbage man' to someone who can offer the public more than a warped celebration of sex, drugs and dissipation." (*LFI*)

Bowie and Iggy performing 'China Girl' at the China Club, NYC, 1986. The royalties from Bowie's cover version funded Pop's comeback. (*Dominick Conde/Rex*)

Backstage with son Eric – now Iggy's tour manager. (*John Paschal/LFI*)

Iggy with his all-time hero, Keith Richards, 1988. (*Bob Gruen/Star File*)

Iggy in the moshpit. (*Andy Chambers/Rex*)

The World's Forgotten Boy pushes 50.
(*D. Sillitoe/Camera Press*)

Iggy the socialite, attending another celebrity-studded
bash. (*Chris Ashford/Camera Press*)

Iggy in a stage heap with admirers from Sonic Youth and Mudhoney. (*S.I.N./Corbis*)

The highlight of a failed movie career, *The Crow: City Of Angels,* 1996. (*LFI*)

With Johnny Depp, Cannes Film Festival, 1997. (*Axel Grousset/LFI*)

With Warhol collaborator and old friend, Gerard Malanga. (*Gerard Malanga*)

With second wife, Suchi. (*Nick Elgar/LFI*)

Back on the streets, *Beat 'Em Up* promotion, NYC, 2001. (*Jason Homa*)

It takes a big girl to satisfy a big boy, with girlfriend Nena at the *Kerrang!* Awards, London, 2001. (*Marc Larkin/LFI*)

"He really knows how to do it now, and still *does* do it," said Bob Gruen. "A lot of other performers you see tend to drift into a routine at his age, or not to be so interested because they're doing the same songs over and over again. He avoids that trap…" (*Rodolphe Baras/LFI*)

the British. For some reason, I tend to have more in common with the people I meet in London than with American musicians. The American bands I've had usually want to score girls and drugs more than they want to make really good music. Britain is a poor country with a lot of very talented people, so you meet all sorts of very hard-working, hustling guys here."

Guitarist Kevin Armstrong was retained from the *Blah Blah Blah* sessions as band leader and recruiter. Seamus Beghan, a former session player, was put on the keys. The rhythm section featured Phil Butcher on bass and Gavin Harrison on drums. The *Blah Blah Blah* tour began in the US West Coast in late October 1986. After two weeks of American clubs (including two New York shows at the Ritz with Bowie and Mick Jagger in attendance), the band moved on to concert halls and theatres in Europe, hitting Pop's beloved and poverty-stricken London just before Christmas.

A new formula was introduced, a lucrative formula which remained in place for the forseeable future. Pop began doing a steady greatest hits set derived from The Stooges and Bowie-period albums, combined with heavy plugging of his new product. The sound became somewhat standardised no-bullshit stripped down contemporary rawk. In '86 this meant the sort of punk metal championed by The Cult or Guns N'Roses. By 2002 it meant a return to the original Stooges attack with a liberal dose of nu metal *a la* Slipknot or Limp Bizkit thrown in. And then, when that strategy fell victim to the law of diminishing returns, he went right back to the start all over again.

The *Hollywood Reporter* liked the clean new show: "Iggy has weathered incredibly well, considering how much he's abused himself with the excesses of rock life over the years. He's cleaned up his act, he looks good, and his vocals are as fiery as ever."

While rehearsing in London for his first European tour in six years, Pop met up with rising indie darlings and Manhattan boho socialites Sonic Youth. While preparing for an important show at London's Town and Country Club the Youth started rehearsing 'I Wanna Be Your Dog' which they felt would help pad out their set.

Lee Renaldo (Sonic Youth): "It turns out that Iggy himself is down the hall whipping and strutting his Euro band into shape and we see him in the hall. Kim (Deal) peeks into his rehearsal while they're doing 'Dog' in order to see what the third verse is. Later we all meet him and pay respects which is so cool even now, in a kind of a cartoon-ceremonial way. And he asks to come see us tomorrow so we say, well, yeah, we suppose we can manage to squeeze him on the list."

Iggy did go down to the show the following night and joined Renaldo and Co. onstage for a couple of numbers. Members of Sonic Youth and their support act fiREHOSE would subsequently play a major part in reviving the fortunes of the Asheton brothers, to the extent that Pop eventually had to get on that phone, call Ann Arbor, and go back to where he once belonged.

Mike Watt (Minutemen, fiREHOSE, reformed Stooges): "I was opening for Sonic Youth with my band fiREHOSE in 1986. While SY were playing they pulled Iggy out of the crowd to do 'I Wanna Be Your Dog' with him. After the gig I said hi to Iggy and to give him much respect for all the great work he's done. He told me he'd like to talk more but he had a plane to catch and ran out of the place. It looked like he was running all the way to the airport!"

Wayne Kramer: "The things that motivate him are deep. They're not thin 'I want to be a pop star' type motivations. He's got these demons in him and he exorcises them by being a singer, writing songs, and making records."

A one-month break over Christmas and the New Year saw him visiting his parents in their new home at Myrtle Beach, South Carolina. He then went back on the road in January '87, opening for The Pretenders on a Japanese tour. By June he was back in Europe for several outdoor festivals. This concentration on European summer festivals became, like the new formulaic set, a permanent strategy. Just as heavy guitar-driven rock underwent a global revival, Iggy became a welcome festival guest, always located somewhere towards the top of the bill. After the Lollapalooza festivals altered the whole concept of what a rock festival should be, it became compulsory to have at least one credible "Famous Old Guy" act on the bill as window dressing. All over Europe, and elsewhere from time to time, the likes of Pop and The Ramones benefited from this. "Much respect" from the Red Hot Chili Peppers/Beastie Boys generation of brain-dead skate kids and lobotomised mall punks turned into much money for the likes of Pop and The Ramones.

These festival appearances in front of crowds of 20,000 to 50,000 receptive young kids did great things for Pop's demographic spread. With a bona fide hit single and saturation airplay via ads and movies, he was finally somebody that people had heard of. While contemporaries like Lou Reed could afford to rest on their highbrow cultural laurels, to play the museums like some dilettante, Pop was out on the grunge circuit enduring punishing tour schedules, determined in his forties to finally get somewhere.

His next album, *Instinct*, didn't deliver any hit singles but garnered considerable airplay, MTV video rotation, and interest. 'High On You' is an enjoyable homage to Sly Stone's 'I Get High On You'. The tracks worked better live than on record, blending in well with the Stooges material. The producer chosen for this crucial project was Brion Gysin admirer – and Michigan expat – Bill Laswell. A respected industry insider, Laswell played bass with his own avant-jazz project Material, had a major role in the development of hip hop/rock fusion, and produced everybody from The Ramones to Yoko Ono to Mick Jagger to William Burroughs to The Last Poets.

Bill Laswell: "I got the impression that he wanted to do a successful album. That was one of the things he had in mind with *Instinct*. He was very serious about the whole thing, brought a lot of determination to it. But he was never humourless but quite the opposite, very loose, relaxed, and easy to work with. He'd written the songs and taken a great deal of care with them. We did a lot of talking before we started working. Again, this was not complicated music. We worked on guitar sounds, getting a good feel for everything. There were a lot of guitar overdubs to be considered, just to make things bigger sounding. We spent a lot of time judging the various performances by the band. But this was not exactly difficult music so it was more about the overall feel and energy than about a precision performance. I leaned towards the two Bowie-produced Berlin albums as a reference more than anything else because I thought that Iggy had a quality in his voice that wasn't raw like a punk singer, that was a sort of mutant Frank Sinatra. He definitely had that possibility with the low end; down at the low end of his voice he definitely had a very real sound. I think one day he will do ballads and things where he can really use his voice. His sense of pitch, his approach to pitch, is not a trained academic one. It's more expressive. There is something there that people really want to hear, but I think it depends on the material that he chooses to sing. He still has a big future with that voice he has. He can still do a lot of things."

Iggy subsequently contributed readings of texts by his old pal Brion Gysin and William Burroughs to a Laswell-produced album – *Hashisheen* – concerning the Bin Laden-like leader of the Cult Of The Assassins, Hassan I Sabbah. The idea for the album came from the now-discredited counterculture guru Hakim Bey, a supporter of the North American Man Boy Love Association sometimes described as a "counterculture criminal". Bey wrote an influential essay on the Assassins and was, at that time, a peripheral influence on Laswell.

Iggy's Burroughs reading was accompanied by music from Techno

Animal. The project also featured Patti Smith, the unpleasant cult leader Genesis P. Orridge, and pussy-powered poet cum rock biz PR Nicole Blackman. These were not great performances by Pop. He showed neither enthusiasm nor sympathy for the intellectual material he was handed, sounding like an indifferent George W. Bush reading from the writings of Bin Laden. Matters of mythology, subversion and conspiracy clearly didn't register with the same resonance as deals with Converse, Reebok, or Virgin Atlantic. *Hashisheen* was subsequently issued on the Belgian indie label, Sub Rosa.

Bill Laswell: "I wanted him to do the readings because he just has a great speaking voice. And his name doesn't hurt when you're trying to sell a project. People like to see his name. And he is also interested in that whole area. That's the real reason. He related very much to the project."

With a new album on the market, it was time to hit the road again. The *Instinct* Tour completed the cycle which began when Pop cleaned up his act. The strong new band was lead by Andy McCoy, the notorious one-time guitarist with Finnish Boulevard of Broken Dreams leaseholders Hanoi Rocks. Yet another Keith Richards wannabe, McCoy was an interesting player and there were people in several towns – London, LA, Tokyo – willing to pay money to go and see McCoy playing in his own right. Captured on the influential semi-bootleg *Live At The Channel* album, the *Instinct* tour was a seamless blend of Stooges classics, well known solo songs (mainly from *Lust For Life* and *The Idiot*), and large chunks of *Instinct*. For the second time in two years Iggy was promoting a release that he'd reason to believe his audience would actually be familiar with.

McCoy suggested to Pop that former UK Subs bass player Alvin Gibbs would be good for the band so an audition was agreed upon. After some to-ing and fro-ing, the summons to meet with Iggy came via McCoy, who showed up at Gibbs' LA front door with the good news: "Come on, we're meeting Iggy in 30 minutes and I want to drink a beer with you first."

The site of this meeting was an upmarket Hollywood apartment inhabited by one of McCoy's LA pals. Gibbs and McCoy decamped to the balcony where they sipped beer until a candy apple red sports car ground to a halt in front of the apartment complex. "Shit man, that's Jim's car," McCoy spluttered. "Quick, get these beer bottles out of here." The owner of the apartment went to receive Iggy while the young punks for hire dropped the beer cans into a quickly hidden bin liner.

Alvin Gibbs: "I was shocked when I first met him, which was when I went to do a sort of interview for the gig as bass player. I'd only seen him prior to that on the *David Letterman* show when his previous record had been *Blah Blah Blah* and *Instinct* was just out. I'd seen him do 'Real Wild Child' on *Letterman*. He looked great, his hair was kind of short, he had a black turtleneck shirt on and a nice leather jacket. He looked like somebody healthy, slightly affluent, but not garish. It just suited him, his personality. Then suddenly he walks in through the door and he looks like he'd been hanging around with Steve Jones and his biker pals for too long. He has this leather vest on, these ripped up jeans, his hair has gotten really long and all over the place. He was wearing all these kind of studded rings. I just thought, 'Hmmm . . . trying too hard.' I was a bit taken aback. Then when I started working with him I saw that that was another way of twisting and turning, trying to do the David Bowie thing of constantly changing. But it seems to me that since then it's kind of stuck, that rockist image, that he's not bothered twisting and turning again. It's been very flat."

Pop's main question during what was obviously a very casual job interview concerned the equipment Gibbs favoured – he wanted to know what Gibbs played. Gibbs told him he used a Gibson Thunderbird put through an old Ampeg valve amp "for a loud fat sound". Pop deemed this to be "cool" and shortly afterwards started looking at his watch; they'd been talking for an hour and now he was running late for an important MTV interview. He told Gibbs he'd heard good things about his playing, and that he'd be giving him a call. As he made his way back to his car he asked McCoy to join him for a moment.

A few minutes later McCoy came back into the room. "You're in, man. Jim likes you. Expect a phone call tomorrow." Gibbs asked McCoy why they'd had to go to so much trouble to hide the beer before Pop arrived, and McCoy kind of grimaced and muttered, "It's politics, man, fucking politics."

Another detoxed rock'n'roll "survivor", Steve Tyler from Aerosmith, maintains a strict backstage substance ban. While life was not quite as puritanical in the Pop camp, the chemical behaviour of band members was carefully monitored by roadies and by Pop himself. The musicians were instructed that "this was to be a clean tour, with no drink or soft drugs before rehearsals or performances, and hard drugs forbidden at all times." One day when the conventionally hedonistic McCoy showed up three hours late for rehearsal with a strong smell of booze coming from him, Iggy exploded, telling McCoy: "You little fucker, if you mess me around I'm going to fuck you up real good." McCoy mumbled something to the effect that he'd been held up in traffic, to which his employer replied, "No drinking before rehearsals, you know the rules.

Either get your shit together or you get out." Then Pop launched his mike stand through the drum kit, kicked over a Marshall amp, and stormed out of the rehearsal room in a fit of pique, later to return much calmed down.

The first task for the new band was to make a video for the first single to be issued from *Instinct*; 'Cold Metal', a Billy Idol/Cult-style rocker which invokes the spirit of Jimi Hendrix in an exceptionally implausible and plastic MTV manner. The shoot was directed in Eighties rockist style by *Evil Dead/Spiderman* director Sam Raimi. Steve Jones, who played all over the *Instinct* album, was there for the video though his participation in the forthcoming world tour was confined to a few cameo appearances at high-profile showcase gigs like LA's Whisky A Go-Go and the important industry gathering, the New Music Seminar in New York.

Alvin Gibbs: "We had a whole list of characters showing up for rehearsals. We had this guy Axl who'd worked and trained under Salvador Dali. Axl made jewellery. Really surreal and beautiful stuff. He'd known Iggy back in the late Sixties. He'd bring stuff for Iggy to wear onstage. He turned up again later in New York with still more stuff for him to wear. I remember one was like an eyepatch with an eye on the outside of the eyepatch, this silver eye with liquid in it which moved around, causing a really strange effect. Penn and Teller the magicians would turn up. They were good friends of his. One of them, the tall one, had a request. Would Iggy do 'Five Foot One' because the line in that song 'I just wish life could be Swedish magazines' was, he thought, the best line ever in rock'n'roll. The actor James Russo was there once. We had a guy come around whose dad owned a sports manufacturing plant or something, he brought golf clubs for Iggy. We just had a carnival of people wandering around, colourful characters moving in and out."

The tour had the backup of a Starliner bus where Iggy had a back room complete with video, stereo, kitchen and shower. The vehicle moved across America from gig to gig but was rarely used by the band because, in America, it was thought that the drives between shows were too long for that style of travelling. Instead the band would fly from gig to gig and the driver would show up with the Starliner. A sideline presence throughout the rehearsal period, who later came more into focus as the tour progressed, was Iggy's wife Suchi.

Alvin Gibbs: "We would always go out to dinner together afterwards. It was never a case of 'Oh, the promoter has invited Iggy out to dinner. You guys are going back to the hotel.' Often it was the other way round.

We would end up going to these things that were primarily laid on for him and he would say, 'Oh, I'm too tired,' or 'I want to go back and rest with Suchi.' And we would end up going and drinking all the champagne, having a great time. People would be going 'Where's Iggy?' and we're going, 'Oh, he's gone back to the hotel but we're here!!' Most days we would usually socialise at dinner with the promoter.

"The thing that got to me, the thing that I thought was uncalled for, was the people surrounding him. The road manager, roadies. I liked Henry McGroggan a lot, he was around for a very long time. I think he has now eased himself out of the Iggy situation a bit and is working with The Corrs. Iggy's son Eric has taken over his job. There were a couple of roadies who'd been with Iggy a very long time, and their attitude was, 'Well, you guys are in the band now, next tour it's probably going to be somebody different, why should we take you seriously?' There was one particular guy there and from rehearsal stage on he was getting on my nerves. He used to come pick us all up from our various places in LA, to go to rehearsal. I remember one morning we were in the bus with him. I said, 'Hi,' and he just sort of grunted. One of the guys in the band asked me what I'd been up to over the weekend. I said, 'I went and bought some clothes and things this weekend because we're going to be gone off for quite some time. I need new duds to take with me.' The next day I get a call from Art Collins saying, 'I hope everything is going all right and everything, but I hope you're getting all these songs down and you're not spending all your time shopping.' I was like, 'Whaat!! Where did you hear this?' He goes, 'Oh, you know, something was said. There's a lot of songs you've got to learn. It's like 35 songs.'"

The *Instinct* world tour was a monument to the precision micro-management that was Art Collins' specialty. First they did about 20 US club dates to get the band warmed up. Then there were big shows in Europe, ice hockey stadiums in Scandinavia, plus bigger venues in France, Germany, and England. On the East and West coast of America there were prestige gigs. In New York he played the Beacon Theater (holding 4,500 people) and The Pier (7,000 capacity). The major LA show was at the Palladium, preceded by a showcase at the Whisky A Go-Go. As the tour headed towards the American South, some of the club gigs were slightly smaller, but these too were well attended.

Trigger (owner, The Continental, a 200-capacity Lower East Side punk venue 10 minutes walk from Iggy's Avenue B apartment): "I saw him walk through the club, which he was checking out. I'd been here a year or two at that time and the club had a bit of a buzz, bands were being signed out of here. I was leaning against the bar, Iggy walked over to me, said, 'Are you Trigger?' I said, 'Yeah.' He said, 'Hi, I'm Iggy Pop.' I knew of course who he was but he said it so sweetly and humbly which was nice. 'Could I play here?' So I said, being I guess the New York smartass that I am, 'Well, bring me a demo. Let me hear what you sound like.' I was, of course, kidding but Iggy, being the sweetheart that he is, said, 'OK, man, I'll bring you a demo tomorrow.' I'm going, like, 'Only kidding Iggy, you can play here anytime.' Then we talked with Art Collins, figured out a night. It was the best night of my life here. He was so prepared. We were all in awe during the soundcheck, trying not to act like it. He took it real seriously, did the show like he was playing a stadium, did all The Stooges songs you'd want to hear.

"The place was already full when Art Collins walked up to me and said, 'Hey Trigger, here's the guest list.' I did a double take. It was a list of about a hundred people! In fairness to Art he said, 'See what you can do.' There were already 20 of my friends behind the bar to make some space, I had journalists from the *Village Voice* and Lisa Robinson behind there too because you couldn't move. Iggy had played about an hour and 20 minutes when the Fire Department showed up. They said to me, 'The show has gotta stop or at least we've got to come inside and see what's going on.' I said, 'Well, let me go and talk to the artist.' When I eventually got to Iggy, it took a while to get through the crowd to the stage, he said, 'Don't worry about it. If they close us down the club will become legendary. You'll be open again in a few days or a week at the most.' The Fire Department waited another 10 or 15 minutes, then they came in and turned off the PA. Iggy just threw the mike behind him and kept on singing without it. Eventually they put the house lights on, and started walking through the crowd."

Alvin Gibbs: "My understanding of Iggy Pop and the whole mythology was that here was this kind of wild guy who lived life at a ferocious pace, was self-destructive. Obviously at a prior time in his life, probably five or six years before I got involved with him, he realised that it was change or die, that he had to reinvent himself, to make a break with all of that, because people in the business were not prepared to take a risk with him any more. He had become like a Johnny Thunders–style character. He actually told me that at one point he was going to get a band together with Thunders, when Iggy was at his most drugged out and crazed. Just the idea of those two in a band working together . . . the mind boggles!"

Backstage in San Francisco, Gibbs introduced Iggy to his brother-in-law who'd been a big fan for years. He introduced Iggy as "Jim". As the name passed from his lips he was almost sure that he saw a flicker of annoyance in Pop's eyes. Jim, he realised, was now a name reserved for his close business associates, family and friends.

Supporting cock rocker Jimmy Barnes in New Zealand, Iggy found himself confronted with corporate onstage advertising in the form of a huge banner which proclaimed the good news: Pepsi Cola – The Voice Of A New Generation. On either side of the stage where he was expected to perform were two 10-foot banners boasting the trademark Pepsi logo. For some reason Pop took huge umbrage at this sight, giving his audience reason to believe that he was opposed to both corporate life, and the interconnection between major corporations and his music. Given the remorseless range and number of business connections he was forging between his own art and multinationals like Reebok and Nike, this was pure hypocrisy. He nevertheless painted himself as the anti-corporate man of the people with great aplomb. Up to a point. He knew before he walked on stage that Pepsi were the show sponsors.

After opening his set with 'TV Eye' he addressed the crowd, pointing at the banners, saying, "See that? I'd rather drink my own piss than touch that vile shit." Later it was, "If those fuckers are the voice of the new generation, then I'm glad I'm a fuckin' old fart." Still later there was an anti-corporate soliloquy: "Those evil sons of bitches at fuckin' Pepsi want to rot your guts and brains with their poisonous shit. They want to fill your veins full of their pus, filth and garbage, and turn you into non-thinking bloated fucking consumers. Well . . . fuck them, fuck them, fuck them!"

He then called for 'Search And Destroy', commenting, " 'Cos that's what I'm gonna do to the assholes who expect me to sing with that on my stage." A representative of Pepsi approached tour manager Henry McGroggan with a word of warning. At the end of the set Pop was about to deliver another principled anti-multinational diatribe, but a word in the ear from McGroggan drove him over the edge. Pointing to the spot where the local Pepsi head honchos were seated, Pop shouted, "Fuck you, you fuckers! Corporate pieces of shit . . . fuck you all," before jumping onto the Pepsi banners and tearing them to the ground while the audience goaded him on.

The next date on the Pepsi tour was Auckland. Before the show two lawyers from Pepsi approached McGroggan and registered a formal complaint in the strongest possible terms about Pop's anti-Pepsi comments and the damaging of their hoardings. More to the point, they made it clear that if there was any recurrence of the "vile, inflammatory and patently untruthful comments" about their product or any further attempted destruction of their property, they would sue Pop for defamation and criminal damage. To this end, they told McGroggan, they'd be bringing their own film crew to the next show to collect evidence of any such infringements. This had the desired effect. Apart from some minor league posturing, Pop withdrew from his war against the corporation.

Alvin Gibbs: "When we toured Suchi was with him quite a lot. There were one or two occasions when she stayed behind in New York. We did a Canadian section to the American tour which was about two weeks long. She didn't come out on that. Apart from that and perhaps one other occasion, she was always there. I still find it kind of difficult to think of him without her. They seemed so close. The rare occasions when she wasn't there he would take advantage. One time Suchi had gone home that morning and we drove from the USA into Canada. I think we were playing in Toronto, this place called the RPM, where we were doing three nights. We did the soundcheck, he came offstage and there were these two hideous looking bruisers hanging around. They were hideous, they had caked make-up on, they must have weighed about 400 pounds each. They were just truly terrible. Even Andy McCoy was going, 'Oh, man! Look at these monsters.' And Iggy came down the steps from the stage, saw them lurking there, grabbed them both and said, 'Two of the best in the house!!' took them backstage and fucked them during the soundcheck.

"I was just like, 'My God! Has the man no shame?' Suchi had just gone home that morning. I just knew he didn't use protection. He just got right in there. I asked him about it later on. I said, 'How was those two . . . things! The groupies you were with?' He was like, 'Oh, yeeeah, man. Ah, God! They were horrible, weren't they? Yeah, but you know, sometimes you just want to get down and dirty.' I kind of know what he meant. His life had become good, he had this beautiful wife. Sometimes he just wanted to get back in the dirt and roll around, like his song, 'Some Weird Sin'. Things get too straight and you can't bear it. He still has that instinct in him, when things are cool and going well, he still needs to get down and do things that are outrageous and not necessarily going to embellish his reputation or new-found professionalism. But he pulls back from that quite quickly, whereas before that sort of incident would have lead to a major lapse. The same with the drugs thing."

In Sao Paulo Iggy got pissed off when he found he'd been booked into a hotel which didn't meet his standards. The building looked like a Warsaw tower block, had no room service, bar, or swimming pool. Pop told Henry McGroggan that, quite simply, this was not good enough; he, his wife, and his band needed to be someplace nice. McGroggan passed on his displeasure to the local promoter – who was obviously expecting a rock'n'roll dude, not this older, hard working, somewhat dried up and out entertainer – explaining that the band were all worn out and needed to relax.

There are two sides to this coin. It might seem somewhat petulant or prima donna-ish to demand swimming pools in each and every hotel, and many people visit hotels from one end of their lives to the other without ever calling for room service. But long band tours are genuinely heavy going and the artist always looks forward to slumping into the womb-like comfort of a well-ordered hotel. The Sao Paulo promoter, after digesting McGroggan's request, proceeded to stomp up and down the foyer, waving his hands around and speaking very rapidly in Portuguese, implying that the whole lot of them were a gang of arrogant, spoilt, foreign bums who could fuck off out of there on the next available flight.

"What the fuck is he saying, Henry?" Iggy asked. "Tell him I'm tired, my wife and band are tired, and we want a better hotel now!" This brought further abuse from the promoter, causing Iggy to break a low table in the lobby with a stamp of his heavy right boot. Then the hotel concierge leapt over his desk and waved a fist in Iggy's face. Iggy pushed the concierge in the chest and was all set to go for him when McGroggan got in between them. Suchi was pleading with her husband to calm down when suddenly, like a scene from a Keystone Cops caper, a bunch of local media and paparazzi appeared upon the scene to capture the chaos for the local papers. The timing seemed a little too good. The next day the local *Illustrada* newspaper carried the headline "Rock Star Iggy Pop Physically Assaults Promoter Over Hotel Accommodation And Threatens To Cancel Show" along with five photographs of Pop – all bug eyed and spiky haired – in various stages of barely controlled dementia, looking old, worn out, frayed, and undignified.

The ensuing shows at Sao Paulo's 4,000-seater Projecto Theatre were infested by crowds of privileged local rich kids since the price of a ticket was more than the average Brazilian worker earned in a month. With this little statistic in mind, and the hotel incident still irking him, Pop proceeded to deliver a rant against his elitist audience: "Yeah, you've got money all right . . . big cars, houses, servants . . . but really, you ain't got shit, you ain't got heart, you ain't got balls, you ain't got nuthin'," before directing the band: "Play for these zombie motherfuckers, 'Your Pretty Rich Face Is Going To Hell'."

The next adolescent outburst against adult authority figures took place in London, during the taping of an appearance on Channel 4's *Wired* show. When the band showed up on the set for rehearsals, they found flash bombs, firework effects, and flashing disco lights everywhere. This was standard rock industry crap in the Eighties and Pop was promoting *Instinct*, an album of quintessentially Eighties rock. What did he expect? The band set themselves up, and Pop positioned himself in front of the lead singer's mike.

"Mr Director, where are ya?" he asked into the microphone.

"How can I help you, Mr Pop?" inquired the director, all concerned to assist the star of the moment.

"You can help me by getting rid of all this shit," remarked Pop, waving his hands in the direction of the special effects. "And while you're at it, change these fucking Mickey Mouse lights, will ya?"

"What we're trying to do here is make the whole show look exciting," explained the director. He claimed that he was seeking to achieve a stimulating visual image. Next thing Pop threw his mike stand into the air and onto a camera where it bounced off the cameraman's head and smashed through part of the plastic stage set.

"You hire a rock'n'roll singer and his band to perform and entertain and then you insult them," Pop shouted as he walked around the stage kicking over amps, drum kit, and set. "You wanna see excitement? You wanna see something stimulating. Is that fucking stimulating enough for ya?"

He told *Creem* that his hobbies included tracing his roots, "Clairol #7 – Ash Blonde". He claimed to be reading *Theories and Techniques of Conceptual Art*. His message to the world was "You paid five bucks and I'm makin' $10,000, baby, so screw ya!" In an episode of *Tales From The Crypt* he played himself. The storyline concerned a dodgy showbiz promoter who puts on a benefit gig with Iggy as the main attraction.

On his way to a show at the University of Wisconsin, about to enter the venue by a back door, a grinning student jock yelled at Pop, "Where did you get the wig from, freak?" The touchy Pop, whose faintly receding hairline can be spotted in photographs taken many years before, and whose then-spiky hairdo certainly had a synthetic look about it, delivered a right hook to the jock, screaming, "Get up, motherfucker. Come on . . . Get up!" before cooler heads intervened to restore peace.

When the time came to play Japan the film star and composer Ryuichi Sakamoto – whose 'Risky' track had featured Iggy the year before – invited Pop and Suchi to join him for dinner in a place way across the other side of Tokyo from where his team were staying. Pop and wife headed off into the rainy night to meet the high profile musician with great expectations for the social evening ahead. Sakamoto proceeded to blow them out unceremoniously. The somewhat singed Osterberg couple showed up back at a restaurant where the backing band and crew were dining. "It was fucking embarrassing," Pop admitted. "Sakamoto pulled up in his limo just as we arrived at the restaurant. He got out, said he had something else on and that we'd get together another time. Then he drove off in the limo leaving Suchi and me just standing there in the fucking rain."

This kind of confrontational touring took its toll on his psyche and his body. Although he'd moderated the chemical aspect of his behaviour, his shows were as out-there as ever. He would still leap into the crowd, get naked, burn off energy like a teenager. Halfway through the tour he pulled a thigh muscle, had a gash across his left eye, a deep wound to his chest plus endless bumps and bruises over his entire body. One night after a show, when Pop walked off, covered in blood from a head wound and black and blue from diving off the drum riser into wire mesh covered monitors, a stage hand shouted, "How goes the war?"

"Can't you see?" Pop replied, without breaking his stride. "The bad guys are winning."

CHAPTER 21

I Got Bored So I'm Making My Millions – *Brick By Brick*

"By the time you get to Green Day or Blink-182 and ones like that, there's no difference between that and a Lesley Gore record like 'It's My Party' or 'Yummy Yummy Yummy I Got Love In My Tummy'. It's inoffensive and personally, I dunno, I like music that's more offensive. I like it to sound like nails on a black-board, get me wild. Get me liquored up wild, that 'I'll do anything' feeling. That's kind of gone out of it now, though. The most successful stuff is sold to you as indispensable social information. The message in the music is, 'We are terribly, terribly slick and suave, and if you listen to us, you can probably get a leg up in society too.' That's sort of your R.E.M. and your U2."

– Iggy to *The Big Takeover*, 2001

"He probably doesn't have any friends. I think he always likes to have a young girlfriend; that's important to him."

– Dee Dee Ramone

BETWEEN 1990 and 2001 Iggy Pop rose to the occasion presented to him by his management and the massed entertainment industries. Gone were the days of small projects ignored by an indifferent public. The kid who began his career with Andy Warhol and David Bowie dancing attention grew up to be a man who pandered to the tastes and prejudices of lowest common denominator middle America. He became a hero to the shelf stackers of this world and three or four of his best songs could be heard regularly in white trash bars, amusement arcades, and the occasional shopping mall.

This was an achievement of sorts given the tough sound on some of those songs, given the profoundly chaotic conditions in which they were originally recorded, given the indifference with which they were originally greeted. Not every Nineties project he got involved with was excellent, not every performance he gave was great. Obviously clear of his past drug problems, Iggy worked at making up for lost time. Something got lost in the translation, but he was obviously in a clean-up-or-die situation.

Iggy, Virgin Records autobiographical sketch: "NYC permanent headquarters now, got a place in Mexico to go to when I can't stand it any more, love my garden, my wife, my dog and cat, a lot. But also love noise aggravation, girls, regular guys, music as much. Drink beer and wine sometimes, hate publicity whores, hokey music, people who wanna use me, and conceited dicks. Ambition is to make better, live life in peace, and then die. Check out my fucking record because it's really good. When I play around your town check that out too, because that'll be the same, only more."

Iggy to Nick Kent: "The young girls who turn up to my shows in LA for example . . . They all think they're living in a rock video all the time. Those girls torment me when I perform. They act like little kittens, 'Maybe you'd like to fuck me!' And I know I'm not going to fuck them, so I'm going crazy! That shit drives me nuts."

The new Iggy drank alcohol occasionally, but he had a strict rule, which was that there was no rule. Once, after doing a line of coke, he realised he didn't particularly enjoy it. He smoked a little pot after a gig at Coney Island High. He didn't know what he was doing because he was slightly drunk after downing three gin and tonics. His alcohol consumption in his day-to-day life was confined to a glass of wine with dinner. And not two drinks. One.

Iggy: "I think people should get as messed up as they can. But I know what I can do and what I can't. Some people can't do it at all. And I respect that and understand it and applaud them that they can't. Having said that, I've got to say, even the little bit that I do, I do notice there are times when I don't really do any. Which is usually if I go visit my mother or father. For those four or five days, even though I don't stay with them, I never have a drink. I just don't do anything for those four or five days and I always notice at the end of that period, I have a kind of shine, an energy, a feeling that I never have otherwise. So there's something to be said for abstinence."

One Danish journalist made the mistake of drinking beer before an 11 am appointment to interview Pop. The hack was shaking when he asked, "So, on this new album you are just using those same old rock chords?" to which Pop's understandable response was, "What chords do you want me to use, motherfucker?" The next Danish inquiry was, "How does it feel to be old? Do your knees hurt?"

He did a lot of flying and grew tired of taking limos out to JFK, listening to drivers who wanted him to help them out with their music careers. All this flying gave him a penchant for flight attendants, a penchant he would subsequently indulge to the hilt. It was one of his big ambitions to fuck a flight attendant, an experience he'd yet to have. He figured that back in his wild days he was just *too* wild for the flight attendants of this world, that he wasn't flight attendant material.

Brick By Brick, 1990's follow-up to *Instinct*, was powerful and un-expected. Producer Don Was knew how to restore legendary Old Guys to their former cultural glories. The dreary-but-worthy Bonnie Raitt and the far from dreary B-52s became pop chart superstars under his guidance. Dylan, Willie Nelson, Kris Kristofferson and The Highway-men were amongst his hirsute successes. Was would subsequently super-vise a vast tranche of late-period Stones masterpieces. And he was from Detroit. He brought all of his skills to bear on *Brick By Brick* and pro-duced an album which didn't outwardly resemble anything else in Pop's canon. He was boldly going where he had never gone before.

Was assembled a few unexpected musicians for the sessions. There were two basic bands, representing musical chalk and cheese. One – semi-acoustic, radio friendly, and surprisingly effective – centred around AOR heavyweights like Jackson Browne's mandolin playing collabora-tor David Lindley and guitarist Waddy Watchel. The other – adopting a more traditional kickass punk approach – featured guitarist Slash and bassist Duff McKagan from Guns N'Roses.

There is more depth and guts to *Brick By Brick* than there had been in either *Blah Blah Blah* or *Instinct*. Most of the songs deal with the music business, celebrity, America, or urban life. These themes stuck, Pop making them his own as he progressed through the Nineties. Kate Pierson from the B-52s was lured in to do a warm pop duet with Iggy on the Blondie-like 'Candy', a Sonny & Cher-style single which got lots of airplay but which didn't deliver the big hit that might have been expected.

'The Undefeated', claiming that life is just "a bag of pot", is a celebra-tion of the rugged individual fighting a world swiftly turning into one giant gaol, a clear reference to the progressively corporate nature of con-temporary rock'n'roll. The sharp hostile lyric is somewhat undermined by the presence in the studio of a massed male choir including high level record company guys and dudes from music publishing companies who chant the "We're the Undefeated" chorus behind Pop. It was a classic stunt, Iggy and Art Collins at their fancy footwork best, all the execs getting vocal credits on the liner notes. Tagged on unexpectedly at the end of *Brick By Brick* is 'Living On The Edge Of The Night' – the Scott Walker-like theme song from the Michael Douglas hit thriller, *Black Rain*.

Iggy's drifting son Eric Benson, sometimes affectionately known as Ewreck, who'd tried his hand at many different things, was now reported to be fronting a band, proving what a great job his Dad had done in keeping him out of the rock'n'roll menagerie. "His pitching's a little suspect," said the proud indulgent father, betraying his age, "but all the girls want to fuck him and that's 80 per cent of the deal taken care of right there.

"My son's mother is gay. And she's a really cool chick, right? And I respect her. I was with him the other day and we were in a cab and we were out in like bumfuck land in Arizona. This cab driver . . . Melissa Etheridge was singing . . . so I went, 'Wow, she can really belt out a tune.' I wasn't sure it was her, and I said, 'That chick's got a lot of voice,' and the cab driver went, 'Yeah, her girlfriend thinks so too.' And I went, 'Woah!' And of course, it really offended my kid too, 'cause you know, he's sensitive to that. We didn't say anything. I guess we were supposed to buddy-in and say, 'Hey, yeah,' but we didn't and the guy, he looked just like a normal human being, he looked clean – he actually said, 'Yeah, when I read that it made me sick. It made me sick.' And I was like, 'Woah,' y'know?"

One night he was relaxing at home watching TV when the phone rang. He didn't answer because he was in the middle of watching something. The caller was Kurt Cobain who was then at the height of his fame, success, and confusion. He left a message saying it was Kurt from Nirvana and, 'Why don't you call me and maybe we can get in the studio or something to kick around some shit together?' At that stage Iggy was wary of proposals of this sort. Rubbing up against chart-topping younger punkish guys in the hope of getting a little demographic traction was still a little way down the road. "I didn't wanna be produced or done up or be a Nirvana mascot or something," he said. "But I had enough respect for him to call him back. But when I called him back it was like, 'This is the Four Seasons Hotel . . . Mr Cobain is hanging upside down like a bat from the ceiling for the next 32 hours' or whatever. So I said, 'Great, just leave a message that I called.'"

He started work on a new book, recounting memorable moments from his sex life. He wrote down the names of 52 girls he recalled being with because there are 52 cards in a deck. When he'd remember some dirty little occurrence to do with one of those girls he'd write it down in explicit detail; what he did with her, plus the emotional aspect of it if there was an emotional aspect, plus any weird shit that might have gone down.

Iggy: "Each girl gets her name, and what I call her story, an explicit tale of what it was like to be with her, and what it was like for her to be inside me, metaphorically speaking, and what the circumstances were and what I felt about the whole thing. I gave it to some publishers, three men and one woman. Two of the men came back with, 'Well, this is not a book yet, but it could develop into something.' And the female came back with, 'I like sexy writing as well as the next woman, but this lacks a certain subtlety.'"

He wrote 10 of these vulgar vignettes before he had to turn his attention towards a new album. The intense *American Caesar* became a sometimes raucous meditation on American imperialism, by way of comparison with the ancient Roman Empire. The idea came to him back in '82 after he'd read an abridged version of *The Decline and Fall of the Roman Empire* by Gibbon. In the middle of the night, in a dilapidated cheap hotel room, he'd curl up in bed with the book, sustained by booze and drugs. Back then he savoured the clash of beliefs, personalities and values being played out on antiquity's stage by inelegant crowds led by huge archetypal characters. "And that was the end of that," he said. "Or so I thought. Eleven years later I stood in a dilapidated but elegant room in a rotting mansion in New Orleans and listened as a piece of music strange to my ears pulled me back to ancient Rome and called forth those ghosts to merge in hilarious, bilious presence with the Schwartzkopfs, Schwarzeneggers and Sheratons of modern American money and muscle-myth. Out of me poured information I had no idea I ever knew, let alone retained, in an extemporaneous soliloquy I called 'Caesar'."

Lacking the nastiness of 'Dum Dum Boys', *American Caesar*'s 'Character' is a mellow elegiac meditation on musicians Pop used to work with when young. He recalls old rock compatriots who may have driven him nuts with their antics but who certainly had some character. He says that those long-forgotten longhair junkies screwed up but that at least when they played the guitar they meant it, unlike the contemporary "white bread boys" of punk metal who "don't even know how to puke".

'Wild America' is a thick juicy slice of American Gothic, *a la* Raymond Carver. It deals with an anonymous sexual encounter which gets going because of a chance meeting between the narrator/hero and a Mexicana who has a butch girlfriend, whom the hero thinks is a man. The two dykes take the hero down an alley to have a little talk with him. There they encounter the dregs of street corner society furtively busy doing this and that in Wild America. The narrator ends up in a lucky situation; driving around in a black car with the Mexicana who offers him methedrine when all he wants is good old-fashioned marijuana.

American Caesar, recorded in New Orleans and partially conceived in Miami, took on board for the first time Pop's burgeoning interest in Hispanic/Latino culture and sexual manners. 'Mixing The Colors' is about the fact that America is turning into a place of race war games, a multicultural kaleidoscope, and about the ameliorating aspect of music. The American South would swamp his life and art over the next few years.

It was around this time that he started displaying a tendency to make long albums with lots of tracks on them. There are 17 tracks on *American Caesar*, which comes in at 76 minutes long. Such fecundity led to one dud, the schmaltzy and dated 'It's Our Love', but this is mainly a very good album. Special guests included unhitched hardcore singer Henry Rollins, Lisa Jermano, and Katell Keineg on backing vocals.

Pop was now two excellent albums away from his successful foray into MTV crossover territory, and he was once more bringing fresh meat to the table.

By the time *American Caesar* hit the shops in '93, Iggy Pop and Jim Osterberg were finally closing in on one another. Both were well into middle age. Wildman Iggy was now as interested in sitting around reading a book as scholarly Osterberg had always been. "Iggy Pop" was now a lucrative, marketable, foul-mouthed, wild American circus act, and the industrious, serious, hard-working Midwestern spirit of Jim Osterberg – and of his father Newell – was in the ascendant. The Iggy Pop show was a money orientated no-bullshit effort with no room for druggy fuck-ups or – the other side of the same coin – wild moments of unprecedented inspiration. He had possessions and responsibilities all around him. It might have been a good time to pause and reflect.

1995's *Naughty Little Doggie* probably had less impact than any album since the Arista years. The cover – a witty black and white photograph of a raddled Iggy – can't have helped. For the first time the record buying public saw a man who was no longer the tight skinned Adonis of legend. He had, of course, been growing noticeably older for a very long time, and uncomplimentary photographs had been appearing in the papers since '78, but the penny didn't drop until, getting on for 50, he appeared on his own album cover looking like a shrivelled up old guy in a long hair wig.

"I am married, yes," he told one journalist flatly. "But I've been on my own working for a few months now. I haven't had a break." The recording process took him away from Suchi at a time when their relationship was crumbling. Pop attributed the end of his marriage, in part, to his inability to keep his fly zipped.

He admitted that 'Look Away', the last song on *Naughty Little Doggie*, was basically about Johnny Thunders, dead since 1990, and Thunders' old girlfriend, Sable Starr. It dealt with them living dangerous fringe lives while getting whacked by society. "The guy gets whacked," Pop said. "The girl says, 'I think I'll go home to the folks.' The other guy in it, me basically, chooses another road and finds stability but the price I pay is I have to hold my feelings down and that's a big price to pay. Maybe too big. That's why I call it 'Look Away' because it's basically when I can't deal with someone, I just look the other way."

Naughty Little Doggie is good but lacks force and focus because – in addition to his marital problems – Iggy was devoting his mature attention to Hollywood. A generation of "young" directors and movie stars who were gradually assuming industry clout had grown up admiring The Stooges and the Berlin-period Iggy. Now, for a fee, they had an opportunity to work with him, to give him work, to eat dinner with him, or to use one of his cool-dude old tunes on their soundtracks.

Despite an early Ann Arbor initiation into the world of movie making via François de Menil, it wasn't until he'd abandoned live gigs and started making money from Bowie's cover versions that Iggy put his considerable back into Hollywood-related matters. He started off by landing cameo roles in movies made by credible directors (and Iggy fans) like Martin Scorsese (*The Color Of Money*, 1986), Alex Cox (*Sid And Nancy*, 1986), and John Waters (*Cry Baby*, 1990).

After his ugly and off-putting performance in *Cry Baby* he realised just how bad his acting was. He went away, worked on the craft, and learned a few things about relaxing in front of the camera. In '95 he landed a decent role with a sympathetic director. The savvy Jim Jarmusch cast him as a possum skinner in *Dead Man*. That same year he appeared in Oscar Aibar Ano's low-budget *Atolladero* – a kind of avant-garde gay Spanish western with a touch of *A Fistful Of Dollars* thrown in for good measure – about, appropriately, a sexually deviant fossil. "We shot it on a NATO training ground in Northern Spain," he said. "Really beautiful, giant, giant pasture, where all you ever see are bulls and shepherds with the flocks . . . And the latest fighters going overhead practising strafing and dropping bombs on everyone."

After *Dead Man*, he took to regarding movie acting as a worthwhile pastime and a solid way of making a buck, even if the work was sometimes exhausting. He soon put all those tasteful, intelligent, independent or auteur directors behind him and decided, as with his thriving modelling and advertising careers, that it was time to make some predictably mainstream and mindless crap. Next up was *Tank Girl* (1995), a poor fantasy based on a punkish riot grrrl cartoon character, starring Ice T and Malcolm McDowell, which was a famously monumental flop. Pop played the aptly-named Rat Face.

1996's *The Crow: City Of Angels*, the movie in which he made the biggest impact, appealed to the nu-metal/jock community that he'd determined to claim as his own. In this sequel to cult hit *The Crow*, Pop played a cold-blooded killer going about his business while the Mexican Day of The Dead explodes all around him. A trendy soundtrack featured Hole, White Zombie, Tricky, and a live version of 'I Wanna Be Your Dog'. Like *Tank Girl*, *The Crow: City Of Angels* was aimed at lowest common denominator middle American metal morons and skatepunks but, unlike *Tank Girl*, it was vaguely successful. He lived alone in Los Angeles for two months while shooting the movie and was proud of himself for making it through without fucking up completely. He didn't have a car accident, and didn't succumb to the allure of heavy drugs, although he admitted to getting into some trouble, "but nothing like the kind I used to." One day, during the movie shoot, he got grief from an LA cop who came upon him practising Tai Chi, an oriental martial arts discipline favoured by recovering junkies and dysfunctional males.

Iggy: "I was on the way to a closed set downtown for the filming of *The Crow II* and I was next to the MTA yard. I pulled my car over, I was a little groggy, it'd been a really tough shooting schedule and before I was going to get to work and have all sorts of stuff happen to me, I said to myself, 'I'll do a little Tai Chi and get some energy going.' I was standing there going like that and this cop car passed me and I thought, 'He's going to come back.' And he came back and said through the loudspeaker, 'Freeze! Hands away from your body,' like I was some kind of heavy criminal. Then I said to him, 'Look, I'm an actor.' I have a SAG card, but not with me, so I showed him the directions to the set on a Universal letterhead. Then he said, 'Well, you should know better, that looks weird when you do it.' A big crew-cut beefy weightlifter. It's OK to do his exercise, but mine looked weird."

In 1997, Johnny Depp (whom Pop had worked with on *Cry Baby* and *Dead Man*) approached him to do a film score for *The Brave*, a Depp-directed/starring project, allegedly about American Indians, with a cameo from Marlon Brando. The teenage Depp had been bass player in a band, The Kids, who'd supported Iggy at the Main Street club in Gainesville, Florida on November 7, 1981. This was during the Follow The Sun tour when Iggy was dressing like a woman onstage. Back then the movie star had been young, drunk and lippy. Now he spouted end-lessly positive press release movie star vibes about the Godfather of Punk. No contemporary Hollywood star has ever been known to say in public anything bad about anybody else working in the industry.

Johnny Depp: "We started to work immediately and Iggy brought me a few demos to listen to. It's strange, you know, Iggy has this kind of image that generally doesn't stick to what he is. People only see him as the punk inventor – that is true but also so reducing. He certainly is a musician but before all he is a poet, an artist. He's such a great guy, so clever and witty. He's like a scientist. I don't know if people can feel about him that he has such an unbelievable sensitivity and that sharp sense of melody too. We do see each other rather often when I stay in New York. We actually met in 1989 on the set of John Waters' *Cry Baby*. But I had already met him long before. We were in a bar in 1980 [sic]. At that time I was part of a band that played the first part of his show. I was 17. It was in Gainesville, Florida. After the gig we all gath-ered in a bar and I absolutely wanted to draw his attention to me. When they closed the bar I was totally drunk and I started yelling obscenities at him. He didn't react at first but after a while he came close to me, looked me straight in the eyes, and said, 'You little scumbag!' Then he left. I felt on top of the world. At least he knew I existed."

"It called for some folky and ethnic shit," Pop said about his soundtracking labours, which he kind of related to his declining mar-riage, "so I started working with acoustic guitar a lot. I always thought, 'Oh, I can't do this shit, it's too much trouble.' I sat down and started trying to master some craft that I had not heretofore really had access to in my work. At the same time I was living alone for the first time in a long time, and my orientation became alone – I'd have friends for a while, and I'd double up at night once in a while, and then I'd end up on my own again. So I was spending more time with the acoustic guitar, which is warm, and songs started comin' out based on the things I was living."

This introspective acoustic behaviour would soon have unfortunate results in the shape of his next album.

Having rubbed shoulders with the best of Hollywood's gilded elite there were no longer any avant-garde gay Westerns on the agenda. Iggy was offered all manner of low budget roles appropriate to the persona of "Iggy Pop" but there was little money in that sort of thing. The future lay in kids' movies, cartoon voice-overs, and dubious mainstream cash cows. While content to appear in low-rent crap like *Crocodile Dundee II* and *Star Trek: Deep Space Nine*, when approached by maverick indie movie-makers, the in-effect No More Mr Nice Guy attitude came into play.

Iggy: "Since I did *The Crow*, I've read tons of scripts and I only accepted one other, *Devil Dear*, which is the story of a stag who kills campers and hunters because he hates people. It's a very funny B-movie. The victims will be seen through the eyes of the stag. Me, I get to play a redneck who tells horrible jokes and who thinks the strangers are all Chinese. I'm all excited. We shoot this movie in NYC. Otherwise I only receive scripts in which I play a vampire or a guy who rapes children, a stock car racer or a psychopathic schoolteacher, or a killer who harasses a Soho artist who works in a nice flat. I also get propositions from young, broke suckers who think they'll get their budget by telling me, 'Wouldn't it be great to have a movie with you, Nick Cave, David Bowie, and who knows, Patti Smith, for a quick appearance?' And I answer them, 'That's funny, but I don't think it's such a good idea, why don't you just die here and now?'"

The movie career, which was supposed to achieve all manner of crossover and financial miracles for Pop, gradually dwindled into a series of inappropriate and mundane roles in secondary films. It'd been a huge effort – he'd entered into movie-making with his now-customary professionalism and willingness to work hard – but it never really went anywhere worthwhile. During a conversation with *Interview* magazine in August 2001, he announced that he had no more plans to make movies. The last offer he'd received called for him to perform oral sex on camera. Art Collins was so totally insulted and offended by this proposal that he didn't even send Pop the script. Oral sex, it seems, was no longer the sort of practice that his client could be associated with.

Iggy: "It was pretty funny. I ran into the director, at a VIP hotel, actually, at a celebrated hotel, because he is a celebrated director, and he said, 'Oh, I sent you a script, didn't you get it?' And I played dumb. The last thing I'd done before that was a kids' movie, *Snow Day*, with people like Chevy Chase in it. I was the guy they hired to stick my hand in a toilet bowl."

More successful than his acting efforts was the extent to which classic

Iggy music was now used on movie soundtracks. The most important event in his career was the inclusion of 'Lust For Life' in the 1996 Scottish heroin comedy *Trainspotting*. As that saga of fringe junkie life became an underground hit all over the world, 'Lust For Life' entered into the public's consciousness in much the same way as The Door's 'The End' had benefited from its inclusion in Coppola's *Apocalypse Now*. *Almost Famous* (2001), the Cameron Crowe comedy in which the Lester Bangs character lauds The Stooges, flashing the cover of *Raw Power* and playing it loud, is a fair example of just how much of middle America Pop was able to reach via Hollywood. By 2002 he was invited to attend the Oscar ceremonies, an honoured guest at an event which included a Tom Cruise-introduced documentary featuring celebrities such as Mikhail Gorbachev, Iggy Pop, and Lou Reed telling the world what their favourite movies were. This was just about the most extraordinary career turnaround imaginable.

Not everything to do with movies, however, went his way. One relatively small budget film was about to bring Ron Asheton lumbering out of the boondocks, like the Kraken awakening, and back into the frame. It instigated a series of events which led to an eventual Stooges reunion, *and* reminded the world that in 1977 Iggy had allegedly been bed-hopping with David Bowie. Just when he'd abandoned the independent movie sector, it rose up to bite him in the form of 1998's *Velvet Goldmine*, the most telling analysis yet of the world's forgotten boy with the tough torso and the loose morals. It came out at a time when "born-again regular guy" Iggy was implausibly denying all rumours of any homosexual past, even a minor one involving David Bowie.

A gay read on a vaguely bisexual time seen through the eyes of a competent gay director, *Velvet Goldmine* tangled accurately enough with the twisted sexualities of its epoch, the glam early Seventies. Director Todd Haynes first came to critical attention through his *Superstar: The Karen Carpenter Story* in which Barbie dolls re-enacted the MOR singer's anorexia nervosa-driven decline and death. It was not a movie which went down too well with Richard Carpenter, Karen's brother and musical partner.

In *Velvet Goldmine*, the puppets were human. One of the film's basic premises is the idea that, somewhere in between all their raucous gigs, emotional triumphs, and aimless wanderings around Berlin, David Bowie and Iggy Pop had a homosexual relationship. The Iggy character, Curt Wylde, was played by Scottish (*Trainspotting*) star, Ewan McGregor, an in-demand actor who shared with Iggy a predilection for flashing his penis for his art. The Bowie persona, Brian Slade, was ably summoned up by Jonathan Rhys Myers, an idiosyncratic Irish actor. The Stooges became The Wylde Rattz. In one scene Wylde and Slade are "eyelash close" when Wylde whispers to Slade, "The world is changed because you are made of ivory and gold. The curves of your lips rewrite history." This passionate relationship was supposedly reflective of a similarly bisexual spirit on the loose in the early Seventies adolescent world.

McGregor claimed that the only way he could reach the required Iggy-like level of intensity during his onstage scenes was by throwing himself around the stage during rehearsal just to see what happened. To get into the mood he watched loads of concert videos including footage from the 1970 Cincinnati Pop Festival. Then he went through Iggy's footsteps with choreographer Lea Anderson, who created for him a dance work based on Iggy's physical movements. "Then it was a case of getting three cameras set up and lighting the stage," explained McGregor, "because they never knew where I would be at any moment. And I would go. I was completely taken over by it. When they said, 'Cut!' I was rather surprised to find myself in front of a camera. I'd lost the plot entirely." McGregor does a trouser-dropping scene copied exactly from the well-known footage on Iggy in the late Seventies, complete with cock and balls leaping into the air along with their owner. Though thin, he looks beefy in the role as compared with Pop's own durable, unyielding air of carnality.

Iggy was predictably prickly about this somewhat unwelcome blast from his past, especially since, in his new role as post-punk totem, he couldn't exactly ignore or denounce the powerful industry types who gave *Velvet Goldmine* their backing. Part produced by R.E.M.'s Michael Stipe, with Thurston Moore of Sonic Youth in charge of the soundtrack, the project came to the screen laden down with indie rock credibility. It can't have helped that the makers shipped in Ron Asheton – now a B-movie actor himself and still musically active with the well-regarded Dark Carnival – to work on the soundtrack. After two lost decades the Ashetons were crawling out of the woodwork onto the fringes of Iggy's universe. They would come closer and closer over the next five years.

It is easy to see why Pop might have found *Velvet Goldmine* invasive or, at the very least, downright cheeky. One scene, cut from the completed film, takes place in a Michigan trailer park in 1946. There is a long shot of a luminous silver trailer home. According to the script, "A pack of black wolves leave a bundle at the door and saunter off, looking back as they go. We hear a baby's cries and the door opens. A handsome white trash family peer out."

Moving forward in time to 1960 when white trash Curt Wylde (Iggy was never white trash, he just grew up surrounded by them) is 14, we find ourselves in Wayne County Sanitarium, Michigan. "Curt is strapped down onto a gurney, hooked up to electrodes, hillbilly Ma and Pa looking on, Pa saying, 'The doctors guaranteed the treatment would fry the fairy clean out of him.'" The characterisation of the Osterberg parents as being a hillbilly Ma and Pa is more than a little condescending since they were obviously the very opposite kind of people. Louella Osterberg, her son's staunchest supporter for 50 years, had died two years before the movie came out. And Iggy had spent at least 10 years frying the fairy out of himself before *Velvet Goldmine* reminded the world just what an exciting character he'd once been. "Well, you know, it's dark," said Thurston Moore. "Todd's stuff is always kinda dark, and it does have the homosexual overtones, but I like it."

Ron Asheton: "I went out and did two songs for a movie soundtrack, *Velvet Goldmine*. They were putting together a band that was Stooge-esque, because the movie's loosely based on the relationship of Iggy and David Bowie. So they got Thurston Moore and Steve Shelley and Mike Watt and Mark Arm. They were looking for a guitar player and Don Fleming (Sonic Youth cohort, Gumball) had just recorded the Dark Carnival CD, *The Last Great Ride*, and he goes, 'Gee, I just got done working with Ron Asheton. How about Ron Asheton? Is he Stooge-esque enough?' So he went back, took the idea to Michael Stipe, and the record company said, 'Yeah, good idea.'

"I went out and I wrote a couple of new original songs, and we jammed for about two or three hours. Just kinda went through and did all the old Stooges songs, the ones that Mark Arm and Mike Watt and Thurston Moore knew, and they wound up putting 'TV Eye' in the movie, and a little bit of an original song I wrote. It'll get limited theatrical release because it has homosexual overtones . . . I mean Todd Haynes is gay, he's openly gay, and he has a gay agenda, and Michael Stipe is gay, and he's executive producer. So that's it . . . it's a love story with no women in it. The only woman who's in it, who plays like the Angie Bowie character, she's kinda dumped on. But in reality, they treated the Angie character properly, because Angie did have a lot to do with creating David Bowie but she got dumped on in spite of that . . .

"Todd Haynes and I actually sat down and did an interview, just the two of us. He (Haynes) actually said that Miramax said, 'Hey, listen, you take all this fag shit out of there, and we'll really go gung-ho, we'll really put it in the theatres.' But of course, that's not Todd's vision, and he had integrity enough to say, 'No'."

Bob Gruen: "That movie was just way too much, it's just one big gay fantasy. A queen's vision of Glam Rock. None of us were there with them so who knows what went on but what we *do* know is that the intimacy caused between two guys who are doing those sort of drugs together is a very strong and fierce bond. Stronger in many ways than any sort of sexual bond. So who knows what may have happened on some given night but I was talking with a lot of friends of mine who were around at that time and I was saying to them: 'My recollection of things is that it was nothing like this. Things were not so gay.' They were agreeing with me that *Velvet Goldmine* is just what some gay people have to say about a scene they had no part in, and little understanding for.

"You've got to remember too, that we're talking about a pre-AIDS world. I mean, herpes was virtually a rumour then. This venereal disease that you couldn't shake off. We thought herpes was the end of the world when we first heard about it, but AIDS changed the whole book of rules, naturally. There was a lot of stuff going on then that was of its time, there was a little window of time that David Crosby talks about which existed when anything went. But this whole gay fantasy which *Velvet Goldmine* paints is just totally inaccurate."

The film is not necessarily about what it was to be a New York rock photographer in the time of glam, or what it was like to be the zeitgeist rock star of that epoch. Or about what it was like to be his consort. It's really about what it was like to be a sexually ambiguous teenager and music fan back then. While far from being a cogent commentary on the Glam Rock explosion, or on the Iggy/Bowie relationship, *Velvet Goldmine* is a surprisingly bold recreation of the messy emotional nature of those times, of the wishful thinking that a lot of adolescent males indulged in, and of the cunning manner in which that thinking was manipulated by the likes of Bowie and Iggy.

When Iggy was asked by journalist Barney Hoskyns to comment on a *Velvet Goldmine* sex scene between Wylde and Slade he claimed that he hadn't seen the film, that he was a "hard sell when it comes to cultural product" (such as *Crocodile Dundee II*), and that he thought Ewan McGregor was a little too porky to play him. "It didn't seem that compelling to me," he frostily commented though he'd not seen the film. "I can give you no comment about the scene in question."

Important chemistry commenced with *Velvet Goldmine*. Ron Asheton got a taste for the contemporary venue-stuffing All Tomorrow's Parties indie scene which looked up to him and his brother as much as it admired the increasingly awards ceremony-attending and catwalk-prancing Iggy. Ron spent time in the studio with, amongst others, former Minuteman and indie jack-of-all-trades Mike Watt. It was time for the Ashetons to leave home. The kernel of an idea commenced in that studio, an idea that, five years later, would push the Ashetons back into the spotlight and instigate the re-formation of The Stooges.

CHAPTER 22

The Guy On The Phone –
Avenue B

"Somebody threw a bottle. Hit him on the head. It was at an outdoor gig in Greece. He went ape, started bleeding and climbed up the lighting pole on the side of the stage like King Kong, waving his arms around like little airplanes were attacking him, then started screaming, 'You can't kill me. I'm fucking Iggy Pop.'"

– Whitey Kirst

"Nothing I sing on there has anything to do with my marriage other than the one passing reference to 'being on the verge of a divorce'. Lyrically the record is about a guy that finds himself alone – it's post-marriage – and he has a finite amount of time allotted to him and he has an inability to rest easily with other people and he's trying to figure out what to do. Musically the record's a big old motherfuckin' giant step for me. If you listen to my last two records before this, which were basically four-chord rock'n'roll records, then that was just as much of a catharsis for me."

– Iggy to Barney Hoskyns

AWAY from his media career, in his Mexican hideaway, Iggy looked after a Siamese cat that was bow-legged as a result of not being fed properly as a kitten. He found that the animals in Mexico ran a little smaller because they didn't have the same concept of "pet" down there. His pet dog was a street stray when he found him, so Pop ferried him between Mexico and New York but eventually the dog settled back in Mexico because New York drove him crazy. When he walked the streets of Manhattan the dog wanted to smell women and eat rubbish. Much, indeed, like his owner in years gone by.

One time he had too many old clothes so he had to get rid of some. He was packing up the stuff to send to the lucky thrift store when he started remembering how he felt when he got each garment, what he did while wearing it and why he was now getting rid of it. His heart, obviously, was no longer full of napalm, and he thought a lot about the past which made him his living and the future which was an adventure yet to be enjoyed. If fortune smiled on him, and the person was right, he reckoned, he could visualise fathering a little girl who might look up to him and go, "Oh, Daddy!" But if the kid turned out to be a boy he might have gone, "Oh bummer, another fucking dick in the family."

Twenty years after the British punk rock explosion which they dominated, The Sex Pistols re-formed for the global Filthy Lucre tour which kicked off at London's Finsbury Park during the summer of '96. Iggy opened for former employees, now reborn Pistols, Steve Jones and Glen Matlock at this huge open-air show. It was supposed to be a historic reunion – very few people had ever actually seen the legendary Pistols in their heyday – but international gig attendance figures proved poor. The London show *was* successful and the general consensus seemed to be that, while it was interesting to see the Pistols, it was Pop, by now the veteran of many an open field full of beer-crazed rock types of all shapes, ages and sizes, who won the day.

Chris Alberti (videomaker): "I always stay in this beautiful small hotel in Notting Hill when I'm working in London or passing through. The first time I visited the place was when I was over there to see The Sex Pistols reunion in Finsbury Park with Iggy Pop in support. My girlfriend at the time was an old pal of Jim's so we went to see him there. He had this really cute room up the top floor of the hotel, which is just this small family run place with maybe 15 bedrooms. Jim invited us up and it was a totally comfortable sort of place. I don't know exactly what the status of his marriage was at that moment of time but he had this really sweet thing with him. I don't know what age she was but I doubt if she was 18. And you just knew . . . the things he must have been up to in there with her. I was just looking at her and that's all that was going through my mind. I'd look at him, I'd look at her, I'd look at the bed. Anyway, next time I was in London I rang this hotel and booked the same room. But I found it hard to get to sleep, thinking of him and her in there. The various positions. She was just such a honey, and, knowing him, what he would have been like, this was all I could think about all night. I could smell her from the room. The two of them."

Bob Gruen: "You're talking to Jim one minute and the next thing he goes to get ready for the show and is just kind of standing in the corner.

It's sort of like the Incredible Hulk. His body gets bigger and the muscles get hard, and he just turns into this other identity. Iggy comes charging out from nowhere and hits the stage running. Look out! Don't be in his way. I went over to London to cover The Sex Pistols reunion and to catch Iggy. Just before he went on there was something I wanted to say to him but his manager Art Collins said to me, 'Don't bother him just now.' The transformation had taken over. Then, when he came off the stage after doing that show, which really put it up to the Pistols despite the historic nature of their reunion, that persona kind of leaves him in waves as he prances towards the dressing room. He is still this kind of crazed monster who is now kind of pacing around going slower and slower. Within three or four minutes you find yourself in the company of Jim once again, and there he is going, 'Hey! How are you? What's going on? Read any good books lately?' He was laughing about the show while demonstrably bleeding. 'Hey, Bob, how bad is it? Do you think I should go get stitched up?' Because he'd just banged his head off of an amp or something. I told him on that occasion that he should get it stitched, that it was pretty bad!"

In '96 Virgin Records cashed in on their investment in Pop by issuing *Nude And Rude; The Best Of Iggy Pop*, which featured a fair cross-section of his work stretching back as far as The Stooges plus a welcome appearance on the cover of Gerard Malanga's much bootlegged full frontal nude Iggy portrait, albeit with the world famous cock discreetly cropped.

Gerard Malanga: "Iggy's manager Art Collins got in touch with me. They wanted to use my nude portrait of him on the cover of *Nude And Rude*. Unfortunately they cropped it which I thought was stupid on their part, really dumb. I am very discreet about using those nude shots. I think it had appeared two or three times in sanctioned publications prior to *Mojo* magazine in London using it. I only used it in very well-placed circumstances. When *Mojo* wanted to use it on the cover I told them I'd sell them the reproduction rights but that they'd have to get permission from Iggy's management first. I didn't want Iggy to feel, I know he wouldn't really, but I didn't want him to feel that I was exploiting it. I've exhibited the print in shows, which is perfectly reasonable because it's a fine art, artistic situation. But when it gets into kind of commercialised situations I feel that I just want to cover my bases first. Out of politeness. The Belgian record label, Sub Rosa used that shot on one of their albums without my permission. I was a little bit upset with them about that at the time. When he was living down on Avenue B before he quit New York I used to see him at a club called The Cooler which was run by a pal of mine. It would usually be a really rock'n'roll sort of backstage atmosphere, not a lot of room for serious talking. I actually made an exhibition print of the nude shot, 16 x 20, and messaged it over to where he was on Avenue B. His manager told me that he was really excited to get it."

"It's gonna look good in convertible BMWs driven by people who listen to rock today," said Iggy of *Nude And Rude*, "or in the Walkmans of the suckers who go training in gyms and enjoy 'this tough rock'n' roll!' No, I'm joking; that's cool if today's boys with short hair have a hard-on when they listen to that stuff."

With all of his crossover achievements firmly in the bag, Virgin were anxious to water down their product as best they could. Iggy was only allowed to approve Virgin's choice of tunes and to voice suggestions about the photos they'd put on the sleeve. The record company wanted to include 'Bang Bang', his profoundly compromised disco effort from *Party*, a song he'd "never considered as very important", and they also wanted to include his version of James Brown's 'Sex Machine'. Then, when the compilation was just about ready to go, Arista said they didn't want to license certain tracks anymore. For a while it looked like there'd be no tracks from *Fun House* because Elektra said, "It's your choice. Either songs from the first LP or from *Fun House*." Then Sony, who had *Raw Power*, said: "We'll give you nothing." Eventually Iggy told Virgin: "Hey, let's stop it. If I can't put a track from *Raw Power* on my compilation, I don't wanna hear about it. I called my manager and he got on to Sony. So they gave away 'Search And Destroy' and another title that could not be 'Raw Power' itself. In return for that I had to spend two weeks remixing *Raw Power* for them with today's technology. Not bad!"

The way it was put to Iggy was that Sony/Columbia were going to remix it with or without him, and he could get involved if he wanted to. He reckoned that it needed the remix, that the available CD version was, if anything, worse than the original vinyl copies.

Iggy: "The way the project was presented to me, it would be coming out on Columbia/Legacy, and the key word is the legacy. There were things The Stooges had to offer as a band of musicians that do not come out on the original and are not made legible. But they do come out on this new one. And I think that functions as a legacy. I hear this version as being of more interest to musicians who are in bands, and coincidentally it just happens to be that almost everybody in the entire Western world is in a band! Or has a guitar or some musical instrument and thinks they're a musician. So this is the musician mix and I made it very much that way, thinking, 'What about this guy who plays guitar and really wants to hear what Williamson's doing, hear how the guitar sounds through the AC-35, or what about that guy who plays drums and wants to hear the rhythm section, etc., etc.'"

When Iggy went to listen to the troublesome tapes, still stored in the library at London's Olympic Studios, he found that they were in fine shape, sounded beautiful, especially the guitar and drum tracks. He reckoned that the bass was very well played but that it would need more work to improve Ron's sound. The sound on the rhythm guitar was "just insane". The middle-aged Pop was not a modest man so he confidently announced that the vocals just blew his mind because, listening back, the guy he heard was just rabid and out of it. He worked on the tapes with a good engineer, Danny Kadar, who had a lot of affection for the material at hand and who would later be involved in *Beat 'Em Up*, Pop's 2001 album. Iggy was there in the studio for the digital remastering too.

Iggy: "I was right there for every step of this. They printed it unbelievably hot at my behest and then toward the end of the day the mastering guy got cold feet and said, 'No, we can't do this!' I said, 'Just shut up and do it. Aaarrggh!' So I got home and I loved it but they had a panic attack. They heard it and it just freaked them out. It sounded like the speakers were gonna explode, bleeding and melting and distorting. Then they did a 'nice' version which I refused to even listen to. And they listened to it and they were embarrassed, they didn't even like it. So we ended up with mine minus maybe a half db. I heard it and it was actually better than mine, because I had mine all the way up, everything's always in the red all the time, that was in keeping with what I tried to do on the original mixes. I said, 'Look, that's not in the red, why isn't that meter in the red? That should be over there in the red with the rest of those meters!' "

Ron Asheton: "Oh, boy! . . . I heard it was being done, but I actually hadn't spoken to Iggy in a long time. Iggy called me up – and I wasn't there – he called me at like 3 am because he was up early to catch a flight. So, someone just left me a message . . . his manager ended up sending me an advance copy of the remix . . . It was so funny. When I was in New York Don Fleming said, 'When Iggy's remix of *Raw Power* comes out, we're all gonna say, 'Boy, do we love that first mix of *Raw Power*.' And sure enough, it came true. What Iggy did was bring up every little yip and yell. Brought all his shit up. He didn't know much about guitars, so he took all of the ambient sounds off of James' guitars . . . people were disappointed with *Raw Power*. All the cool stuff Bowie did with the guitar sounds was gone. Don Fleming was right. But people think it's fun – just in the sense that it's another interpretation of that record. Something for real Stooge-o-philes."

Iggy: "You had a rip-snortin' super-heavy nitro-burnin' fuel injected rock band that nobody in this world could touch at that time, nobody could rock like that band does, no band that anybody had, when we were on and together, wow, it was powerful. This did not come through on the record for lack of technology and money and time and equipment to make the sounds come out correctly. And to bring out that rhythm section, especially, and to bring those guitars out fully, and to have it really sound like it should. The sound of the thing is weedy. It's a beautiful weedy little record and I don't think that a new version improves the record, it just gives people who admire a strong rock band, and particularly people who are used to hearing things at today's standards of technology, a chance to hear that band in a way that's legible, audible, in a way that the original record was not.

"Being the person I am today, this is like the guy with 30 years experience making rock'n'roll, singing rock'n'roll, drumming five years before that, helluva lot of experience, in the prime of my life, at the top of my game, looking basically at the time in my life when I'm gonna have to start – I'm now becoming history – saying, 'OK, this is how this piece of work should sound to be legible to people and to show what the band could do, to show what was really there.' There's a quirky, off charm to the original, like a car you have to crank up to start, and that's a beautiful thing, and I like that. But this is more like a Nineties version, an end of the millennium version, that's the best way I can put it. This will become the version that people will know, and I'm fine with that, 'cause when you put it on your speakers it'll knock you down, you can hear the band and it's very powerful. And I think it'll stand right up there with your Smashing Pumpkins and your Pearl Jams and your Nirvanas and – what are the ones with the heroin singer? – Stone Temple whatever-their-name-is."

It is one of the least reliable remixes of an iconic rock album around. This is not Pop's fault – he was painting with a tiny restrictive palate. The original tracks had been sloppily recorded and no amount of digital knob twiddling was going to make it sound like the bozo frat punk/metal that Iggy wanted it to resemble. His first mistake was to undertake the task without the other Stooges, and his second was to mess with a good thing. He had little business remixing the album alone, since all the other members of the group were still alive and kicking. This pointless exercise in revisionism for revisionism's sake ensures that future generations will have to pay vast amounts of money buying original vinyl copies of *Raw Power* if they want to know what the critical fuss was all about.

Ron told journalists that he hadn't spoken to Pop since their conversation concerning the remix. Iggy didn't call him and he didn't know where Iggy was. The distant star was always changing his phone number but, occasionally, Ron talked with manager Art Collins. "I always loved 'Search And Destroy' and 'Penetration'," he said of the *Raw Power* remix. "Iggy took out some of my baby boy vocals on his mix, which I was pissed off about 'cause I did all the high things. I learned to hate those songs incredibly much. I had to play them over and over after we were dropped by Mainman . . . We played those goddamn songs over and over so many times that when I hear them, it almost makes me physically ill. 'Gimme Danger', they wanted us to do it for *Velvet Goldmine*. That was one thing Todd requested and I said no way."

James Williamson: "I personally think it (Iggy's remix) sucked. I gotta tell ya that I like the idea of what he tried to do, and I talked to him about it, and there's a lot of factors involved, but at the time, none of us liked Bowie's mix, but given everything, Iggy, when he went in to mix it, he found out that the guy who had recorded it originally had not gotten a lot of level on certain things, like the bass and drums, especially the bass, so he didn't have a lot to work with. Then Iggy, on his mix, he left a bunch of guitar stuff on there that probably shouldn't have been left in, and just odds and ends. Bowie's not my favourite guy, but I have to say overall, I think he did a pretty good job."

Ron Asheton on James Williamson: "I've finally forgiven him. I saw him about a month ago. He actually came here to Ann Arbor. I thought I'd never wanna see him again. He called up and said he was going to be in the area. I thought, 'Ah, well.' We had a nice time. We talked and he didn't apologise for anything, which he didn't have to, but I could tell he was being humble and there was friction and there was some stupid things done by him. The beauty of it was that we didn't have to say a word. He's got a great job with Sony. He's got a wife and two kids. He's doing very, very well. Goes all over the place with his job."

Ron reported that his brother Scott was "kind of Ann Arbor-ed and Detroit-ed out, he's kinda had his fill of slummin' around here . . . His girlfriend and his child live in Florida, so he just went back down to Florida for the winter. They usually come up here for the summer. He has a house by the lake, so that's basically what he's doing – huntin' and fishin'. Fishing is the most, it's his favourite thing . . . he really is an outdoorsman; he's spent a lot of time outdoors. As children we always enjoyed it, 'cause my father liked fishing. But for me . . . well, I like being on the water and stuff, but . . . I can't kill anything, so I don't like hunting anymore. I like eating fish, but I don't like them flopping around when I pull them out of the water. But he likes it . . . it's relaxing for him to sit out on the boat with a can of beer. He's got a boat, it's his own lake, or he'll go to friends who have lakes, they're all private lakes, so he has a good time. And he's got his drums set up in a place where he can go and bang on them once or twice a week. His chops are pretty good. I didn't get to see him actually record, but like I said, I was in after he was done tracking and got to mix some stuff and he sounded good as ever."

Iggy's past surrounded him; retrospective compilations, remixes of old projects, movies about his early career and, to cap it all, serious talk of a Stooges reunion. Hip hop/metal producer Rick Rubin (in the business, like Don Was, of making oldies like Mick Jagger and Johnny Cash sound like their old selves) proposed to Pop that he do a new Stooges album. Given Rubin's sensitive intellectual ear, this would undoubtedly have been a valid project. It didn't happen just then, but it certainly set tongues, including Iggy's, wagging.

Back in May '96, speaking about a possible reunion to David Yow from the group Jesus Lizard, Iggy said he regarded Scott Asheton as his friend, and that Scott was always on to him about wanting to do something together. He was only interested in doing something that was new. He didn't have the time or the interest to go out and play old Stooges tunes with The Stooges. Seven years later he'd find all the time and interest in the world to do just that. Yow more or less put it to him that he seemed happy enough to pepper his solo set with his own versions of those classics. He defended this by saying they were substantially different versions, *his* versions.

He had a point. At his shows the long-ago noise anthems were all ground down into a pretty homogenised grunge by his ongoing backing band made up of hot-shot B-division LA metallers. To do this was entirely his valid prerogative. The artist with whom he bears closest comparison, Lou Reed, spent a whole decade doing the exact same thing – a crowd-pleasing set largely made up of cranked out Velvets classics with a few solo tracks thrown in for good measure.

He told Yow that he saw Ron Asheton maybe twice a year, which wasn't true, adding that Ron still lived with his mother in the same house, with the same phone number, as he had 30 years before. When asked who would replace Dave Alexander in a putative reunion, Pop suggested Gary Rasmussen, his one-time bass player from The Up and

Fred "Sonic" Smith's Rendezvous Band. "Because Gary's the exact kind of personality. He'd say, 'I don't take no shit,' and he's musically exactly in tune with that sound."

A few months later, in October '96, Ron Asheton was washing the dishes in his mother's house. In the kitchen with him was Larry Steele, the drummer with his band, Dark Carnival. Steele was staying with the Ashetons' at the time and expecting a call so when the phone rang he picked it up. He turned to Ron and said, "There's a guy on the phone that says he's Iggy." Since Steele was not really familiar with Iggy's voice, Ron said, "Yeah, right. Just hang up on him," because he received similar crank calls all the time. "No, no," Steele said, "he says he's Iggy." So Ron picked up the phone and it was indeed the real Iggy Pop – significantly not Jim Osterberg – anxious, after some small talk, to discuss the possibility of a Stooges reunion.

Pop and Asheton had sometimes been pals, but at other times they were substantially estranged. Ron said that Iggy phoned him occasionally to tell him how cool he was and how well he was doing. Iggy said they'd been friendly up to a point. "I like this guy, he's nice," he said. "But we had never been close friends and it was really more a thing where I had got him to be in my band. I conned him into it." After the surprise call, Asheton didn't hear from Pop for years. When he eventually tried to phone Art Collins about the putative reunion, Collins' phone number had been changed.

Iggy: "We had all kinds of possibilities to do The Stooges in a movie or we were offered a Doors movie, to open for The Doors. I'm glad I didn't do it or do a reunion tour. I don't want to do anything like that. But to try to create some new music with these same people that they are now, that interests me. Since both Ashetons are really active as musicians, that's legitimate to me. And I know it would mean a lot to Scott particularly. He's been wanting to do it for years and I care for Scott a lot. I don't see him but I care for him a lot."

It can't really have mattered to Iggy whether The Stooges re-formed right then or not. Things were comprehensively going his way and he had the liberal rock establishment eating out of his hands, believing his every pontification or assertion. In '96 he did an important interview with London's neo-liberal *Guardian* newspaper, anxious to prove what a sophisticated and well-read guy he was; ploughing through books nobody else had the time to read while listening to music nobody else had the inclination to listen to. The night before the interview, he confided, he'd cooked, invited friends over for dinner and excused himself around midnight because he had important interviews to do in the morning. He read for a while before going to bed, a chapter from *The Big Money* by John Dos Passos, and passages from Malcolm Bradbury's book, *The Modern American Novel.* He'd listened to some Benedictine monks singing "this 14th-century work". After that, the mighty Iggy Pop went to bed thinking about what Bradbury had to say about the hero in Hemingway's fiction.

In his interview with David Yow he confessed that his big project was buying "shit" at auctions. "Some antiques and some high-class junk, ranging from rugs to furniture to lithographs, and also African and oceanic tribal art. A week prior to the auction, you go look at the exhibit. It's like having your own little museum. I never go to the auction, I always do it by phone, 'cause it's more fun to not actually sit there. I like being the guy on the phone."

It was a long way from clearing his own shit off the back porch of Stooge Manor. "To be a member of the middle class," he opined in his best son-of-a-teacher's didactic tone, "there's a certain mercantile defi-nition of safety and favourable position to which one aspires, and once you're there at the goal line you're happy to go around that spiral again, and I know a lot of people like that, but they ain't artists, they don't live with my compulsion."

1997 brought with it still more reworking of his back catalogue, this time combined with an important slice of contemporary music biz diplomacy. On the *We Will Fall – The Iggy Pop Tribute* CD a variety of early tunes were covered – with varying degrees of success – by big shot rockers such as the Red Hot Chili Peppers and Monster Magnet, origi-nal punks like Blondie, Joey Ramone, Lenny Kaye and Jayne County, and a peculiar selection of contemporary major label no-counts. Most of the profits went to LIFEbeat, a music industry-approved AIDS charity which seeks to raise awareness of the illness and to provide financial help to members of the music industry suffering from HIV/AIDS. Rick Rubin got the opportunity to show what he might achieve on a new Stooges album when he produced the Chili Peppers' elegant reading of 'Search And Destroy'. Blondie, masquerading for some reason as Adolph's Dog, were poised and sultry as ever on 'Ordinary Bummer'. Joey Ramone got together with Ramones collaborator Daniel Ray and The Misfits to do '1969'. It would subsequently appear on his post-humous *Don't Worry About Me* album.

In '97 Pop fronted the unsuccessful faux-Lollapalooza ROAR summer tour of America beginning on May 24 and scheduled to continue until July 19. Featuring the consummate rockabilly of the Reverend Horton Heat, Sponge, and the misunderstood underestimated Bloodhound

Gang, ROAR was musically strong but short on box office appeal. The Bloodhound Gang, for instance, had yet to become a commercial force. A "wide demographic of fans" was predicted but never materialised. The effect of cigarette company sponsorship was to keep the price of tickets remarkably low. $10 to catch Iggy, Horton Heat, the Bloodhound Gang and others was a pretty good deal — tickets for U2 were about $50 that same year — but it just didn't work out. ROAR wasn't a bad name for a rock festival, but it was a necessary abbreviation of a rather pompous full title, Revelations of Alternative Rhythms.

Just before the tour kicked off, the first of many problems emerged. The Washington-based National Centre for Tobacco-Free Kids said that the tour sponsors, Skoal smokeless tobacco, were an inappropriate sponsor for a venture aimed at indie kids and otherwise alienated youth. "These are alternative rock bands," announced the anti-smoking fanatics, "and alternative rock is aimed at young people. This is clearly a way for US Tobacco to entice younger people to use their product."

Then the papers reported that Pop pulled out of the tour two weeks before it concluded, having performed with an injured shoulder for several weeks after stage diving into one of the many gaps in the thin crowd at the ROAR show at the Polaris Amphitheater in Columbus, Ohio. Art Collins met up with Pop early in July and decided his client should pull out. The tour had been playing to well publicised empty houses all over America, and this can't have done much for Pop's status or ego. His last ROAR appearance was on July 5 in Jackson, Missouri. The tour struggled on without Pop, who headed off for a month or more of physical and ego therapy.

Whitey Kirst (Iggy Pop band): "It was in Columbus, Ohio, lots of kids on summer vacation, don't think they knew much about us. Probably there to see some newer groups. We were playing down on the street and all these really young kids were in the front. Iggy was probably freaking them out or something; I think they were scared. Anyhow he gets a little scary looking sometimes — somebody once told me 'tales of the cryptish'. So he saw these kids in the front and he dove out at them but they were so scared I guess they moved out of fear or something so he went straight into the concrete head first. Our guy Jos pulled him out of the crowd and got him back onstage. He was bleeding a lot and had only one arm. He crawled a little, grabbed the mike and started saying all this weird cool shit on his knees, singing and talking at the same time, really cool stuff. Then he started fading. Jos came on stage and threw him over his shoulder like a bag of potatoes and walked off. We played a while longer then we split too. He was backstage with an ambulance. He was freaking out saying he wanted to keep playing and finish the gig but he had a dislocated shoulder and his head was split so they took him to the hospital. We kept doing gigs after that a little while. Jos the roadie would gaff tape his arm to his side around his waist so he couldn't move it."

The endless touring, the remorseless promotion of his increasingly lucrative back catalogue, was now a yearly ritual. The bigger the field or the arena, it seemed, the better. He was famous, but nobody was entirely sure what he was famous for. Was it for his modelling assignments, his movie appearances, *Trainspotting*, the Grolsch ads, the tunes he helped create 20 or 30 years before, the Heineken ads, his dick, his self-mutilation, or his relationship with David Bowie? He was certainly not known for the good albums he continued to churn out; all part of the procedure by which he reminded the public, via endless media interviews, that he existed.

During November 1998 *Rolling Stone* journalist and Iggy fan David Fricke was on the road with Stooges freaks Mudhoney in Camden, New Jersey: "Iggy Pop and his entourage walk past the open door on the way to the stage. His wiry frame clad only in leather pants and Cuban heels. Pop's prissy gait and simian posture make him look like a hard-ass hair-dresser. He is shorter than he looks on television. His band's live sound is muddy and diffuse, and Pop compensates by jumping around like the firecrackers in his pants just went off. The crowd seems utterly confused by this old, longhaired dude until 'Lust For Life'. The teenage girls react immediately, breaking into that patented teenage white-girl dance. Soon a wave of recognition passes over the crowd. At this point, Pop proves why he's still worth a million in prizes. Midway through the song, he jumps off stage into the front row. His son, a younger version of his dad, cheers him on. A sweet young thing, probably not even a spermatozoon in her daddy's vas deferens when Pop wrote the song, slinks up and bumps and grinds with the Idiot. He puts his hand on her ass. The crowd swarms round him, ecstatic to be so close to this guy who's famous for some reason or other. The song ends as Pop climbs back onstage and bids the crowd adieu in his own special way: 'Thanks a lot, cocksuckers!' "

He was still back in the Stone Age when it came to attitudes towards women. *Bust* magazine asked him whether he'd ever had any women in his bands. For a man as eloquent, savvy and smart as Pop, his response was remarkably confused and wide of the mark: "No. I don't think I ever have. I've worked with them before, but I don't think I've ever had them in the band. I think I could now, at this point. In fact, I may use a keyboard the next time I go out because there's a lot of my stuff I can't cover without it. And if I did, there's some girls that know how to play that, 'cause I hate guys that play licks, you know? A lot of the best bands now are girls, anyway.

"It's shifted right now because what's happened is that the men have gone bankrupt. It's a down period for guys and they don't know what the fuck to do. Whereas the girls are somewhat fresh to it, and also people aren't used to looking at girls in that role and, you know, they look better. So you can see them and go, 'Oh wow, that's interesting.' But you know, I think it's just a time link thing, I don't think that's necessarily gonna last. I think it just means that, in the end, it can equal, it will balance out. Or else maybe everyone will just stop doing it, and do something else. They'll all get bored."

Iggy on Courtney Love: "There is certainly a case to be made that there is a role for a blonde that was invented a long time ago and has been recycled into an American archetype. Marilyn would be one that everybody knows. There is a blonde role and somebody has to fill that role, and Courtney's doing it right now and Madonna did it a little before her. Of course the requirements, what you have to be able to do to fulfil that role, shift and change constantly. She's done a good job of seeing what that is, and doing it. To me, that sort of thing is ultimately not gonna be as interesting as what the music is gonna sound like five years from now . . . I'm more interested in how it looks up the line, because I'm older, and my orientation is different, and it will be really interesting to see the ups and downs. I've seen so many come and go now. I can remember idols from 25 years ago that absolutely, like if they shit people wanted to eat it and wear it and now, nobody cares."

Could this possibly be a reference to Bowie, by now a grinning regular on middle-of-the-road chat shows, playing his many old hits in arena shows stuffed full of aging fans, while nobody really cared?

Iggy met riot grrl-style feminism head on when he encountered Courtney Love at a Lemonheads gig where she was hanging out. The incendiary grunge rock icon must have altered Pop's old school notion that "girls" in bands should play keyboards and look good, and his rather condescending notion that she was the latest in a long line of busty blonde American stereotypes. It was the first time he'd seen her play; she came out and did two songs alone. "And it was very, very high quality," he later admitted. "It's very hard to do, to deliver a song alone. Particularly to a large room, particularly one that's just been through a rock concert, but she did it. That is a genuine talent, to be able to deliver the serious goods . . . I'm really experienced with divas, I know lots of them, so I thought, 'Oh, God, it's gonna be diva time,' but she wasn't diva-esque, which I really enjoyed. She was just sort of regular. And since then, like everyone else, if you see anyone ad nauseam in the media you start to get sick of 'em. I'm sure she knows that too, but she has something to sell out there right now, so she's gonna be as visible as she possibly can be to sell more units."

It was also at the Lemonheads show that Courtney Love approached him with the proposal that he should cover a previously unavailable Kurt Cobain song written with Iggy in mind. He said, 'OK, great, I'll listen to it.' Perhaps he wasn't sufficiently overcome with gratitude. Love went onto MTV where, in her usual gunboat diplomacy style, she announced that she had this unreleased Kurt song and that she was trying to make up her mind whether she should give it to Iggy or to Patti Smith. A remarkably odd condescension, given that both Smith and Pop have consigned to the waste basket songs much better than Cobain's finest efforts. Indeed, one of the reasons Cobain killed himself was because he thought, correctly, that he was no good at this rock thing. "She started playing games and I'm not interested!" Pop snapped. "And then somebody called my manager and wanted to talk about meeting about the song . . . I didn't really care. I do my own music, and I like Kurt's music, but I have no interest in doing Kurt's music. If I did do any of his music, I'd be more likely to do something off *Bleach* which I liked a lot more than the later stuff."

1999 saw the release of the soporific *Avenue B*, which was hyped as Pop's most personal and self-revelatory album yet. Iggy grows up or Iggy grows old seemed to be the marketing spin. It is certainly the most boring album in his canon, and not a whole lot better than *Party* in terms of songwriting. He was now divorced from Suchi and – like the marriage itself – the separation proved to be a mightily convenient marketing tool. Work commenced in May 1998 with Don Was once more at the controls but proceedings ground to a halt when Iggy headed off to do his annual dollar-hoovering round of the summer festival circuit. In August they got back together in a New York studio to tie up some loose ends. Then, a few months later, Pop came up with a new song and got Was to return from LA. Was persuaded Pop that the best way to approach this new moody piece – a Beat Generation-like spoken word meditation on his wrecked marriage – was to draft in sedate Blue Note jazz act Medeski, Martin & Wood.

The Stooges had always been a jazz-respecting band – John Sinclair had educated them well about Pharaoh Sanders and John Coltrane.

They'd shared cocaine with Miles Davis and he was a big admirer of their work. Subtle jazz influences informed many of Pop's better solo albums like *Soldier* and *Kill City*. The idea of a Blue Note approach to Pop's difficult new material was essentially sound, as was the use of aging child prodigy David Mansfield on fiddle.

"He's very youthful," enthused John Medeski, keyboard player with Medeski, Martin and Wood. "His body is like a young kid and just his attitude, his approach to things. We did some tunes of his. I don't know if they recorded it, but we also did 'Autumn Leaves' and 'Willow Weep For Me'. We were just doing them for fun, but he sounded great. He was crooning. He could be the Frank Sinatra for the new millennium."

Iggy: "There was one particular song, 'Avenue B'. I was originally doing it solo – just me and an acoustic guitar and it was three times more depressing than the result you hear on the album. Don Was had a vision to do it with a big organ sound and he was pushing either Medeski, Martin and Wood or the guys from The Young Rascals. I sort of vetoed that – I ain't working with the fucking Young Rascals, OK? Don kept thinking of the song 'Groovin' On A Sunday Afternoon' because it had some of the same chords. Anyway, he touted Medeski, Martin and Wood and I did it out of respect for him."

On *Avenue B* Pop rejects grunge, white noise, and the shattered relics of his youth in favour of a determinedly "adult" approach. The result is generally self-important and mediocre, exactly the sort of thing one might expect from an antique buying, primitive art collecting, cat loving, penthouse inhabiting rock star. He certainly drew inspiration from Ginsberg or Kerouac, but Ginsberg and Kerouac were poor writers and, on the spoken word aspects of *Avenue B*, Pop was guilty of some very ordinary writing.

A high point is the title track which refers honestly to the author looking down onto the real world from his Christadora "castle", on the verge of his divorce, at a rapper on the street corner. Equally valid are 'She Called Me Daddy', a brutal account of a relationship breaking down, tinged with a weird David Mansfield-supplied melancholy, and Spanish-language 'Espanol', in many ways the most enjoyable track on the album, a rolling jazzy gem reminiscent of *Zombie Birdhouse* or *Soldier*. Unfortunately Pop takes his whole Latino thing too seriously and contributes his own Santana-style guitar solo to the track. *Avenue B* is many people's favourite Iggy album but, despite a lot of publicity and many really positive reviews, it sold about 30,000 copies.

During one radio interview he was asked, "What if Jack Kerouac and William Burroughs had been pop stars? Would they have been making records like *Avenue B*?" "It's verbally more advanced than a lot of what I've done in the past," he incorrectly replied, "so yeah, I know what you're saying. It kind of owes something to those guys which makes sense because I listened a lot to them both. In fact there are tapes of Kerouac rappin' his poetry . . . in fact there's one very good one of him accompanied by the comedian, Steve Allen, who's also known as being a very good jazz pianist."

Free from Iggy, Suchi Asano (as she now traded) wrote, and had published, a novel, *In Broken Wigwag*. It concerned a cool Japanese girl hanging out in Manhattan's rock clubs and art galleries. Filed under Japanese-American Fiction, it was, impressively enough, extracted in the *Evergreen Review*. She grabbed the apartment.

"I had a divorce," he said. "The lovely lady that I'd lived with preferred to have the place, and I was fine with that. I wanted to get a place just with parity, what I'd paid for that, and realised that things had gone way up since I'd moved there. I went and looked at places for the same money and they were all dog houses." While he was doing all this househunting he started spending time in Miami. He had this desperately in need of cash pal who wanted to sell him some paintings by Robert Williams, a good cartoon artist whose best known painting is the cover of *Appetite For Destruction* by Guns N'Roses.

Pop – an enthusiastic art collector – already had some paintings by Williams. His dodgy impoverished pal also had a Miami condo so Iggy said he'd buy that off him. It was a cheap and nasty place in a cheap and nasty part of Miami Beach. He began commuting there to get away from New York because trips to his home in Mexico – he was also an enthusiastic collector of homes – were complicated. It took 10 hours to get there and there were no direct flights. This remorseless moving from home to home, as he circled the metaphorically important age of 50, made him feel homeless and disjointed.

The divorce didn't just result in one lesser album – it also resulted in Pop relocating from New York to Miami, where the vice is nice at half the price. He was weary of Manhattan anyway because everybody he met seemed to be some kind of wannabe artist or creative type. He felt sure that he didn't want to live in an art colony of two million people. The reality of artistic life in New York, it seemed to him, was that it was a good place to promote yourself, and a good place for people who wished to push themselves. Manhattan was now a whitewashed theme park and the things which first attracted him to the city had disappeared without trace. When he'd moved onto Avenue B, it'd been a virtual war zone, a no-go area for middle-class white kids. By the time he moved out it was rancid with skate geeks, cyber cafes, and dreadlocked, patchouli-oiled, legalise dope, anti-globalisation types.

On the Lower East Side, as nosy a village as you could possibly imagine, a living shrine to the myth of New York punk, he was a recognisable face unable to walk the streets anonymously. One day he was sitting in a cafe drinking coffee while two students with a movie script were discussing their big plans at the next table. One of them dropped a piece of paper on the ground and Iggy picked it up. It said, "That's Iggy Pop. Ask him – he has money." He reckoned that, unlike Manhattan, the people in Miami were not going to ask him what he did for a living during the first five minutes of a conversation.

He'd gone to New York in the first place to hang out with dark, vulgar, swarthy, shady people speaking amazingly bad English. Now he had to live in Miami, which he said was five degrees north of redneck, to enjoy that particular ambience. In New York he couldn't go out to get some food without somebody pitching him a bad film script or asking him to save a Yogi or buy a dubious Nepalese shirt.

Miami, by way of sharp contrast, was full of the poor and the dispossessed, a cultural collision in progress. He reckoned that the city was becoming the capital of Latin America, a jungle environment full of lizards and bugs and trees. He found, in his "later years", a great exit for himself in the Spanish language – he learned to speak Spanish when he was almost 48. He liked speaking the language because he liked having sex with Hispanics. Miami was home, as it happened, to the global headquarters for Royal Caribbean Cruises, the old folks cruise firm which had famously used 'Lust For Life' on an advertising campaign. Maybe part of his deal with them got him a good rate on Senior Citizens' trips.

The city satisfied the amateur historian/psychogeographer which was part of his make-up. It was home to a condo belonging to Seymour Stein of Sire Records. "I was up there once," he said. "Expensive and very tacky." (It used to be said of the personable and entertaining Stein, "Seymour Stein. See less money.") He sometimes drove by The Cameo, an old theatre where he'd played in '89. "You could smell the pee," he told *Rolling Stone*. "And now it's a hip-hop bar. And that's the stinkiest, nastiest strip bar in Southern Florida. They put a big red throne out front and girls sit on it – scantily clad, repulsive girls. This town is diverse shit. I like it here a lot."

Buying a cheap condo from a pal was a reasonably simple real estate negotiation but, when he decided to make Miami his permanent base, he had a whole new experience – he had to go and buy a real home. He'd never before looked for or secured a rental or bought a house.

There'd always been someone else who'd do that for him. Or else he'd tell a roadie, "Put me somewhere and then get me the key." Or he'd be crashing on somebody's floor or holed up in a hotel or his booking agency would find a short let apartment.

He couldn't keep living that way now that he was getting on for 50, the proud owner of lots of art and other old stuff. He took to driving himself around Miami Beach looking for a home. He'd been to the city many times before and had always regarded the area he was cruising through as beautiful. He was looking for one of those degenerated mansions right out of Tennessee Williams. What he had in mind was a big old Mediterranean-style crumbling house in the middle of grounds which might include jungly private lawns, lizards and possums. Eventually he found, in an old Jewish district, exactly what he was looking for. The owner was a "wild old queen". Not for the first time, he managed to strike a mutually satisfactory deal with a wild old queen.

The old queen sold him a Chekovian Mediterranean Revival-style house surrounded by a small forest of ficus trees and featuring a once-grand palm tree. He filled his new home with Haitian voodoo art, Early American furniture, and a Louis XVI couch. Every rock star needs at least one Louis XVI couch. A self-portrait hung in his bedroom, which boasted black-velvet curtains. The painting features mischievous gremlins tempting the central character. "The face is me in my torment," he explained, "and the pointy object to the left of the face – I call it The Flaming Tit of Temptation – is talking in my ear. He's like, 'Just go do it. Take that fuckin' coke. Get rid of that girl. You don't need her.'"

"I got this car when I went to Miami," said Mr Jim Osterberg, ardent consumer. "I've got a '68 cherry-red Cadillac convertible deVille with a white top. It's beautiful and it cost nothing. It cost $5,600 and it's a bomb. I smile when I see it and people yell and cheer when I drive around, because people don't make cars that optimistic anymore. Now they make all these little cars and people say, 'I'll be safe and I'll just blend right in and it locks automatically!' With a Cadillac, it's like Jayne Mansfield, bustin' out all over . . . It's vintage like I am. It looks great, it runs great, and it rides great, but then one day you'll be out in the rain and 'poof!' All the lights go on and you gotta call the tow truck."

Out in Hollywood his myth was now taking on a theatrical form. Well-connected playwright Susie McDonnell wrote a play – *Waiting For Iggy* – which was staged at the Lost Studio during March '99. The work was based on the exploits of one of the dramatist's friends, a member of an all-girl LA punk rock band who once got to support Pop on a tour.

The comedy, set in 1982, concerns a punkette called Blue who convinces herself that Iggy is her father. Her mother, a one-time Sunset Strip cool chick who knew all the guys back in the days, can't remember exactly who Blue's father was. "You always forget Peter Fonda!" Mom admonishes her daughter when Blue lists off Dylan, Jack Nicholson and Jim Morrison as other possible parental candidates.

The play garnered some pretty glitzy support from within the local creative community. The Red Hot Chili Peppers headlined a benefit – also featuring members of The Circle Jerks and Thelonious Monster – organised to pay for theatre rental. It was a night devoted entirely to covers of Iggy songs. Joey Ramone and actor John Cusak caught the play, while one of its angels was Roger Kumble, director of *Cruel Intentions*, a teensploitation hit.

Life in the real world continued apace. Appearing in commercials for corporate products occupied his time, as did providing old tunes for new ad campaigns. He said that when he'd written a lot of those old songs he was paying attention to radio jingles which he felt had a beautiful simplicity to them. Funnily enough, he hadn't written the music for the songs that the ad guys really wanted. Most of those tunes had music by Bowie, Ron Asheton or James Williamson.

In August 2001 it was announced that comedian Stephen Fry and Iggy Pop were to join "it" girl Lady Victoria Hervey for a multimillion pound TV campaign to promote Virgin Atlantic's Upper-Class service. The new ads would play up the stars' personalities to push different aspects of the airline's luxury service, with Fry enjoying a massage. Iggy's scenario left him propping up the bar. Lady Victoria was shown enjoying an in-flight beauty treatment, saying, "Call me superficial, but I like to fly with the beautiful people." This particular campaign died something of a death in the aftermath of Osama Bin Laden's September 11 attack on America.

It was nevertheless a typically busy period for Pop, ad-wise and otherwise. He allegedly amazed the organisers of a Scottish rock festival when he forwarded a dressing room rider which demanded *The New York Times*, broccoli, and seven dwarves. The dwarves had to be dressed like the ones in *Snow White*, which he mistakenly described as *Cinderella*. More conventional rider requirements included pizza, ginger beer, good red wine and organic cigarettes. The festival organisers, delighted with the last-minute publicity spree generated by the dwarves request, said, "Getting hold of seven dwarves isn't exactly a tall order, but it won't be easy."

It was reported that Iggy was to be one of the stars in a new Reebok ad campaign. Reebok, perhaps the least cool of the major sports gear manufacturers (he had already endorsed Converse, the coolest of trainers), planned to use Pop in a print advertising blitz, which also featured former NWA rapper Ice Cube. A compliant media gushingly reported that this brilliant scheme was dreamed up by the New York office of advertising agency BBH. John Wardley, VP of "brand communication" at Reebok was well pleased with his investment in rap'n'roll trashy cultures: "The idea for this campaign is grounded in the power behind simple black and white imagery, something that truly resonates with the timelessness and elegance of Reebok Classic shoes. We're hoping the portraits will stir people's emotions as they realise that Classic is about a timeless touch of humour, surprise, comfort, mystique or fear that knows no barriers and crosses all cultures."

Iggy defends himself: "It's been real nice, because that's the way people got to hear my songs. They still don't make an inroad on American commercial radio. It's been overseas socialist radio, movies and adverts. So it's been great for me. Otherwise my music goes unheard. The film soundtrack, ads stuff, ensures that I have enough money to say 'fuck you' and that's nice, but not enough that I don't have to work. Because like everybody else, I have divorces and my old managers to pay, and my fuckin' car needs an oil change. I have shit like everybody else has."

CHAPTER 23

I Won't Grow Anymore –
Beat 'Em Up, Skull Ring,
Stooges Reunion

*"Out came The Stooges. They blasted out with their fury and the crowd just
stood there looking at them. I couldn't believe it. It reminded me of Iggy's stories
of early Stooges performances where the audience just stands there in disbelief.
This crowd was not in disbelief, however. They just didn't know who or what
they were witnessing. The sound system was excellent. I was at Coachella and
this was far superior. You could hear everything well, even up pretty close. Iggy
immediately recognised the audience's indifference. He yelled at no one in particular, 'Radio weasels!' After a couple of songs Iggy screamed at the audience that,
"You (the audience) won't hear The Stooges on FM radio or see them on TV."
He spent quite a bit of time trying to get a rise out of the crowd and even singled
one guy out for yawning during his performance."*

– Steve Bartels, San Antonio, Texas, 2003

THE fifties are a difficult time in the life of a rock superstar. The years
are rushing by and 60 looms. Contemporaries fall off the perch with
increased regularity – just like back in the Sixties – only they're not
snuffing due to drug overdoses these days. Your pretty face is going to
hell. The only decent gigs you get offered are as a semi-Famous Old
Guy, in the middle of the bill at open-air festivals or as a special guest at
some TV awards show. Not quite up there like Mick Jagger but not
quite down there like Roky Erickson either.

He began to sport a beard, looked like a younger, handsomer Willie
Nelson, only without the Liberal Democrat credentials. He had no

shame. During the 1998 VH-1 Fashion Awards he scraped the bottom of the aesthetic barrel, joining Lenny Kravitz to sing Bowie's 'Rebel Rebel'. He could now be found fifth on the bill at festivals where he'd been a headliner five years earlier. By 2003 nearly everybody in the whole wide world who wanted to see Iggy Pop live had taken the opportunity to do so – at least twice.

Somewhat out of the blue, in 2001, he released what is possibly his best album since *Zombie Birdhouse*. The self-produced *Beat 'Em Up* explores the fucked-up sound of The Stooges informed by the more creative end of nu metal – the Red Hot Chili Peppers or Slipknot. Recorded close to home in Miami, with help from *Raw Power* remix co-conspirator Danny Kadar, *Beat 'Em Up* is another long album – 15 tracks over 72 minutes. Some songs are beautifully constructed noise sculptures, and the quality of the songwriting harks back to thoughtful masterpieces like *Zombie Birdhouse* or *Kill City*. There is some wear and tear on Pop's voice, but that is normal in singers of popular song heading up towards 60, especially those who insist on doing too many live shows. For the first time, and not before time, this great singer whose persona is entirely street corner hip took on board the world of hip hop/rap which had been altering the rest of American rock music for 20 years at this stage.

The band – Whitey Kirst, Lloyd "Moose Man" Roberts, Alex Kirst, Pete Marshall and Danny Kadar – delivered for the singer a melodically winning mixture of rhythm and nasty aggression. He'd been playing shows with many of these guys for years so – like Dylan's touring band on *Love And Theft* – they knew exactly what their boss wanted and was capable of. The boss, on this occasion, was at his competitive best so he rose to the occasion. To get some idea of what contemporary radio-friendly heavy rock was sounding like he checked out, despite his public declarations that new punk was limp as a Dali clock, a Sum 41 CD. He needed to find out what was the skill level and recording technique level of a band like that. He later admitted – though he didn't listen to whole songs on the album because he didn't want to take their influence on board – that he was somewhat taken aback to find that they were "a little too good".

Iggy: "It's Seventies-inspired, I think, handmade, kinda somewhere between hard rock and proto-metal, the music that later became codified as metal but before it was called that. But it's not quite all the way to metal. There's more to it, there's a little more song-iness and structure than I associate with a lot of heavy metal. Within that format, we fuck around with it. It gets an urban twist from the basically South Central ghetto bass player and then it gets a little bit of an academic twist from me, 'cause that's what I do, word-wise."

The man giving it that South Central hip-hop funk was Moose Man Roberts, formerly the bassist in Ice T's rap-metal project, Body Count. Moose Man was supposed to do the promotional tour but was shot dead in South Central two months before the tour started. He was, like many a gunned down urban resident, just in the wrong place at the wrong time. The story of his death became an important part of the spin surrounding the marketing of his last record.

There are numerous genius songs on *Beat 'Em Up*. 'Football' is as good as a rock ballad gets, reminiscent in its musky way of 'Beyond The Law' from *Kill City* or 'The Passenger' off *Lust For Life*. Iggy is a football being passed from hand to hand while trying to score. Life is a football game as every chump and champ knows, people kicking one another where it hurts while setting up the big play. 'Mask' was inspired by a Slipknot gig that Pop attended. The arena-stuffing band, normally masked up on stage, naturally moved around backstage without their masks. Iggy noticed this 16-year-old girl who'd managed to get into the exclusive area. She walked up to one of the Slipknot members and said to him, "Hi. Which mask are you?"

"What a beautiful phrase!" Iggy thought. "So I used it to describe the whole music scene. It took only 20 minutes to write that rant in the second half." The second half rant – which a younger man might call a rap or something closely resembling one – is a free-flowing attack on the MTV music universe. He assaults the insatiable demands of society, frat boys in their shorts, sensitive college graduates, and a world which has irony in place of balls, balls in place of brains, and brains in place of soul. 'Mask' has integrity but, of course, that integrity is substantially undermined by the fact that its author rose to wealth and fame of a sort by pandering to the power elite within the MTV universe.

On the Detroitish 'L.O.S.T.', which leans conspicuously on Iron Butterfly's 'In A Gadda Da Vida', he walks through the sterile wasteland before being thrown on the scrapheap to die while even the animals are running away. "I got my work," goes a vaguely familiar refrain, for the American work ethic was something he'd been singing about since his Reagan-loving Arista days. 'VIP' is a 13-minute slab of vitriol presaged by a Beatnik spoken word narration in the *Avenue B* vein. It's about how flight attendants, whom he's always wanted to screw, are interested in him now because, being a rock star, he is effectively a young executive. The rock star of popular mythology has the money, the fame, can get into the right restaurants, and knows lots of other famous people just like himself. 'VIP' is a witty, observant meditation on the perks and priv- ileges that go with being a major B-list superstar surviving in a sterile, cold, corporate world of drum machines.

Iggy and his regular touring band featuring guitarist Whitey Kirst, his brother Alex Kirst on drums, with Iggy veteran Pete Marshall replacing Moose Man on bass, went out on the road to promote the new material when the album was released that July. "It's just my own little personal band. No big stars," said Iggy. Around this time the backing band became known as The Trolls. They would, very soon, be in need of that unique identity. Iggy was about to hear tales, as he made his way from town to town, of another touring band made up of big stars, a band he knew like the back of his hand who knew him the exact same way, with whom he would soon be doing business.

Iggy & The Troll's set opened with tracks off *Beat 'Em Up* which held up well live, followed by a brutal attack on Stooges classics like 'Raw Power' and 'Search And Destroy'. Critic Jim De Rogatis complained that, "Huge tracts of his discography go untouched in favour of the familiar anthems. In fact, of the 20 tunes delivered during a gripping 90-minute set, almost half dated from The Stooges and the early Seventies." De Rogatis said the Pop audience was "a nice mix of grey, grizzled veterans and young punks."

When Iggy reached New York, he played the chic indie Irving Plaza. The beautiful people, like Aerosmith's Steve Tyler and his daughter Liv Tyler (whose mother Bebe Buell had been one of Iggy's celebrated lovers), came out in strength to be reminded of exactly how it used to be done a long time ago when New York gave birth to punk rock.

Bob Gruen: "Liv Tyler said she was coming down to see the show and mentioned that her dad was in town. I said to her, 'Tell him to come down and see the show. Maybe he's too high maintenance these days to come Downtown.' I knew that'd get him and that he'd be there. It was great because he really enjoyed it and he doesn't get to really come out and see a cool rock show that often these days. Later, after the encores, he was kind of asking me to help organise it for him to get backstage. I've known Steve a long time but he was saying he'd never known Iggy which a lot of people might find strange. It turned out he'd never gotten to see Iggy since the Seventies. He was very much impressed by what he saw. As you had to be. It was very, very impressive."

Iggy, on selling the noisy *Beat 'Em Up* to his label: "The way the music business works is they have to give you enough money to fly everybody where they're going, and get the project off the ground and pay the studio. And they wanna hear shit, they wanna hear what you're gonna do in advance. So, I let 'em hear the stuff on the first half, which is a little more formal. There are a couple that are medium-tempo songs, and they hadn't heard 'Mask'. They heard cuts two through eight, something like that, and then they gave me the green light. Then I did stuff like 'Drink New Blood' and 'VIP' and all that shit, and nobody'd heard it. We got checked halfway through and they said, 'OK, go ahead and finish it.' "

Like *Avenue B, Beat 'Em Up* only sold in the region of 30,000 copies, mighty slim pickings for a living legend on a major label. After a quick look at the sales figures Virgin declined the opportunity to put out another whole album of Iggy and his no-stars backing band belting out take-no-prisoners rock'n'roll. It was then, perhaps, that Art Collins and his client turned their attention towards gathering together a few stellar names, some credible players, and two old friends for the album that became *Skull Ring*.

At first he was living alone in Miami amid the decayed splendour of his Mediterranean-style villa. One day when he was out cruising around South Beach in his cherry-red Cadillac convertible with the top down he spotted two babes on the street. These Miami beauties were heading towards a pizza parlour so he decided that he'd pull up and go into another pizza parlour right next door so that he could observe his prey.

"We spotted him right away," says Nina Alu, the full-figured local girl who shortly afterwards became his live-in lover. "He was wearing slippers and was all alone, looking pensive. We felt kind of sorry for him." He didn't know exactly what to do about this promising situation so he got back into his Cadillac, drove over to where the ladies were and said, "You girls want to go for a ride?" The girls, it transpired, *did* want to go for a ride. Shortly after the ride, Iggy started dating Nina, a USS Airways flight attendant who'd made the unusual decision not to go into broadcast journalism, her university major where, according to Pop, she graduated "summa cum fucking laude".

Nina Alu, a half-Irish, half-Nigerian in her mid-30s, looks like something out of the movies, though nobody's saying what kind of movies. She has variously been described as a busty dream girl, built, stacked, healthy, an ornamental work of art, statuesque, and manly. Less complimentary commentators say she is "like a Marine in drag", or "a Brazilian transvestite" or "Is she for real?" No doubt she is real enough. Her assets have been a marketing godsend for her man.

Iggy had never been particularly coy about his family life. Since the day he got going he'd been giving journalists a running commentary on his parents, his son, his lovers. When he was married to the alluring Suchi she became an intrinsic part of his photo-opportunity promotional package, albeit a classy component. Nina, whose approach is more brazen and in-your-face, has appeared in his last two CD booklets and has pouted and preened for the paparazzi at the countless award ceremonies that they religiously attend as if their lives depended on it. Early on in their relationship paparazzi shots of the two of them skinny dipping appeared in the tabloids – Nina Alu was a walking, talking photo opportunity.

Taking a leaf out of Suchi's book, she superglued herself to Pop's side. She was even present during press interviews, causing one female journalist to protest that she felt self-conscious working in front of an audience. "No you don't get to be alone with me," Pop explained as rudely as only he can. "This is formal, it's a meeting and I don't know you and I'm comfortable with someone here." He claims to have sex with Nina about 10 times a week when he's not working, When he's touring it tends to be less often, because of all that nervous energy that gets burned up on stage and because on the road you end up spending a lot of time in bed anyway. He never goes on the road without her because he couldn't stand the "physical and emotional loneliness of it." She says, "It works that way."

Nina, *Rolling Stone*: "I love Iggy Pop and I respect him, but I don't think I could live with him. But Jim, Jim is sweet and peaceful and romantic; when we're having dinner or making love that's Jim, and sometimes I'll catch him just looking at the trees and birds. It's endearing and almost childlike, just the way he looks at the world with those big eyes."

When not screwing Nina or looking at the world through his big eyes he likes, being something of a bookish intellectual, to watch the *Discovery Channel*, the *History Channel*, and *C Span*. He eats bacon and two eggs sunny side up most mornings for breakfast, claims to have no friends in Miami, only acquaintances like Lamar the gardener, Harry at the gas station, and the guy at the car wash. "One of my legs is shorter than the other," he told *Rolling Stone*, "and I was recently told to start evening things out or I'm going to be fucked up later in life." Nina cooks his meals, packs his bags, pays his multiple parking fines. She says he never lifts the toilet seat before peeing.

"I don't use the toilet much to pee in," he defended himself. "I almost always pee in the yard or the garden because I like to pee on my estate. But inside I would, like, never go, 'Oh, before I pee, I must lift the seat.' Why would I think of that?"

"You're good that way," Nina conceded. "You never leave any residue."

Perhaps, after all, it hasn't been such a long strange trip from the days when he was leaving his shit out to dry on his balcony back in Ann Arbor.

Out in Ann Arbor Ron Asheton got a summons which harked back to *Velvet Goldmine* but which was about to propel him back onto centre stage. Mike Watt, former Minutemen and fiREHOSE bassist, was touring with The Fog, a new band formed by Dinosaur Jr. guitarist J Mascis. Watt had worked with Asheton on the *Velvet Goldmine* soundtrack, and with Mascis for almost 10 years. Mascis was of the opinion that the Stooges songs were the folk music of his generation, and told *Mojo* magazine that *Fun House* was his all-time favourite album. Watt was the link between the retired Stooge and Mascis, a guitarist with a global cult following. Early in 2001 Mascis undertook the first in a long series of shows all over the world billed as "J Mascis and The Fog with special guest Ron Asheton."

The nightly formula saw Mascis do his regular set of solo songs and Dinosaur Jr. oldies until, towards the end, Mike Watt summoned Asheton to the stage. Overweight and outwardly indifferent, but self-evidently the long-lost guitar hero to the blank generation, Asheton always got a hero's welcome before leading the band into some of the noisiest music anybody'd ever heard. He usually did about seven numbers, all drawn from the first two Stooges albums.

Lesser contemporary luminaries queued up to special guest with the special guest. At New York's Wetlands the room was so rammed to capacity that nobody could see the band properly. The Lemonheads' Evan Dando got his chance to be Iggy for a night during that show. In London the celebrity singer at a sold-out Shepherd's Bush Empire was Primal Scream's Bobby Gillespie who got so carried away with his Iggy impersonation that he violently attacked a teenage boy in the audience who was dissing his performance. Even Steve Mackay, written off as dead by some commentators, showed up in San Francisco to reprise his *Fun House* work.

This could have gone on forever so it took root in people's imaginations. When Sonic Youth were asked to curate the impeccably cool All Tomorrow's Parties avant-rock festival in 2002, they wanted this Mascis plus Asheton show on board. Mascis asked Ron if there was any chance of his brother Scott doing the festival, and Scott readily agreed. "I'm ready to go," he said. "To tell you the truth I don't know anything

about Watt and Mascis. But if Ron likes them, they gotta be good."
Suddenly, and beyond his control, the whole can of worms was opening
up on Iggy Pop once again.

The next question was, "Why is Iggy not doing All Tomorrow's
Parties?" He was referred to in the papers as "the only living original
Stooges not scheduled to appear". He had been very seriously wrong-
footed.

Ron bitched about him. "We had such great times when The Stooges
were doing well and the only drugs anyone took was smoking
marijuana, basically. There were *lots* of good times. You would think
that when Iggy came to Detroit he would call and say, 'Hey, why don't
you guys come down to the show, I'll put you on the guest list.'" He
reckoned that a reunion would be fun but deeply unlikely. He advised
his brother to do the show with Mascis and Watt because that might be
as close as they'd ever get to a reunion. "My brother, he misses Iggy," he
said. "'cause those guys, they chummed a lot, they went through all the
heroin bullshit."

Scott was slightly more diplomatic: "I always felt bad for my brother
because he kinda got the raw end of the deal. Me and James and Iggy
were having some problems, and as a result the band fell apart. But I
have a lot of good memories too. I'd still love to do some type of
reunion. I think the people would like it, I think it would be cool. It's all
up to Iggy."

After laurels and bouquets at All Tomorrow's Parties, there was
another sell-out tour. The billing this time was Asheton, Asheton,
Mascis & Watt. Thunderous music of a sort not heard for 30 years
impressed young and old across Europe and the States. People stared
bug-eyed at Scott Asheton as he pummelled his kit into submission,
viscerally linked to his brother's incessant guitar noise-mongering. It
gave new meaning to the phrase, a blast from the past.

The re-emergence of the Ashetons was as unexpected as it was longed
for and avidly welcomed. The Asheton, Asheton, Mascis & Watt shows
had worked out well commercially. The Dum Dum Boys finally proved
themselves to be ornery, stubborn, resilient customers who'd stayed true
to their original intentions. Where once he'd been the prettiest Stooge,
Scott Asheton was now a lumbering man in middle age but he was still
the motherfucker of all drummers. Ron, who'd remained in music all
through the years, now had the skills and the experience necessary to
play the difficult music that he'd once struggled with. The time had
finally arrived when Iggy Pop – selling minuscule quantities of albums,
acting career on hold, sliding down those festival bills, still famous for

being famous – really needed them, just like he did as a teenager when, though he could certainly do it, he couldn't do it on his own.

Iggy: "What really changed things was that I was out on tour with *Beat 'Em Up* and I heard everywhere I went, 'Hey, Ron's out on tour with Dinosaur Jr. doing Stooges songs and it's real good.' Or I was in Europe and I'd hear 'Ron and Scott are both out with Mike Watt doing Stooges songs at festivals.' And I thought, whoa, they're out there playing the material, so it kind of raised my eyebrow a little bit."

Talk of other Stooges playing Stooges songs at festivals (where you normally get paid at least five figures) must surely have set alarm bells ringing.

Rumours of a Stooges reunion started to circulate on geekish Iggy chat rooms and in the media. There were nights during the *Beat 'Em Up* Tour when Iggy would be playing one side of town while the brothers with their indie pals were gigging elsewhere in the same city at pretty serious venues; rumours of ad hoc get-togethers zapped around the planet. Art Collins eventually confirmed that something was going on. "It's not going to be some grand reunion," Art insisted. "Who knows, maybe it could be. But it's not the intent. It's just for them to get together and do a couple of tracks."

"It's pretty simple and straightforward," said the manager. "Iggy's still signed with Virgin Records and he's working on a new album. He called Ron and Scott and said, 'Hey, maybe you guys want to play on a couple of tracks and see what comes out of it.'" Art went on to say that Iggy and the Ashetons had always remained friends, though it's questionable whether Ron and Iggy were ever truly intimate – they'd certainly been cronies at one time but by 2002 it was 20 years since they'd been in the same room together. Scott had stayed in the frame and he used to visit Iggy from time to time over the years.

The Stooges weren't the only great beast slouching out of the Sixties to be reborn. At this time Pop was made a surprising offer that he could easily refuse; The Doors were re-forming and wanted him to be their lead singer. The loquacious Doors keyboard player Ray Manzarek told the media that, "We're talking to Iggy Pop right now so we'll see . . . how Iggy's schedule works out. But, wouldn't that be great, man? Iggy and The Doors. I'd love that, you know, and Densmore said he'd play too. So, John and Robby and Ray may all play together – the three surviving Doors and Iggy Pop, and I'd really dig that." Pop was lucky not to dig the proposition – he said it would have been impolite to the memory of Jim Morrison.

Despite his much vaunted admiration for Morrison – and despite the cultural sharp practice which'd allowed Danny Sugerman and Manzarek mischievously to repackage The Doors post-*Apocalypse Now* as some sort of punk progenitors – The Doors were yesterday's papers like The Byrds or Creedence Clearwater Revival. Public association with their show-bizzy nostalgia-drenched reunion would've dashed Iggy's credibility at a time when that credibility was his strongest card. And maybe the money deal wasn't so hot either. Manzarek eventually managed to cobble together The 21st Century Doors, as they were forced to call themselves after legal threats from founding member John Densmore, with the fifth rate ex-Cult singer Ian Astbury breaking on through to the other side at the cock-rocking helm.

The first Stooges sessions were short but sweet. Four tracks were done in 10 days starting on January 13, 2003. The venue for these historic sessions, close to Pop's bayfront home on North Bay Road, Miami Beach, was North Miami's popular Criteria Studios where the Bee Gees once did 'Tragedy' and Brook Benton cut 'Rainy Night In Georgia'. It was at Criteria that Pop did *Beat 'Em Up*.

The initial meeting between the Ashetons and Pop was understand-ably tense. "The first meeting was a little awkward," leaked Ron. "We were at the hotel and he came to meet us and it was a little strange. I felt a little nervous because I hadn't really seen him for 20 years. My brother had seen him but I hadn't. I knew it was a little awkward for Iggy, too. But it melted away very quickly. And everyone relaxed. It was like old times. Iggy opened up and laughed a lot more. At first he was all business. By the time we left the first trip it was going fine." Iggy later admitted that, "I didn't expect jack shit from it. I really underestimated my own group."

That first night, not having been picked up in the airport by their old pal and having had an "all business" hotel reunion, it was only natural that they didn't go to dinner at Pop's home. Instead they went to the 11th Street Diner, close to the Ashetons' hotel. Ron, who now looks a little like Michael Moore after six months dining at McDonald's, and who was subsequently described by diplomatic music industry journals as beefy, obviously took a liking to this eatery. "I was going there for my pre-studio food and when we were done I'd go back," he said. "I was spending about $100 a day there. I loved the diner, and I was stuck on it."

Punk rock, these days, clearly marches on a full stomach.

"They're hungry," said Iggy. "They've had a long time to wait for this and they're ravenous. Because of that they've managed to muster some-thing that passes for maturity when we're working." They can't have been all that ravenous if they were spending $100 a day in a diner. And Iggy still couldn't resist the temptation to knife them with the stiletto of back-handed compliments. He also managed to explain to a journalist that he had a lot more money than them.

"Scott can still sell a song as a drummer, and Ron has really grown as a guitar player," puffed Iggy correctly. "When the two of them lay down tracks in the studio just alone, guitar and drums together, they have the authority of old blues players, the kind of authority I associate with Junior Kimbrough, or R.L. Burnside . . . Sometimes I just left them alone and they came up with whole tracks, and I came in and constructed vocals as we went along."

The Stooges reunion had kicked off for real. Alexis Petridis, writing in British paper, *The Guardian*, pointed out that reunions of legendary bygone acts like The Sex Pistols were invariably fraught with credibility problems. He cited the grimmest of all reunions, that of The Velvet Underground, the only Sixties band with whom The Stooges can be compared. He wrote of "the sight of Lou Reed on stage with the Velvet Underground in the early Nineties, smoking a cigar and embellishing songs with wildly inappropriate whoops and extemporary lyrics: 'Shiny shiny, shiny boots of leather, WOOH YEAH momma!'" Petridis went on to say that something better could be expected from The Stooges.

He was absolutely right – this would prove to be an astute, fly reconciliation.

At the same time that he was turning back the clock or pushing back the aural envelope one more time, Iggy was busy constructing the rest of the *Skull Ring* album. The overall sound was a welcome continuation of *Beat 'Em Up*'s Fuck You attitude but it didn't flow so well, maybe because of the necessary presence of a variety of special guests – Green Day, Sum 41, and Peaches – who were youngish and hopefully commercial. The Stooges' tracks sound authoritative and upmarket. The Trolls' songs come across kind of goofy, adolescent, demo-like, and occasionally Ramones-ish. The Peaches duets are unnecessary, and the tracks featuring the superstar punks, appallingly catchy, sound like Iggy stranded in bubblegum punk hell. In subsequent interview blather promoting the album, Pop was his usual positive-about-the-product self. He had his own band – The Trolls – that he had commitments to and he liked collaborating with other artists, "some pretty fucking estimable ones at that".

"I've been out making a living, playing in the flesh, doing the real dirty deal with these guys," he said about The Trolls. "And if they're there when you piss and they're there when you sweat and they're there on the stinking bus, and next to you when you raise your arm in glory and everybody says, 'Yeah, he's great,' and you know the gig's going great – then they need to be there on the record." The implication of this is that Iggy travels around in stinking buses, whereas in reality the musicians travel by bus while he favours limos.

Despite his fraternal support, The Trolls must've felt somewhat disturbed and insecure about what the future held. Their boss was now moving fast. He recorded 'Little Know It All' with chartbusting Sum 41 on April 29, 2003, two days after The Stooges, at the huge Coachella Festival, did their first triumphant live show together since the Michigan Palace affray back in '74. 'Little Know It All' subsequently became the first single from *Skull Ring*.

Iggy had got to know Sum 41 in November 2002, when he did a two song set with the band at a Canadian awards ceremony. "They sent me a demo of something," he said. "They didn't want it to sound like another one of their songs so they said it was in the mould of early Social Distortion." He joined them in LA at a crummy, seedy demo studio in a bad part of Hollywood. The thing that impressed him about this band was how comfortable and totally relaxed they were being in the room together. They were "a quiet, efficient, serious machine, and they were there to work". Deryck Whibley, Sum 41's singer and guitarist, was impressed with the irascible old greybeard punk too. "I was kind of nervous at the beginning," he said. "I didn't know what to expect from him. But he was one of the nicest guys ever. It was like talking to an old friend."

He became pally with Green Day on the lucrative European festival circuit where he is pretty much a permanent annual fixture. Billy Joe Armstrong, Green Day's leader, was given two sets of Iggy lyrics so that he could write music for them. Then the other guys in the band wanted in on the deal. He got together with Green Day in Berkeley's Studio 880. "The stuff's kind of rockabilly in a way although it doesn't feel like it. I think that's where it comes from. Billy Joe is really talented so anything I could get him to do, an idea about the vocal, an extra guitar riff, a mix, anything. I just said, 'Do it. Do it.' He is a genuine key talent, really the first American writer to uncover the roots of what had become neo-punk and emo. Frankly it all comes from that one band."

Clearly the "key talent" Green Day whom Iggy encountered in pursuit of his career in 2003 had improved in leaps and bounds since 2001 when he compared them, in his interview with *The Big Takeover*, to the worst excesses of bubblegum pop and offensively inoffensive MOR pap like Lesley Gore's 'It's My Party'. Back in '93 the likes of

Green Day and Sum 41 were lampooned on *American Caesar*'s 'Character' for being "white bread boys" who didn't even know how to puke.

When the album came out, it was The Stooges who rightly got pride of place on the little CD sticker which boasted the big shot guest stars. *Skull Ring* is a dolly mixture. The Stooges tracks, along with an acoustic Iggy number, are the best things there. The Stooges manufacture a sort of music no longer made in the mainstream, partly because so much of it has been made over the last 20 years. They need a real producer to bring out the best in them. Confronted with the absolute wall of sound that the Ashetons were giving him to play with, Iggy's voice, which had served him so well for so long, wasn't always there. He sometimes struggled to keep up with the noise. All those live shows had taken their toll of his most dependable asset.

One of the Green Day collaborations, 'Supermarket', deals precisely with his dubious career as a product endorser and a provider of music for advertising campaigns. The Sum 41 tune is the best example of Pop compromising his art in the hopes of getting radio airplay since *Blah Blah Blah*. It's not clear what purpose the Peaches duets serve but she was getting a lot of publicity around then with her tinny electropop-rock, popular with gay audiences. She sounds way out of her league alongside the heavyweight chart acts and the still heavier Stooges.

Alexis Petridis, *The Guardian*, October 2003: "Weirdly, given that he is the one with the ongoing career, Iggy emerges as the weakest link. On the original Stooges albums, his vocals and lyrics offered a barely controlled howl of youthful rage and self-disgust. Rightly surmising that to try anything similar at 56 would sound fairly ridiculous, he is forced into self-parody, making the appropriate fizzing and cracking sound effects on 'Little Electric Chair', offering some self-consciously overblown shrieking on 'Loser'. Only on their final track together, 'Dead Rock Star', does everything gel perfectly. As The Stooges hammer away, Iggy dredges up some remarkably clear memories of the last time the trio shared a stage, back at the Michigan Palace. 'I'm so afraid of failing, I hang on to the railing,' he booms. 'I gather awful knowledge you cannot get at college . . . I'm a dead rock star.' Tinged with regret and hard-won wisdom, it's moving in a way that the original Stooges never were."

With an album in the shops Iggy, virtually on autopilot, took to the road. This time he mainly toured with The Stooges but some gigs featured The Trolls. The Stooges used Mike Watt, left over from the Asheton brothers own tours, on bass with saxophonist Steve Mackay from the *Fun House* period back in the saddle. Material was restricted to the two pre–James Williamson Stooges albums, and to the stuff the band did on *Skull Ring*. Rumour had it that Ron Asheton nixed any reunion role for James Williamson and, if this is true, he was quite entitled to do so.

Williamson had been a famous music biz recluse for decades. The vibe was that he'd become incredibly wealthy as a straight technology executive. He'd been coming up for air in recent years, granting the occasional interview, always making great play out of the fact that he was entirely finished with both guitar playing and showbiz. Now that a reunion was actually happening, he was clearly miffed not to be invited.

Fanclub website www.iggy-pop.com asked him if he'd be willing to play with the band again. "Hard to say . . ." he responded hopefully. "Anything and everything is possible. We'll have to see how things turn out." The website wondered how he felt about being left out in the cold, with none of his songs in the set, and about Ron's role in this omission. "I doubt if it was Ron's decision," Williamson responded testily. "But anyway, actually, I don't know the real answer. Maybe they just wanted to do the original line-up. I have no idea." The last time he'd spoken to Iggy had been six or seven years previously when he was doing a show in San Francisco.

The New York Times, when The Stooges came to town, thought that, "Mr Pop made his countless latter-day imitators look like poseurs." Punk rocker turned writer Richard Hell said that the show he saw "was one of the best shows I've seen for as long as I can remember. Actually I hardly ever go to any shows . . . but I caught him at Jones Beach. He's the real thing. Every fibre of him is devoted to making those few minutes on stage to take you out of yourself."

Veteran Iggy watcher Nick Kent was impressed when he caught up with them at the Coachella festival, viewing them through middle-aged rose-tinted glasses: "The reformed Stooges stole the show and completely obliterated the performances of younger stars such as The White Stripes, The Strokes and The Hives. This was quite a feat when you consider that the three Stooges were all in their mid-fifties and their singer, Iggy Pop, exhibited a pronounced limp throughout the performance."

The Detroit gig, likely to be a phenomenally emotional affair for the generations of Michigan fans who'd grown up with nothing more than a myth and various Asheton bar band projects to hang on to, was cancelled because of a power cut which enveloped much of the Northeastern US that night. Pop ended up eating some cold beef sandwiches back in his hotel, worried that the power might come back on after the cancellation, and that the band would "look like fuckin' pussies". They eventually did their Detroit show some time later, and blew the home-town crowd away. (This homecoming show was subsequently released as a DVD, *Iggy And The Stooges Live In Detroit 2003.*) The European shows were the first ever played on the continent by the band.

In a Spanish hotel before one show Mike Watt reported sharing a fish meal with the Asheton Brothers. Scott went out and bought some tins of local sardines and some bread. Ron and Watt then used the complimen-tary combs provided to them by the hotel to dish out the sardines onto the bread. Scott also provided pistachios which he brought all the way from Michigan with him.

Ron and Scott hung out with the roadies. Iggy travelled in separate vehicles from the band. He had his own dressing room. He never soundchecked with them. There was a fair bit of running off stage and right into a limo where Nina was waiting for him so that they could be whisked directly off to the airport. It is not entirely clear that he is big enough a star to need this kind of Elvis Has Left The Building behaviour for any reason other than enormous ego gratification. The Ashetons and Mike Watt would reach the airport afterwards in a van. It was, however, a very real reunion – on stage they were equal partners – but Pop clearly continued to tour as a solo act, with all that this implies as regards the carve-up on the money coming in. The Ashetons both got songwriting credits on the four tracks they contributed to *Skull Ring.*

It must have been quite difficult for him on a human level. He had, whatever the implications, become a man of wealth and taste. It is perhaps understandable that he wanted to travel separately, and maintain separate dressing rooms, from chaps who would eat sardines off plastic combs, import nuts from Ann Arbor, or spend $100 a day in a diner. He'd been solo a long time and, especially since things started going well for him, his backing band had been just that, younger hired guns glad of the gig and the prestige factor.

Now he was out on the road with two guys who'd known him since he was a child, people who'd known his parents, whose family he knew, who were still seeing on a regular basis people from Ann Arbor that he'd moved on from a long, long time ago. He'd straightened himself out pretty seriously finally to fulfil his social climbing instincts to the hilt. He'd run away from that trailer park and never looked back. He was snobby, pretentious, an arriviste connoisseur of good wine and good living, a charming socialite with a pop porno promo babe on his arm. They were still the unruly hamburger-eating kind of guys who'd missed the train and stayed behind on a going-nowhere provincial indie scene; nice and off the wall and utterly without malice. He had shat on them in a serious way when he threw it all away on their behalf. It can't have been easy. The Ashetons had so much to offer him by way of musical excellence and career enhancement. It was good to see him allowing himself to be so fundamentally challenged again.

Bob Gruen: "He has the best abs and the best stomach of anybody in the business. Lou Reed wrote this funny piece about Iggy. They were playing the same festival somewhere and staying in the same hotel. Lou wrote about how he saw Iggy walking across the foyer of the hotel and just looking at Iggy made him feel real low about himself. He'd just spent the previous two years working out to get some shape together and all that work had failed to make him look even remotely close to the condition Iggy was in. The thing about him is that he makes it all look natural. He just has the best muscles and figure there is."

Nyna Symmonds-Burright (Iggy fan): "I met Iggy in the immigration line in San Juan, Puerto Rico on April 7, 2002. He was dressed in faded jeans, no shirt, a brown vest, and boots. He was travelling with a very tall, attractive black woman and they seemed to be together. She was kind of leaning into him. I approached him and asked him if he was in fact Iggy Pop. He smiled and said, 'Yes.' I told him what a big fan I was, and had been for many years. He quite surprised me because he was quite gracious. Knowing how he can be, I almost expected him to be nonchalant, perhaps even rude. He was so nice to me. As I spoke he just continually thanked me, shook his head, and seemed most appreciative. Then I left him alone and went back to my place in the queue. Later I saw him and his companion coming down the escalator into baggage reclaim. They both got pulled out of line by customs to be searched by hand."

Michael Erlewine: "Back in the early days, when he was with the Prime Movers, Iggy had this kind of unofficial personal manager who was also a very close friend of his, David 'Panther' White. Panther was a wonderful comedian who, if he'd gotten the breaks, could have been a comedian of national importance. He and Iggy used to hang out together a lot. A couple of years back Panther, who is now living in the Boston area, bumped into Iggy, who was doing a local show. Iggy arranged for him to have passes and all that stuff for the show. When Panther showed up Iggy treated him just like any other fan. There was no crossing of the barriers of time, there was no sense of Iggy giving him a fraternal embrace. These guys had been very close friends. Panther was stunned and offended that Iggy would be such an asshole."

Michael Erlewine (to Ken Shimamoto): "Iggy invited him (Panther) to ride in his limousine with him, and told him that he hardly lets anyone ride with him. Then, when they got to the concert, Iggy said he would issue him with a complete pass, so that Panther could come back and visit with him, during intermission or whatnot. But when Panther attempted to access the backstage area, he was told he was not on the list. Of course, he said that he *was* on the list and that Iggy put him there. He was rebuffed and had to go back to his seat. After the show, when he *did* meet up with Iggy, Iggy said to Panther, and I quote, 'I decided you should wait and see me like the rest of my fans . . . I've got real friends now, like Keith Richards and David Bowie.' As if anyone could buy or hire an old friend. Priceless."

At the 2003 *MTV Video Awards Show* in New York, Iggy and Nina stepped out of a limo on Sixth Avenue. His name was announced over the PA but the large crowd of teenybop kids, waiting for their favourites like Britney and Justin Timberlake, didn't know who he was. Iggy smiled for the cameras like a professional and made his way into the lobby. He later said that the hip-hop guys like DMC and Big Boi and Dr Dre were friendly, that James Hetfield from Metallica expressed an interest in getting together to do something with The Stooges.

Bob Gruen: "He really knows how to do it now, and still does do it. A lot of other performers you see tend to drift into a routine at his age, or not to be so interested because they're doing the same songs over and over again. He avoids that trap, partially I think because he attracts an all-ages crowd and can't necessarily rest on his laurels. He has people out there from his own age right down to mid-teens, all of whom he works up into a roaring frenzy."

Danny Fields: "Iggy played five or six years ago at a theatre in Times Square and it was a great show. There was a party afterwards and there was a table that said, 'Reserved for Iggy Pop,' so I just went and sat there. They said, 'That's reserved for the stars,' and I said, 'It's all right.' Iggy came bounding in. He pulled me over after a while, real confidential, and said, 'I have to ask you something.' I said, 'Well, what?' He said, 'Do I owe you any money?' I said, 'Yeah, but I don't know how much. Forget it.'

"I thought 'God! We've never talked about that before!' It must have been on his mind. It'd been 20 or 30 years ago, and, 'Do I owe you any money?' I wish I could calculate how much money it was with interest over the time but don't worry about it. I did a thing on VH-1 because they were doing something on him and I heard myself saying, 'What was the problem? Oh, that's right, he was a junkie.' I just went off ranting and I think they cut to a commercial break because I was sitting there screaming and ranting, 'He was a junkie! He was a junkie!' I saw him backstage at Irving Plaza and I said, 'Gee, I should apologise.' Iggy said, 'Nah, I should apologise to you. I *was* a junkie.'"

Mike Watt: "He is the crux, the absolute singularity. So much stuff comes to us second, third, fourth, fifth, umpteenth hand and here I get to have a direct line on the primary source. I feel totally blessed. He's totally aware of everything onstage – what's happening, what's getting played, and how. Yet he has total abandon with his emotions – it's quite a righteous talent he has. I get so scared playing in front of people but with Iggy at the bow of the boat, how can one be afraid? He is a lightening rod for emotion, just drawing it into you as you try and let loose your own fury. Still all the while he has total focus and perspective. He is quite the inspiration, bringing out the best in me that I can deliver. He is one of the most happening folks I have ever been on stage with."

He is heading up towards 60, 140 pounds compared with the 160 pounds he was when he finished high school. His son is finally up and running. Educated, rehabbed, and married with a kid. Iggy Pop is a grandfather. The last time he did heroin was 1981, he took his last opium in '83. If he drinks two glasses of wine at dinner he loses the plot a little and starts talking about his penis.

Iggy: "I like to go to the beach. I like to stare at the clouds. I like to ride around. I got an old used car, a convertible Caddy. I like to ride around and listen to music, or just have a quiet dinner. I like to go to the supermarket. I like to shop for food. I've got a library, but I don't read a lot; I like to play with the books."

Acknowledgements

Chris Charlesworth at Omnibus suggested that I write this book and showed great patience with me. François de Menil made the time to put me right about his movie. Nina Antonia turned down the opportunity to biographise Pop and was generous and gracious beyond the call of duty with her contacts and her comments. Her books on Johnny Thunders and the New York Dolls are unique. Her own Iggy book is small but perfect. Bill Laswell, whose musical explorations are downright heroic, helped me out although there has been a lot of water under the bridge. Barry Neuman at the Modern Culture gallery was exceptionally helpful, not to mention being the source of many entertaining New York conversations. Jack Rabid took the time to show me around Alphabet City and to explain something of the NY hardcore scene to me. His magazine *The Big Takeover* is a cultural bible. When I asked Frank Rynne if he thought Iggy and Bowie ever did it in Berlin, he opined, sensibly enough, "Of course they did. At least once. They must've done something!" Gerard Malanga was a real human in the way he told me about taking that famous photograph. Tav Falco from Panther Burns told me about the time he worked on a movie with Iggy, and the time they were label–mates thanks to Chris Stein. Helen Donlon was a good friend throughout this book's somewhat fraught gestation.

I'm indebted to Ira Cohen, Chris Campion, Mick Farren, Billy Name, Penny Arcade, Jack Sergeant, the great biographer Ulick O'Connor, Tony White, Tim Wheeler, Goofy Sufi, Joel Pereira, Hayley Ann at Codex, Elaine Palmer (www.pulp.net), Wayne Kramer, Glen Matlock, Brendan Maher and Grace Wells at/and South Tipperary Arts Centre, Bob Gruen, James BL Hollands and Roger K Burton at The Chamber Of Pop Culture, Declan O'Reilly, Billy Name, Nourredine Batchi, The Parkinsons, Carwyn Ellis, Anita Pallenberg, Marek Pytel, Kevin Barrington, Michael Murphy, Lydia Lunch (who, one day in Norway, taught me how to truly disrespect), Gary Valentine, OBL, Alvin Gibbs, Jean Michel Reusser, Jacopo Pandolfi, Tavis Henry, Jon Mozes, Seb Tennant, Stephen Robinson at the Hot Press, Gene Gregorits, Richard Morgan, Malcolm Kelly, Al Orensanz at the Angel

Orensanz Centre, Carl Stickley, Michael Simmons, Terry Wilson, John Brett, and Cor Neven for help with the discography. R.I.P. Nigel Preston, Hamri, Rachid Batchi, and Andrew Clandermond.

Leee Black Childers was funny and sharp about the Manhattan fag scene into which Iggy enthusiastically tumbled. Martin Arthur, Margaret Hurley, and Barry Cannon were the close Dublin pals who first turned me on to Iggy, with everything which that eventually involved. Rodney Bingenheimer opened up his address book and we talked for hours about Iggy, the Chelsea Hotel, and much else besides.

Trigger at The Continental took a lot of persuading before he agreed to talk. "How do I know you're not some kind of Iggy stalker?" he asked. "He's not my type," I assured him. The Continental is now New York's punk Central. Victor Bockris, author of many of my favourite books, proved to be as good a talker as he is a writer. The MC5 tearing down forests metaphor in my Foreword comes from him. Michael Erlewine has a profound sense of the history that he was involved with. Kandia Crazy Horse shared The Anita Pallenberg Story and Manhattan's best soul food with me.

With Regina Weinreich I tried out the lobster place across the road from the Chelsea. Roberta Bayley met me on the street where she lives. She is part of the local physical graffiti herself. Mick Rock went to London when I went to New York but he eventually stormed into the Chelsea full of enthusiasm and things to do. "Blue" Gene Tyranny put me on the right track about Iggy, especially about his sexuality. Danny Fields talked brilliantly about the roots of music, accidentally explaining why The Stooges were so important. I never understood Field's contribution to the music that I love until I met him. He has a special vision of the genre; he should write a book of his own about his musical theories. Spencer Kansa was his usual generous self, offering up his unique research into the Berlin/Hansa days. Aziz Number One from the Minzah Hotel, Tangier was my number one guide. John Sinclair took time off from album making and was kinder to Pop than I would've been in the circumstances. John Dunning pointed me in the direction of Berlin information. Jonathan Kearney reminded me of *The Sex Revolts*.

All quotes from Iggy Pop contained in this book have been credited other than those which derive from live radio/internet and other secondary sources. www.iggy-pop.org did interviews with Whitey Krist, James Williamson, Mike Watt, and Ricky Gardiner. Scott Westerman interviewed Russ Gibb. Ben Edmonds wrote Jeep Holland's obituary. Mike Watt's home page – wherein his online on the road reflections on the reformed Stooges can be found – is at www.hootpage.com. Pam

Brown did the *Punk* interview with Iggy. Other Iggy interviews used were done by Jaan Uhelszki, Colin McDonald, and Erik Hedegaard. John Griffin did a radio interview with Ron Asheton which was used in the hardback edition of this book without John getting a credit. Chris Parcellin and Jason Gross also did Ron Asheton interviews that went unacknowledged. Ken Shimamoto interviewed Gary Rasmussen, Ron Asheton, Scott Morgan, Michael Erlewine, and James Williamson for a series of important articles. His material was used in the hardback without a credit going to Ken. This was unfortunate since, in particular, his interview with James Williamson, which I've leaned on, was something of a scoop. Chapter 14 owes a great deal to Danny Sugerman's *Wonderland Avenue* book and to an enjoyable afternoon I spent with Sugerman discussing Iggy. Per Nilsen and Dorothy Sherman's earlier Pop biography, *The Wild One*, contained invaluable interviews with Jimmy Silver, Louella Osterberg, Ron Asheton, and Chris Ehring. They did sterling spadework on Iggy's mid-period. *Jesus – This is Iggy* is a DVD/video documentary which features the original TV transmission of The Stooges' *Cincinnati Pop* performance.

The bulk of this book was written in Morocco, in the company of people who had never heard, or heard of, Iggy Pop before I showed up. Neither were they overly familiar – beyond the usual suspects – with rock music. The comments of people entirely new to the artist and (to some extent) the genre gave me an invaluable insight into Pop. I did most of the interviews while staying at New York's Chelsea Hotel where, as usual, Stanley Bard was a fine host. I am indebted to Helen Carey and Anna Doherty at the Centre Culturel Irlandais in Paris where I stayed while working on this substantially revised paperback edition.

Gimme Danger is dedicated to the guy I was with at the Ron Asheton/ J Mascis gig who had his head smashed by Bobby Gillespie from Primal Scream.

Joe Ambrose.
joedigger@hotmail.com

Bibliography

Ambrose, Joe, Rynne, Frank, & Wilson, Terry. *Man From Nowhere; Storming The Citadels Of Enlightenment With William Burroughs and Brion Gysin* (Delinquente, Dublin, 1992)

Antonia, Nina. *Johnny Thunders: In Cold Blood* (Jungle Books, London, 1984)

Antonia, Nina. *The New York Dolls: Too Much Too Soon* (Omnibus Press, London, 1998)

Antonia, Nina. *Iggy Pop* (Virgin Publishing, London, 1997)

Briot, Marie-Odile. *Brion Gysin 23* (23, Paris, 1992)

Bockris, Victor. *Patti Smith* (Fourth Estate, London, 1999)

Bockris, Victor. *Beat Punks* (De Capo Press, New York, 1998) aka *New York Babylon* (Omnibus Press, London, 1993)

Cale, John & Bockris, Victor. *What's Welsh For Zen* (Bloomsbury, London, 1999)

Colegrave, Stephen, & Sullivan, Chris. *PUNK. A Life Apart* (Cassell, London, 2001)

Evans, Gavin. *Biopic – Iggy Pop* (Canongate, Edinburgh, 2003) (photo study)

Farren, Mick. *Give The Anarchist A Cigarette* (Jonathan Cape, London, 2001)

Gibbs, Alvin. *Neighborhood Threat; On Tour With Iggy Pop* (Britannia Press Publishing, UK. 1995/ Codex, Brighton, 2001)

Graham, Bill. *Bill Graham Presents* (Da Capo Press, 2004)

Harry, Debbie, Stein, Chris, & Bockris, Victor. *Making Tracks: The Rise Of Blondie* (Elm Tree Books, London, 1982)

Heylin, Clinton, *From The Velvets To The Voidoids* (Penguin Books, London, 1993)

Kent, Nick. *The Dark Stuff: Selected Writings On Rock Music 1972–1995* (Penguin Books [UK], Da Capo Press [US], 1995.) Foreword by Iggy Pop.

McLaughlin, David. *Mothers And Others: The Rock And Roll History Of Romeo, Michigan* (Details unknown)

McNeil, Legs & McCain, Gillian. *Please Kill Me: The Uncensored Oral History Of Punk* (Penguin Books, US, 1996)

Melnick, Monte & Meyer, Frank. *On The Road With The Ramones* (Sanctuary, London, 2003)

Nilsen, Per. *Blah Blah Blah Tour* (Rosebud, 1987)

Nilsen, Per with Dorothy Sherman. *Iggy Pop: The Wild One* (Omnibus Press, London, 1988)

Pop, Iggy with Anne Wehrer. *I Need More; The Stooges And Other Stories* (Karl-Cohl Publishing, New York, 1982; Two Thirteen Sixty-One Publications, 1997)

Ranaldo, Lee. *jrnls80s* (Soft Skull Press, New York, 1998)

Reynolds, Simon & Press, Joy. *The Sex Revolts: Gender, Rebellion, And Rock' n'Roll* (Serpent's Tail, London, 1995)

Rock, Mick. *Raw Power – Iggy And The Stooges 1972* (Creation Books, London, 2000). Foreword by Iggy Pop.

Sugerman, Danny. *Wonderland Avenue; Tales Of Glamour And Excess* (Sidgwick & Jackson, London, 1989)

Thompson, Dave. *Beyond The Velvet Underground* (Omnibus Press, London, 1989)

Valentine, Gary. *New York Rocker: My Life In The Blank Generation* (Sidgwick & Jackson; London, 2002)

West, Mike. *The Lives And Crimes Of Iggy Pop* (Babylon Books, 1982; second edition, 1987)

Discography

Selected US/UK discography. Only foreign releases of interest are included.

ALBUMS

(with The Iguanas)

THE IGUANAS
1996 (US) Norton ED 251
TRACKS: Mona/I Don't Know Why/Again And Again/Out Of Limits/
California Sun/Twist And Shout/Walk Don't Run/Things We Said Today/
Surfin' Bird/Louie Louie/Wild Weekend/Tell Me/Slow Down/Johnny B.
Goode/Tequila/I Feel Fine/Pipeline/If I Had A Hammer

(The Stooges)

THE STOOGES
August 1969 (US) Elektra EKS 74051
September 1969 (UK)
Reissued March 1977 (UK) as Elektra K42032
TRACKS: 1969/I Wanna Be Your Dog/We Will Fall/No Fun/Real Cool
Time/Ann/Not Right/Little Doll

FUN HOUSE
August 1970 (US) EKS Elektra EKS 74101
December 1970 (UK) EKS Elektra EKS 74071
Reissued March 1977 (UK) as Elektra K42051
TRACKS: Down On The Street/Loose/TV Eye/Dirt/1970 (aka I Feel
Alright)/Fun House/LA Blues

(Iggy & The Stooges)

RAW POWER
May 1973 (US) Columbia KC 32111
June 1973 (UK) CBS 65586
Reissued (UK) as CBS Embassy 31464, May 1977 and
                CBS Embassy 32083, November 1981

TRACKS: Search And Destroy/Gimme Danger/Your Pretty Face Is Going
To Hell/Penetration/Raw Power/I Need Somebody/Shake Appeal/
Death Trip

METALLIC KO
1976 (France) Skydog SGIS 008
1977 (US) Import IMP 1015
TRACKS: Raw Power/Head On/Gimme Danger/Rich Bitch/Cock In My
Pocket/Louie Louie (all tracks live Michigan Palace 1973/74)
Reissued as METALLIC 2xKO (double album)
(France) Skydog 62232-1
TRACKS: Raw Power/Head On/Gimme Danger/Search And Destroy/
Heavy Liquid/I Wanna Be Your Dog/Open Up And Bleed/
I Got Nothing–I Got Shit/Rich Bitch/Cock In My Pocket/Louie Louie
(all tracks live Michigan Palace 1973/74)

(Iggy Pop)

THE IDIOT
March 1977 (US/UK) RCA PL 12275
Reissued (UK) as RCA International INTS 5172 October 1981 and
                RCA NL 82275 October 1984
TRACKS: Sister Midnight/Nightclubbing/Funtime/Baby/China Girl/
Dum Dum Boys/Tiny Girls/Mass Production

LUST FOR LIFE
September 1977 (US/UK) RCA PL 12488
Reissued (UK) as RCA International INTS 5114 October 1981 and
                RCA NL 82488 October 1984
TRACKS: Lust For Life/Sixteen/Some Weird Sin/The
Passenger/Tonight/Success/Turn Blue/Neighborhood Threat/Fall In Love
With Me

(Iggy Pop & James Williamson)

KILL CITY
November 1977 (US) Bomp BLP 4001
February 1978 (UK) Radar RAD 2
TRACKS: Kill City/Sell Your Love/Beyond The Law/I Got Nothin'/
Johanna/Night Theme/Night Theme (reprise)/Consolation Prizes/
No Sense Of Crime/Lucky Monkeys/Master Charge

(Iggy Pop)

TV EYE LIVE 1977
May 1978 (US/UK) RCA PL 12796
TRACKS: TV Eye/Funtime/Sixteen/I Got A Right/Lust For Life/Dirt/
Nightclubbing/I Wanna Be Your Dog

NEW VALUES
April 1979 (UK) Arista SPART 1092
October 1979 (US) Arista 4237
TRACKS: Tell Me A Story/New Values/Girls/I'm Bored/Don't Look
Down/The Endless Sea/Five Foot One/How Do Ya Fix A Broken Part/
Angel/Curiosity/African Man/Billy Is A Runaway

SOLDIER
February 1980 (UK) Arista SPART 1117
            (US) Arista 4259
TRACKS: Loco Mosquito/Ambition/Take Care Of Me/Get Up And Get
Out/Play It Safe/I'm A Conservative/Dog Food/I Need More/Knocking
'Em Down In The City/Mr. Dynamite/I Snub You

PARTY
June 1981 (UK) Arista SPART 1158
            (US) Arista 4278
TRACKS: Pleasure/Rock And Roll Party/Eggs On Plate/Sincerity/
Houston Is Hot Tonight/Pumpin' For Jill/Happy Man/ Bang Bang/Sea Of
Love/Time Won't Let Me

ZOMBIE BIRDHOUSE
September 1982 (US) Animal Records APE 6000
                (UK) Animal CHR 1399
TRACKS: Run Like A Villain/The Villagers/Angry Hills/Life Of Work/
The Ballad Of Cookie McBride/Ordinary Bummer/Eat Or Be Eaten/
Bulldozer/Platonic/The Horse Song/Watching The News/Street Crazies

BLAH BLAH BLAH
October 1986 (UK) A&M AMA 5145
                (US) A&M 395 145-1
TRACKS: Real Wild Child/Baby, It Can't Fall/Shades/Fire Girl/Isolation/
Cry For Love/Blah Blah Blah/Hideaway/Winners And Losers

INSTINCT
June 1988 (UK) AMA 5198
                (US) LP: A&M/395198-1
                CD: A&M/395198-2

TRACKS: Cold Metal/High On You/Strong Girl/Tom Tom/Easy Rider/
Power And Freedom/Lowdown/Instinct/Tuff Baby/Squarehead

BRICK BY BRICK
July 1990 LP: Virgin/VUSLP19 CD: Virgin/CDVUS19
TRACKS: Home/Main Street Eyes/I Won't Crap Out/Candy/Butt Town/
The Undefeated/Moonlight Lady/Something Wild/Neon Forest/
Starry Night/Pussy Power/My Baby Wants To Rock & Roll/Brick By
Brick/Livin' On The Edge Of The Night

AMERICAN CAESAR
September 1993 VUSLP 64/7243 8 39025 1 4 (double vinyl)
CD: Virgin/CDVUS64/7243 8 39025 2 1
TRACKS: Character/Wild America/Mixin' The Colors/Jealousy/Hate/
It's Our Love/Plastic And Concrete/Fuckin' Alone/Highway Song/
Beside You/Sickness/Boogie Boy/Perforation Problems/Social Life/
Louie Louie/Caesar/Girls Of N.Y.

NAUGHTY LITTLE DOGGIE
February 1996 LP: Virgin/VUSLP102/7243 8 41327 1 2
CD: Virgin/CDVUS102/7243 8 41327 1 2
TRACKS: I Wanna Live/Pussy Walk/Innocent World/Knucklehead/
To Belong/Keep On Believing/Outta' My Head/Shoeshine Girl/Heart Is
Saved/Look Away

AVENUE B
Released: September 20, 1999 CD: Virgin/CDVUS 163/7243 8 48216 2 3
TRACKS: No Shit/Nazi Girlfriend/Avenue B/Miss Argentina/Afraid To
Get Close/Shakin' All Over/Long Distance/Corruption/She Called Me
Daddy/Felt The Luxury/Espanol/Motorcycle/Facade

BEAT 'EM UP
Released: June 18, 2001 CD: Virgin/CDVUS 200/7243 8 10574 2 1
TRACKS: Mask/L.O.S.T./Howl/Football/Savior/Beat 'Em Up/
Talking Snake/The Jerk/Death Is Certain/Go For The Throat/
Weasels/Drink New Blood/It's All Shit/Ugliness/V.I.P.

SKULL RING
Released: UK – September 29, 2003
          US – November 4, 2003
          CDVUS246/7243 5 80774 2 1
Little Electric Chair – (with The Stooges)/Perverts In The Sun/Skull Rings
– (with The Stooges)/Superbabe/Loser – (with The Stooges)/Private Hell –
(with Green Day)/Little Know It All – (with Sum 41)/Whatever/Dead
Rock Star – (with The Stooges)/Rock Show – (with Peaches)/Here Comes
The Summer/Motor Inn – (with Peaches)/Inferiority Complex/

Supermarket – (with Green Day)/Till Wrong Feels Right/Blood On My
Cool/Nervous Exhaustion – (hidden track)

SINGLES

Selected US/UK Discography. Only foreign releases of interest included.

(*The Iguanas*)

Mona/I Don't Know Why
1965 (US): Forte 201

(*The Stooges*)

I Wanna Be Your Dog/1969
1969 (US): Elektra 45664

Down On The Street/I Feel Alright
1970 (US): Elektra 45695

(*Iggy & The Stooges*)

Search And Destroy/Penetration
1973 (US): Columbia 45877

I Got A Right/Gimme Some Skin
1977 (US): Siamese PM 001

I'M SICK OF YOU (EP)
I'm Sick Of You/Tight Pants/Scene Of The Crime
1977 (US): Bomp EP 113

(I GOT) NOTHING (12" EP)
Gimme Danger/Heavy Liquid/I Got Nothin'
1978 (France): Skydog/62233-6
                    Skydog SGIS 12

(*Iggy Pop & James Williamson*)

JESUS LOVES THE STOOGES (EP)
Consolation Prizes/Johanna/Jesus Loves The Stooges
1977 (US): Bomp EP 114

Kill City/I Got Nothin'
1978 (UK): Radar ADA 4

(*Iggy Pop*)

China Girl/Baby
1977 (UK): RCA PB 9093

Sister Midnight/Baby
1977 (US): RCA 10989

Success/The Passenger
1977 (UK): RCA PB 9160

I Got A Right (live)/Sixteen (live)
1978 (UK): RCA PB 9213

I'm Bored/African Man
1979 (UK): Arista ARIST 255
      (US): Arista ARIST 0438

Five Foot One/Pretty Flamingo
1979 (UK): ARIST 274 (picture disc ARIPD 274)

Loco Mosquito/Take Care Of Me
1980 (UK): Arista ARIST 327

Bang Bang/Sea Of Love
1981 (UK): Arista ARIST 407

Pumpin' For Jill/Time Won't Let Me
1981 (US): Arista ARI 8112

Run Like A Villain/Platonic
1982 (UK): Animal/Chrysalis CH/FLY/2634

Cry For Love (edit)/Winners And Losers
1986 (UK): A&M AM 358
      (US): A&M AM 2874

Cry For Love (extended dance mix)/Cry For Love (7″ edit)/
Winners And Losers (12″ single)
1986 (UK): A&M AMY 358

Cry For Love (extended dance mix)/Cry For Love (7″ edit)/
Little Miss Emperor (12″ single)
1986 (US): A&M AM SP-12203

Real Wild Child (Wild One)/Little Miss Emperor
1986 (UK): A&M AM 368

Real Wild Child (Wild One) (extended)/Real Wild Child/Little Miss
Emperor (12″ single)
1986 (UK): A&M AMY 368

Real Wild Child (Wild One)/Fire Girl
1987 (US): A&M AM 2909

Shades/Baby, It Can't Fall
1987 (UK): A&M AM 374

Shades/Cry For Love (extended)/Baby, It Can't Fall (extended) (12″ single)
1987 (UK): A&M AMY 374

Fire Girl/Blah Blah Blah (live Zurich, 12/12/86)
1987 (UK): A&M AM 392

Fire Girl (remix)/Fire Girl/Blah Blah Blah (live Zurich, 12/12/86) (12″ single)
1987 (UK): A&M AMY 392

Isolation/Hide Away
1987 (UK): A&M AM 397

Isolation/Hide Away/Fire Girl (remix) (12″ single)
1987 (US): 12″: A&M/392205-1

Cold Metal/Instinct
1988 (UK): A&M AM 452

Cold Metal/Instinct/Tuff Baby (12″ single)
1988 (UK): A&M AMP 452

High On You/Squarehead
1988 (UK): A&M AM 475

High On You/Tuff Baby/Squarehead (12″ single)
1988 (UK): A&M AMY 475

Livin' On The Edge Of The Night (edit)/The Passenger
1990 (UK): Virgin VUS18

Livin' On The Edge Of The Night (edit)/The Passenger/Nightclubbing/
China Girl (12″ single)
1990 (UK): Virgin/VUSTG 18 (pic disc VUSTE 18)
    (US): Virgin/VUST 18A

Livin' On The Edge Of The Night (remix)/Livin' On The Edge Of The Night/The Undefeated (acoustic)/Butt Town (acoustic)/My Baby Wants To Rock & Roll (acoustic) (12″ single)
1990 (UK): Virgin/VOZEP 02

Livin' On The Edge Of The Night/Lust For Life/China Girl/The Passenger
1990 CD: Virgin/96497-2

Home/Lust For Life
1990 (UK): Virgin VUS 22

Home/Lust For Life/Pussy Power/Funtime (12″ single)
1990 (UK): Virgin VUST 22

Home/Lust For Life/Pussy Power/Sister Midnight
1990 (US) CD: Virgin VUSCD 22 PM 515

(*with Kate Pierson*)

Candy/Pussy Power (acoustic demo)
1990 (UK): Virgin VUS 29

Candy/The Undefeated (acoustic demo)/Butt Town (acoustic demo) (12″ single)
1990 (UK): Virgin VUST 29

Candy/Pussy Power (acoustic demo)/My Baby Wants To Rock'n'Roll (acoustic demo) (10″ individually numbered limited edition coloured vinyl in gatefold sleeve)
1990 (UK): Virgin/VUSA 29

Candy/The Undefeated (acoustic demo)/Butt Town (acoustic demo)
1990 (UK & US) CD: Virgin/VUSCD 29

Candy/Pussy Power (acoustic demo)/My Baby Wants To Rock'n'Roll (acoustic demo)
1990 CD: Virgin VUSCD 29

Candy/Neon Forest
1990 (UK) cassette single: Virgin VUSC 29

Candy/Pussy Power
1990 (US) cassette single: Virgin VUSC 29

LOUIE LOUIE EP
Louie Louie/Evil California/Home (live, Feile Festival '93)/Fuckin' Alone
1993 (Holland) 12″: Virgin VU PM 212
          CD: Virgin/LLCD1 (7243 8 92218 2 4)

WILD AMERICA EP
Wild America/Credit Card/Come Back Tomorrow/My Angel
1993 (UK): Virgin VUS 74
     12": Virgin: VUST 74

Wild America (LP version)/Credit Card/Come Back Tomorrow/My Angel/
Sodom
1993 (Holland) CD: Virgin EP VUSCD 74 (7243 8 92106 2 0)

Wild America/My Angel/Credit Card/Evil California
1993 (US) CD: Virgin V25H – 38409

Beside You/Evil California/Home (live, Feile Festival '93)/Fuckin' Alone
1993 CD: Virgin VUSD 77 (7243 8 92199 2 0)

Beside You/Evil California/Home (live)/Fuckin' Alone
(Ltd edition individually numbered 10")
1994 (UK): Virgin VUSA77 (7243 8 92199 0 6)

Beside You/Les Amants/Louie Louie (live)/Beside You (acoustic)
1994 CD: Virgin EP VUSCD 77

Heart Is Saved/(Get Up I Feel Like Being A) Sex Machine/Hate*/
The Passenger*
1996 CD: Virgin/VUSCD-102 (7243 8 93405 2 5)

Lust For Life/Sex Machine
1996 (UK): Virgin VUS 116 (pink vinyl)

Lust For Life/(Get Up I Feel Like Being A) Sex Machine/Lust For Life (Feile
Fest '93)/I Wanna Be Your Dog (live Rock For Choice '96)
1996 (UK) CD: Virgin VUSCD 116 (7243 8 93844 2 0)

Corruption/Hollywood Affair
1996 (UK): Virgin VUS 155 (red vinyl)

Monster Men/Gorgeous/Monster Men Remix edit (Mr. Clean version by 2
Lazy)/Etno/Candy/Bad Luck Blues/Space Goofs (Interactive track)
1997 (EU) CD: Virgin/LC 3098 (7243 8 94914 0 1)

The Passenger/Lust For Life/Nightclubbing
1998 (UK) CD: Virgin/VSCDT 1689 (7243 8 94921 2 5)

Corruption/Rock Star Grave/Hollywood Affair (featuring Johnny Depp)
1999 CDS: Virgin/243 8 96243 2 8

---

* Live at the Feile Festival, Ireland, 1993.

GUEST APPEARANCES:

VARIOUS ARTISTS
REPO MAN (LP Soundtrack)
– vocals on 'Repo Man' –
1984 (UK): MCA MCF 3223
    (US): San Andreas SAR 39019

RYUICHI SAKAMOTO
NEO GEO
1987 (UK & US): CBS 460095 1
– vocals on 'Risky' –

THE CULT
SONIC TEMPLE
1989 (UK/US): Sire 2587
– vocals on 'New York City' –

VARIOUS ARTISTS
'Spirit Of The Rainforest'
1989 (UK/US) CD single: Virgin VS 1191
– vocals –

VARIOUS ARTISTS
RED WHITE AND BLUE
1990 (UK & US): Chrysalis CHR 1799
– vocals, with Deborah Harry, on 'Well, Did You Evah!' –

WAS NOT WAS
ARE YOU OK?
1990 (UK & US): Fontana 846-351-1
– backing vocals on 'Elvis's Rolls Royce' –

THE CRAMPS
LOOK MOM NO HEAD!
1991 (UK & US) CD: Restless/7 72586-2
– vocals on 'Miniskirt Blues' –

VARIOUS ARTISTS
PEACE CHOIR (VARIOUS ARTISTS)
'Give Peace A Chance'
1991 CD single: Virgin GPAC 1114 096
– backing vocals –

RAINDOGS – BORDER DRIVE-IN THEATRE
1991 LP: ATCO/7567-91680-1 CD: 7567-91680-2
– speaking part on 'Dance Of The Freaks' –

JOHN MORAN
THE MANSON FAMILY: AN OPERA
1992 CD: Point/432 967-2
– *vocals as Jack Lord – 'The Prosecutor' –*

WHITE ZOMBIE
LA SEXORCISTO : DEVIL MUSIC VOL. 1
1992 CD: Geffen/GED24460/GEFD24460/424460-2
– *vocals on 'Black Sunshine' –*

OFRA HAZA
KIRYA
1992 CD: Warner/903176127 2 & CA851 (FR) & SH64034
– *narrator vocals on 'Daw Da Hiya' –*

LES RITA MITSOUKO
1993 CD (France): DE 724383914-623
– *vocals on 'Easy Lover' –*

VA MOURIRE
1995 CD (France): PL 9522
– *vocals on 'I'm A Man', 'Nightclubbing', 'Dirt', 'Sister Midnight', 'Ballad Of Hollis Brown', 'Sell Your Love', 'I'm Sick Of You' –*

DEATH IN VEGAS
THE CONTINO SESSIONS
1999 CD: Concrete/74321 661992/HARD41/CD
– *vocals on 'Aisha' –*

LENNY KRAVITZ
2000 CD single: Virgin
– *vocals on 'Rebel Rebel' (live from VH-1 Fashion Awards, Oct. 1998) –*

AT THE DRIVE-IN
RELATIONSHIP OF COMMAND
2000 CD: Grand Royal/Virgin/CDVUS184/7243 8 50351 2
– *vocals on 'Rolodex Propaganda' –*

VARIOUS ARTISTS
THE BEST OF KING BISCUIT LIVE VOLUME 2
1991? CD: Sandstone/D2330066-2
– *featuring Iggy 'Real Wild Child' (Rec: live, New York Nov. 20 1986) –*

UNPLUGGED
1993 CD: EMI/8966029
– *featuring Iggy 'Brick By Brick' (Acoustic Demo) –*

BACK TO THE STREETS
celebrating the music of Don Covay
1993 CD: Sanachie/9006
– featuring Iggy's cover version of 'Sookie Sookie' –

NORWEGIAN WOOD
1996 CD: Special Limited Edition, available during the Norwegian Wood
Festival, June 15–16, 1996
– featuring Iggy track 'To Belong' –

THE CONCERT FOR THE ROCK AND ROLL HALL OF FAME
1996 CD: Columbia/4837932
– featuring Iggy track 'Back Door Man' (live with Soul Asylum) –

CLOSED ON ACCOUNT OF RABIES
Poems and tales of Edgar Allan Poe
1997 CD: Mouth Almighty/Mercury/314 536 480-2
– featuring Iggy reading 'The Tell-Tale Heart' –

JAZZ A SAINTGERMAIN
A tribute to the free spirit of 50s jazz in Paris
1997 CD: CDVIR7072/7243 8 452622 1
– featuring Iggy Pop & Francoise Hardy track: 'I'll Be Seeing You' –

SHAKEN AND STIRRED
The David Arnold James Bond Project
1997 CD: WB/3984 20738 2
– featuring Iggy track 'We Have All The Time In The World' –

FATHER FUCKER
Peaches
2003
– featuring Iggy duetting with Peaches on 'Kick It' –

SOUNDTRACKS

REPO MAN
1984 CD: MCA/MCD39019
– featuring Iggy on 'Repo Man' –

DOGS IN SPACE
1986 LP: Mercury/832748-1 & CD: Mercury/832748-2
– featuring Iggy on 'Dog Food' and 'Endless Sea' –

SHOCKER, NO MORE MR. NICE GUY
1989 LP/CD: SBK 064 793233
– featuring Iggy on 'Love Transfusion' –

FREDDIE'S DEAD: THE FINAL NIGHTMARE
1991 CD/LP (Europe): Zorro 33
– featuring Iggy on 'Why Was I Born?' –

SHORT CUTS
1993 CD:
– featuring Iggy on 'Evil California (These Blues)' –

ARIZONA DREAM
1993 CD: Mercury/5121122
– featuring Iggy on 'In The Deathcar'/'TV Screen'/'Get The Money'/'This Is A Film' –

FAST TRACK TO NOWHERE – SONGS FROM REBEL HIGHWAY
1994 CD: A&M 314 5402-402
– featuring Iggy on 'C'mon Everybody' –

THE CROW : CITY OF ANGELS
1996 CD: MH 62047 2
– featuring Iggy on 'I Wanna Be Your Dog' (live) –

TRAINSPOTTING
1997 CD: EMI/8212652
– featuring Iggy on 'The Passenger'/'Nightclubbing' (Baby Doc Remix) –

BORN TO LOSE
1997 CD: Bomp/Alive Records/LOSE6997
– featuring Iggy & The Stooges track 'Tight Pants' –

GREAT EXPECTATIONS
1997 CD: Atlantic/7567-83058-2
– featuring Iggy track 'Success' –

WILD AMERICA
1997 CD: label & cat no. unknown
– featuring Iggy track 'Real Wild Child (Wild One)' –

WHATEVER
1998 CD: label & cat no. unknown
– featuring Iggy track 'Gimme Danger' –

THE RUGRATS MOVIE
1998 CD: Interscope/IND90181
– featuring Iggy track 'This World Is Something New To Me' –

LOCK, STOCK & TWO SMOKING BARRELS
1999 CD: Island/CID8077/524578-2
– *featuring Iggy track 'I Wanna Be Your Dog'* –

IMPORTANT REISSUES

I'M SICK OF YOU
1981 (Germany): Line LLP 5126
TRACKS: I'm Sick Of You/Tight Pants/I Got A Right/Johanna/
Consolation Prizes/Scene Of The Crime/Gimme Some Skin/Jesus Loves
The Stooges

I GOT A RIGHT
1983 (US): Invasion/Enigma E 1019
TRACKS: I'm Sick Of You/Tight Pants/I Got A Right/Scene Of The
Crime/Gimme Some Skin/Kill City/I Got Nothin'/Johanna/Consolation
Prizes/No Sense Of Crime/Lucky Monkeys

RAW POWER
1997 Columbia-Legacy/485176 9
– *remixed by Iggy Pop & remastered* –

NEW VALUES
CD: (2000) Buddha/74465 99662 2
As well as original album, remastered CD features two previously unreleased
bonus tracks: Chains, and Pretty Flamingo.

SOLDIER
CD: (2000) Buddha/74465 99660 2
As well as original album, remastered CD features two previously unreleased
bonus tracks: Low Life, and Drop A Hook.

PARTY
CD: (2000) Buddha/74465 99661 2
As well as original album, remastered CD features two previously unreleased
bonus tracks: Speak To Me, and One For My Baby.

ZOMBIE BIRDHOUSE
CD: I.R.S./X2-13063
As well as original album, CD features bonus track: Pain And Suffering.

BLAH BLAH BLAH
CD: A&M/395145-2
As well as original album, CD features bonus track: Little Miss Emperor.

Index

Single releases are in roman type; albums are it italics

Index